Permanent Campaigning in Canada ....

COMMUNICATION
STRATEGY
AND POLITICS

Communication, Strategy, and Politics

THIERRY GIASSON AND ALEX MARLAND, SERIES EDITORS

Communication, Strategy, and Politics is a ground-breaking new series from UBC Press that examines elite decision making and political communication in today's hyper-mediated and highly competitive environment. Publications in this series look at the intricate relations between marketing strategy, the media, and political actors and explain how this affects Canadian democracy. They also investigate such interconnected themes as strategic communication, mediatization, opinion research, electioneering, political management, public policy, and e-politics in a Canadian context and in comparison to other countries. Designed as a coherent and consolidated space for diffusion of research about Canadian political community, the series promotes an interdisciplinary, multi-method, and theoretically pluralistic approach.

Other volumes in the series are:

Political Marketing in Canada, edited by Alex Marland, Thierry Giasson, and Jennifer Lees-Marshment

Political Communication in Canada: Meet the Press and Tweet the Rest, edited by Alex Marland, Thierry Giasson, and Tamara A. Small

Framed: Media and the Coverage of Race in Canadian Politics, by Erin Tolley

Brand Command: Canadian Politics and Democracy in the Age of Message Control, by Alex Marland

See also:

Canadian Election Analysis 2015: Communication, Strategy, and Democracy, edited by Alex Marland and Thierry Giasson. Open-access compilation available at http://www.ubcpress.ca/CanadianElectionAnalysis2015/ CanadianElectionAnalysis2015.pdf

Permanent Campaigning in Canada

•••••• Edited by Alex Marland,
Thierry Giasson, and
Anna Lennox Esselment

UBCPress·Vancouver·Toronto

26 25 24 23 22 21 20 19 18 17   5 4 3 2 1

Printed in Canada on FSC-certified ancient-forest-free paper
(100% post-consumer recycled) that is processed chlorine- and acid-free.

___

Library and Archives Canada Cataloguing in Publication

Permanent campaigning in Canada / edited by Alex Marland, Thierry Giasson, and Anna Lennox Esselment.

(Communication, strategy, and politics, ISSN 2368-1047)
Includes bibliographical references and index.
Issued in print and electronic formats.
ISBN 978-0-7748-3448-3 (hardcover). – ISBN 978-0-7748-3449-0 (softcover)
ISBN 978-0-7748-3450-6 (PDF). – ISBN 978-0-7748-3451-3 (EPUB)
ISBN 978-0-7748-3452-0 (Kindle)

1. Political campaigns – Canada. 2. Politics, Practical – Canada. 3. Communication in politics – Canada. 4. Canada – Politics and government. I. Giasson, Thierry, author, editor II. Marland, Alexander J., author, editor III. Esselment, Anna Lennox, author, editor IV. Series: Communication, strategy, and politics

JL193.P47 2017   324.70971   C2017-901042-5
                                                               C2017-901043-3

___

Canadä

UBC Press gratefully acknowledges the financial support for our publishing program of the Government of Canada (through the Canada Book Fund), the Canada Council for the Arts, and the British Columbia Arts Council.

This book has been published with the help of a grant from the Canadian Federation for the Humanities and Social Sciences, through the Awards to Scholarly Publications Program, using funds provided by the Social Sciences and Humanities Research Council of Canada.

Printed and bound in Canada by Friesens
Set in Scala and Minion by Artegraphica Design Co. Ltd.
Copy editor: Lana Okerlund
Proofreader: Dianne Tiefensee
Indexer: Noeline Bridge
Cover designer: David Drummond

UBC Press
The University of British Columbia
2029 West Mall
Vancouver, BC V6T 1Z2
www.ubcpress.ca

Maclean's *National Leaders' Debate,*
CITY studio complex, Toronto, August 6, 2015

"The *Fair Elections Act* turns out to be full of surprises.
One of the things it did was allow you to extend the
election campaign to 11 weeks and prorate expenses
to match. Did you have this kind of long election
campaign in mind for two years?"

    –Paul Wells, national leaders' debate moderator

"Everybody knew an election would be on. The other
parties were out campaigning. It's very simple: if we
are going to be in an election campaign, we should
be under the rules of the *Election Act*, not using
parliamentary resources but using resources that
our party raises."

    –Rt. Hon. Stephen Harper, Conservative leader

"So why were you putting up 24/7 [PMO videos] on
your website, Mr. Harper?"

    –Justin Trudeau, Liberal leader

Source: Maclean's. 2015. "Tale of the Tape: Read a Full Transcript
of Maclean's Debate." August 6. http://www.macleans.ca/politics/
ottawa/tale-of-the-tape-read-a-full-transcript-of-macleans-debate/.

Contents

Figures and Tables

Foreword

•••••• *Tom Flanagan*

When I was campaign manager for the Canadian Alliance and the Conservative Party of Canada in the years 2002–5, our campaign team introduced to Canadian politics many of the practices now usually known as the permanent campaign. At the time, I never heard that term mentioned. We were just trying to win power, not trying to create or imitate a model of campaigning. It wasn't until later that I realized we had generated a Canadian version of permanent campaigning, which other parties have also begun to practise.

Political parties in Canada are now using the same techniques of communication and persuasion outside the writ period as within it, including:

- paid advertising, now employed in the pre-writ period by all parties that can afford it
- direct voter contact through telephone solicitation, direct mail, email, and social media for voter identification as well as grassroots fundraising
- strategic visits by the leader to ridings and areas of the country thought to be marginal in the coming election
- coordinated travel by the leader's surrogates as a boost to local fundraising and team building (the main reason that some senators used to be appointed; we will have to see how Prime Minister Trudeau's pledge to appoint non-partisan senators works out in practice)
- policy announcements designed to win support from designated groups essential to building a winning coalition in the next election, making policy an obvious tool of politics
- frequent opinion polling, even nightly tracking during critical periods
- war-room-style rapid response at all times
- extension of leaders' debates into the pre-writ period, considered for the 2015 federal election but overtaken when the election was called early on August 4.

To be sure, electioneering is far more intensive during the writ period, with much higher spending on advertising, non-stop travel by leaders and surrogates, release of a comprehensive platform, and ramped-up telephone solicitation and social media contact for voter identification, persuasion, fundraising, and get-out-the-vote activities. Also, the legal environment of the pre-writ and writ periods differs, depending on the jurisdiction. At the federal level, third-party advertising is unlimited in the pre-writ period but strictly regulated during the official campaign, whereas in Ontario, third parties are able to spend freely in the writ period (though Premier Kathleen Wynne has pledged to change the law in that regard). In most jurisdictions, the party in power is able to run unlimited "government advertising" and make highly political policy announcements in the pre-writ period, but comes under strict regulation once the writ is dropped. So party strategies and competitive dynamics of the writ and pre-writ periods are not identical, but the tools employed to carry out these strategies are increasingly similar.

It is plausible to believe that this mode of comprehensive permanent campaigning contributes to the polarization of the electorate. Parties are in frequent contact with their donors, members, and supporters, bombarding them with mail, phone calls, and electronic messages almost daily. These messages are not designed to enhance civic literacy; they are designed to boost partisanship and raise money, elicit volunteer activities, and win votes. They almost always attack opposing parties and their leaders while extolling the virtue of their own party and leader.

This message bombardment interacts with the polarizing effect of the Internet, on which many authors have commented. By vastly multiplying the available sources of news and commentary, the Internet allows partisans to seek out comfortable sources of fact and opinion that reinforce their existing partisan biases. Partisans come to inhabit an echo chamber where they hear supportive messages repeated over and over, with little intrusion of other viewpoints. Party communications enhance the effect when they include copies of, or links to, strategically chosen news stories, editorials, opinion columns, and videos.

In a fairly pure two-party system such as that of the United States, polarization promotes not only a lot of bad temper, but political gridlock, as elected members of the two main parties find it difficult to compromise with each other. Even those whose disposition favours compromise must fear the wrath of the more radical base within their parties. The days of Ronald Reagan and Bill Clinton, when presidents could reach out to opponents to get important legislation passed, have given way to never-ending trench warfare within Congress and between Congress and the president.

The effects in a multiparty system such as Canada's are rather different. With several parties contesting for office, it is rare for any party to gain, or even approach, a majority of the popular vote. It is much more common for the leading party to get about 35 to 45 percent of the popular vote, which the magic of the first-past-the-post electoral system may translate into a majority of seats. The strategic implications of this fact are immense. To win, you don't have to try to build an electoral coalition containing the fabled median voter. Against divided opponents, you can win by holding your core support together and adding some carefully selected geographic and demographic voter segments to produce a minimum winning coalition that is smaller, often much smaller, than a majority coalition. Stephen Harper's Conservatives followed this strategy in their rise to power. Historians will record that Harper grasped the logic of multiparty competition and imposed it on the fractious right wing of Canadian politics, thereby making himself prime minister for a decade.

The Roman maxims *divide et impera* and *divide ut regnes* do not precisely describe what Harper did. He did not need to cunningly divide his opponents, because he found them already divided. But, after ending divisions on the right, he saw how to build a party and pursue strategies that could take maximum advantage of division among opponents. Permanent campaigning did not create this outcome; Canada, after all, has had a multiparty system since 1921. But permanent campaigning allows a practitioner of divide-and-conquer politics to play that game more efficiently by keeping core voters more closely bound together. "It is no accident," as Marxists like to say, that under Harper's leadership, the Conservatives were the first Canadian party to pull together existing techniques of communication and persuasion into a coherent model of the permanent campaign, which other parties are now taking even further in their Darwinian competition for power.

The Liberals have been particularly imaginative in their use of social media, erasing the advantage that the Conservatives held for a time in direct voter contact. During the Harper years, the Conservatives built a voter contact and fundraising machine that depended heavily on direct mail and telephone solicitation. It worked well for a decade, but is rapidly becoming as obsolete as the Soviet army. The Conservatives will have to retool to remain competitive in the age of social media.

The "change" rhetoric of Liberal leader Justin Trudeau may seem more inclusive than Stephen Harper's appeals to selected demographics, but beneath the surface, one can see the same process of building a minimum winning coalition (39.5 percent of the popular vote, similar to what the Conservatives received when they won a majority government in the previous election). Analysis of the Liberal platform and campaign will show how they targeted voting blocs that were dissatisfied under the Conservatives (public servants, Aboriginal people, youth) as well as groups that the Conservatives had temporarily captured (suburban families, recent immigrants).

A related phenomenon is the transformation of political support from a family or tribal loyalty to something resembling a consumer brand preference. When I immigrated to Canada in 1968, it was easy to predict a person's political support. Francophones, Roman Catholics, and Jews skewed Liberal, as did most other ethnic groups except for some Central and Eastern Europeans who hated Communism. Protestants and inhabitants of the Prairies skewed Conservative. Trade unionists voted disproportionately for the NDP. Of course, these preferences were susceptible to change. Sir John A. Macdonald's Conservatives had once had the support of French Canadians, Sir Wilfrid Laurier's Liberals had once ruled the Prairies, and significant new parties, such as the Progressives and their CCF/NDP heirs, had occasionally arisen. But party loyalties were mostly stable across generations.

All that has changed, at least at the federal level of politics, since the election of 1984, when Brian Mulroney's Progressive Conservatives detached Francophone voters in Quebec from their traditional Liberal moorings. Since then, Francophones in Quebec have shifted three times again, to the Bloc Québécois in 1993, to the NDP in 2011, and away from the NDP but to no single party in 2015. In Western Canada, and to a lesser degree in rural Ontario, the Reform Party took over traditional PC support, turned itself into the Canadian Alliance, then merged with the Progressive Conservatives. The new Conservatives started to get substantial support from traditional Liberal voting blocs, such as Roman Catholics, Jews, and recent immigrants, until those trends were reversed in the Liberals' victorious campaign of 2015. The Green Party has also become a factor in federal politics, although thus far it has elected only one member.

Although timetables have been different at the provincial level, the general trend has been the same, especially in Quebec and the western provinces – collapse of old parties, sudden rise of new parties, merger of existing parties, dramatic shifts of voting blocs. A few highlights:

- British Columbia – the collapse of the previously governing Social Credit party, the rise and fall of a provincial Reform party, and the final emergence of the Liberals as a consolidated party of the right
- Alberta – the demise of the ruling Social Credit party, the rise (and recent collapse) of the Progressive Conservatives as a long-term governing party, the emergence and then obliteration of the Liberals as the official opposition, the birth of several new parties (most prominently Wildrose), and finally the unexpected victory of the NDP, which had long toiled on the fringes
- Saskatchewan – the demise of the Progressive Conservatives and the slow death of the Liberals, with the rise of the Saskatchewan Party as a consolidated governing party on the right
- Quebec – the death of the Union Nationale, the rise and fall of provincial Social Credit, the emergence of the Parti Québécois as the main (but not only) party of the left, and the coming and going of other parties such as the Equality Party, the ADQ and CAQ, and Québec solidaire.

All of this is well known to students of Canadian politics. I recite these examples of change only to emphasize the frequency with which modern voters are confronted with new parties, new labels, and new competitive configurations or cooperative alliances. "You can't tell the players without a scorecard," said Harry Stevens, the inventor of the baseball scorecard. The same could be said of modern Canadian politics. From one election to the next, voters face differing menus of parties, party labels, and realistic options. From the gradual transitions for which plate tectonics was an apt metaphor, we have moved into an era of sudden and unexpected changes better symbolized by the kaleidoscope.

The act of voting is now like a shopping trip. "Hey, let's go buy a new car, computer ... government. Who's offering the best deal this time? Are there any new makes to try out?" And as with other shopping excursions, voters' final decisions are often postponed to the very end, thus ruining the reputation of pollsters who don't poll late enough in the campaign to pick up last-minute surges. In the 2015 national election, pollsters who kept polling on the final weekend correctly foresaw a Liberal majority, but no one picked up the extent of the NDP collapse in Quebec. Many Québécois voters must have reached their final decision as they were driving to the polls.

Permanent campaigning did not cause this mutability, but it harmonizes with it and reinforces it. Winning political strategy now usually means holding your base together while reaching out to selected demographic and geographic segments. The non-stop messaging and highly politicized appeals of the permanent campaign are ideal for this purpose. Moreover, the employment of commercial sales technology for political purposes sends the not-so-subtle message that politics is just another form of commerce – "let's make a deal" conducted with votes rather than dollars. Thus, it becomes ever more logical for voters to act like consumers. Declining turnout also fits nicely into this tableau. Those who always or usually vote are disproportionately older people raised in an age when voting was an unquestioned civic duty. Those who seldom or never vote are disproportionately the young, who have grown up in an era when voting is treated as a consumer decision – and if there is nothing you want to buy, you don't need to bother going shopping. It remains to be seen whether the rise in turnout of young people in the national election of 2015 was a temporary event or the beginning of a new trend.

Is all of this regrettable? Many observers seem to think so (Delacourt 2013). But I am not so nostalgic for an idealized past. The pioneers of voting studies taught us that there were very few rational, independent voters who made a careful study of all available evidence before casting a civic-minded vote for the common good. Given the existence of large and stable blocs of tribal voters, elections were usually decided by poorly informed, not very interested floating voters responding to short-term stimuli. Most minds were closed, and the minds that were open were not very well informed. Today, more minds are open. They may still not be very well informed by the standards of scholars, but they are exposed to enormous amounts of information, not least from the political parties whose permanent campaigns bombard them with messages. If that's not progress, at least it's not regress.

REFERENCE

Delacourt, Susan. 2013. *Shopping for Votes: How Politicians Choose Us and We Choose Them*. Madeira Park, BC: Harbour Publishing.

...... Acknowledgments

This book came about because, to anyone paying attention to the news, it is clear that Canadian politics and governance have been changed by an unrelenting mentality among political elites of non-stop political marketing, communication, and strategic thinking. It is the third in a series looking at the inner workings of Canadian politics and governance. The first, *Political Marketing in Canada* (UBC Press, 2012), examined the ways that Canadian democracy is changing as public sector elites use market intelligence and marketing tactics. The second, *Political Communication in Canada: Meet the Press and Tweet the Rest* (UBC Press, 2014), explored the ways that political communication and political behaviour are profoundly changing. A fourth volume is in development to examine the behaviour of Canadian political elites themselves in the digital age. All of this is part of the UBC Press series *Communication, Strategy, and Politics*, for which a description can be found on an earlier page. The open-access compilation *Canadian Election Analysis 2015: Communication, Strategy, and Democracy* (available for free public download at www.ubcpress.ca/CanadianElectionAnalysis2015) is also affiliated with the series, as are a number of other publications.

The editors would like to thank Tom Flanagan for authoring the foreword. Flanagan is a prolific University of Calgary academic who has published about permanent campaigning in Canada, often drawing on his experience running a number of leadership and election campaigns. His work is cited throughout this book. Budding journalist Laura Howells performed an outstanding copy edit of draft chapters. The contributors to this collection were outstanding to work with, putting up with our relentless drive for content symmetry and cohesion, and meeting our deadlines in a manner that evokes the spirit of non-stop campaigning. At UBC Press, we would like to thank senior editors (past and present) Emily Andrew and Randy Schmidt, and the usual high standards of professionalism exhibited by many fine people including Megan Brand, Holly Keller, Lana Okerlund, Dianne Tiefensee, and Noeline Bridge. We also have come to appreciate the efforts of others who are involved behind the scenes after a UBC Press book has been published, such as Laraine Coates, Harmony Johnson, Kerry Kilmartin, and Melissa Pitts. All of us owe a debt of gratitude to the three anonymous reviewers who took the time to offer suggestions for improving an earlier draft of the manuscript.

Permanent Campaigning in Canada has been published with the help of a grant from the Canadian Federation for the Humanities and Social Sciences, through the Awards to Scholarly Publications Program. The authors also wish to acknowledge funding assistance provided by the University of Waterloo, Faculty of Arts.

Abbreviations

CIMS	Constituent Information Management System
CPC	Conservative Party of Canada
CRA	Canada Revenue Agency
DNC	Democratic National Committee
DND	Department of National Defence
EAP	Economic Action Plan
EPC	election planning committee
GOTV	get out the vote
LPC	Liberal Party of Canada
MEP	message event proposal
MP	member of Parliament
NDP	New Democratic Party
NPG	New Political Governance
OLO	Office of the Leader of the Official Opposition
PAC	political action committee
PCO	Privy Council Office
PIPEDA	*Personal Information Protection and Electronic Documents Act*
PMO	Prime Minister's Office
PPP	party–press parallelism
PSB	public service bargain
VAN	Voter Activation Network

Permanent Campaigning in Canada ....

PART 1

Theoretical Parameters ....

1

Welcome to Non-Stop Campaigning

•••••• *Alex Marland, Anna Lennox Esselment,*
and Thierry Giasson

> Per·ma·nent cam·paign
>
> *noun*
>
> Electioneering throughout governance, which often
> involves leveraging public resources. This is more
> prevalent with fixed-date election legislation because all
> political parties maintain a state of election readiness
> that builds as the election approaches. Non-stop
> campaigning is most pronounced in the final year of
> a four-year cycle, during by-elections, and during the
> uncertainty of minority government when the possibility
> of a sudden election campaign is ever-present.
>
> *(from the glossary)*

The requirements of election campaigns were once viewed as quite separate from the responsibilities of governing. In the early to mid-twentieth century, the separation between campaigning and governing was relatively clear. In large part, political parties had a solid membership base on which they could rely for votes and electioneering from one campaign to the next. News cycles were long, and political parties provided newspaper scribes with inside scoops with a quid pro quo expectation of favourable treatment. Campaign funds were secured through party bagmen, and local campaigns were controlled by party bosses. The lubricants of patronage and pork-barrelling kept party machines running. These party attachments began to unravel in the latter half of the twentieth century, and political elites were faced with more difficult terrain. Political scandals, particularly in the United States, gave voters and journalists legitimate reason to be skeptical of decision makers. Political correspondents, adhering to a new watchdog philosophy in political reporting, became more critical of parties and government. By extension, journalists and citizens became less deferential to authority. The media engaged in aggressive investigations of government and reported on any misconduct or suspicion of wrongdoing. Stricter campaign rules and public tendering processes were installed to reflect the changing political ethics. A philosophy of catering to party supporters was no longer possible without also considering public opinion polling to gauge voter sentiment. Maintaining a high public approval rating improved the chances of re-election; however, staying on top of the polls required calculated effort akin to the type of planning demanded by an election campaign.

Nowadays, political parties are embroiled in constant electioneering – a non-stop competitive mindset to win the onslaught of media battles, to raise funds, to persuade public opinion, to push an agenda, and to generally maintain a state of election readiness. It has become the norm for political parties that have just won an election to carry on as though the campaign never stopped. Moreover, they do not shy away from taking advantage of the multitude of publicly funded levers at their disposal. Political leaders and strategists have always done this, but not with such ferocity or calculated purpose.

This book explores the phenomenon and industry of permanent campaigning in Canada. We lack information about "when permanent campaigning began in this country, how pervasive it has become within government and how permanent 'the permanent campaign' style of governing will be" (Thomas 2013, 66). We even lack a strong understanding of what the concept encompasses.

What Is Permanent Campaigning?

It is commonly understood that the first priority of any government is to secure re-election (Benoit 2006, 178), and leaders have such a penchant for conflating governing with campaigning that one becomes indistinguishable from the other. While political actors have always sought to leverage their office to secure re-election, the concept that we are concerned with here originated in the 1970s in the United States. Political consultant Patrick Caddell believed that it was a mistake to divorce politics from government, because those in power tend to forget the reasons why they were elected. Apolitical government results in the enactment of policies that grate against the wishes of the public and make re-election more difficult. Instead, Caddell insisted that "governing with public approval requires a continuing political campaign" (Blumenthal 1980, 39). With that simple thesis, the concept of governing with the intensity of an official election campaign was born.

Permanent campaigning and its many synonyms – constant, continuous, perpetual, non-stop, inter-election, and never-ending campaigning, to name some – describe a mindset that efforts to win the next election begin immediately after election day. This is fuelled by a desire to achieve positive media coverage that treats all manner of political issues as mini-contests with winners and losers. Public opinion polls, by-elections, legislative votes, policy announcements – they all must be won as though the outcome of the next election is at stake. At a deeper level, the concept refers to political actors maximizing all available resources to achieve their electoral goals, and in particular to members of the political government accessing public resources. In this sense, permanent campaigning refers to an approach to governance whereby the partisan elites who control the government apply strategies and techniques usually found in a campaign setting to the process of governing itself. The thinking is that to implement a political agenda and to be re-elected, it is imperative that the government party be seen to be more often on the winning side.

Concern about this phenomenon is warranted when public administration is entwined with electioneering. Governing is combined with disciplined political communication to the point that it can be difficult to discern what is apolitical, what is political, and what is partisan. The use of public resources for government advertising, branding, direct voter contact, social media, and public opinion research warrants scrutiny. In particular, there is growing reliance on – and influence of – political staff within government, and a creeping politicization of the public service the longer that a party is in office. All of this raises questions about the democratic nature of government.

The study of permanent campaigning and its effects on American politics blossomed after Caddell's view for maintaining power began to take shape. One point of scholarly intrigue was the observation that presidents increasingly sought to persuade congressional representatives of their policy goals by appealing directly to the American electorate for support (Jones 1998; Kernell 1997). President Franklin Roosevelt's fireside chats in the 1930s and 1940s were an early example of this. Rallying the voting public to build support for presidential legislative initiatives or foreign policy operations became commonplace, particularly once television was a stock item in most

American households. A more recent illustration was President Obama appearing as a regular guest on late-night entertainment shows, news stations, and other media platforms when his health-care reform bill was making its way through Congress (Baum 2012, 183). Other academics observed that pollsters, armed with the latest opinion research, are frequent visitors to the White House, demonstrating the increasing dependence on – and weight given to – public views by the executive when making decisions (Bowman 2000; Murray and Howard 2002). The extent to which party expenditures are set aside to pay for polling data solidified the suspicion that the executive is keenly interested in the various opinions of American voters (Tenpas and McCann 2007).

A further area of research is the role played by political staff in government. The Office of Political Affairs was created in 1980 by President Jimmy Carter, to whom Caddell's advice was offered. The office's explicit purpose is to provide political, partisan advice to the president. In large part it is staffed by strategists, consultants, polling experts, and other political staff charged with the responsibility for providing "assistance in mid-term elections and the early planning for the president's re-election campaign" (Tenpas 1996, 512). It keeps close tabs on issues that arise in the various states so that the president is apprised of political developments. Due to the throng of publicity that accompanies a president, another angle for analysis is the way that presidential touring is planned. The White House crafts the president's travel schedule in a manner designed to bolster public support for policy initiatives and to target large, competitive states (Cook 2002; Doherty 2012). A further area of interest is the relationship between constant campaigning and political communication. This includes an emphasis on carefully crafted messages that are deliberately targeted to different segments of the electorate (Burton and Shea 2010; Johnson 2011). Using numerous forms of media, the political executive can improve its ability to direct and manage its messages. In short, there is an increasing propensity for political elites to take Caddell's prescription to heart and to practise an innovative way of politicking and governing in the United States.

Understanding permanent campaigning also requires recognizing what it is not. As both a mindset and a political context, it should not be confused with marketing. Political marketing frames the permanent campaign; it defines the polling, communication, and policy initiatives that parties engage in during the inter-election period. Market research carried out between elections, both by government and partisan formations, dictates how continuous campaigning is undertaken. These data provide information to set the agenda of issues, help segment and target receptive voters, and inform communications strategy. Political marketing sets the objectives for which the permanent campaign is designed and implemented.

Permanent campaigning should also not be equated solely to political communication. As many chapters of this book demonstrate, persuasion is a central tenet, employing such strategic tools as advertising, speeches, image management, online presences, policy announcements, leader's tours, and media relations. However, the reach of permanent campaigning extends to other political phenomena that are not directly related to communication activities. These include the centralization of executive decision making, the politicization of public administration, and the instrumentalization of parliamentary rules and institutions for partisan and electoral purposes. Therefore, both political marketing and political communication are closely associated to the concept of permanent campaigning, but should rather be understood as contributing factors to its relevant success. The subject matter of this book is concerned with the contextual environment of perpetual election preparedness and with the institutionalization of strategic actions in the inter-election period – whether political, marketing, or communication in nature – that at one time were exclusive to the official election period.

Permanent Campaigning in Canada: Conceptual Nuances and Distinctions

In Canada, Justin Trudeau has arguably been in a perpetual state of campaigning since before he became leader of the Liberal Party of Canada and ever since he became prime minister. Political commentator Andrew Coyne observes as much, writing that "the governing style of Justin Trudeau's government is coming into focus. It is one part not being Stephen Harper, one part symbolic gesture, one part wriggling out of campaign promises, and one part saying yes to everybody. You thought the Harper government was all about the permanent campaign? Get used to it" (Coyne 2016). The list of politicking is so long that it is confusing what constitutes legitimate government business and what is about image and persuasion with an eye on winning votes, and whether there can be any separation. Prime Minister Trudeau participated in a live Q and A with citizens that was televised on CBC. He flew with an entourage to a state dinner in Washington, DC, and reciprocated by hosting President Obama. His cabinet held retreats at resorts in New Brunswick and Alberta, and the government has paid British consultants to counsel ministers about how to deliver on election promises (Dyer 2016). He has instructed Liberal MPs to focus on getting re-elected by delivering top-quality services to constituents and being good grassroots communicators. As one MP put it, "It's got to be all about helping people ... That's where the votes come from" (Rana 2016). Supporters might assert that these and many other actions embody a democratic spirit of accessibility and transparency and are legitimate government business. Detractors might reason that it is mostly about spin and media management and prioritizing the needs of the political class. We argue that it all constitutes permanent campaigning.

Prior to the Trudeau Liberal era of governance, the federal Conservative Party was an aggressive adopter of marketing practices and methodically deployed government resources to further its needs. A strong argument could be made that the practice of non-stop campaigning emerged with force in Canada during the minority governance era of 2004 to 2011. All political parties were cognizant that an election could occur at any time, and this spurred a greater degree of preparedness for a potential campaign. This was especially true for the Conservatives. Harper and his team understood the importance of being prepared for electoral warfare at any moment, and they were in power alongside major developments in social media, such as YouTube, Facebook, and Twitter. The party implemented a disciplined and fused style of communication messages and resources in its bid for election, to stay in power, and to win the next election with a majority of seats. The ferocity of permanent campaigning in this country may therefore well be related to Harper's tenure as leader of the Conservative Party from 2004 to 2015 and as prime minister for nearly a decade. That period is thus a formidable source of data. We are also in the early throngs of permanent campaigning by interest groups and other political actors. In Canada as elsewhere, the delineation between electioneering and governing was clearer before the prominence of opinion surveys, before the advent of twenty-four-hour news channels and digital media, and before the relentless effort to win the hearts and minds of narrow pools of floating voters.

Yet there is other evidence that perpetual campaigning extends to other political parties. There is a history in this country of partisans seeking to exploit the perks of office for political-electoral gain through patronage, gerrymandering, changed election rules, advertising, buying votes with budget goodies, and so on. We need only look at the Liberal administrations that immediately preceded the Harper Conservatives to illustrate that permanent campaigning is an art form in which many Canadian political elites have become master artisans. The Commission of Inquiry into the Sponsorship Program and Advertising Activities (Gomery Commission) identified a number of themes within the upper echelon of the Chrétien/ Martin Liberal governments that set the scene for the advent of permanent campaigning. Most notably, normal reporting processes were bypassed to award bogus advertising contracts to Liberal-connected advertising agencies, which was at the heart of the sponsorship scandal. The Gomery report enumerated a number of far-reaching partisan activities within government, ranging from senior government officials exploiting their influence, to the alignment of government communication with party messaging (Public Works and Government Services Canada 2005). Evidence also exists that parliamentarians engage in permanent campaigning at the most microscopic levels. The circulation of a message from a New Democratic Party MP's parliamentary email account inviting supporters to participate in a weekly phone bank and weekend door knocking is a case in point. An independent MP criticized that error in judgment thusly:

> The Parliament of Canada is not a partisan institution. It's the legislative branch of the Government of Canada. It is paid for by all taxpayers, not taxpayers that support a particular candidate or a particular party. So, to deploy taxpayers' resources to recruit individuals to an imminent political campaign is inappropriate and if I was a taxpayer, which I am, I'm offended when my tax dollars are used by individuals to promote partisan causes that I don't support. (Rana 2015)

Complaints about how elected officials exploit public resources for their own political gain are common in Canada, particularly as an official election approaches.

The practice of permanent campaigning appears to be connected to the speeding up of political communication. Whatever the reasons, it is now accepted that "the frenzied, headline-grabbing approach of the election period" is "carried over into the governing process" in this country (Thomas 2013, 66). Public administration scholar Donald Savoie (2010, 96) summarizes the many factors that contribute to permanent campaigning as a byzantine mix of political marketing practices, including

> the new media; the blogification of the media; political reporting; negative campaigning; the rise of political consultants and professional campaigners and spin specialists; single issue movements; the use of focus groups to review policy issues; the larger and more senior partisan political staff in ministerial offices; the staff and increased resources allocated to members of Parliament; the growing number of swing voters and those unwilling to identify with a political party; increases in spending on government advertising and public opinion surveys; the development of a voter data base; and spending restrictions during elections [*sic*] campaigns but none outside the campaign period.

A number of developments have brought forth such a frenzied atmosphere. None of these are attributable to any one political party, but rather are an outcome of broader trends.

The first development that we observe is the intensifying concentration of power at the centre of Canadian politics, namely the Prime Minister's Office (PMO) and its supporting agencies (Marland 2016; Savoie 1999).[1] A second development is the greater use of political marketing techniques by Canadian political parties (Delacourt 2016; Flanagan 2014; Marland et al. 2012). Most parties and their strategists realize the advantage provided by adopting sophisticated sales and marketing practices in today's competitive political environment. Changes in political communication are a third development. Sticking to a script and staying on message has been a standard campaign orthodoxy for many years now. With the twenty-four-hour news cycle and the advent of social media, disciplined communication practices both on the campaign and in government have never been more important or harder to manage (Elmer et al. 2012; Marland et al. 2014). A fourth turn of events was changes to legislation overseeing political party finance and fundraising rules, in 2003 and 2011.[2] The reforms dramatically affected the way in which Canadian parties seek and spend money. A banning of corporate and union donations coupled with the phasing-out of public subsidies means that parties adept at raising small amounts from a large number of citizens are better positioned to fund their elections. The Conservative Party mastered this new method first (Flanagan 2014), but the other major parties gained ground. For some time, this was a formidable position of strength for the Conservatives, who had both the funds and gravitas to deploy negative advertising to "de-brand" opponents outside of the election writ period, when usual rules over electoral communication expenses do not apply (Flanagan 2012; Rose 2012). With the Liberals now in power, the ability to fundraise from the seat of government has changed hands. The fifth development we observe was the advent of fixed-date election legislation. This effectively shortened the normal electoral cycle for a majority government to four years from the constitutionally allowed five years. The first minister reserves the right to seek the early dissolution of the legislature but is constrained by the publicly known scheduled date of the next election. This shift puts political parties in a state of heightened election readiness, particularly in an election year. The situation is even more frenzied during a minority Parliament. Equally, in 2015, the intensity of pre-election campaigning pushed Prime Minister Harper to set in motion one of the longest official campaigns in Canadian history, ostensibly to constrain third parties' ability to advertise and to bleed the resources of his opponents.

These five developments – prime ministerial power, political marketing strategies, disciplined communication, party finance changes, and fixed-date elections – are not the only factors at play. For instance, the growth in hyperpartisanship is a contributing factor, as are changing communications technologies, successive minority governments, and parties' obsession with message cohesiveness. When considering these and other variables, we can see how the contours of the permanent campaign have taken shape both within and outside of government in this country.

One need only look at news coverage of Canadian politics and government for evidence of permanent campaigning. In the executive branch, there is a constant stream of news stories about communication management. For instance, social media posts of text, photos, and video developed by the PMO that present the prime minister in a positive light avail of the government communications infrastructure and are recirculated by the party. Members of cabinet make announcements at pseudo-events that look similar to campaign-style events. More ministerial regional offices have been created around the country. Ministers travel as part of consultation processes, and cabinet meetings are periodically held outside of the capital. Party officials and government officers who are publicly off message with leadership are sanctioned and dismissed, just as candidates are axed with alarming frequency during a campaign for past social media indiscretions.

These are in public view; many other ways of manipulating public resources go on behind the scenes or are discovered years later. One little-known example is the revelation that the Government of Canada paid over $8,000 in hospitality expenses for former Australian prime minister John Howard to spend three days in Ottawa, during which time he met with government officials – though ostensibly the reason for his visit was to speak at the Manning Centre Conference that is mostly attended by Conservative partisans (Smith 2016). Others are hidden in plain sight, such as the Ontario Liberal government spending nearly $600,000 on advertising during the federal election campaign to promote a stronger pension plan scheme, a topic that Premier Kathleen Wynne advocated while stumping with Trudeau (Canadian Press 2016). We are left to wonder how many other activities occur without public knowledge.

A permanent campaigning mentality extends to the legislative branch, where MPs avail of their franking privilege to distribute partisan mailings, including during by-elections. Political parties maintain parliamentary research bureaus – known as the Conservative Resource Group, Liberal Research Bureau, and NDP Caucus Services – that receive funding to support the caucus but in turn conduct opposition research and coordinate party messaging. When an election is called, the bureaus dissolve and become party-funded war rooms. The New Democrats created satellite party offices with parliamentary funds and allows its parliamentary staff to draw on their overtime to continue to collect a paycheque when they take time off to volunteer for by-elections. Partisan activities have been an essential component of a senator's work, so it follows that senators have billed the Senate for travel expenses for attending events where they prop up their party and urge political donations. In the legislature, all political parties attempt to exploit existing rules and collectively make decisions on legislative committees that favour their own circumstance or attempt to constrain their opponents' campaigning and resources. Parliamentary debate exercises strict party discipline and message control, even when leaders publicly profess otherwise. Legislation and convention are altered to enhance the government's partisan advantage. At times, the government refuses to produce requested documents that could derail its agenda. As an election approaches, government bills are introduced that form the basis of political messaging. "One could ultimately say that there is the legislative agenda, and then there is the spin agenda, or the election agenda ... I believe the driving push within the House of Commons from a legislative and just a debate perspective is going to be focused solely on the election," remarked the Liberal House leader in early 2015 (Aiello 2015). Likewise, parliamentarians introduce private members' bills so that they have something to campaign on.

Permanent campaigning in government is also marked by increasing numbers of communications personnel. Government advertising is a tool of mass persuasion that blurs partisan messaging. Websites promote visuals that convey a cohesive brand that makes it difficult to differentiate party from state. Meticulously planned pseudo-events advance the governing party's communication priorities. Public servants, including government scientists, who publicly speak their minds do so at their own risk. Government departments are encouraged by senior mandarins to use social media to promote policy using the governing party's sloganeering and policy commitments. To name one example of this coordination, in 2014, a leaked email authored by an assistant deputy minister of finance asked contacts across government to "re-tweet the Department of Finance tweets from @financecanada on the announcement over the following 72 hours. Most of our tweets will contain the hashtags #StrongFamilies ou #Famillesfortes" (Canadian Press 2014). As the election approaches, budget goodies are dispensed, from big-ticket pan-Canadian initiatives to government pork for local community ventures. Languishing policy issues are neutralized with promises to take future action.

Early signals from the Trudeau government suggest that hyperpartisanship, and by extension permanent campaigning, are no longer in vogue. Some of the Harper government's most acrimonious forms of communication and governance are being undone. During that period, media relations were confrontational and governance was a highly disciplined machine with a partisan messaging mentality. Journalists had reduced access to most members of cabinet and fewer scrum opportunities. They experienced delayed responses to inquiries and access to information requests. They were directed to submit questions by email, which prompted a controlled electronic response, sometimes without regard for what was asked. News conferences were replaced with photo opportunities only and with seated Q-and-A–style events on a stage with a friendly handpicked moderator. When Prime Minister Harper did take questions from journalists, only those picked by the PMO were invited, and even then only a handful of questions were accepted. Information about high-level meetings, such as with premiers, was announced after the fact, so journalists could report only what was allegedly discussed. Digital media acted as a powerful method to bypass traditional news media and communicate directly with supporters and stakeholders. Meanwhile, the fourth estate grew dependent on the contrived electronic information even as it bristled at the practice. Time will tell whether Trudeau's sunny ways can penetrate the forces of political communication that have beset all of those who have previously headed the PMO. It is one thing for sunlight to be a disinfectant when first occupying the highest public office; it is quite another matter the longer that one occupies that office. Permanent campaigning in the Liberal government is prone to mount as controversy ensues, as the list of political enemies grows, as poll results suffer, and especially as the next election campaign approaches.

A permanent campaigning mindset is most evident among political parties, irrespective of leader. Major planks of an election manifesto are released long before the official campaign. Perpetual fundraising occurs through electronic media appeals and database management. The strategy of microtargeting subsegments of electors in communication carries over into the development of public policy. Centralized training modules are offered in preparation for the next election, and candidates are rigorously screened. Nominated candidates begin campaigning months if not years before the signing of the writ. "It was almost four years ago when the last election [took place] and I haven't stopped," remarked a Liberal candidate planning to contest an electoral district whose boundaries were adjusted under redistribution (quoted in Lord and Rana 2015). Electioneering was so pronounced in 2015 that it was pretense for that year's extraordinarily long seventy-eight-day official campaign period, as the exchange between Harper and Trudeau in the epigraph on p. v serves to illustrate.

The activities of interest groups in this environment are better described as constant communication. There is increased coordination of political advocacy, more government monitoring of protests, and growing susceptibility to leaked information that can discredit a group's perceived legitimacy. The threat of left-wing super PACs (the American term for political action committees that pool their resources) and union-funded pre-campaign advertising were other reasons why Harper headed to the polls early. The one area that has, to date, been hands-off is the judicial branch. The Conservative prime minister's unprecedented public volley against the chief justice of the Supreme Court, whom he alleged made an inappropriate phone call to the minister of justice, may be an isolated case. Or it may indicate that a permanent campaigning mentality leads to testing new boundaries.

While there is ample evidence of permanent campaigning in Canada, there is minimal theorizing about the concept in the Canadian context, which has a unique combination of institutional factors, principally the concentration of power at the apex of government combined with stringent party discipline. Public administration scholar Peter Aucoin spent much of his last academic efforts on the New Political Governance (NPG) model (2011, 2012). The NPG concept effectively captures the changing dynamics of core executive operations in light of new media pressures, the imperative placed on strategic communication, an enhanced decision-making role for political staff, the demand for transparency, and the hyperpartisan/political polarization between parties and within the electorate. Aucoin's model emphasizes the political and partisan aspect of party government, which provides some insight as to why a political party would be both susceptible to and welcoming of the permanent campaign. His intent was to more purposefully combine observations and analyses about the political/electoral imperative of parties with scholarship on the nature of public administration. This extended the theory of executive dominance to its logical conclusion in what is now a media-driven marketplace that requires a deft command of electoral preparedness, political communication, and governance. The NPG model thus sets out a useful framework for greater scrutiny of permanent campaigning, particularly in the section devoted to governance and the permanent campaign. But the model may not apply as readily to all areas under study here, and it holds greater relevance for a government that has been in office for a while than for one freshly installed.

A recent collection edited by Kirsten Kozolanka (2014) about what is termed "the publicity state" offers the most direct intersection between the permanent campaign and government communication, mostly considered through advertising expenditures. Its contribution relies more on its critical and normative approach to the subject matter, and less on an analysis of empirical, data-driven cases. Another recent contribution, *The Permanent Campaign: New Media, New Politics* (Elmer, Langlois, and McKelvey 2012) also reflects on the concept. Its authors investigate more narrowly the notion from the angle of "networked political communication," where transformations in online technologies impact the way political actors, news media, and citizens alike take part in a hybrid, accelerated, and partisan campaigning process. As well, Tom Flanagan's *Winning Power: Canadian Campaigning in the Twenty-First Century* (2014) addresses permanent campaigning more directly, with an entire chapter dedicated to the concept. Building the book's argument from his past experiences as a Conservative campaign strategist, he brings a finer conceptual definition and details the practice's implications for governance and electoral preparedness in Canadian politics. This includes the centralization of operations, message discipline, pre-writ negative advertising, and obsession with fundraising, which have become core preoccupations of political parties. *Winning Power* mostly focuses on parties' electioneering efforts and somewhat less on the use of governmental institutions, policy design, and communication practices as tools of permanent campaigning by governments. As with other contributions, the emphasis tends to be on changes within party politics or governance, rather than on permanent campaigning's relationship with public administration.

The concept of the permanent campaign has also been introduced and studied in volumes published in the *Communication, Strategy, and Politics* series of UBC Press. Chapters in both *Political Marketing in Canada* and *Political Communication in Canada* contribute to the definition of this reality within the Canadian context. Contributions in the first collection use political marketing theories to describe how market research and communication activities (such as government communication and advertising or partisan use of social media) are integrated in strategic designs aimed at ensuring electoral success. Anna Lennox Esselment's (2014) work provides a rich review of the literature on permanent campaigning and describes how, from 2006 on, Conservatives in Ottawa had modified four features of government communication (professionalization, centralization, polling, and partisan polarization) to bring a permanent-campaign ethos in governance.

In the absence of a general theoretical model, our approach here is that permanent campaigning comprises five interrelated strategic objectives. These are carried during the inter-election context by political parties to improve electoral outcomes: communication control, resource exploitation, redefinition of norms, database management, and coalition building (Table 1.1). This framework highlights the hybrid nature of permanent campaigning in Canada, which combines older and newer types of strategic objectives undertaken through older and newer forms of electioneering. These and other activities are dotted throughout the book; in Chapter 16 we return to them, offering examples of electioneering in the lead-up to the 2015 election call. We believe that they tell a story of the institutionalization of a permanent electioneering ethos, combined with the broad scope of inter-election tactics that have been implemented in recent years.

Table 1.1

Strategic objectives of permanent campaigning in Canada

Component	Description	Examples of inter-election activities
1 Communication control	Communication practices that at one time were confined to the official campaign period but are now routinely practised in the inter-election period.	• Candidate screening and training • Direct marketing with supporters • Fewer opportunities for going off script • Information constraints • Political advertising • Tighter media protocols • Unforgiving message discipline
2 Resource exploitation	State resources are leveraged for campaigning purposes between elections, in particular to support new approaches.	• Government advertising and polling • More communications personnel • Partisan mailings through MPs' offices • Politicization of public administration • Satellite offices • Touring and pseudo-events
3 Redefinition of norms	Attempts are made by political elites to circumvent or change rules and norms to accommodate the practice of permanent campaigning.	• Altered conventions or legislation • Fusion of party and government messaging and visuals • Ignoring normal processes • Discrediting critics, libel suits • PMO digital media production
4 Database management	Fundraising and data mining are key roles for the extra-parliamentary party operations as a means to drive agendas throughout the parliamentary mandate.	• Email fundraising • Information collection about electors • Political marketing research, segmentation, and microtargeting
5 Coalition building	Governing party's willingness to engage with or court particular stakeholders, groups, or constituents – while ostracizing opponents – is increasingly tied to its larger electoral goals.	• Appeals to select subsegments of the electorate while ignoring others • Mobilization of supporters • Monitoring of protests

Permanent Campaigning and Democracy

Before turning to the potential implications for Canadian democracy, and to set up an assessment of what can be done to address concerns, we must consider institutional arrangements. As indicated, changes in information and communication technologies are responsible for hurtling forward the political cycle. The unprecedented connectivity of political actors and citizens is having profound implications for political life and government business. The exponential effect of the volume and speed of information transfer is too profound to discuss here, as are the implications for traditional media (but see Elmer et al. 2012; Marland et al. 2014; Marland 2016). Suffice it to say that the volume and speed of information transfer are responsible for the intensification of political advocacy and obsessive issues management.

The electoral system is a static institutional consideration that affects the way that permanent campaigning is carried out. A prime minister has little incentive to distribute pork or travel to ridings that are firmly held by incumbents, especially members of opposition parties. However, there is an enormous impetus to visit battleground ridings where a seat is at risk of being lost or a gain is possible, particularly in the period surrounding by-election campaigns. The winner-takes-all feature of the single member plurality system requires only a minimum winning coalition. Majority governments have been formed with less than 40 percent of the national vote, meaning that policy proposals can be advanced even if a majority of Canadians are opposed. The importance of fixed-date election legislation is to raise political parties' consciousness of a pending campaign. The rule itself is not always relevant given that first ministers do not necessarily abide by it and because minority Parliaments will almost certainly collapse beforehand.

Voter behaviour is a further consideration. The best predictor of voter behaviour is partisanship. In Canada, a decline in durable partisanship began in earnest in the 1960s and 1970s, and today this country has a comparatively greater number of flexible partisans than its US counterpart (Clarke et al. 1979; Clarke et al. 2009). Flexible partisans are citizens who lean towards identifying with one party, but are more susceptible than durable partisans to short-term factors, such as issues and leadership, and tend to switch their vote from one election to another. The decline in party memberships is connected with the rise of partisan flexibility, as well as with the decline in Canadians' deference to institutions, leaders, and elites generally. Because parties have shrinking pools of hard and fast partisans to rely on, the need to identify supporters and to assemble coalitions of voters is increasingly important (Flanagan 2014; Gidengil 2012). This means that parties have to not only look after their base, but also reach out to floating voters, a segment whose composition changes from one election to the next.

Election and political financing regulations have a profound influence on the way that permanent campaigning is carried out. Because these rules shape activities during the official campaign, by extension they influence how that campaigning persists. Among the most influential is the leader's veto over candidate nominations, which makes all local campaigns flow through the upper echelon of the party and is the basis for exacting message discipline. It is doubtful that a party leader's inner circle truly relinquished this power after the passage of the *Reform Act*, in effect as of the 42nd Parliament, which stipulates that regional agents must sign a candidate's nomination papers. Another Canadian practice of significance is the *Canada Elections Act* provision that electors' contact information from the National Register of Electors be regularly provided to political parties and MPs. This forms the basis for database marketing and non-stop fundraising. Limits on campaign spending, which are particularly rigid for third parties, make pre-writ advertising a necessary practice for well-funded organizations. Strict annual donation limits encourage political parties to raise money every single year, not just in election years. A former member of the Harper PMO describes the pre-writ situation as a period when "there are no spending limits, no advertising limits, no polling limits, no blackout periods, and no one has to determine what is or is not an election expense ... All of the work that has gone into developing the *Canada Elections Act* over the years to limit the influence of the almighty dollar goes out the window in this extended pre-writ period" (Carson 2014). That a prime minister would seek refuge in the regulations of an extraordinarily long official campaign speaks volumes about the practice of pre-election politicking across a wide spectrum of political interests.

As indicated, a further institutional consideration is the clout of the executive branch of government over the legislative branch. The centre of government is a compilation of influential political actors who work in concert with public servants in central agencies. Cabinet and powerful cabinet committees, such as Treasury Board and Parliamentary Affairs, work in concert with the PMO. So does the Agenda and Results Committee (formerly Operations), which we note that the Trudeau government further renamed as Agenda, Results and Communications three months into office to integrate strategic communications functions. Political directives flow to the Privy Council Office (PCO) and the Treasury Board Secretariat. All departments and agencies, boards, and commissions act as arms of the government, with the Department of Finance and the Department of Public Services and Procurement playing a more centralized and conformist role than the rest. These are overseen by ministers and their exempt political staff, who work in ministers' offices. Coordination of this monolith must be balanced with the political executive enjoying the continued support of the government party's caucus and, more broadly, a majority of MPs.

Members of the PMO and PCO, alongside ministers and their staff, face the unenviable challenge of mobilizing the public service. Increasingly, this involves a whole-of-government approach to public administration that unites departmental resources under a shared programming umbrella, such as the Canada 150 celebrations. The PMO and ministers issue directives via the government whip to ensure that MPs are mouthpieces who promote desired messages and vote in synchronized fashion. However, there is more two-way communication with caucus than people appreciate. A prime minister who ignores caucus risks losing power, as happened with Jean Chrétien; one who provides a critical mass with active roles in governance gains a stronghold over the party, as with Stephen Harper and his caucus advisory committee system (Wilson 2015).

There are several potential democratic implications that are well worth considering. First and foremost, partisan misuse of public resources not only presents an ethical concern but in fact poses a significant risk to Canadian democracy. In the Westminster parliamentary system, a non-partisan public administration is considered as a safeguard to abuse of powers from elected officials and their political staff. Public servants should not be expected to become cogs in the marketing and public relations apparatus of a government's agenda. They act as impartial policy advisors to the governing elite, as protectors of the common good, and as service providers to citizens. They are also tasked with explaining to Canadians what government is doing and then implementing it. Therefore, the politicization of public administration may endanger the non-partisan nature of the public service necessary to safeguard the public interest. This speaks to an underlying premise that most political actors are less concerned with promoting broad democratic tenets, such as enhancing civic literacy, than they are with advancing their own interests and one-upping their opponents.

In the same vein, partisan use of public funds, particularly on government advertising and research, during the inter-election period goes against the spirit of electoral expense regulations. Political parties, both in government and opposition, circumvent electoral regulations by engaging in persuasive communication spending aimed at conditioning public opinion for the next electoral cycle. Canadians are exposed to pre-electoral advertising, often in the guise of government information campaigns destined officially at selling the policies and programs of the party in power. Such spending works around the regulatory framework regarding election expenses to the benefit of the party in power. Bans on partisan advertising outside of the official electoral campaign and a redefinition of the period under which expenses – both for research and communication – are considered as electoral in nature have been considered in other jurisdictions as effective mechanisms to ensure the integrity of electoral regulation frameworks. Early indications are that these are the sorts of reforms that may transpire under the Trudeau government.

Another set of complications arises with the concentration of power within the central agencies of government. This centralization of decision-making processes within the prime minister's close guard diminishes the role of individual elected representatives from the governing party. In the disciplined communication context of the permanent campaign, government MPs act as both docile supporters expected to vote along party lines and as customer service agents who promote policies and programs to their constituents. Concentration of power within the executive also dilutes the legitimacy of Parliament and its elected members as core actors of the legislative process. Recent governments have limited parliamentary debate over policies, introduced mammoth omnibus bills or budget legislation containing hidden hyperpartisan provisions and regulations, and made information less accessible for policy evaluation in parliamentary committees. This suggests that cooperation, moderation, and negotiation in the legislative process are often sacrificed.

Finally, as the permanent campaign is carried under the guides of political marketing principles, it is aimed at aiding parties to assemble a minimum winning coalition of specific segments of targeted voters. During the inter-election period, government officials and opposition parties cater to the narrow interests and needs of the voters that they court to win the next election. Interest representation is therefore limited, and political responsiveness is calculated in ways that were not possible prior to the age of data analytics and narrowcasting.

This raises the spectre of permanent campaigning as an insidious phenomenon. In the United States, political parties can mobilize to shut down the government until political compromise is worked out in Congress and with the executive branch. In Canada, the fusion of the executive and legislative branches has other implications, including the ability of the prime minister (via the governor general) to shut down the legislative branch. The government party has significant advantages over opponents because of the rich resources at its disposal and an ability to act without negotiating with the opposition parties. This authority is magnified in a majority government situation. Whether this results in peace, order, and good government is a matter of opinion.

The Structure of *Permanent Campaigning in Canada*

The chapters in this book address a number of democratic implications related to permanent campaigning in Canada. Our concluding chapter presents potential remedies to those issues. *Permanent Campaigning in Canada* aims to bridge a void in the Canadian literature by bringing together the different components of the permanent campaign (e.g., political marketing and election preparedness, political communication, governance) through data-driven, empirical case studies. Whereas past Canadian publications have used more segmented or narrow theoretical, epistemological, and methodological approaches to investigate the concept, this one offers an integrated perspective. It explores the permanent campaign through general lenses of how it is marketed, how it is communicated, and how it affects how Canadians are governed. An overarching research objective is to assess whether the advent of perpetual campaigning in the inter-election period has enhanced or diminished key features of democratic governance. The following key questions are considered:

1   To what extent are the tactics, tools, or channels used by political actors in Canada during governance the same or different than what occurs during the official election campaign period?
2   To what extent does permanent campaigning result in a more informed, engaged, or cynical citizenry in Canada?

3 What are the corresponding implications of permanent campaigning for political parties, the media, parliamentary government, and Canadian democracy?

Permanent Campaigning in Canada is positioned to test parts of the NPG model by closely examining different aspects of permanent campaigning in Canada, as well as to contribute to broader theorizing. It further develops and refines the five key strategic objectives that we associate it with – communication control, resource exploitation, redefining norms, database management, and coalition building – as they apply to the Canadian context. The book features contributions from a variety of scholars who offer fresh perspectives about the Canadian political marketplace.

The first section of the book deals with theoretical parameters. In Chapter 2, Jonathan Craft sets the groundwork for how a non-partisan public service ought to interact with its publicly accountable political masters. Steve Patten builds on this in Chapter 3 by cautioning about the democratic implications of political strategy and data analytics. Chapters in Parts 2 and 3 follow a common organizational format of reviewing theory, presenting a case study, and considering what it means for permanent campaigning in Canada. Part 2 is about permanent campaigning by political parties. In Chapter 4, Andrea Lawlor looks at the media's treatment of political party messaging. The use of digital media by parties during the permanent campaign is tackled next. Alex Marland and Maria Mathews examine how email communication is used for fundraising, while in Chapter 6, Thierry Giasson and Tamara Small look at the strategy behind the online communication of Canadian opposition parties. Chapter 7 by André Turcotte and Simon Vodrey complements that work by dissecting the role of Liberal Party pollsters during the inter-election period. The section is rounded out by David McGrane, who in Chapter 8 discusses the mindset of a constant state of election readiness that seized the New Democratic Party of Canada in recent years.

Part 3 is about governance. In Chapter 9, Philippe Lagassé considers the use of prerogative powers of the Crown and offers an analysis of the policy implications of Canada's fixed-date election law. Chapter 10 sees Denver McNeney and David Coletto test whether government advertising influences viewers' impressions of the governing party. This is followed by a

discussion about the role of branding in the Obama and Harper administrations, by J.P. Lewis and Kenneth Cosgrove. In Chapter 12, Anna Lennox
Esselment and Paul Wilson peel back the curtain on how permanent campaigning is directed from the highest levels of government offices. The role
of digital media in the Canadian public service is considered in the next
two contributions. Amanda Clarke and Mary Francoli look at ways that the
Canadian public service have been slow to embrace digital media, while
Mireille Lalancette and Sofia Tourigny-Koné find evidence of how political
personnel exploited public resources to produce cutting-edge digital video
productions about the prime minister. Finally, in Chapter 15, we purposely
sought an understudied area that is of important social concern and looks at
political actors on the fringes of permanent campaigning. Mario Levesque's
study of the activities of disability organizations offers much-needed insights about how small outside interests struggle to be heard. The book's
concluding chapter brings all of these perspectives together and reconsiders
the questions raised in this introductory chapter.

The empirical analyses within the chapters cover a broad range. Some
examine how a permanent-campaign mentality has affected the opposition
parties, particularly how developments such as voter microtargeting are now
ubiquitous given the low level of partisan attachment among Canadian voters. Others investigate the imperative of perpetual fundraising, the use of
government advertising as it relates to strong leadership, and the challenge
that a competitive atmosphere poses for the traditional separation of political and bureaucratic spheres. This volume is different from others in that
we are foremost concerned with the inter-election period and its treatment
as a campaign context. Whereas political behaviour studies emphasize the
effects of party or media behaviour on electors during the official campaign
period, we expressly seek to explore the nature of party and media behaviour outside of the electoral period and the effects of institutions on the behaviour of political elites. Importantly, we are concerned with understanding
the effects of party elites' behaviour on the permanent government and the
fourth estate, and vice versa. As a result, we anticipate that this body of work
will fill a gap at an intersection between the increasingly fused literatures of
political behaviour, political communication, and public administration.

NOTES

1 For more information about many of the concepts discussed in this opening chapter, see Marland (2016).

2 In 2004, the *Canada Elections Act* was amended to prohibit donations from corporations and unions. To offset the revenue decline, a new per-vote state subsidy regime was introduced, and a more generous tax credit for limited personal donations became available, which ended up being phased out by the 2015 election. In 2006, the amount that Canadians were allowed to donate to each political party was lowered to $1,000, which is subject to an inflation provision. In 2015, Canadians were eligible to donate up to $1,500 annually to each political party and at the riding level (in effect, up to $3,000 per party), of which the first $400 was eligible for a 75 percent tax refund. A further stipulation is that fundraising communication constitutes an advertising expense during the official election campaign, whereas there are no such spending constraints during the inter-election period.

REFERENCES

Aiello, Rachael. 2015. "MPs Say Remaining Weeks in House All about Positioning, Posturing Pre-Writ Period." *Hill Times*, April 13, 1.

Aucoin, Peter. 2011. "New Political Governance." In *Approaching Public Administration: Core Debates and Emerging Issues*, edited by R. Leone and F. Ohemeng, 301–8. Toronto: Emond Montgomery.

–. 2012. "New Political Governance in Westminster Systems: Impartial Public Administration and Management Performance at Risk." *Governance: An International Journal of Policy, Administration and Institutions* 25 (2): 177–99. http://dx.doi.org/10.1111/j.1468-0491.2012.01569.x.

Baum, M. 2012. "Preaching to the Choir or Converting the Flock: Presidential Communication Strategies in the Age of Three Medias." In *Presidential Communication Strategies in the Age of Three Medias*, edited by R.L. Fox and J.M. Ramos, 183–205. Cambridge: Cambridge University Press.

Benoit, Liane E. 2006. "Ministerial Staff: The Life and Times of Parliament's Statutory Orphans." In *Commission of Inquiry into the Sponsorship Program and Advertising Activities, Restoring Accountability: Research Studies Volume 1 – Parliament, Ministers and Deputy Ministers*, 145–252. Ottawa: Public Works and Government Services Canada.

Blumenthal, Sidney. 1980. *The Permanent Campaign: Inside the World of Elite Political Operatives*. Boston: Beacon Press.

Bowman, Karlyn. 2000. "Polling to Campaign and to Govern." In *The Permanent Campaign and Its Future*, edited by N. Orstein and T. Mann, 54–74. Washington, DC: American Enterprise Institute and the Brookings Institution.

Burton, Michael J., and Daniel M. Shea. 2010. *Campaign Craft: The Strategies, Tactics, and Art of Political Campaign Management*. Santa Barbara: Praeger.

Canadian Press. 2014. "Public Servants Asked to Promote Conservative Tax Proposal on Twitter." *Globe and Mail*, November 21. http://www.theglobeandmail.com/news/politics/public-servants-asked-to-promote-conservative-tax-proposal-on-twitter/article21705733/.

–. 2016. "Ontario Spent $600K on Ads Touting Pension Plan during Federal Election: Taxpayer Group." *Huffington Post*, February 8. http://www.huffingtonpost.ca/2016/02/08/ontario-spent-600k-on-pension-plan-ads-during-federal-election-taxpayer-group_n_9189744.html.

Carson, Bruce. 2014. "Unintended Consequences of a Fixed Election Date: Year-Long Campaign." *Hill Times*, October 27, 12.

Clarke, Harold D., Jane Jenson, Lawrence LeDuc, and Jon H. Pammett. 1979. *Political Choice in Canada*. Toronto: McGraw-Hill Ryerson.

Clarke, Harold D., Allan Kornberg, and Thomas Scotto. 2009. *Making Political Choices: Canada and the United States*. Toronto: University of Toronto Press.

Cook, Corey. 2002. "The Permanence of the 'Permanent Campaign': George W. Bush's Public Presidency." *Presidential Studies Quarterly* 32 (4): 753–64. http://dx.doi.org/10.1177/0360491802238707.

Coyne, Andrew. 2016. "Trudeau's First Three Months in Power Big on Symbolism, Short on Substance." *National Post*, February 5. http://news.nationalpost.com/news/canada/trudeau-first-three-months-in-power.

Delacourt, Susan. 2016. *Shopping for Votes: How Politicians Choose Us and We Choose Them*, 2nd ed. Madeira Park, BC: Douglas and McIntyre.

Doherty, Brendan J. 2012. *The Rise of the President's Permanent Campaign*. Kansas: University Press of Kansas.

Dyer, Evan. 2016. "'Deliverology' Guru Schools Trudeau Government for 2nd Time at Cabinet Retreat." *CBC News*, April 26. http://www.cbc.ca/news/politics/deliverology-liberal-cabinet-retreat-1.3553024.

Elmer, Greg, Ganaele Langlois, and Fenwick McKelvey. 2012. *The Permanent Campaign: New Media, New Politics*. New York: Peter Lang.

Esselment, Anna. 2014. "The Governing Party and the Permanent Campaign." In *Political Communication in Canada: Meet the Press and Tweet the Rest*, edited by A. Marland, T. Giasson, and T.A. Small, 24–38. Vancouver: UBC Press.

Flanagan, Tom. 2012. "Political Communication and the 'Permanent Campaign'." In *How Canadians Communicate IV: Media and Politics*, edited by D. Taras and C. Waddell, 129–48. Edmonton: Athabasca University Press.

–. 2014. *Winning Power: Canadian Campaigning in the Twenty-First Century*. Montreal/Kingston: McGill-Queen's University Press.

Gidengil, Elizabeth. 2012. "The Diversity of the Canadian Political Marketplace." In *Political Marketing in Canada*, edited by A. Marland, T. Giasson, and J. Lees-Marshment, 39–56. Vancouver: UBC Press.

Johnson, Dennis W. 2011. *Campaigning in the Twenty-First Century: A Whole New Ballgame?* New York: Routledge.

Jones, C. O. 1998. *Passages to the Presidency: From Campaigning to Governing*. Washington, DC: Brookings Institution.

Kernell, Samuel. 1997. *Going Public: New Strategies of Presidential Leadership*, 3rd ed. Washington, DC: Congressional Quarterly.

Kozolanka, Kirsten, ed. 2014. *Publicity and the Canadian State: Critical Communications Perspectives*. Toronto: University of Toronto Press.

Lord, Craig, and Abbas Rana. 2015. "Candidates Campaigning in Full Election Mode for Months, Some Years, ahead of Oct. 19 Election." *Hill Times*, April 27, 1.

Marland, Alex. 2016. *Brand Command: Canadian Politics and Democracy in the Age of Message Control*. Vancouver: UBC Press.

Marland, Alex, Thierry Giasson, and J. Lees-Marshment, eds. 2012. *Political Marketing in Canada*. Vancouver: UBC Press.

Marland, Alex, Thierry Giasson, and Tamara A. Small, eds. 2014. *Political Communication in Canada: Meet the Press and Tweet the Rest*. Vancouver: UBC Press.

Murray, Shoon Kathleen, and Peter Howard. 2002. "Variation in White House Polling Operations: Carter to Clinton." *Public Opinion Quarterly* 66 (4): 527–58. http://dx. doi.org/10.1086/343754.

Public Works and Government Services Canada. 2005. "Who Is Responsible? Summary." Commission of Inquiry into the Sponsorship Program and Advertising Activities. http://epe.lac-bac.gc.ca/003/008/099/003008-disclaimer.html?orig=/100/206/301/ pco-bcp/commissions/sponsorship-ef/06-03-06/www.gomery.ca/en/phase1report/ summary/es_full_v01.pdf.

Rana, Abbas. 2015. "Rival MPs Question NDP MP Morin's Use of Parliamentary Email for Partisan Purposes." *Hill Times*, April 6, 1.

–. 2016. "PM Tells Grit MPs to Keep a Close Eye on Constituencies." *Hill Times*, February 1, 1.

Rose, Jonathan. 2012. "Are Negative Ads Positive? Political Advertising and the Permanent Campaign." In *How Canadians Communicate IV: Media and Politics*, edited by D. Taras and C. Waddell, 149–68. Edmonton: Athabasca University Press.

Savoie, Donald J. 1999. *Governing from the Centre: The Concentration of Power in Canadian Politics*. Toronto: University of Toronto Press.

–. 2010. *Power: Where Is It?* Montreal/Kingston: McGill-Queen's University Press.

Smith, Marie-Danielle. 2016. "Harper Government Subsidized Ex-Australian PM's Trip for Conservative Conference." *Embassy*, January 13. http://www.embassynews.ca/ news/2016/01/13/harper-government-subsidized-ex-australian-pms-trip-for -conservative-conference/48082.

Tenpas, Karen. 1996. "Institutionalized Politics: The White House Office of Political Affairs." *Presidential Studies Quarterly* 26 (2): 511–22.

Tenpas, Kathryn Dunn, and James A. McCann. 2007. "Testing the Permanence of the Permanent Campaign: An Analysis of Presidential Polling Expenditures, 1977– 2002." *Public Opinion Quarterly* 71 (3): 349–66. http://dx.doi.org/10.1093/poq/ nfm020.

Thomas, Paul G. 2013. "Communications and Prime Ministerial Power." In *Governing: Essays in Honour of Donald J. Savoie*, edited by J. Bickerton and B. Guy Peters, 53– 84. Montreal/Kingston: McGill-Queens University Press.

Wilson, R. Paul. 2015. "Minister's Caucus Advisory Committees under the Harper Government." *Canadian Public Administration* 58 (2): 227–48. http://dx.doi.org/10.1111/ capa.12112.

2

Governing on the Front Foot: Politicians, Civil Servants, and the Permanent Campaign in Canada

Jonathan Craft

Once elected, governments must govern. They must engage with the apparatus of the state to close the loop on the constant campaign, work with the public service and the formal policy-making processes, and confront accepted public administration and management structures and norms. This endogenous or inside-of-government aspect of the continuous campaign has received some treatment (Aucoin 2012; Savoie 2013, 2015), but as detailed in the introductory chapter of this volume, it remains far less scrutinized than its external-facing and predominantly communication-based counterpart. Analysis is stymied in large part by a lack of access to political and bureaucratic elites, particularly those associated with a sitting government, and by the fact that permanent campaigning is a nascent research subject in Canada.

For some time now, scholars and media accounts have begun to raise concerns of the significant dangers to traditional policy making and governance arrangements that may accompany the permanent-campaign mode in Canada. Continuous campaigning is argued to privilege partisan-political electoral interests and politicize the public service and the policy process. This takes shape through greater attention from and involvement by the political arm in senior public service appointments and in aspects of the policy-making process – like implementation – that have traditionally been considered the purview of the public service, a growing reliance on appointed partisan-political staff throughout government, and efforts to align the content of policy development with current and future partisan-political electoral objectives (Aucoin 2012; Savoie 2013). The cumulative result is that governments are increasingly governing on the front foot. They are pressuring the public service for greater responsiveness to the partisan-political policy agenda of government. More than ever, a governing political party leverages the tools of office to favourably position itself for the next election.

Few argue with the primacy of politics or the democratic legitimacy of the political class in Canada's system of responsible government (Aucoin 1995; Craft 2010). Rather, the concern is that the permanent campaign will at best challenge and at worst diminish public service impartiality or its provision of detached competence – that is, competence that serves the public interest rather than exclusively the priorities of the government of the day (Montpetit 2011; Savoie 2003; Zussman, 2015). What precisely constitutes the public interest, and what role the public service plays in its determination or protection from partisan but democratically elected actors, remains contested. Some suggest that the public service has a constitutional obligation to protect the longer-term public interest from partisan short-termism (see Sossin 2006). Others have argued for the primacy of politics and against the public service serving as platonic guardians of the public interest (Rhodes and Wanna 2007). So how can we critically appraise the endogenous impacts and implications of Canada's purported adoption of the permanent campaign?

One approach to evaluating the health of the Canadian governance arrangement – the relationship between democratically elected officials, the citizens they represent, and the permanent professional non-partisan public service – is to think of it as a public service bargain (PSB). Canada's traditional arrangement was modelled on the British Shafferian bargain. The name emanates from its author Bernard Shaffer, an early proponent of the PSB, who sought to capture the idealized agreement that long governed the respective entitlements and duties tacitly agreed on by British politicians and public servants. In Canada, Savoie (2003, 6) argues, a similar arrangement endured from Confederation until the prime ministership of Pierre Trudeau, where:

> public servants exchanged overt partisanship, some political rights, and a public profile in return for permanent careers, or at least indefinite tenure, anonymity, selection by merit, a regular work week, and the promise of being looked after at the end of a career that did not require paying close attention to their own material self-interest. Politicians meanwhile exchanged the ability to appoint or dismiss public servants and change their working conditions at will for professional competence and non-partisan obedience to the government of the day.

This chapter integrates PSB and permanent-campaign literature to theorize the key tensions and pressures facing Canada's bargain(s) given the dynamics of the permanent-campaign era. The analysis is anchored by three overarching research questions: How are the key components of the PSB (rewards, competencies, and loyalty) operationalized in a permanent-campaign context? Second, what are their likely implications for political–administrative relations and the policy-making process? Third, assuming the permanent campaign is in fact a new feature of contemporary Canadian governance, will it result in a new bargain(s) or adaptation of existing bargain(s)? Given the burgeoning nature of the permanent campaign and the paucity of attention given to how the permanent campaign will impact the machinery of government, some theorizing is needed to better attend to its implications for political-administrative relations and the policy process.

The central argument advanced here is that the permanent campaign is a specific subsidiary type of bargain that will be layered on existing bargains. That is, it is one of a successive number of bargains that have been struck as Canadian institutions, actors, and governing practices have evolved (Benzies and Lodge 2015; Lodge 2010). The result is an era of contemporary bargains characterized by departures from Shafferianism, but not a complete overthrow of it (Bourgault and Van Dorpe 2013), and greater hybridity as aspects of the permanent-campaign mode are accommodated and rejected.

The communication and marketing–heavy analysis of the permanent campaign masks important policy and governance implications. As the editors of this volume put it in Chapter 1, the permanent campaign refers to "the contextual environment of perpetual election preparedness and with the institutionalization of strategic actions in the inter-election period – whether political, marketing, or communication in nature – that at one time were exclusive to the official election period" (this volume, p. 7). Similarly, Anna Lennox Esselment (2014, 29) identifies four key features of the permanent campaign in Canada:

1 use of campaign strategists in government for communications advice
2 use of command-and-control-style message discipline
3 reliance on market research and polling
4 use of a communication style that reflects sharp partisanship.

To these definitions and features, two additional internal characteristics are posited here and developed in this chapter. They marry the advent of the permanent campaign with bargains thinking to better grapple with polit-ical–administrative relations and policy-making in a constant campaign mode. They are:

5 heightened partisan-political policy agenda management
6 selectively contentious political–administrative relations.

The permanent-campaign bargain will likely involve heightened compres-sion of the policy-making cycle, where a handful of key electoral and partisan policy agenda items of government are privileged and expedited through the machinery of government. The remaining day-to-day or housekeeping policy matters are left largely to the public service. This trend has already been iden-tified (see Savoie 2003) and predates the 2004–11 minority governments of Stephen Harper, which are often credited with the advent of continuous cam-paigning in Canada. However, this reality is arguably going to become even more acute as governments seek to drive their electoral agendas through the machinery of government and begin to position their subsequent electoral priorities while in office. This further broadens the first trend identified by Esselment (2014) above, in that partisan-political interests will be satisfied and privileged not only in communications but, crucially, also in the develop-ment and implementation of policy (Lathrop 2003). The Conservatives' 2005–6 campaign promise to gradually reduce the goods and services tax by two percentage points is a good example. It was widely argued to be a suboptimal policy choice, reducing consumption versus income taxes, but was intended to curry electoral favor to facilitate implementation of the broader Con-servative agenda (Geddes 2009; Carson 2014, p.90). Other examples include income splitting, child-care benefits, and various boutique tax measures designed to privilege certain segments of the electorate (Wells 2013). Put differently, the governing party's continuous campaign necessitates com-munication of what it has done and expects to do – but requires an ability to marshal the resources of government to accomplish continuous campaign goals while governing. For its part, the public service assumes greater respon-sibility for the files the government of the day deems *not* to be a priority, with the political arm engaging only when they become politically salient (Savoie 1999). That is, when governments must reactively firefight or manage issues or when policy matters become opportunities for partisan electoral advantage.

Second, the permanent campaign is likely to give rise to sharp bursts of contentious political–administrative relations. Contentiousness to some degree is a product of the inherent tensions of Canada's adoption of a Westminster-style system of responsible government (Aucoin 1995). The political arm of government seeks to make things move, while the institution of the public service is designed to slow policy making through various processes and routines to prevent errors and maladministration (Axworthy 1988). The concern is that the permanent campaign is a threat to impartial public administration; as senior public sector appointments become increasingly politicized, all public servants are expected to be enthusiastic promoters of government policy, and all forms of scrutiny and oversight become perceived as hostile. Given the breadth of policy matters in play at any time and the need for the public service to implement and realize policy, the likelihood that governments would be prepared to die on every hill is low. Instead, it is reasonable to posit that contentiousness would be selective: focused on a government's key electoral promises, where it is instrumentally useful to government for policy priorities or the mitigation of electoral fallout.

This second internal impact of the permanent campaign can be hypothesized on two fronts. The first is linked to the above tension, where the political arm of government seeks to mobilize its key partisan-political policy items, while the public service seeks to balance political responsiveness with its professional non-partisan standards, and statutory and fiduciary duties. Second, governments may use contentiousness instrumentally as a rationalization for their real or perceived inabilities to advance particular priority policy files. This is not merely theoretical. There are well-documented examples of the public service being accused of being "bloated, expensive, unresponsive, a creation of routine deliberately resistant to changes, and largely incapable of dealing with new challenges" (Peters and Savoie 1994, 419). This chapter explores how these twin dynamics will likely impact the loyalty, competency, and rewards components essential to PSBs.

The Permanent Campaign and Canada's Evolving Ecology of Bargains

Broad agreement exists that Canada's Shafferian bargain is under duress (Hood 2000a; Savoie 2015). The causes for the breakdown include a laundry list of broader contextual matters as noted in Chapter 1, but also internal machinations tied to domestic political–administrative relations (Hood and Lodge 2006a; Savoie 2003). Therefore, it is important to emphasize that their decline precedes the emergence of the permanent campaign. In Canada, this typically involves the contention that Canadian prime ministers and their courtiers (their close circle of public service and political advisors analogous to a royal court) have displaced Parliament and cabinet and have fundamentally altered governance and policy-making arrangements (Aucoin 2012; Savoie 1999). The result, from a policy-making perspective, is that one policy process exists for the priorities and pet projects of the first ministers and their courtiers, and a second process exists for the day-to-day or housekeeping public service activities and policy files (Savoie 1999, 2003). In addition, both sets of elites are argued to engage in various forms of cheating that see them skirt their respective responsibilities and obligations under the traditional bargain (Hood 2002; Hood and Lodge 2006a). For example, the increasing penchant for politicians to avoid blame and/or to lay responsibility for unpopular matters directly at the feet of public servants, occasionally naming them directly. For their part, public servants, described by some as unresponsive or self-interested policy actors, have become more visible and are unwilling to accept and implement the policy preferences of their political masters (Savoie 2004).

A return to pure Shafferian bargains seems unlikely (if it ever existed), and the permanent campaign is now a potential reason why (Aucoin 2012; Savoie 2013). A first step is to recognize that different types of PSBs exist. Some of these, along with their subtypes and variants, are detailed in Table 2.1 based on the function and purpose of the public service (Hood 2002). The bargain can represent a broader social or constitutional covenant where the public service fulfills a representative or social cohesion function (consociational bargains), or where it is understood as a quasi-autonomous actor or trustee (Hegelian/Confucian bargains). In contrast, pragmatic bargains and their subtypes are rooted in more specific and localized agreements between political and administrative elites – for instance, in the Canadian case. On one end of the spectrum within the pragmatic category are Shafferian bargains, and on the other end are managerial/regulatory bargains. Hybrid-type bargains fall in between.

Second, observers have noted that such accommodations can and do evolve. Christopher Hood (2000a), for instance, has convincingly argued that pragmatic bargains are more sensitive to adaption and change and that in many jurisdictions, successive public sector reforms have shifted Shafferian bargains to managerial types. In the managerial bargain, public servants are provided increasing autonomy and managerial space but are also subject to public blaming for misadministration (Hood 2000a). Others,

TABLE 2.1

Public service bargain types and subtypes

Bargain archetype	Subtype	What politicians get	What public servants get	Cases
"Systemic" bargains (part of a broad constitutional or social bargain)	Consociational	"Social glue" or bonding through representative bureaucracy in a divided society	Share of administrative power	Belgium, India, Lebanon, Trinidad, EU
	Hegelian or Confucian	Trustees with quasi-judicial autonomy acting to protect the constitution or advance general public welfare	Status (and for Hegel, career-long material comfort)	Germany; self-proclaimed role of military in some states
"Pragmatic" bargains (specific politician-bureaucrat bargains)	Shafferian	Loyalty and competent service to government of the day	Permanent tenure, trust by ministers, avoidance of public blame for policy	Canada, UK, and classic Westminster-type systems
	Hybrid	Competent service with party or personal loyalty to government, minister	Some degree of trust by political superordinates, limited public blame for policy	French cabinets; Latin American patrimonial systems
	Managerial/ regulatory bargain	Public servants are blameable for regulatory/ operational errors	Operational autonomy or managerial space	US city managers, autonomous regulators, etc.

SOURCE: Adapted from Hood (2000b).

borrowing from the neo-institutional theory, contend that PSBs can themselves evolve through a process of layering, where new specific types of bargains are grafted to existing bargains (Benzies and Lodge 2015). Therefore, rather than a single static bargain, governance arrangements are characterized by one evolving bargain or by multiple bargains co-existing in various states of harmony and discord. The result is a mix or "ecology of bargains" that operates in any given jurisdiction and at particular conjunctures (Lodge 2009, 2010).

Determinations of duties and entitlements are then central to analysis of these bargains, with examinations centring on the rewards, loyalty, and competencies involved (Hondeghem 2011; Hood and Lodge 2006a). They too have been broken down into subsidiary types; see Table 2.2. In general, rewards are what public servants receive for their labour by type and stage of their career. They may include financial remuneration but also non-financial considerations such as promotions and participation in policy making. Competencies represent the abilities, skills, and knowledge that public servants are expected to have and to demonstrate in exchange for their rewards and the more basic ability for them to share in power. In Hood and Lodge's (2006a) elaboration the third criterion is loyalty and responsibility – that is, the agreed-on division of labour and responsibility in government and who is to be loyal to whom and in what ways.

The managerial bargain involves a "turkey race" with rewards based on individual competition, and "deliverer" competencies emphasizing skills in getting things done, and favours executive types of loyalty where bureaucrats act to pursue defined goals in a defined or limited policy space (Van der Meer, Van den Berg, and Dijkstra 2013). Hybrid bargains provide increased scope for one-off arrangements between politicians and civil servants regarding these aspects of PSBs (Bourgault and Van Dorpe 2013). These three components and their characteristics therefore allow us to theorize and anticipate what a permanent-campaign bargain involves and its fit with other existing bargains.

Recent analysis has found that Canada is moving towards a managerial bargain as a result of "Conservative minority governments and managerial reforms" (Bourgault and Van Dorpe 2013, 57). This raises direct linkages to the permanent campaign given that minority governments are less stable and typically result in more frequent elections, as has been noted in Canada's recent flurry of electoral activity (Flanagan 2014). Others have long argued that Canada's bargain is best characterized by hybridity. Some aspects of the

TABLE 2.2

Public service bargain reward, competency, and loyalty components

Key aspect	Subtypes	Characteristics
Rewards	"Lottery-of-life" bargains	Non-automatic or predictable rewards
	"Pyramid and escalator" bargains	Structured pattern of reward
	"Turkey race" bargains	Variable rewards; agreement to rewards based on individual competition
	"Noblesse oblige" bargains	Relative self-restraint at the top; agreement to a double-imbalance structure with relatively less generous pay at the top
Competencies	"Sage" bargains	States people in disguise; skills; provision of intellectual or moral insight
	"Deliverer" bargains	Skills of (creative) execution; ability to get things done
	"Wonk" bargains	Provision of technical knowledge and judgment
	"Go-between" bargains	Boundary-spanning skills, ability to work across different worlds
Loyalty/ obligations	"Jester" bargains	"Irritating" loyalty; acts as reality checker for rulers (e.g., truth to power)
	"Judge" bargains	Loyalty to the state and the law; acts as semi-autonomous player with loyalty to some higher entity
	"Executive" bargains	Loyalty within a specified brief; acts to pursue defined goals in some limited and revocable space of action
	"Partner" bargains	Loyalty as confidant and co-ruler; acts as interlocutor and collaborator with rulers, with right to be heard

SOURCE: Adapted from Hondeghem (2011).

Shafferian bargain are retained due to Canadian aversions to some tenets of managerial reforms and organizing principles (e.g., creating special operating agencies), while others are adopted in part or in full (e.g., performance-based pay) (see Aucoin 1995; Hood 2002). These assessments also raise clear links with the permanent campaign, as Canada's more pronounced use of appointed political staffs for policy purposes in ministers' and prime ministers' offices has been well documented. As a crucial instrument of the political arm of government, political staffs very existence is to attend to the politics of policy making and governing (Craft, 2016; Lodge 2010; Savoie 1999). The scholarship on PSBs, however, predates the permanent campaign, and the pathologies of the permanent campaign and its effects remain underspecified. Focusing on PSB loyalty, competencies, and responsibility is helpful in this regard.

Rewards for deputy ministers remain governed by long-standing practices of peer-to-peer public service evaluation. Financially, analysis is cut and dried. Salaries and bonuses have trended upward since 2000, and performance evaluation rooted in individual performance is a hallmark of managerial-type bargains (Bourgault 2011; Bourgault and Van Dorpe 2013). In concrete terms, recent reporting has found that the average performance pay envelope for executives in 2015 had risen 46 percent since Prime Minister Stephen Harper came to power in 2006 (Thompson 2015). However, rewards also involve non-financial benefits, and here the picture is not as straightforward. Jacques Bourgault's (2014) leading analysis over some twenty-five years suggests that the public service process for senior appointments remains fair and merit-based, but the politically appointed status of deputies, and the more recently created associate deputy cadre, allows for politics to muddy the waters. Indeed, the Liberals' return to power in 2015 was also marred by perceptions of public service politicization when a non-public servant with 2015 Liberal platform development credentials, was appointed to the Privy Council Office (PCO) as deputy secretary to cabinet for results and delivery (May 2016).

With respect to loyalty, the implications of the permanent campaign are also significant. Research has found there is still strong support amongst deputy ministers for an understanding of the obligations of the public service to be impartial, loyal, and offer its best free and frank advice to government. However, the same research finds that "deputy ministers are now removed from office when their superior has little confidence in their capacity to cope with the agenda" (Bourgault and Van Dorpe 2013, 55). There are of course some well-publicized examples of contentious political–administrative relations that emerged during the Conservative Party's tenure. These examples underscore that loyalty is a complex notion that involves loyalty to the government of the day and, above all some argue, loyalty to the ethos a professional non-partisan public servant who serves the public interest (see Sossin 2006). A well-known example is the highly publicized resignation of Canada's head statistician, Munir Sheikh, in July 2010. Sheikh publicly stated his opposition to the rationale offered by the government for the end of the mandatory long-from census in favour of a voluntary survey (Chase and Grant 2010). In Sheikh's case, his loyalty to the principles of non-partisan professional public service meant that he had to resign given he was unable to loyally serve the government of the day by supporting their policy preference. As prime ministerial appointees, deputy ministers and associate deputy ministers' loyalty will likely increasingly be put to the test under a permanent-campaign bargain. The Sheikh example demonstrates one of the subsidiary hypotheses advanced above: that the degree to which the permanent campaign will impact the bargain will depend in part on the electoral salience of any given issue and how public servants live up to traditional expectations of their non-partisan and professional status. All the more so in a minority government context where the stakes are high with the next election looming around every corner. Indeed, as Bourgault's recent analysis of deputy ministers suggests, minority parliaments reinforced continuous campaigning tendencies. As he puts it, "Increasing tensions and declining trust between ministers and their deputies, along with a reluctance to embrace an ambitious agenda because of risk aversion" (Bourgault 2014, 398).

This finding is also germane to the competency component of the bargain. It supports the notion that the core competencies sought in a constant campaign bargain will be sensitivity to politically important policy matters and error-free administration (Savoie 2003). Analysis has for some time revealed a broader trend in Westminster systems of senior ranks of the public service shifting from substantive subject matter experts with long-standing experience to shorter-lived policy management and process generalists (Rhodes, Wanna, and Weller 2010; Howlett, Craft, and Wellstead 2017). Bourgault's (2011, 2014) findings confirm that, overall, the senior ranks of the Canadian public service are no different. That deputy ministers fit that bill, generally speaking, underscores the important changes to competency aspects of the bargain. Here too the public record is instructive, with high-profile episodes like that of Linda Keen and Louis Ranger being relieved of duties (or retiring) for what was publicly stated, or rumoured to be, a lack of political responsiveness. In the case of Keen, then chair of the nuclear regulatory safety board who had been appointed by the previous Liberal administration, the government was said to have dismissed her for a "lack of leadership" (Harris 2014). Keen shut down one of the world's leading nuclear isotope generators over maintenance and safety concerns despite clear pressure and preference for its reactivation from the governing party. In another case, Deputy Minister Ranger was a long-serving public servant in charge of a massive infrastructure spending program that was rumoured to be moving too glacially for the political arm. The perceived obstructionist deputy was replaced with a new executive able to "deliver" (Campion-Smith 2009). These are, of course, only two isolated examples and perhaps the exceptions to the rule. They are, however, indicative of the types of shifts in the competencies that may be expected by elected officials in the age of the permanent campaign. Competencies for successful implementation are prized given that policy priorities and decisions made in campaigns are revised in government based on campaign-like strategy and tactics. Bourgault and Van Dorpe (2013, 63) go so far as to suggest that contemporary governance contexts, without invoking the permanent campaign, lead to a need to recruit a new kind of senior official. As they put it, one who embraces "a decrease in law and technical expertise for the job; greater manager-leader competencies; a capacity to cope with the increasing role of the political centre (accompanied by more administrative accountability); a greater sensitivity to governmental political agendas; a new role of policy advisor; a capacity to envision and cope government-wide; and a greater degree of attention paid to service delivery." The Liberal elected in 2015 moved quickly and decisively to reorient the internal machinery and culture of government to one centred on delivery and results by appointing an assistant secretary of cabinet in the PCO for "results and delivery." Also dubbed deliverology, this is a results-based management approach pioneered by British official Michael Barber, former head of UK prime minister Tony Blair's "delivery unit." Deliverology seeks to advance the government's agenda by tasking departments with clear targets, coupled with strong oversight and coordination provided by a central delivery unit. From a permanent-campaign perspective, the Trudeau appointment of an individual with firsthand involvement in the Liberal platform as the head of the PCO delivery unit leaves open the perception that responsiveness has been prized above all else and raises the spectre of an even more empowered centre of government.

Permanent Campaigning in Canada

If it is in fact an enduring fixture of Canadian political life, permanent campaigning will result in a new specific bargain being layered on existing Canadian bargains. In keeping with the thematic questions raised by the editors in Chapter 1, several implications can be distilled. As argued at the outset of this chapter, tactical implications are twofold. First, political-administrative relations will be marked by spurts of contentiousness on key issues when the government believes the electoral stakes and future prospects warrant the instrumental use of contentiousness. As a result, the public service needs to manage attempts to align partisan-driven policy making with traditional public service norms. Second, the policy-making process itself will be further oriented to a handful of key partisan-political policy goals of governments (past, present, and future). This will likely involve the continued focus from the centre of government on managing the policy agenda and the continued use of appointed political staffs and perceived supportive senior officials to do so.

Much of the bargains literature focuses predominantly on the public service, but politicians are part of the arrangement as well, a point to which the permanent campaign highlights. The above analysis suggests new realities for both sets of actors. Politicians benefit from an accelerated and partisan-aligned policy process where they can emphasize their key electoral policy issues. They will benefit from continued use of appointed political staff to drive that agenda and manage its implementation in concert with the public service, particularly the newly empowered delivery unit within the PCO. Politicians will also benefit from a governance context dotted by contentious political–administrative relations when needed. They will seek to avoid blame by shifting it to the public service or use them instrumentally to legitimize their policy failures or delays. For its part, the public service will benefit from a small and clearly demarcated set of policy issues, and it will continue to exert influence and benefit from partial independence over housekeeping policy matters. These will of course vary depending on who forms government and their particular style and policy priorities. Nonetheless, these policy matters represent more broadly the administration of government programs or services that are valence issues – that is, those policy matters that attract little public debate or positioning among political parties. This includes, for example, the administration of public service human resources, official languages programs, or the collection and processing of government revenue. The public service will, however, be at greater risk of being publicly attributed a role and its share of blame when things go wrong, but will benefit from seemingly increasing individual performance-based pay. Table 2.3 sets out the characteristics of the permanent-campaign bargain that is argued to be a type of hybrid bargain.

Following Hood and Lodge (2006a, 153), the argument of this chapter has been that PSBs are "not necessarily stable or self-reinforcing." It is therefore erroneous to think of the effect of permanent-campaign dynamics in absolute terms. Rather, it may be more accurate to think of them as part of a spectrum, with the permanent-campaign bargain contributing to the movement of one or a mix of PSB components, or the overarching ecology or set of bargains, towards hybridity. That is, while a pure permanent-campaign

TABLE 2.3

The permanent campaign bargain as hybrid bargain type

Bargain archetype	Subtype	What politicians get	What public servants and the public get
"Pragmatic" bargains (specific politician-bureaucrat bargains)	Shafferian	Loyalty and competent service to government of the day	Permanent tenure, trust by ministers, avoidance of public blame for policy
	Permanent campaign (hybrid bargain)	Accelerated and partisan-aligned policy process; increased use of appointed political staffs in policy making; contentious political-administrative relations when politically useful (blame avoidance, legitimation with electorate)	Clear government policy priorities; increased but partial policy-making autonomy (e.g., policy housekeeping); performance-based rewards, increased risk of blame; contentious political-administrative relations as public servants seek to live up to professional obligations
	Managerial/regulatory bargain	Public servants are blameable for regulatory/operational errors	Operational autonomy or managerial space

mode may involve the complete politicization of the public service, there is a high likelihood that many or some of the Shafferian bargain components will remain (e.g., permanence of tenure, ministerial responsibility) while others adapt (e.g., delivery competencies being prized over advice giving or rewards styled in pay-for-performance terms to support the permanent-campaign objectives). The point is that while the Shafferian bargain is homogeneous for all public servants, the permanent-campaign bargain allows for managerial and hybrid-like bargains to be struck along the three principal bargain components with individuals and particular sets of actors. It retains aspects of Shafferianism, but it layers on the traditional bargain new imperatives, norms, and practices that flow from the continuous campaign.

In theory, there may also be shades of grey along this spectrum as governments selectively deploy permanent-campaign tactics and practices and as the public service – or particular subsets thereof – is able to retain its administrative traditions or determine where it must adapt (Halligan 2010). The permanent-campaign bargain will likely involve layering effects that impact senior public servants more directly. Students of public management have, for instance, questioned the implications of pay-for-performance regimes that provide massive bonuses for deputy ministers based on their ability to meet politically determined objectives (Bourgault 2011, 2014). These arrangements, however, do not apply to mid- to lower-level public servants who can be expected to live up to a stricter Shafferian interpretation. Therefore, the ecology of bargains may involve a further bifurcation of the compact or arrangement between political and bureaucratic actors, depending on their role within the system of government. While attention has been paid to the bargains that have emerged for regulators, agency heads, political staffs, and central agency officials (Hood and Lodge 2006b; Savoie 2003), there has been less study of how mid- to lower-level public servants are impacted. On the competency front, recent studies suggest that policy analytical competencies of mid- to lower-level Canadian public servants are also trending towards generalists (Howlett, Wellstead, and Craft 2016). The other components, loyalty and rewards, remain empirical questions.

We can see the impact not only of the layering of the permanent-campaign bargain on governance arrangements, but also of the evolving institutional contexts within which competing loyalties, competencies, and rewards interact (Lodge 2009). However, the impact of the layering is likely to be contingent on how partisan elected governments behave when in office – or how well the government understands its function once elected and how well the public service of the day understands its obligations and functions and is able to navigate the boundaries between responsiveness and detached competence (Montpetit 2011). Finally, as already observed, the continuous campaign is likely to be more acute when a known election date approaches and more generally during the intense jockeying of minority government contexts (Flanagan 2014). Yet the move to fixed election dates in Ottawa makes plain when elections are going to be and may have implications for electoral readiness; some close Ottawa observers note that these implications are already fast becoming a reality (Hébert 2015). The permanent campaign should thus be understood as one of several contributing factors to the movement of the broader set of bargains towards further and different types of hybridization or managerialism. As one recent assessment concludes, while Canada is moving away from Shafferianism, "important elements of the old bargain still remain. The Canadian case seems to support Hood's hypothesis about the sensitivity of pragmatic bargains to change, due to conservative minority governments and managerial reforms" (Bourgault and Van Dorpe 2013, 57).

In summary, permanent campaigning should be viewed itself as a hybrid type of bargain that combines managerial and Shafferian principles as well as the practices associated with the permanent campaign detailed above. In addition, it can be understood as one of several specific subsidiary bargains that now exist, with the cumulative effect being a shift towards hybridity in the overall mix of bargains. Continuous campaigning is, however, a nascent phenomenon, and its implications remain unknown, particularly the internal political-administrative issues that may accompany it. The barrage of Economic Action Plan advertising or subsequent equivalents will serve as ready reminders of how governments seek to maximize government resources and levers for optimal policy positioning. We must, however, also think about how the permanent campaign manifests itself for governing and how rewards, competencies, and loyalties may change both for political and bureaucratic actors with implications for governance arrangements and the policy process. The secondary literature examined in this chapter points to the tensions that are already apparent, but others may emerge as the permanent-campaign bargain ebbs and flows and interacts with other existing bargains. Its layering may be the straw that breaks the camel's back, or it may be part of a new *pas de deux* that the public service and political actors undertake in an era when the government increasingly governs on the front foot. Other chapters in this book bear this out.

REFERENCES

Aucoin, Peter. 1995. *New Public Management: Canada in Comparative Perspective.* Montreal/Kingston: McGill-Queen's University Press.

–. 2012. "New Political Governance in Westminster Systems: Impartial Public Administration and Management Performance at Risk." *Governance: An International Journal of Policy, Administration and Institutions* 25 (2): 177–99. http://dx.doi.org/10.1111/j.1468-0491.2012.01569.x.

Axworthy, T. 1988. "Of Secretaries to Princes." *Canadian Public Administration* 31 (2): 247–64. http://dx.doi.org/10.1111/j.1754-7121.1988.tb01316.x.

Benzies, Phillipe, and Martin Lodge. 2015. "Civil Service Reforms, Public Service Bargains and Dynamics of Institutional Change." In *Comparative Civil Service Systems in the 21st century*, 2nd ed., edited by F. Van der Meer, J. Raadschelders, and T. Toonen, 136–61. New York: Palgrave Macmillan.

Bourgault, Jacques. 2011. "Canada's Senior Public Service and the Typology of Bargains: From the Hierarchy of Senior Civil Servants to a Community of "Controlled" Entrepreneurs." *Public Policy and Administration* 26 (2): 253–75. http://dx.doi.org/10.1177/0952076710391517.

–. 2014. "Federal Deputy Ministers: Serial Servers Looking for Influence." In *Deputy Ministers in Canada: Comparative and Jurisdictional Perspectives*, edited by J. Bourgault and C. Dunn, 364–400. Toronto: IPAC/University of Toronto Press.

Bourgault, Jacques, and Karolien Van Dorpe. 2013. "Managerial Reforms, Public Service Bargains and Top Civil Servant Identity." *International Review of Administrative Sciences* 79 (1): 49–70. http://dx.doi.org/10.1177/0020852312467739.

Campion-Smith, Bruce. 2009. "Trouble at Transport: Clashes over Spending." *Toronto Star,* June 20.

Carson, Bruce. 2014. *14 Days: Making the Conservative Movement in Canada.* Montreal/Kingston: McGill-Queen's University Press.

Chase, Steven, and Tavia Grant. 2010. "Statistics Canada Chief Falls on Sword over Census." *Globe and Mail,* July 21. http://www.theglobeandmail.com/news/politics/statistics-canada-chief-falls-on-sword-over-census/article1320915/.

Craft, Jonathan. 2010. "Do Politicians Control Government?" In *Approaching Public Administration: Core Debates and Emerging Issues*, edited by R. Leone and F. Ohemeng, 54–64. Toronto: Emond Montgomery.

–. 2016. *Backrooms and Beyond: Partisan Advisers and the Politics of Policy Work in Canada.* Toronto: University of Toronto Press.

Esselment, Anna. 2014. "The Governing Party and the Permanent Campaign." In *Political Communication in Canada: Meet the Press and Tweet the Rest*, edited by A. Marland, T. Giasson, and T.A. Small, 24–38. Vancouver: UBC Press.

Flanagan, Tom. 2014. *Winning Power: Canadian Campaigning in the Twenty-First Century.* Montreal/Kingston: McGill-Queen's University Press.

Geddes, John. 2009. "Ian Brodie Offers a Candid Case Study in Politics and Policy." *Maclean's,* March 27. http://www.macleans.ca/politics/ottawa/ian-brodie-offers-a-candid-case-study-in-politics-and-policy/.

Halligan, John. 2010. "The Fate of Administrative Traditions in the Reform Era." In *Traditions in Public Administration*, edited by M. Painter and B.G. Peters, 129–41. Basingstoke: Palgrave Macmillan.

Harris, Michael. 2014. *Party of One: Stephen Harper and Canada's Radical Makeover*. Toronto: Viking.

Hébert, Chantale. 2015. "Fixed Election Date Making Public Policy Debate Yield to Partisan Interests: Hébert." *Toronto Star*, January 14. https://www.thestar.com/news/canada/2015/01/14/fixed-date-election-law-could-hamper-stephen-harper-hbert.html.

Hondeghem, A. 2011. "Changing Public Service Bargains for Top Officials." *Public Policy and Administration* 26 (2): 159–65. http://dx.doi.org/10.1177/0952076710387039.

Hood, Christopher. 2000a. "Paradoxes of Public-Sector Managerialism: Old Public Management and Public Service Bargains." *International Public Management Journal* 3 (1): 1–22. http://dx.doi.org/10.1016/S1096-7494(00)00032-5.

–. 2000b. "Relationships between Ministers/Politicians and Public Servants: Public Service Bargains Old and New." In *Governance in the Twenty First Century*, edited by B.G. Peters and D.J. Savoie, 176–206. Montreal/Kingston: Canadian Centre for Management Development/McGill-Queen's University Press.

–. 2002. "Control, Bargains, and Cheating: The Politics of Public-Service Reform." *Journal of Public Administration: Research and Theory* 12 (3): 309–32. http://dx.doi.org/10.1093/oxfordjournals.jpart.a003536.

Hood, Christopher, and Martin Lodge. 2006a. *The Politics of Public Service Bargains: Reward, Competency, Loyalty – and Blame*. Oxford: Oxford University Press. http://dx.doi.org/10.1093/019926967X.001.0001.

–. 2006b. "From Sir Humprey to Sir Nigel: What Future for the Public Service Bargain after Blairworld?" *Political Quarterly* 77 (3): 360–68. http://dx.doi.org/10.1111/j.1467-923X.2006.00807.x.

Howlett, Michael, Adam Wellstead, and Jonathan Craft, eds. 2017. *Policy Work in Canada: Professional Practices and Analytical Capacities*. Toronto: University of Toronto Press.

Lathrop, D.A. 2003. *The Campaign Continues: How Political Consultants and Campaign Tactics Affect Public Policy*. Westport, CT: Praeger.

Lodge, Martin. 2009. "Strained or Broken? The Future(s) of the Public Service Bargain." *Policy Quarterly* 5 (1): 53–57.

–. 2010. "Public Service Bargains in British Central Government: Multiplication, Diversification and Reassertion." In *Tradition and Public Administration*, edited by M. Painter and J. Pierre, 99–113. Basingstoke: Palgrave Macmillan. http://dx.doi.org/10.1057/9780230289635_8.

May, Kathryn. 2016. "Perception of Politicization of the Public Service Is Problem for the Liberals." *Ottawa Citizen*, March 7. http://ottawacitizen.com/news/national/perception-of-policitization-of-the-public-service-is-a-problem-for-liberals.

Montpetit, Eric. 2011. "Between Detachment and Responsiveness: Civil Servants in Europe and North America." *West European Politics* 34 (6): 1250–71. http://dx.doi.org/10.1080/01402382.2011.616663.

Peters, B. Guy, and Donald Savoie. 1994. "Civil Service Reform: Misdiagnosing the Patient." *Public Administration Review* 54 (5): 418–25. http://dx.doi.org/10.2307/976426.

Rhodes, R.A.W., and John Wanna. 2007. "The Limits to Public Value, or Rescuing Responsible Government from the Platonic Guardians." *Australian Journal of Public Administration* 66 (4): 406–21. http://dx.doi.org/10.1111/j.1467-8500.2007.00553.x.

Rhodes, R.A.W., John Wanna, and Patrick Weller, eds. 2010. *Comparing Westminster*. Oxford, UK: Oxford University Press.

Savoie, Donald J. 1999. *Governing from the Centre: The Concentration of Power in Canadian Politics*. Toronto: University of Toronto Press.

–. 2003. *Breaking the Bargain: Public Servants, Ministers, and Parliament*. Toronto: University of Toronto Press.

–. 2004. "The Search for a Responsive Bureaucracy in Canada." In *Politicization of the Civil Service in Comparative Perspective*, edited by B.G. Peters and J. Pierre, 139–58. London: Routledge.

–. 2013. *Whatever Happened to the Music Teacher? How Government Decides and Why*. Montreal/Kingston: McGill-Queen's University Press.

–. 2015. "The Canadian Public Service: In Search of a New Equilibrium." In *The International Handbook of Public Administration and Governance*, edited by A. Massey and K. Johnson, 182–98. Cheltenham: Edward Elgar. http://dx.doi.org/10.4337/9781781954492.00015.

Sossin, Lorne. 2006. "Defining Boundaries: The Constitutional Argument for Bureaucratic Independence and Its Implication for the Accountability of the Public Service." Paper commissioned by the Inquiry into the Sponsorship Affair (Gomery Commision).

Thompson, Elizabeth. 2015. "Performance Pay, Bonuses for Public Service Executives up 65 per cent under Harper." *iPolitics* (blog), August 18. http://ipolitics.ca/2015/08/18/performance-pay-bonuses-for-public-service-executives-up-65-per-cent-under-harper/.

Van der Meer, Frits M., Caspar F. Van den Berg, and Gerrit S. Dijkstra. 2013. "Rethinking the 'Public Service Bargain': The Changing (Legal) Position of Civil Servants in Europe." *International Review of Administrative Sciences* 79 (1): 91–109.

Wells, Paul. 2013. *The Longer I'm Prime Minister*. Toronto: HarperCollins.

Zussman, David. 2015. "Public Policy Analysis in Canada: A Forty-Year Overview." In *A Subtle Balance: Expertise, Evidence, and Democracy in Public Policy and Governance 1970–2010*, edited by E. Parsons, 11–36. Montreal/Kingston: McGill-Queen's University Press.

3

Databases, Microtargeting, and the Permanent Campaign: A Threat to Democracy?

Steve Patten

A technological revolution is currently transforming political campaigns and, going forward, is sure to have a significant impact on the processes of governance. Access to massive databases and developments in data analytics and predictive modelling are revolutionizing parties' strategic calculations, while data-driven microtargeting is transforming political communication. Moreover, there are now signs that party databases, big data, and data mining are also influencing the characteristics of parliamentary politics, governing, and public policy. New technologies and a new generation of technologists have emerged alongside the rise of the permanent campaign, and these developments are sure to have consequences for the character and quality of democracy. Unfortunately, while the data revolution, data sciences, and microtargeting are rapidly evolving – and are sure to look dramatically different just a few years from now – social scientists are only beginning to grapple with the significance of these developments.

Data-driven microtargeting is made possible by increases in computing power and sophisticated information technologies that facilitate the collection, storage, and analysis of vast amounts of information regarding individual citizens. Political party databases – sometimes known as voter files – now have the capacity to include hundreds of pieces of information on individual voters, ranging from their contact information to their ethnicity, employment status, views on key policy issues, voting record, and much more. In this era of big data, parties also have access to the research of data analytics consultancies that work with vast amounts of data from surveys, government and commercial sources, and social media. Moreover, the strategic value of these data is increasing with enhancements in statistical techniques designed to discover previously unrecognized relationships between, for example, demographic information, lifestyle choices, consumer habits, and political attitudes. The variety of correlations that data miners examine allows for a much finer-grained segmentation of the electorate than traditional polling. Replacing small, randomly selected samples of the population with vast data sets shifts the predictive modelling from generalizations regarding the median voter to identifying targeted clusters of voters who can be appealed to with highly individualized campaign communication (Murray and Scime 2010).

The term "microtargeting" was coined in the 1960s by marketing professionals and entered political lexicon in the 1990s, when American campaign strategists applied the lessons of commercial marketing to the challenge of understanding, connecting with, and mobilizing persuadable voters (Nielsen 2012). What is significant about microtargeting is not only the use of data analytics to identify target voters, but the opportunities to supplement traditional phone banks and door-to-door canvassing with computer-based communication and new media (ranging from email to text messaging, social media, and web ads) to reach identifiable voters with targeted messages. Unlike broadcasted messages and traditional advertising, the capacity of microtargeting to occur out of view of the news media has led some to characterize it as "stealth marketing" (Spiller and Bergner 2014). These techniques are particularly efficacious in tight races, when concentrating on a relatively small group of mere hundreds of voters sharing particular values or demographic profiles is enough to ensure victory.

It is common – and not entirely incorrect – to assume that technological changes shape the tactics, strategies, and practices of political parties (McKelvey and Piebiak 2014). Technological advances can reshape institutions (such as political parties) by enhancing certain capacities and facilitating certain activities, while constraining others. But there is more going on than simple technological determinism. The actual impact of the data revolution is mediated through existing party institutions and shaped by, among other things, dominant understandings of the norms of party politics, the powerful interests that work within parties, the political economic context, and the constitutional and legal environment in which technological advances are taken on board. Because it was American political parties that pioneered data-driven microtargeting, the literature in the field is peppered with assumptions rooted in the American experience. Turning to an examination of the evolution of voter databases, data analytics, and microtargeting in the American Democratic Party will provide a sense of cutting-edge practices while deepening our understanding of the field of data-driven microtargeting. Readers must be cautious, however, about assuming that Canadian parties have followed exactly the same path in terms of database development and the implementation of microtargeting.

The American voter file industry emerged in the 1980s when computer-literate campaign professionals began collecting voters lists on mainframe computers and designing programs for managing these lists and inputting basic data. Entrepreneurial politicos marketed their software to candidates, and by the lead-up to the 1992 Democratic primaries, all of the major candidates were using computerized voter file databases for voter identification and voter information management. The first major development in this emerging industry came in the mid-90s, when the computing power of personal computers allowed for downsizing from mainframes to PC-based networks (Blaemire 2012). By the turn of the century, a number of companies – Democrat, Republican, and non-partisan – were competing for business and pushing advances in both database management and software programs that brought the practices of customer relationship management software from the commercial to the political world.

At this time, software companies also moved onto the Internet with online voter file interfaces that provided clients with quick and easy access to data. This made it possible for national party organizations to coordinate an integrated data-driven microtargeting strategy at the local, state, and national levels. When Howard Dean assumed the chair of the Democratic National Committee (DNC) in 2005, the creation of a national database and microtargeting program was a central feature of his fifty-state strategy. The Democrats relied heavily on Voter Activation Network (VAN), a commercial enterprise, to develop VoteBuilder, a national database and software for managing voter files and voter contact programs. As VoteBuilder evolved, the software was expanded to facilitate volunteer management, event organizing, fundraising, and increasingly sophisticated use of new media. In 2010, VAN merged with NGP Software to form NGP VAN, Inc., which is now the undisputed leader in the provision of database software and contact programs for organizing and fundraising (including compliance management) to Democrats, American unions, and progressive organizations in the United States and beyond. There are other firms in the Democratic universe as well as non-partisan firms and, of course, equally large and sophisticated Republican firms. But in this highly privatized area of campaign management, NGP VAN is a leader.

The Democrat's VoteBuilder contains thousands of identifying details in profiles of nearly every registered voter and many unregistered potential voters. The core of the database are the US voter registration lists – which include names, addresses, voter turnout histories, and, in many states, party affiliation, birth dates, and racial and ethnic identity. To this is added a range of publicly and commercially available data on credit card purchases, home and auto ownership, marital status, magazine subscriptions, web browsing history, charitable contributions, membership in professional organizations, occupation, hunting and fishing licences, and more. Traditional door-to-door canvassing, telephone banks, and surveys (conducted by both live callers and automated interactive voice response systems) also gather vast amounts of additional data on voting intention, values, policy interests, and other matters deemed relevant by the data analysts. VoteBuilder's software developers have provided the Democratic Party with a web platform called Dashboard and, more recently, a phone and tablet app known as MiniVAN that allows campaign workers to generate lists of voters to be canvassed or telephoned. Dashboard and MiniVAN also allow for virtually instantaneous inputting of data gathered by volunteers.

Analysts employ the sophisticated algorithms of predictive analytics as they trawl the VoteBuilder database in search of politically relevant patterns that allow the electorate to be segmented into dozens of groups with particular characteristics, political values, and propensity to turn out to vote for the Democratic candidate. Knowing clusters of characteristics that identify potential supporters allows the campaign to make stunningly accurate individual-level predictions of how likely a person is to vote, whom they will vote for, and what issues will inform their voting decision. This information – market intelligence – is then used to craft highly targeted voter contact campaigns. The manner and media of communication used in these campaigns continue to evolve. Precinct volunteers are regularly provided with lists of specific voters (such as core Democrats or persuadable swing voters) and scripts that provide guidelines for their conversations with those voters. Some clusters of voters might be targeted in a direct mail campaign, while others will be covered by focused email or text blasts. But in all cases, the key to effective microtargeting is getting the right message to the right people. Data mining helps identify which issue themes will appeal to particular clusters of voters.

In 2008, the Democrats found that unprecedented numbers of individuals were using the campaign website to volunteer for the Obama campaign (see also Chapter 6 by Thierry Giasson and Tamara Small). This development presented the campaign with a new opportunity to combine microtargeting with old-fashioned person-to-person campaigning. VoteBuilder could be used to generate lists of persuadable voters living in a particular neighbourhood, and the Neighbor-to-Neighbor project allowed people to sign up online to get involved in the campaign. Volunteers were provided with a list of neighbours identified as persuadable, a script to use in their conversations, flyers to distribute, and instructions for reporting the results of their outreach efforts through Dashboard or MiniVAN (Sullivan 2012). In 2012, the Obama campaign extended their organized person-to-person microtargeting to the world of social media. When a supporter signed on to Dashboard through Facebook, the campaign would seek permission to access that individual's list of Facebook friends. A central computer would then search VoteBuilder to see if any of those friends had been identified as voters the campaign wanted to persuade or mobilize to vote. The campaign called this "targeted sharing," and it was used to encourage and assist 600,000 supporters who reached out to more than 5 million friends the campaign had targeted as persuadable, potential donors, or unregistered supporters. The success of this peer-to-peer digital persuasion was a major take-away from the 2012 campaign and is certain to feature prominently in the future of microtargeting (Scherer 2012).

While less information is available regarding the Obama administration's use of data-driven microtargeting in the processes of governance – either in defining agendas, reaching out to supporters, or mobilizing to influence Congress – the DNC took action after the 2008 election to keep their volunteers engaged in a sort of permanent field campaign and ensure that their extensive database was employed to mobilize Obama supporters. In early 2009, they established Organizing for America (OFA) as a non-profit organization under the control of the DNC. While never considered extremely effective, OFA engaged in legislative outreach, the coordination of lobbying, and selective microtargeting to mobilize voters around issues like healthcare reform (Melber 2010). In 2013, OFA was renamed Organizing for Action and registered as an officially non-partisan community organizing project in support of President Obama's legislative agenda. With staff from the 2012 campaign and the White House, this new version of OFA is an example of what Sasha Issenberg (2012) suggests is the Democrat's effort to apply the lessons of data-driven grassroots organizing and targeting to governance.

The ultimate purpose of this chapter is to consider the impact of data-driven microtargeting on the permanent campaign and the character and practice of democracy in Canada. While this is not the core focus of the literature, a number of observers contend that databases and microtargeting are positive for democracy because they expedite the flow of information between voters and their representatives, facilitate new forms of individualized and virtual face-to-face contact that can promote political participation, and allow politicians to connect with voters on the issues they are most concerned about (see Kang 2005; van Onselen and Errington 2004; Taylor cited in Delacourt 2013, 262). The alternative view is that using massive databases to craft highly targeted campaign communication raises privacy concerns, challenges the ideal of a vibrant and democratic public sphere, and incentivizes changes in the character of political parties and campaigning that should concern strong democrats (see Bennett and Bayley 2012; Howard and Kreiss 2010; Serazio 2014).

Those of us who embrace an interpretivist epistemology assume that, as individuals, we cannot separate ourselves – or our political interests – from our intersubjectively constructed understanding of the social sphere in which we live. Appreciating this discursive dimension of identity formation and the public sphere illuminates the importance of how we are appealed to and called into politics. Quite simply, the electoral appeals of political parties are important because they influence the social construction of political identities and interests, including the public interest. Put differently, the methods and content of strategic political communication has consequences for how we understand and experience politics and democracy.

Social egalitarians who appreciate these insights regarding the power of discourse and ideas understand that democracy requires, among other prerequisites, that people are free and equally capable of engaging in collective processes that define political identities. Moreover, they produce the shared text that determines the norms, values, issues, and perspectives that feature prominently in civic and public affairs. It is the role of the public sphere, not private communication, to define – and perhaps resolve – the substance and nature of political conflict. While some scholars argue that new communications technologies are enriching the public sphere by promoting civic education and engagement (Cogburn and Espinoza Vasquez 2011), others note the potential for stealthy communication and worry about the increasing power of campaign professionals who seek electoral gains through targeted communication that encourages the rise of ever more distinct issue publics and, all too often, a politics that is more combative and polarizing

(Serazio 2014). Indeed, the rise of polling, data analytics, market segmentation, and targeted political communication serve to increase the power of campaign professionals – many with roots in public relations, data analytics, and polling – who believe that political parties exist only to wage and win campaigns. These campaign professionals have been seized by the notion that electoral success is most easily achieved and maintained by targeted political communication – and, often, divisive wedge politics – that aims to motivate relatively narrow segments of the electorate in key battleground constituencies. There is, therefore, good reason to be concerned that the era of data-driven microtargeting by political parties poses a threat to the richness and vibrancy of democracy. These concerns will be taken up later in this chapter.

Case Study

Canadian political parties have always had an interest in amassing and organizing data for political purposes. Local constituency associations were producing poll maps of past election results and marking voters' voting intentions on paper voters lists well before the age of personal computers. In the 1980s and 1990s, delegate tracking for leadership conventions provided the first opportunities for the parties to work with databases to store information that would be used in targeted strategic communication. The embrace of direct mail fundraising during this period also required computerized mailing lists, including supplemental lists purchased from commercial list brokers. But parties did not develop modern databases or employ data analytics and microtargeting until after the turn of the century.

The data revolution took hold in Canada's federal party system between 2004 and 2015. The Conservative Party of Canada was first out of the gate with the development of their Constituent Information Management System (CIMS) in 2004. Essentially a modified version of the Ontario Progressive Conservative's Trackright system, which is similar to the American Republican's Voter Vault, CIMS allowed the Conservatives to implement the innovative voter contact program that helped them win a number of close local races beginning in the 2004 election (Flanagan 2007). By 2011, the New Democrats and Liberals had developed their own national databases: NDP Vote and Liberalist. But in the 2011 election, the Conservatives were able to maintain their position as the most sophisticated in terms of data analytics and the most effective in terms of voter targeting and contact.

By the time of the 2015 election, however, the NDP had overhauled their data strategy with the help of 270 Strategies Inc., a consultancy with ties to the Obama presidential campaigns, and relaunched their database under the name Populus (see David McGrane's chapter in this volume). The Liberal Party, for its part, had engaged in a monumental effort to train volunteers and get local buy-in. Moreover, both parties hired experts to develop in-house analytics operations, as the Conservatives had years before (McGregor 2014a).

Thus, the 2015 election took big data campaigning to new levels. Of course, it was not the first campaign in which data analytics had featured prominently. Indeed, in addition to developing their own databases before 2015, all of the major federal parties had previously contracted with private analytics and data building firms, such as Environics Analytics, which uses voter segmentation tools that identify unique groupings of voters based on income level, age, occupation, ethnicity, family type, and key social values, and then offers political clients valuable insights into the political attitudes, desires, and motivations of these groups (Jimenez 2008). What was unique about 2015 was that all three major parties had sophisticated national databases, in-house analytics capacity to support the development of microtargeting strategies, and user-friendly programs and apps that ensured local campaigns were updating data and using the database in their own voter identification, persuasion, and mobilization efforts. While the academic literature and media coverage of data-driven microtargeting in Canada has focused heavily on the Conservative Party's CIMS database, this chapter draws on information regarding the Liberal Party's database to shed further light on the nature of party databases and how they are now integrated into the process of campaigning and campaign management at the national and local level in Canada. In addition to being most open with the media regarding their investment in database technologies (Bryden 2015; Ormiston 2015), the Trudeau Liberals have made their online platform and training manual publicly accessible, providing a unique window into how these databases function. Much of the discussion below is informed by an examination of these training manuals and demonstrations of Liberal database technologies offered to the news media by party officials.

Shortly after the 2008 general election, the Liberal Party of Canada entered into talks with NGP VAN to design and develop a version of the VoteBuilder database used by the Democrats in Obama's first successful presidential campaign. The result was Liberalist, an Internet-based database with downloadable apps that allow campaign workers from across the country to access and work with centrally stored and protected voter files and campaign management tools. Liberalist is designed with multiple account levels so that people in different positions within the campaign will have access to only the tools that are appropriate to their position and role. Those working on the front lines of local campaigns as door-to-door canvassers or staffing phone banks are limited to accessing the voters list they require and, importantly, inputting the results of their work. Those with greater levels of responsibility for managing volunteers or planning campaign events are given access to more advanced tools. The senior members of the local campaign team are able to work with voter files and volunteer lists, oversee the work and measure the progress of canvass and phone bank teams, create scripts for phone banks and canvassers, produce texts for email blasts, design surveys for collecting information to be added to the database, access analytics modules, and export approved data to the central database. Only a select group of senior party and campaign staff has access to the entire national database and the full array of campaign surveillance and analytics tools.

As one would expect, the core of the Liberalist database is the voters list provided by Elections Canada. The Liberal Party's publicly accessible website allows Canadians to learn that Liberalist contains information from party membership and donor lists, campaign records pertaining to volunteers and voters' willingness to take a lawn sign, and intelligence on voting intentions and issue priorities that is gathered by canvassers and phone banks. For each voter file, Liberalist includes "vital statistics" (such as sex, age, and preferred language), "activist codes" (identifying, among other things, a voter's cultural background and occupation), and responses to surveys generated by the local campaign. Further information on what is contained in the national database and the methods used to gather additional data and attach them to names on the voters list is not shared publicly by analysts within the central campaign team.

It is well established that all major parties contract with firms that engage in large-scale calling programs to gather information to build their databases. It has been reported that the Liberal Party has used software that identifies an individual's likely cultural background based on their last name (Delacourt 2013), and all political parties are closely following advances that private data analytics firms are making on the challenging task of matching social media accounts with people on the voters list. A data analytics firm working with the Quebec Liberal Party, ZeroPi, has reported that, with the use of multiple tools, they were able to reliably attach additional information to 60 percent of the names on the provincial voters list (McGregor 2014b). The Liberal Party of Canada has claimed that it is committed, in principle, to not capturing any information gathered by MPs in the course of their interactions with constituents, but this does not stop the party from actively gathering information from public petitions and publicly stated views – in the blogosphere or on social media, for example (Bennett and Bayley 2012). We do know that, unlike in the United States, the volume of commercially available data is limited by restrictions that Canada's *Personal Information Protection and Electronic Documents Act* (PIPEDA) places on the disclosure of personal information by commercial enterprises. Thus, while our picture of the data in Liberalist may be incomplete, there is no doubt that much of the data are self-generated and, particularly in the case of the data that are accessible to local campaign teams, comprise information knowingly provided by individual voters while speaking with campaign volunteers or visiting the party's website.

The opportunities Liberalist creates for data analysis and microtargeting at both the national and local levels are our primary interest here. But Liberalist also has implications for what has always been the primary function of the local campaign: voter identification and mobilization. Possessing a permanent, computerized voter file for each voter has transformed door-to-door canvassing and voter contact through telephone banks. Campaign volunteers now possess useful background information on the voters they will be speaking with, and they can immediately update the information regarding voters' voting intentions – and other matters they've been instructed to gather information on – using the MiniVAN app on their phone or tablet or, alternatively, by scanning bar codes on their printed lists. Local canvass managers have the capacity to monitor the canvassers' progress in real time and then make necessary adjustments in the allocation of volunteers to ensure the local team has the information required for an effective get-out-the-vote (GOTV) effort on election day. Similarly, the central campaign's capacity to monitor local campaigns and take action to provide the supports that will ensure the party's capacity to mount thorough and effective GOTV efforts is maximized (Radwanski 2015).

While a database such as Liberalist provides more limited opportunities for data analytics than the Democrats' massive VoteBuilder database, the analysts working at the national level are also mining polling data, social media activity, and publicly available data – such as census records and data from the National Household Survey – pertaining to specific demographic and geographic clusters of voters, and the resulting insights inform both the data mining performed on Liberalist and the microtargeting that results. Moreover, while the insights of big data analytics are invaluable for parties developing strategic intelligence, it is the information about individual voters that, going forward, will allow for increasingly effective microtargeting. While the Liberals were initially slow to populate Liberalist's voter files with data (Delacourt 2013), they have made great strides in the level of detail and comprehensiveness of information in their database in recent years, investing three times as much in data and data analytics in the 2015 election than in 2011 (Bryden 2015; Ormiston 2015). The data analysis options Liberalist makes available to local campaign teams are limited to simple counts and crosstabs. They cannot engage in the more sophisticated regression analysis and other analytical operations that would be performed by the central campaign team. Indeed, many local campaigns still use data analysis primarily to chart progress with voter identification, determine where to focus canvassing efforts, and prepare a game plan for GOTV. But, in battleground constituencies, this is sufficient to alter the election results.

In 2015, for example, the Trudeau Liberal's central analytics team employed their research to develop a predictive model that identified the personal characteristics of voters who were, first, highly likely to vote and, second, highly likely to vote Liberal. This model was then employed to construct a six-tier ranking system that guided the voter identification and GOTV efforts of local campaigns. In one Alberta-based battleground constituency, the local campaign team found that there was a 60 percent chance that a visit or telephone call to a tier-one voter would result in the campaign identifying a supporter who they would want to mobilize on election day. The corresponding results for tiers two and three were in the 35 to 40 percent range, and numbers dropped off after that. Thus, the decision was made to focus the canvass campaign on households with tier-one through tier-three voters. Using an app designed for smartphones and tablets, Liberal canvassers were provided with the addresses (or telephone numbers) of the tier-one through -three voters they were to contact. Then the canvassers were able to upload to the central Liberalist database the information they had collected on newly identified Liberals, and mobilizing these voters on election day was enough to ensure a narrow Liberal victory in that constituency.

The Liberalist software's functionality includes a capacity to generate letters to be mailed to voters or send email or text blasts to specific groups of voters. This has been essential to improved fundraising and persuasion efforts (for more on this, see Chapter 5 by Alex Marland and Maria Mathews). In 2015, canvassers in some local campaigns were armed with a variety of centrally produced issue cards, and information extracted from Liberalist determined which card they would leave with the voter. Although Canada's parties are still learning how to make the most of their databases and voter management software, there is no doubt that microtargeting has facilitated campaign innovations. As the scope and detail of the information in databases expand and parties become more proficient at employing microtargeting in voter persuasion, highly personalized targeted campaign messages will rival the importance of the messaging of the national campaign and party leader tours. In fact, the potential for local campaigns to use Liberalist to improve voter contact and microtargeting is limited only by the central campaign's ability to provide the training necessary to ensure campaign managers have a sophisticated understanding of Liberalist and appreciate the strategic vision and priorities of the national campaign.

Permanent Campaigning in Canada

The rise of data-driven microtargeting is tied – in a range of direct and indirect ways – to the permanent campaign, both in the sense of perpetual campaigning and in the ways that the application of the strategies and tactics of elections are increasingly applied to the processes of governance. As party databases have become increasingly important to all aspects of politics and governance, parties are less and less likely to ignore opportunities to gather information that could enhance their understanding of the electorate or be used to facilitate microtargeting. Indeed, while Liberal and New Democratic MPs have long claimed that they maintain a wall between constituent information and their parties' databases, Conservative MPs and their staffs are expected to collect information during routine dealings with constituents for inputting into the CIMS database. In 2006, Conservative MP Cheryl Gallant sent birthday cards to a number of constituents, only to have it later revealed that she had acquired their birth dates from passport applications. After former minister of citizenship and immigration Jason Kenney sent out an email blast extolling the Conservative government's efforts to offer protection to gay and lesbian refugees, it was revealed that he had collected the names and email addresses from a 10,000-name petition calling on the government to reverse the deportation of a gay artist from Nicaragua (Bennett 2013b).

In power during the data revolution in Canadian politics, the Harper Conservatives were first to latch onto the value of what observers agree are data-driven boutique policy offerings designed to win over or maintain the support of identifiable clusters of voters. Particularly in the context of the winner-take-all rule structure of Canada's single member plurality electoral system, the incentive structure favours skewing policy to the benefit of small clusters of voters who are important to electoral success in battleground constituencies (van Onselen and Errington 2004). Most prominent has been a series of boutique tax cuts. These include Justin Trudeau's 2015 proposal for a tax credit that would reimburse teachers 15 percent of up to $1,000 in personal expenses on classroom supplies, as well as the Harper Conservatives' children's fitness tax credit, tradesperson's tool deduction, and volunteer firefighters' tax credit (Cullen 2015; Woolley 2011). Similarly, the former Harper government's approach to rolling out its tough-on-crime agenda seemed to be designed to galvanize the support of an identifiable cluster of committed Conservatives who can be counted on for fundraising and electoral support as long as there is evidence that the government is addressing their agenda. While never fully delivering on the demands of this segment of the electorate, and certainly falling short of offering a carefully integrated plan to overhaul our criminal justice system, the government introduced dozens of pieces of tough-on-crime legislation from 2007 to 2015, and followed up many of these legislative offerings with fundraising appeals to targeted supporters (Csanady 2015).

A prominent theme in the literature on the role of databases in politics and governance is the issue of privacy. In Canada, citizens' privacy is protected by two pieces of legislation. PIPEDA regulates the collection, use, and disclosure of personal information by commercial enterprises, while the *Privacy Act* regulates the collection, use, and disclosure of personal information by the Government of Canada and guarantees citizens certain rights of access to personal information possessed by the government. Political parties, however, escape regulation under either of these pieces of legislation. The justification for exempting political parties from these existing legislative frameworks is that democracy is threatened by restrictions on parties' rights to use voters' personal information to communicate, educate, and mobilize citizen participation (Bennett 2013a). However, given how unlikely it is that voters are aware that their doorstep conversations with party canvassers, let alone their interactions with their MP or a minister's office, will result in their views on current issues being recorded and inputted in a database along with their identity and contact information, critics suggest parties and politicians should no longer escape the obligation to be transparent about how personal information will be used or to seek consent regarding its collection (Bennett and Bayley 2012). Without such transparency or consent requirements, political privacy and citizens' rights to engage with elected officials and parties in a context free from the pressures associated with informational power imbalances and surveillance are threatened (Howard and Kreiss 2010).

Employing data analytics to segment the electorate and identify appropriate messages for target audiences has altered the relationship between parties, governments, and the news media. In addition to informing microtargeting practices – which, it is argued, turns political communication into a private affair that challenges the news media's capacity to hold the political class accountable (Jamieson 2013) – the data-based marketing orientation of party and government communications strategies has also encouraged political leaders to take advantage of audience fragmentation and concentrate on narrowcasting over broadcasting (Strömbäck and Kiousis 2014). Working with information on the demographic character of the audiences exposed to particular niche media, narrowcasting strategies involve communication that purposefully bypasses the major electronic and print broadcast news media in favour of selected niche media. For parties and governments, narrowcasting is an opportunity to reach selected audiences, while also asserting greater message control and avoiding news organizations that are viewed as negatively predisposed to their leader or message, a practice embraced by the Harper Conservatives after 2006 (Ditchburn 2014).

The gradual rise of microtargeting within the party system while Stephen Harper was at the helm of the Conservative Party partially de-emphasized broad collective identities and the public interest in favour of private interests. Emphasizing narrow, often private interests over broader collective identities and the public interest undermines the vibrancy of the public sphere and the possibility of a politics animated by a shared text and shared ideas of the general good. Admittedly, so long as we aspire for a politics that respects diversity and difference, the goal of a shared text and a general good is always elusive. But the strategic employment of microtargeting by parties and governments actively nurtures distinct issue publics that, in the absence of a commitment to public-sphere ideals, contribute to social and political polarization (Howard 2005; Howard and Kreiss 2010; Serazio 2014). When political parties divide the country into niche markets that can be won over with targeted communication and boutique policies, politicians can abandon the art of political persuasion and the hard work of building a broad consensus on a national vision. Portions of the electorate are ignored, and public discourse suffers (Delacourt 2013; Yakabuski 2015).

The increased prevalence and importance of data-driven microtargeting have had consequences for the character of Canadian political parties and the party system. In this era of electoral-professional parties, data-driven microtargeting, strategic political communication, and message control now dominate to the point that they determine even the most mundane of party activities (Flanagan 2014). Moreover, the assumed need for disciplined control of databases and the unique requirements of data management have reinforced the centralized character of parties. If Canadian parties ever were brokerage parties with unifying national visions that accommodate core cleavages, this is no longer the case (Carty 2013). Indeed, microtargeting's focus on galvanizing the support of highly motivated target segments of the electorate allows space for a form of wedge politics that is purposefully divisive and polarizing (Barocas 2012). Microtargeting is useful to catch-all parties (van Onselen and Errington 2004), but for parties that have abandoned big-tent politics in favour of building a minimum winning coalition, microtargeting facilitates a trend towards what could be called "catch-enough" politics in the Canadian party system.

In Canada, the rise of data-driven politics and microtargeting coincided with the emergence of the permanent campaign. The demands of data gathering, management, and analysis require perpetual attention to campaign objectives, making politics and governance more partisan and encouraging the continued use of the tactics and tools of campaigning in the processes of governance. The Conservative Party of Canada was out in front on all these trends, but as the New Democrats and Liberals have worked to challenge Conservative supremacy in the world of political data analytics and microtargeting, it is increasingly likely that these developments are being normalized in Canadian politics. Unfortunately, the increased potential for stealthy political communication, the fostering of distinct issue publics at the expense of a vibrant public sphere focused on a shared text, and the divisiveness of wedge politics suggest these developments could, over time, threaten the quality of democracy.

REFERENCES

Barocas, Solon. 2012. "The Price of Precision: Voter Microtargeting and Its Potential Harms to the Democratic Process." In *Proceedings of the First Edition Workshop on Politics, Elections, and Data (PLEAD)*, 31–36. New York: ACM. http://dx.doi.org/10.1145/2389661.2389671.

Bennett, Colin J. 2013a. "The Politics of Privacy and the Privacy of Politics: Parties, Elections and Voter Surveillance in Western Democracies." *First Monday* 18 (8). http://dx.doi.org/10.5210/fm.v18i8.4789, http://firstmonday.org/ojs/index.php/fm/article/view/4789/3730.

–. 2013b. "What Political Parties Know about You." *Policy Options* 35 (2) (February): 51–53.

Bennett, Colin J., and Robin M. Bayley. 2012. *Canadian Federal Political Parties and Personal Privacy Protection: A Comparative Analysis*. Report to the Office of the Privacy Commissioner of Canada. Victoria, BC: Linden Consulting Inc. https://www.priv.gc.ca/information/research-recherche/2012/pp_201203_e.asp.

Blaemire, Robert. 2012. "An Explosion of Innovation: The Voter-Data Revolution." In *Margin of Victory: How Technologists Help Politicians Win Elections*, edited by N. Pearlman, 107–20. Santa Barbara: Praeger.

Bryden, Joan. 2015. "How Old-School Volunteer Armies Use Data Analytics to Focus Campaign Efforts." *Globe and Mail*, May 31. http://www.theglobeandmail.com/news/national/how-old-school-volunteer-armies-use-data-analytics-to-focus-campaign-efforts/article24716373/.

Carty, R. Kenneth. 2013. "Has Brokerage Politics Ended? Canadian Parties in the New Century." In *Parties, Elections, and the Future of Canadian Politics*, edited by A. Bittner and R. Koop, 10–23. Vancouver: UBC Press.

Cogburn, Derrick I., and Fatima K. Espinoza Vasquez. 2011. "From Networked Nominee to Networked Nation: Examining the Impact of Web 2.0 and Social Media on Political Participation and Civic Engagement in the 2008 Obama Campaign." *Journal of Political Marketing* 10 (1–2): 189–213. http://dx.doi.org/10.1080/15377857.2011.540224.

Csanady, Ashley. 2015. "NP Explainer: Tough-on-Crime and the Tories, a Brief History by the Numbers." *National Post*, May 31. http://news.nationalpost.com/news/canada/canadian-politics/np-explainer-tough-on-crime-and-the-tories-a-brief-history-by-the-numbers-video.

Cullen, Catherine. 2015. "Canada Election 2015: Justin Trudeau's Tax Credits: Does He Think Teachers Are Special?" *CBC News*, September 1. http://www.cbc.ca/news/politics/canada-election-2015-justin-trudeau-s-tax-credits-does-he-think-teachers-are-special-1.3211998.

Delacourt, Susan. 2013. *Shopping for Votes: How Politicians Choose Us and We Choose Them*. Madeira Park, BC: Douglas and McIntyre.

Ditchburn, Jennifer. 2014. "Journalistic Pathfinding: How the Parliamentary Press Gallery Adapted to News Management under the Conservative Government of Stephen Harper." Master's thesis, Carleton University.

Flanagan, Tom. 2007. *Harper's Team: Behind the Scenes in the Conservative Rise to Power.* Montreal/Kingston: McGill-Queen's University Press.

–. 2014. *Winning Power: Canadian Campaigning in the Twenty-First Century.* Montreal/ Kingston: McGill-Queen's University Press.

Howard, Philip N. 2005. "Deep Democracy, Thin Citizenship: The Impact of Digital Media in Political Campaign Strategy." *Annals of the American Academy of Political and Social Science* 597 (1): 153–70. http://dx.doi.org/10.1177/0002716204270139.

Howard, Philip N., and Daniel Kreiss. 2010. "Political Parties and Voter Privacy: Australia, Canada, the United Kingdom, and United States in Comparative Perspective." *First Monday* 15 (12). http://dx.doi.org/10.5210/fm.v15i12.2975.

Issenberg, Sasha. 2012. "How President Obama's Campaign Used Big Data to Rally Individual Voters." *MIT Technology Review,* December 19. https://www.technologyreview. com/featuredstory/509026/how-obamas-team-used-big-data-to-rally-voters/.

Jamieson, Kathleen Hall. 2013. "Messages, Micro-Targeting, and New Media Technologies." *The Forum* 111 (3): 429–35.

Jimenez, Marina. 2008. "Parties Get Sophisticated in Bid for Immigrant Vote." *Globe and Mail,* October 6. http://www.theglobeandmail.com/news/politics/parties-get -sophisticated-in-bid-for-immigrant-vote/article1063227/.

Kang, Michael S. 2005. "From Broadcasting to Narrowcasting: The Emerging Challenge for Campaign Finance Law." *George Washington Law Review* 73 (5/6): 1701–30.

McGregor, Glen. 2014a. "If the 2011 Vote Was the "Twitter Election," Then 2015 Will Be the "Big Data Election." *National Post,* October 17. http://news.nationalpost.com/ news/if-the-2011-vote-was-the-twitter-election-then-2015-will-be-the-big-data -election.

–. 2014b. "Winning Elections on the Desktop: How the Experts Zero in on Target Voters. *Ottawa Citizen,* October 17. http://ottawacitizen.com/news/national/winning -elections-on-the-desktop-how-the-experts-zero-in-on-target-voters.

McKelvey, Fenwick, and Jill Piebiak. 2014. "Porting the Good Campaign: American Campaign Management Software in Canada." Paper presented at the 2014 Conference of the International Communication Association. Seattle, May 22. http:// paperroom.ipsa.org/papers/paper_31666.pdf.

Melber, Ari. 2010. "Year One of Organizing for America: The Permanent Field Campaign in a Digital Age. *techPresident Special Report* (January). http://papers.ssrn. com/sol3/papers.cfm?abstract_id=1536351.

Murray, Gregg R., and Anthony Scime. 2010. "Microtargeting and Electorate Segmentation: Data Mining the American National Election Studies." *Journal of Political Marketing* 9 (3): 143–66. http://dx.doi.org/10.1080/15377857.2010.497732.

Nielsen, Rasmus Kleis. 2012. *Ground Wars: Personalized Communication in Political Campaigns.* Princeton, NJ: Princeton University Press. http://dx.doi.org/10.1515/ 9781400840441.

Ormiston, Susan. 2015. "Federal Election 2015: How Data Mining Is Changing Political Campaigns." *CBC News,* September 3. http://www.cbc.ca/news/politics/federal -election-2015-how-data-mining-is-changing-political-campaigns-1.3211895.

Radwanski, Adam. 2015. "How Data Are Giving Parties More Control over Local Campaigns." *Globe and Mail*, February 2. http://www.theglobeandmail.com/news/politics/how-technology-is-allowing-parties-greater-control-over-local-campaigns/article22755848/.

Scherer, Michael. 2012. "Friended: How the Obama Campaign Connected with Young Voters." *Time*, November 20. http://swampland.time.com/2012/11/20/friended-how-the-obama-campaign-connected-with-young-voters/.

Serazio, Michael. 2014. "The New Media Designs of Political Consultants: Campaign Production in a Fragmented Era." *Journal of Communication* 64 (4): 743–63. http://dx.doi.org/10.1111/jcom.12078.

Spiller, Lisa, and Jeff Bergner. 2014. "Database Political Marketing in Campaigning and Government." In *Political Marketing in the United States*, edited by J. Lees-Marshment, B.M. Conley, and K. Cosgrove, 44–60. New York: Routledge.

Strömbäck, Jesper, and Spiro Kiousis. 2014. "Strategic Political Communication in Election Campaigns." In *Political Communication*, edited by C. Reinemann, 109–28. Berlin/Boston: De Gruyter Mouton.

Sullivan, Mark L. 2012. "A New Model: VAN and the Challenge of the Voter-File Interface." In *Margin of Victory: How Technologists Help Politicians Win Elections*, edited by N. Pearlman, 133–46. Santa Barbara: Praeger.

van Onselen, Peter, and Wayne Errington. 2004. "Electoral Databases: Big Brother or Democracy Unbound?" *Australian Journal of Political Science* 39 (2): 349–66. http://dx.doi.org/10.1080/1036114042000238555.

Woolley, Frances. 2011. "Why Politicians Love Boutique Tax Credits." *Globe and Mail*, March 24. http://www.theglobeandmail.com/report-on-business/economy/economy-lab/why-politicians-love-boutique-tax-credits/article547999/.

Yakabuski, Konrad. 2015. "The Lost Art of Political Persuasion." *Globe and Mail*, April 25. http://www.theglobeandmail.com/globe-debate/the-lost-art-of-political-persuasion/article24101210/.

PART 2

Political Parties

4
Media-Party Parallelism:
How the Media Covers Party Messaging

Andrea Lawlor

In the era of permanent campaigning, voters can become easily fatigued with the constant torrent of partisan messaging and attacks that mass media deliver directly to their front page. The constant flow of information from political parties may provide useful content for the press, but to citizens, it can be difficult to disentangle whether parties or mass media are driving what they see in the news. However, determining what information comes from parties through the press and what comes from the press about parties – in other words, unravelling what information comes directly from parties who want to govern and what information is mediated through the press, who may have their own political goals – is an essential component of determining party support.

This question of "who leads whom?" in the party–media relationship has been at the centre of the agenda-setting (Bartels 1996; Gans 1979; Soroka 2002) and gatekeeping (Shoemaker and Vos 2009) literatures for the past forty years, yet most conclusions face two constraints: (1) they look at all party communications as a single phenomenon (e.g., social media, speeches, public statements, Hansard) (Bartels 1996; Norris 2003) and (2) they focus only on the election campaign period with the goal of explaining how media might influence voting (Brandenburg 2002; Donsbach 1997; van Kempen 2007). Recognition of the permanent campaign has blown the "who leads whom?" question wide open. Not only is it useful to consider this question in the inter-election period, when parties and leaders mix stumping and sloganeering with trading barbs in the House of Commons, but it also allows us to further explore how parties fulfill their representative role in Parliament and how they leverage media (or vice versa) to do so. Why this question matters to academics is obvious; however, the relationship between parties and the media should also matter to voters. News media are not only citizens' primary source of political information, but also the chief bodies that interpret and convey governments' expressed agendas to the wider public.

Early theories linking the mass media and parties focused strictly on the acknowledged ties between media (typically newspapers) and party organizations. The concept of party–press parallelism (PPP) is defined as the strength of these ties and is typically measured through the content of reporting, press ownership, political or partisan affiliation of journalists, and broad ideological patterns in the readership (Hallin and Mancini 2004; Seymour-Ure 1974; van Kempen 2007). In short, PPP suggests how the press can use this alignment to improve the electoral performance of the party. Lacking a strong clientelistic relationship between the press and parties that might be found in other media systems, liberal market countries such as Canada are unlikely to have a high degree of PPP. Rather, Canada, like other countries with liberal market media systems, is defined by loose, inconsistent relationships between parties and media outlets, where the press may at times be respondent to party interests and behaviours, but equally may find greater reward in remaining expressly non-partisan (Hallin and Mancini 2004).

This arrangement tends to result in loosely cobbled relationships between individual journalists and party organizers or legislators. Occasionally, there are longer-standing relationships between editorial boards or owners; however, even these are arm's-length and mutable. Systems such as Canada's that lack a strong press–party link are relevant to study precisely because there is a higher level of variation in the way that media cover political parties. This helps reinforce perceptions of neutrality to the public. Furthermore, lacking an obvious explanatory factor (such as ideology) for when media cover party messaging, we are presented with an empirical puzzle: when do media pick up on party messaging and on what issues?

For the purpose of this chapter, the degree to which media outlets track party messaging (positively or negatively) can be described as media-party parallelism (MPP). MPP, as it is understood here, is not driven by an ideological connection between media and political parties (partisan conditions), but by how newsworthy media find party messaging and under what conditions they are willing to bolster party messaging by covering the parties' agendas rather than creating their own (media conditions). In this sense, MPP is more of a measure of agenda setting than a measure of an institutionalized, embedded media-party relationship. In the context of the

permanent campaign, where parties are constantly trying to position themselves as the most viable governing option, this link is crucial to conveying
competence to voters.

The standard agenda-setting hypothesis asserts that the salience of any
given issue on the public agenda is a function of how relevant media make it
(McCombs and Zhu 1995). While some scholars have suggested that media
may play a subordinate role to parties on agenda setting for policy issues
(Kingdon 1984), increasingly, the agenda-setting relationship between media
and parties is acknowledged as bidirectional, with the political agenda being
influenced by the interplay between mainstream political actors and major
news outlets (Brandenburg 2002; Williams and Carpini 2000). Similarly, the
gatekeeping argument suggests that media do, at least sometimes, follow parties' leads, particularly when the content generated by parties is sensational-
ist or attention grabbing (Shoemaker and Vos 2009). Recently, however, it
has been suggested that the modern 24/7 news media environment (precisely one of the formulating factors of the permanent campaign) erodes
mainstream media's gatekeeping power because of the many available path-
ways to getting news out to the public (Williams and Carpini 2000). Finally,
the literature on issue ownership has implicated media in promoting both
the associative and competence dimensions of party ownership of a policy
area (Walgrave, Lefevere, and Tresch 2012). Media are documented as having a strong influence in promoting parties as issue owners, as they are able
to mediate communication from political actors to influence voters' issue-
ownership perceptions (Stubager and Slothuus 2013).

In sum, the assumption embedded in the media literature appears to be
that there are no strict rules as to whether and when media or parties lead
the messaging cycle. In fact, they both do. The conditions under which parties may lead are (usually) during campaigns and in party-to-party attacks.
On the other hand, media tend to lead when they bring scandals to the fore
or when the source of new political or policy information comes from outside the legislature or party headquarters. Media may also be more likely to
react to focusing events, particularly those that take place internationally.
While the assumptions above do state that parties will lead messaging
during the campaign, it remains unclear how attentive the press will be to
mediating party messages when it is business as usual (Brandenburg 2002).
In other words, the permanent campaign is currently unaccounted for in
media-party messaging theory. And while the campaign may be permanent,
the relationship between parties and the media is anything but.

Canada's party system has been well disposed to the concept of the permanent campaign (see Chapter 1 this volume). The single member plurality "winner-take-all" electoral system, the rise in adversarial exchanges in the House, the (de facto) lack of fixed election dates until the 2015 election, and the hybridized public and commercial media environment (Iyengar et al. 2010) have resulted not only in an institutional setting wherein competition is promoted and consensus is frowned on, but also in a media environment that thrives on conflict and sensationalism (Mancini 2000). Scholars such as Anna Lennox Esselment (2014), Tom Flanagan (2012), and Jonathan Rose (2012) suggest that Canadian parties have extended their campaign behaviours, including partisan attacks, televised messaging, and extensive fundraising campaigns, to the off-campaign season. Similarly, the continued professionalization of campaign activities and their extension to the inter-campaign period have had a particularly strong impact on the relationship that parties have with news media.

Canadian parties have always relied on the media to inform and persuade voters, and mobilize financial and electoral support to their side, and they have used a variety of communication techniques (e.g., press releases, leader's speeches, campaign platforms) to do so (Norris 2003; Trimble and Sampert 2004). Media have been essential in this process, because most citizens, other than attentive partisans, do not read party communications and instead rely on the mediated and truncated form of the message through mainstream media channels (Taras 1999; Trimble and Sampert 2004). Mediated messaging, therefore, becomes what most Canadians take with them to the polls. The permanence of the campaign period therefore has an impact on what and how much information citizens are able to synthesize. And while parties and media provide a considerable amount of information to those willing to access it, demands on time and cognitive capacity prevent citizens from attending to everything on the political agenda (Norris 2003).

In the (historical) standard campaign period, parties have tended to be better resourced and, without the distraction of parliamentary business, they were able to focus on carefully crafting partisan messages for public consumption. In the inter-election period, parties are waging a war on two fronts: maintaining a strong presence in the legislature and attempting to situate themselves as the party most capable of governing (regardless of whether they are actually doing so at the time). As such, parties are not only reliant on relationships with the media for positive coverage on parliamentary business, but also dependent on them for coverage on prospective policy plans and picking up on partisan attacks to publicize their own strengths and the opposition's weaknesses. This relationship has grown in importance with the advent of the permanent campaign.

Case Study

This chapter puts a new spin on the "who leads and who follows?" question by looking at the party–media relationship in the context of the permanent campaign in Canada. The degree of symmetry between parties and media during the permanent campaign signals the conditions under which media are willing to depart from their own agendas and give parties a messaging boost. By measuring what Justin Grimmer (2010, 3) calls parties' "expressed agendas" – the attention a politician or party allocates to issues in public statements – this study investigates how variation in party messaging can impact what media pay attention to. Based on the arguments set out in the permanent-campaign and media-effects literatures, I offer the following three expectations:

1 Media coverage will follow party press releases on issues related to public policy.
2 Party press releases will follow media coverage on external focusing events.
3 Media coverage will follow party press releases on issues related to partisan attacks.

METHOD

To provide a longitudinal analysis of MPP, I measured how often party press releases and English-language media coverage focused on the same series of topics for a one-year period (May 1, 2014, to April 30, 2015). Ending almost six months prior to the next fixed federal election date (October 19, 2015), this period is firmly within the inter-election period. As such, it incorporates messages that were transmitted while the House was sitting (May and June 2014, September to mid-December 2014, and January to April 2015) and while the House was in recess (July and August 2014). The data, therefore, account for media responses to party messaging when parties had relatively more or less time to dedicate to active campaigning. I covered all press releases from the three major federal parties – the Conservatives (CPC), Liberals (LPC), and NDP. This resulted in a total of 701 press releases. Owing to the comparatively small number of press releases from the

CPC during this time ($n = 33$), press releases from the Prime Minister's Office (PMO) ($n = 184$) were included in the preliminary analysis because of the PMO's strong role in communications strategies for party leaders, particularly the prime minister and his or her office, posited in the Canadian literature (Esselment 2014).

For the media portion of the analysis, coverage was gathered from the same period (with a one-week lead and lag) from the country's two national newspapers, the *Globe and Mail* and the *National Post*. Despite assumptions that the *Globe* and *Post* have a Toronto-centric view of coverage, they best approximate the national mood, they have robust coverage in the national capital, and, though neither paper is overtly ideological, their tendencies towards the left of centre and right of centre, respectively, provide some ideological variation (Trimble and Sampert 2004). Local papers were omitted owing to their tendencies towards region-specific coverage and their reproduction of national coverage from larger sources (e.g., wire services). Using the Dow Jones Factiva database, I captured any article that used the following search terms in the headline or lead paragraph: "Conservative" OR "Conservatives" OR ("Stephen" AND "Harper") OR "Liberal" OR "Liberals" OR ("Justin" AND "Trudeau") OR "NDP" OR ("Thomas" OR "Tom" AND "Mulcair") OR "PMO" OR "Prime Minister's Office." This search yielded a total of 1,370 stories once stories that did not prominently feature federal politics or that fell into the category of opinion or editorial pieces were screened out (see Andrew 2007).

Each party press release was manually coded as belonging to one or more of three categories: public policy, focusing events (i.e., large-scale events that occur outside of routine Canadian domestic politics, such as a war or military conflict), and partisan attacks. I excluded press releases that were exclusively about funding/donation drives, seasonal messages, or holiday greetings and links to party surveys (though these are also included in Table 4.1), as these were less likely of interest to journalists. Four areas of public policy were covered: environment, immigration, foreign affairs, and public safety (other policy domains were coded and are available). These represent issues that are routinely of concern to voters, but typically fail to make the top of the list of most important problems (which are usually the economy, jobs, and health care). Mainstream areas of public policy, such as the economy and social policy, were excluded, as it is anticipated that parties and media will always be covering these domains. The four policy areas evaluated here, however, are more likely to generate intermittent coverage,

TABLE 4.1

Types of press releases issued by the PMO and political parties (May 1, 2014 to April 30, 2015)

	PMO	CPC	LPC	NDP
Attack	0	5	26	125
Focusing event (military conflict, outbreak, etc.)	18	1	19	14
Fundraising	0	5	2	0
Holiday/greeting	18	1	70	2
Policy	62	5	29	154
Other (party business, visiting dignitaries, etc.)	86	16	22	21
Total	184	33	168	316

and therefore MPP effects should be more visible. The four focusing events included were the Russia/Ukraine conflict, the ISIL/Syria conflict, the legalization of marijuana (a topic that became almost synonymous with the leadership of Justin Trudeau, an advocate of the legalization of cannabis, in mid-2014), and the Senate expenses scandal that was propelled to the front pages of newspapers by the RCMP investigation of the spending habits of numerous senators. These events provide a convenient blend (similar to Bartels 1996) of foreign and domestic focusing events, and they received the most coverage from parties and media during the 2014–15 period.[1] Each media article and press release was coded for the number of topic mentions of each policy domain or focusing event.[2] Similarly, media and party communications were coded for the number of partisan attacks within. These included all direct party-to-party attacks, excluding any criticisms of the parties by the journalist, editor, or outside actor (e.g., provincial premier or a non-governmental organization).

FINDINGS

It first bears mentioning that the most convenient and manifest way of recording whether parties follow traditional media or vice versa – simply counting instances where a media article mentions a press release – would result in a very weak analysis. First, parties never mention that they are following the media's lead in any of the press releases captured here. Second, media reference a party press release in only five of 1,370 articles – and only in two instances is the mention relevant to the policies, focusing events, or attacks that are the subjects of the analysis. Therefore, the following analysis looks at the latent symmetry or parallelism in party and media messaging.

Recall the expectations set out earlier in the chapter: media should follow party press releases in areas of public policy and partisan attacks; parties should follow media on focusing events. Presumably, these behaviours are true across all parties (government or opposition). Nevertheless, this is an assumption worth testing. Some preliminary descriptive statistics in Table 4.1 show the content of press releases by party. The overall variation in the volume and allocation of press releases is staggering. The NDP ($n = 316$) released almost ten times as many press releases as the then-governing Conservatives ($n = 33$);[3] the Liberals issued roughly half as many as the NDP ($n = 168$) (see Table 4.1). The modal press release for the Conservatives was related to policy, fundraising, or partisan attacks, but these amounted to only 15 press releases in a year's time. The NDP, on the other hand, released a total of 154 policy-oriented press releases and 125 that featured a partisan attack. The Liberals followed the same pattern, with almost equal focus on policy (29 press releases) and attacks (26). Unlike the other parties, however, the Liberals dedicated the largest number of releases to holiday greeting messages – focused on maintaining party–society relationships rather than more overt permanent campaigning tactics. Interestingly, the PMO's focus was largely on policy (62) and on other messaging (86 press releases, mostly about visits by foreign heads of state). In other words, suggestions that the CPC were not issuing press releases, but leaving the direction of the party to the PMO, might find some support here, but of course, given its official governmental role, the PMO does not use its press releases to engage in the more hostile elements of the permanent campaign (e.g., partisan attacks). Given the central agency status of the PMO, it is more likely that it would do so through less official channels (see Chapter 5 in this volume).

Figures 4.1 through 4.3 illustrate the media-party messaging trends of four policy areas, four focusing events, and partisan attacks by each party. Each panel in the figures represents the number of mentions of that topic per day in an article (media) or a press release (parties). Evidence of leads and follows by media or parties would be, temporally, in short order, one after another. After all, the media messaging cycle is notoriously short even when the issue has been of great concern to groups outside the media (Chadwick 2013). The black line in each panel represents the frequency of media mentions of that particular policy domain in the *Globe* and *Post* (aggregated), while the grey line represents the frequency of mentions in party press releases (aggregated). Party mentions are scaled as half of media mentions to look at symmetry in overall trends rather than actual numbers.[4]

The data in Figure 4.1 suggest that environmental policy was the clearest case of national media-led messaging (see Soroka et al. 2012 for additional support). These data are suggestive of a temporal relationship between party press releases and media coverage of an event. Immigration shows the same trend of media-led messaging. Foreign affairs, on the other hand, appears to show the opposite trend. Parties seem to have been in front of the issue, with media reporting in the days following a party announcement. Finally, public safety follows no specific pattern: there were instances when parties led (July 2014 and February and April 2015, corresponding with the increase of investigations into murdered and missing Aboriginal women and the debate over the controversial Bill C-51) and when media led (May and August 2014, corresponding to the debate over Bill C-13 and the break-in to Liberal leader Justin Trudeau's house). In sum, there is evidence of the proposed MPP relationship, even when the response to the "who leads" question varies.

FIGURE 4.1

Media-party parallelism: Policy messaging

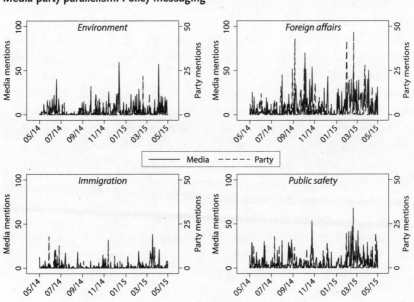

While these patterns work against the hypothesis that media would routinely follow parties on matters of public policy, there may be some nuance in the findings. The policy domains for which media deviated from expectations were in policy areas – environment and immigration – in which focusing events tend to account for small-to-moderate adjustments to subsets of policy (e.g., adjustments to refugee admissions for a discrete amount of time, not a revision of all immigration policy) rather than an overhaul to the entire domain and in which policy change is rarely a top campaign priority for governments or opposition parties. To be clear, this is not to say that these areas are devoid of focusing events or prioritization on the government agenda; they are not, however, typically among the traditional ballot-box issues. The area in which media did align with the expectations forwarded by the literature was foreign policy, an area of high priority for governments that is routinely determined by focusing events (e.g., military conflict). Public safety is, in some ways, a hybrid of these areas: occasionally driven by focusing events (e.g., the Parliament shooting of October 2014) and an election issue (e.g., a tough-on-crime approach). Both areas, more importantly, were priorities for the Conservative government, which might also have dictated the strong presence of the parties in these domains.

Figure 4.2 investigates the MPP relationship for the four most frequently reported focusing events in Canadian national print news: the ISIL attacks across the Middle East, the legalization of marijuana, the Russia/Ukraine conflict, and the Senate scandal. Somewhat counterintuitively, parties were more active on international issues (ISIL and Russia/Ukraine) than they were on domestic issues (marijuana legalization and the Senate), particularly from May to September 2014. The split between domestic and international focusing events may provide some explanation here. All parties were united in the desire to prevent conflict and violence in both the ISIL and Russia/Ukraine events; here, party press releases could be used to reinforce valence positions. However, parties may have been equally cautious about making statements about the legalization of marijuana and the Senate scandal without knowing how public opinion polling or the outcome of the Auditor General's inquiry would impact their parties. It is possible that the Liberals and Conservatives, with senators implicated in the audit of Senate expenses, may have wanted to avoid drawing attention to the issue altogether, while the NDP, which has no sitting senators, would not have had that concern. Compared to policy, focusing events show a weaker degree of MPP.

FIGURE 4.2

Media-party parallelism: Focusing events

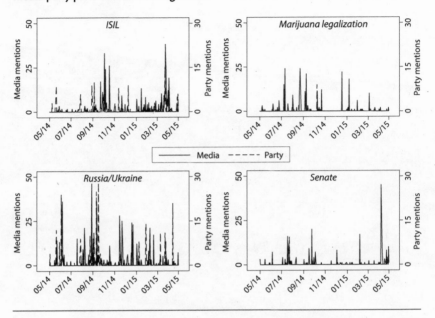

Partisan attacks, a hallmark of the campaign (permanent and otherwise), are likely to provide the strongest evidence of party-led MPP. It is presumed that media will necessarily follow parties when covering attacks simply because attacks invariably originate from the parties themselves (though media are not beyond inciting tensions among parties). Figure 4.3 illustrates these trends by the party delivering the attack. The period under investigation presents a particularly interesting three-way partisan competition rather than the standard competitive two-party-plus model that, until recently, Canadians had become used to. According to Nanos Research (2015), Canadians placed the Conservatives, Liberals, and NDP on roughly the same footing in terms of popularity from 2014 to 2015. The media, however, provided a different view of the competition. When contrasted with coverage of policy or focusing events, party press releases contained comparatively few partisan attacks. Of the three parties, the NDP official opposition most routinely attacked other parties in its press releases. The governing Conservatives, however, did so rarely.

Figure 4.3

Media-party parallelism: Partisan attacks

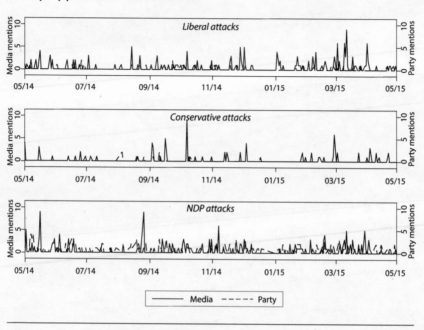

According to Figure 4.3, media appear to have been most attentive to partisan attacks in NDP press releases (possibly because, by comparison, the other two parties infrequently used press releases to attack). In at least five cases – May, August, and November 2014 and February and March 2015 – we see evidence of the NDP levelling attacks and media covering them within a one- to two-day lag. Over 85 percent of these attacks were directed at the governing Conservatives. The four peak points for media-covered attacks were attacks on Justin Trudeau's credibility, criticism of Stephen Harper's condemnation of new Canadians wearing the niqab during citizenship oath ceremonies, the financial responsibility of senators, and the handling of the declaration of attack on ISIL.

Proportionately, however, the media portrayed the Conservatives as "on the attack" more than the other two parties, though there seems to be little evidence that these attacks originated in the party's press releases. This finding contradicts the view that the Conservatives have been the first to go negative in official party messaging (Small 2012). Indeed, it may be true that, as a party, the Harper-led Conservatives were more likely to convey negative partisan messaging than other parties, but they chose not to do so through party press releases; other types of aggressive messaging (e.g., defence of their policies) likely played out in other venues such as question period and media scrums.

Simple observational testing aside, the very nature of the permanent campaign – its length and its consistency – encourages the study of longitudinal responsiveness in agenda setting. The data here permit simple modelling of the variation in day-to-day relationship between party and media messaging on policy, focusing events, and partisan attacks by seeing whether there is a consistent temporal lag between party and media communications (or vice-versa) (Bartels 1996; Brandenburg 2002; Soroka et al. 2012). In plain language, the media might pick up on the content of press releases (or vice versa) shortly after they are released in a more consistent way across time than simple descriptive graphs can illustrate.

Tables 4.2, 4.3, and 4.4 present results from a series of simple Granger causality tests. The Granger test observes the presence of a systematic temporal relationship between the number of media mentions of the policy issue/focusing event/attack and the number of press release mentions of that item.[5] Together, these models can show the extent to which MPP is present in reporting of policy issues, focusing events, and partisan attacks in the Canadian permanent campaign (see Soroka et al. 2012 for an example on the Canadian and US media's coverage of environmental issues).

Each row of data represents the impact (at time t) of the previous day's (t–1) media coverage and party press releases. The cells we are most interested in are those shaded in grey; they represent the media's influence on party press release content and the influence of press releases on media reporting. In Table 4.2, we see that media coverage of all policy areas was related to the previous day's coverage of that issue (statistically significant). The same is true for party coverage of all policy areas (statistically significant), except for immigration – that is, media impacted their own coverage (obviously) and that of parties on all policy areas studied here except immigration. The second row of data shows if the inverse is true: do parties influence media coverage? There is some evidence that a party's mention of a policy area did impact environmental and foreign affairs media coverage, but there is no relationship between party press releases on the subject of immigration or public safety and the preceding day's media coverage on those subjects. In other words, we see a bidirectional MPP relationship on

TABLE 4.2

Policy messaging mentions in press releases

	Environment Media^t	Environment Party^t	Foreign Media^t	Foreign Party^t	Immigration Media^t	Immigration Party^t	Public safety Media^t	Public safety Party^t
Media$_{t-1}$	0.408***	0.074**	0.683***	0.178***	0.357***	0.042	0.569***	0.082*
	–(0.09)	–(0.02)	–(0.07)	–(0.04)	–(0.07)	–(0.04)	–(0.07)	–(0.03)
Party$_{t-1}$	0.561*	0.069	0.308*	0.340***	–0.007	–0.001	0.313	0.113
	–(0.23)	–(0.07)	–(0.12)	–(0.07)	–(0.13)	–(0.07)	–(0.20)	–(0.09)
R²	0.17	0.06	0.46	0.27	0.15	0.01	0.33	0.06

NOTE: $n = 364$; *** $p < 0.001$; ** $p < 0.01$; * $p < 0.05$. Estimates rely on daily data. Cells contain OLS vector regression coefficients; standard errors are in parentheses. Constants were not estimated.

TABLE 4.3

Focusing event messaging mentions in press releases

	ISIL Media^t	ISIL Party^t	Legalization Media^t	Legalization Party^t	Russia/Ukraine Media^t	Russia/Ukraine Party^t	Senate Media^t	Senate Party^t
Media$_{t-1}$	0.536***	0.01	0.436***	0.001	0.276***	0.023	0.213	0.00
	–(0.07)	–(0.03)	–(0.10)	–(0.02)	–(0.08)	–(0.06)	–(0.14)	(0.00)
Party$_{t-1}$	0.860***	0.369***	1.409***	0.103	0.464***	0.169*	0.00	0.001
	–(0.16)	–(0.07)	–(0.41)	–(0.08)	–(0.09)	–(0.07)	(0.00)	–(0.08)
R²	0.41	0.15	0.15	0.01	0.20	0.03	0.01	0.01

NOTE: $n = 364$; *** $p < .001$; ** $p < .01$; * $p < .05$. Estimates rely on daily data. Cells contain OLS vector regression coefficients; standard errors are in parentheses. Constants were not estimated.

TABLE 4.4

Partisan attacks mentions in press releases

	Conservative Media^t	Conservative Attack press release^t	Liberal Media^t	Liberal Attack press release^t	NDP Media^t	NDP Attack press release^t
Media$_{t-1}$	0.097 –(0.07)	0.027 –(0.02)	0.211** –(0.07)	0.036 –(0.02)	0.199** –(0.07)	0.101 –(0.05)
Party$_{t-1}$	0.226 –(0.29)	-0.007 –(0.06)	0.901*** –(0.25)	0.006 –(0.07)	0.281** –(0.09)	0.473*** –(0.07)
R^2	0.02	0.02	0.13	0.02	0.13	0.21

NOTE: $n = 364$; *** $p < .001$; ** $p < .01$; * $p < .05$. Estimates rely on daily data. Cells contain OLS vector regression coefficients; standard errors in parentheses. Constants not estimated.

the environment and foreign affairs, a weak unidirectional media-led relationship for public safety, and no systematic relationship for immigration.

Table 4.3 shows the same type of results for coverage of focusing events. Here we see no media impact on party press releases on any subject; however, there is evidence that when a party focused on some of the events in question (ISIL, the legalization of marijuana, and the Russia/Ukraine conflict), news media picked up on it the following day. The result is strongest ($\beta = 1.409$) for the legalization of marijuana. Notably, there is no relationship between parties and the media on the Senate scandal. This is owing to the dearth of party release activity on the Senate audit, which, as suggested earlier, was likely an attempt to quiet rather than encourage coverage.

Finally, Table 4.4 uses the same test to determine a causal relationship between partisan attacks in press releases and those reported in the media. Here we see the clearest instance of a unidirectional Granger causal effect. In no case is there evidence that media reporting on a partisan attack (in any form) led parties to strike back with a partisan attack in a press release. We do, however, see evidence that national print media coverage of partisan attacks (by the Liberals and NDP, namely) was systematically and positively led by partisan attacks in press releases. Proportionately, however, the media responded to the parties differently, portraying the Conservatives as on the attack more than the other two parties.

Permanent Campaigning in Canada

Press releases are not an artifact of the permanent campaign, but their usage should be carefully considered as one of the tools that can help a party in communicating strategically. During the permanent campaign, parties that are able to lead the news cycle and encourage media to follow may find that they have gained exposure that can typically be provided only through expensive ads and marketing strategies. Using low-cost, low-resource communications tools such as press releases, parties can get traction on issues without having to craft pithy one-liners in question period or pose for expensive photo ops. Though their use may be waning with the rise of digital communications, press releases remain a deliberate style of messaging whose specific intent is to be picked up by media. A party that leads in this style of express messaging, rather than striving to stay on top of the media's agenda, may very well find they can also lead in polling.

The analysis here demonstrates evidence that media clearly drive the agenda in some areas such as the environment. Other areas, such as foreign policy, appear to be party-led. Public safety, on the other hand, lacks clear direction (vector autoregression confirmed a weak media-led relationship). In all cases, we do see media messaging parallelism, even when the leader-follower relationship varies. Issue coverage contrasts with focusing events and partisan attacks, which show stronger party-led messaging for issues of foreign conflict, but no clear relationship in domestic focusing events. This may be on account of parties' desire to stay out of focus in potentially inflammatory situations.

Some party-specific effects are also evident (though results here are limited). There were stark differences in the volume of press releases issued by parties, with the then official opposition NDP as the most active in party message distribution through press releases on types of messages. In this regard, they could be said to have been the most committed to driving media coverage through centralized party messaging. Proportionately, the Conservatives attacked more than other parties, but they did so little by way of press release–based messaging in the first place that it is notable that the media picked up on it more. It may be that their reputation of going negative preceded them, even though the NDP sent out far more press releases that attacked the government than vice versa. In the context of the permanent campaign, this is especially relevant, since it is commonly noted that negative campaign tactics tend to engender apathy and a general complacency towards electoral politics. As much as the goal of the permanent campaign may be to engage voters constantly, it may indeed have the opposite effect. Here, we see the catch-22 of the permanent campaign: in the constant pursuit of media attention, parties may end up supressing interest in their expressed agendas. On the other hand, the reinforcement of apathy, particularly when it results in voter suppression, may be precisely what some parties are hoping to achieve.

The link between media and parties enriches the study of the permanent campaign precisely because the increase in carefully curated political information from parties is at odds with the (presumed) goal of media – to provide a rich, balanced slate of newsworthy items. While parties may produce reams of information in the inter-election period, that is not the same as providing new or useful knowledge for voters. In this sense, party outreach tactics may be more noise than sound. The role that media play is critical. Where media see party press releases as newsworthy simply because of the source, we may expect a narrower agenda and an increase in substituting attacks for relevant policy information. And in the context of the permanent campaign, the relationship with media will likely become an even more pressing concern for parties with ambition to lead not only in messaging, but also in governing.

NOTES

1 The number of days each issue was reported on in a one-year period were as follows: Russia/Ukraine conflict (n = 90); ISIL/Syria conflict (n = 81); marijuana (n = 51); Senate (n = 52).

2 The codebook is a compilation of words and phrases that signal the presence of the issue. Once the dictionary was compiled, an automated search through the text yielded the total number of frequencies per article/press release. These were verified manually.

3 Note that this represents only party press releases, not releases from the PMO. The lower overall numbers for the Conservatives may reflect the change in approach to press releases.

4 Any direct comparison of numbers here is inevitably artificial. Despite the relative freedom parties have in issuing press releases, media still have more opportunity to run multiple articles per day that cover the same subject.

5 The test regresses total current media coverage of the item on the previous day's media coverage, while simultaneously regressing it on the previous day's press release mentions of the item. Therefore, the Granger test results illustrate whether, when controlling for past media coverage, press release coverage systematically leads to increases in media coverage of an issue (or vice versa).

REFERENCES

Andrew, Blake. 2007. "Media-Generated Shortcuts: Do Newspaper Headlines Present Another Roadblock for Low-Information Rationality?" *Harvard International Journal of Press/Politics* 12 (2): 24–43. http://dx.doi.org/10.1177/1081180X07299795.

Bartels, Larry M. 1996. "Politicians and the Press: Who Leads, Who Follows?" Paper presented at the American Political Science Association. San Francisco, August 29–September 1.

Brandenburg, Heinz. 2002. "Who Follows Whom? The Impact of Parties on Media Agenda Formation in the 1997 British General Election Campaign." *Harvard International Journal of Press/Politics* 7 (3): 34–54. http://dx.doi.org/10.1177/1081180 X0200700303.

Chadwick, Andrew. 2013. *The Hybrid Mediasystem: Politics and Power.* Oxford: Oxford University Press. http://dx.doi.org/10.1093/acprof:oso/9780199759477.001.0001.

Donsbach, Wolfgang. 1997. "Media Thrust in the German Bundestag Election, 1994: News Values and Professional Norms in Political Communication." *Political Communication* 14 (2): 149–70. http://dx.doi.org/10.1080/105846097199416.

Esselment, Anna. 2014. "The Governing Party and the Permanent Campaign." In *Political Communication in Canada: Meet the Press and Tweet the Rest,* edited by A. Marland, T. Giasson, and T.A. Small, 24–38. Vancouver: UBC Press.

Flanagan, Tom. 2012. "Political Communication and the 'Permanent Campaign.'" In *How Canadians Communicate IV: Media and Politics*, edited by D. Taras and C. Waddell, 129–48. Edmonton: Athabasca University Press.

Gans, H. 1979. *Deciding What's News*. New York: Pantheon Books.

Grimmer, Justin. 2010. "A Bayesian Hierarchical Topic Model for Political Texts: Measuring Expressed Agendas in Senate Press Releases." *Political Analysis* 18 (1): 1–35. http://dx.doi.org/10.1093/pan/mpp034.

Hallin, Daniel C., and Paolo Mancini. 2004. *Comparing Media Systems: Three Models of Media and Politics*. Cambridge, UK: Cambridge University Press. http://dx.doi.org/10.1017/CBO9780511790867.

Iyengar, Shanto, James Curran, Anker Brink Lund, Inka Salovaara-Moring, Kyu S. Hahn, and Sharon Coen. 2010. "Cross-National versus Individual-Level Differences in Political Information: A Media Systems Perspective." *Journal of Elections, Public Opinion, and Parties* 20 (3): 291–309. http://dx.doi.org/10.1080/17457289.2010.490707.

Kingdon, John. 1984. *Agenda-Setting, Alternatives and Public Policies*. New York: HarperCollins.

Mancini, Paolo. 2000. "How to Combine Media Commercialization and Party Affiliation: The Italian Experience." *Political Communication* 17 (4): 319–24. http://dx.doi.org/10.1080/10584600050178906.

McCombs, Maxwell, and Jian-Hua Zhu. 1995. "Capacity, Diversity, and Volatility of the Public Agenda: Trends from 1954 to 1994." *Public Opinion Quarterly* 59 (4): 495–525. http://dx.doi.org/10.1086/269491.

Nanos Research. 2015. *Weekly Nanos Party Power Index Tracking*. Ottawa: Nanos Research.

Norris, Pippa. 2003. "Preaching to the Converted? Pluralism, Participation and Party Websites." *Party Politics* 9 (1): 21–45. http://dx.doi.org/10.1177/135406880391003.

Rose, Jonathan. 2012. "Are Negative Ads Positive? Political Advertising and the Permanent Campaign." In *How Canadians Communicate IV: Media and Politics*, edited by D. Taras and C. Waddell, 71–108. Edmonton: Athabasca University Press.

Seymour-Ure, Colin. 1974. *The Political Impact of Mass Media*. London: Constable.

Shoemaker, Pamela J., and Tim P. Vos. 2009. "Media Gatekeeping." In *An Integrated Approach to Communication Theory and Research*, edited by M.B. Salwen and D.W. Stacks, 75–89. Mahwah, NJ: Lawrence Erlbaum Associates.

Small, Tamara A. 2012. "E-ttack, Politics: Negativity, the Internet and Canadian Political Parties." In *How Canadians Communicate IV: Media and Politics*, edited by D. Taras and C. Waddell, 169–88. Edmonton: Athabasca University Press.

Soroka, Stuart N. 2002. *Agenda-Setting Dynamics in Canada*. Vancouver: UBC Press.

Soroka, Stuart N., Stephen Farnsworth, Andrea Lawlor, and Lori Young. 2012. "Mass Media and Policymaking." In *Routledge Handbook of Public Policy*, edited by W. Xun, M.M. Ramesh, M. Howlett, S. Fritzen, and E. Araral, 204–14. London: Routledge. http://dx.doi.org/10.4324/9780203097571.ch16.

Stubager, Rune, and Rune Slothuus. 2013. "What Are the Sources of Political Parties' Issue Ownership? Testing Four Explanations at the Individual Level." *Political Behavior* 35 (3): 567–88. http://dx.doi.org/10.1007/s11109-012-9204-2.

Taras, David. 1999. *Power and Betrayal in the Canadian Media*. Peterborough, ON: Broadview Press.

Trimble, Linda, and Shannon Sampert. 2004. "Who's in the Game? The Framing of Election 2000 by the *Globe and Mail* and the *National Post*." *Canadian Journal of Political Science* 37 (1): 51–71. http://dx.doi.org/10.1017/S0008423904040028.

van Kempen, Hetty. 2007. "Media-Party Parallelism and Its Effects: A Cross-National Comparative Study." *Political Communication* 24 (3): 303–20. http://dx.doi.org/10.1080/10584600701471674.

Walgrave, Stefaan, Jonas Lefevere, and Anke Tresch. 2012. "The Associative Dimension of Issue Ownership." *Public Opinion Quarterly* 76 (4): 771–82. http://dx.doi.org/10.1093/poq/nfs023.

Williams, Bruce A, and Michael X. Delli Carpini. 2000. "Unchained Reaction: The Collapse of Media Gatekeeping and the Clinton–Lewinsky Scandal." *Journalism* 1 (1): 61–85. <http://dx.doi.org/10.1177/146488490000100113.

5

"Friend, Can You Chip in $3?" Canadian Political Parties' Email Communication and Fundraising

Alex Marland and Maria Mathews

This chapter aims to understand Canadian political parties' email communication during the permanent campaign. Even amid the presence of social media, email remains a popular fundraising tool and it constitutes a steady stream of direct outreach to electors. We hypothesize that institutional conditions contribute to a preoccupation by political parties to use email for fundraising purposes even when a general election is years away. More meaningful relationship building, such as through the encouragement of civic participation, is sacrificed in the name of positive and negative messaging designed to generate contributions. Studying the emails is an opportunity to observe an otherwise undocumented practice and assess the purpose of the messages.

For political and non-political organizations, enduring relationships are the bedrock of customer loyalty and are nurtured through constant communication (Agariya and Singh 2011; Sheth and Parvatiyar 1995). Email communication begins by building a list of supporters. This involves relentlessly searching for people's contact information and maintaining a customer inventory. List prospecting involves asking people to sign up for newsletters, encouraging supporters to refer others, and offering inducements such as contests; list refinement involves asking people in the database to specify their interests so that customized messages can be developed. Once customers are signed up, they are retained with loyalty inducements. Participation in incentive programs, from returning mail-back forms to collecting frequent-flyer points, is the genesis of building a social bond that supports customer retention. To cite just one retail example, Shoppers Drug Mart regularly distributes a personalized email brochure to members of its loyalty card program (El Akkad and Kerr 2013). Tailored electronic messages offer customized limited-time discounts reflecting the customer's purchase history, a practice designed to encourage more frequent store visits and to stimulate brand loyalty attachments.

Email communication is a critical component of a stealth campaigning strategy that bypasses media filters. Like other forms of direct marketing, it is difficult for opponents to counter because of its undetected precision. In the United States, personalized direct mail was popularized in the 1970s and telemarketing in the 1990s (Sherman 1999). The low-cost appeal of direct marketing grew as campaign expenses mushroomed and as information and communications technology advanced. Today, technology enables organizations to collect, store, analyze, and disseminate information in a manner that matches the right messages with the right audiences. Political campaigns no longer bombard previous donors and ignore non-donors. Instead, they segment audiences and send a constant stream of carefully crafted messages to cultivate relationships with pools of potential supporters, hoping to turn non-donors into donors, episodic donors into regular donors, and so on. Aside from fundraising, the emails perform communication functions (e.g., information, framing, persuasion) and mobilization functions (e.g., activism, election readiness, get out the vote) that are vital to permanent campaigning and a general state of election readiness. Such proactive outreach has the potential to play an important democratic role.

British political communications scholar Nigel Jackson (2005, 2006) theorizes that there is a considerable democratic upside to political email. It is easy to use, convenient, and inexpensive and enables targeting. Greater interactivity occurs through increased dialogue and constant campaigning. Inbound emails constitute a source of market research data; outbound emails offer information in a conversational format, in contrast with the officialese of letters or news releases. In one study, he examined British MPs' e-newsletters, finding that subscribers were offered information about party policy and activities. Engagement included inviting participation in opinion surveys, events, local meetings, and campaigns and encouraging party membership (Jackson 2006, 235–37). In another study, Jackson (2005, 95) suggests that evidence of relationship building should involve coding emails on the basis of their frequency outside of election campaigns, tailoring of messages to the recipient, two-way rather than one-way communication, and the building of engagement networks between elected officials and constituents. In both studies, one-way communication is prevalent, and the messages are personalized by using the recipient's name in emails or by mentioning particular issues of interest.

The Barack Obama campaign machine took email communication to another level. Recipients received messages from political staffers who treated them as confidants to whom campaign strategies could be divulged (Harfoush 2009). Some emails were presented as though they were from Obama himself. Short text and images replaced the clunky, text-heavy emails used by other campaigns. All manner of message considerations were tested to identify what was likely to generate the best response, including the sender's name, the subject line, the call to action, the images, and the time of day. Informal communication seemed to work best; the most successful subject line was "Hey," and mild profanity often generated more clicks (Green 2012). Inducements were offered, such as "free" campaign buttons and bumper stickers for donors. Information was customized by segmenting zip codes so that recipients could be informed about local events and local media coverage. Prompts sought to identify which issues mattered to listserv members and allowed the campaign to send them personalized issue-specific information. The tone and amount of monetary requests were adjusted depending on the recipient's donation history. This type of email communication persists long after a campaign and is part of a new age of personalized communication and mobilization (Nielsen 2012).

What was novel with the Obama campaign, and was subsequently used by the Hillary Clinton and Donald Trump campaigns, has become the norm in Canadian political communication. Software used by service providers like Campaign Monitor and MailChimp allows clients to easily craft reusable email templates that are aesthetically pleasing and that feature embedded URL links and images.[1] An email's message content can be readily customized depending on what is known about recipients, such as inserting a first name in a salutation or sending messages only to certain socio-demographic cohorts. The software enables A/B testing such that two segments of the list receive different variations of subject lines, sender names, and delivery dates/times, and the variation that generates the best response is automatically sent to the rest of the list. Time zone optimization is employed so that messages are delivered only during normal waking hours. Messages are pretested against spam filters; data are collected about people who have opened the emails; messages are automatically scheduled when recipients conduct a specified transaction; and so on. For all of this, scholars know very little about the practice of email communication by political parties in any jurisdiction. As Rasmus Nielsen (2012, 15) observes, "To put it bluntly, we know that personalized political communication happens and that it works, but we do not know how it works and what that means." Matters are particularly opaque in Canada (but see Marland 2016, 155–64).

It is easy enough to see that Canadian governments participate in email communication. For instance, people who sign up at www.pm.gc.ca are added to the PMO's email listserv. Soon afterwards, they begin receiving news releases and weekly video digests. As Mireille Lalancette and Sofia Tourigny-Koné describe in Chapter 14, during the Harper era this included embedded links to the *24 Seven* video magazines. The Liberal PMO sends daily messages with Prime Minister Trudeau's itinerary. This is more transparent than under Harper, though sometimes information is obscured by remarking only that Trudeau will be in private meetings or private appointments.

But the main function of political email communication is for fundraising by political parties. The institutional conditions mentioned in Chapter 1 encourage the use of email to bundle small donations as part of a non-stop permanent campaign. In the past, tiny amounts were collected by passing a bucket around at political events as an election approached, which is a reason why Elections Canada permits anonymous cash donations under twenty dollars. With e-commerce, it is even easier to collect small amounts and to keep asking prospective donors to chip in within the annual contribution limit. Sending an email blast is less work than holding an event, and it generates much richer returns. Throughout the changing institutional circumstances, the Conservative Party built a war chest by leveraging its voter identification practices and by practising direct voter contact with rank-and-file supporters (e.g., Flanagan 2009, 2014; Flanagan and Jansen 2009). The relative sophistication of the Conservatives' fundraising operations is captured in a 2008 remark by Conservative fundraiser Irving Gerstein, who proclaimed that the party practises "complex, leading-edge fundraising techniques such as data mining, segmentation, targeted marketing and relationship management, all in an effort to move our pool of identified supporters up the support pyramid, from supporters to members to donors" (quoted in Chase 2008). For over a decade, the party spent "heavily on voter ID and GOTV in targeted ridings during election campaigns, combine that with door-knocking data and membership sales from nomination races, then fundraise from the list of identified voters using direct mail, email, and telephone solicitation" (Flanagan 2014, 118). Meanwhile, the opposition parties grew dependent on the per-vote subsidy. They had so little database marketing infrastructure that the Conservative government's plan to eliminate the subsidy was an impetus for provoking the 2008 coalition crisis (Topp

2010, 57). In 2011, the Conservatives passed legislation to phase out the subsidy by fifty cents annually, marking a decline by April 2015 from two dollars per vote received to nothing. This gave the opposition parties time to recalibrate their operations. It is likely that they would have modernized by the 2015 election given their need to compete with the Conservatives and a desire to replicate the communications prowess of the Obama campaigns. However the elimination of millions of dollars in state financing provided a dramatic impetus to build an electronic fundraising infrastructure (for more detail about the transformation of digital strategies in recent years, see Chapter 6 by Thierry Giasson and Tamara Small).

The major political parties are now so deeply committed to raising money through email communication that fundraising is a defining component of permanent campaigning in Canada. Regular fundraising reports to Elections Canada act as an added institutional stimulus. Section 433 of the *Canada Elections Act* stipulates that every quarter – that is, the periods ending March 31, June 30, September 30, and December 31 – the parties must submit a financial transactions declaration. The quarterly return identifies the number of contributors and includes information about contributors who donated more than $200. The data are the basis for horserace-style news stories, as political observers routinely treat the number of donors and total amount fundraised as proxies for each party's election readiness (e.g., O'Malley 2015). This institutional rhythm motivates party strategists to generate positive fundraising numbers every three months, regardless of whether or not an actual election campaign is looming. It also encourages them to wage spin wars in their email communication because they know that journalists are paying attention.

Aside from the National Register of Electors, the most common way for a party to build its database is to solicit email addresses from visitors to the party's website. For instance, in May 2015, the Conservative Party's website home page was blanketed with a "Donate Today" message, which if clicked led to a three-step process of identifying the amount of a one-time or monthly donation; entering a name, a mailing address, an email address, and a phone number; and submitting credit card details. Contact information is often gathered under other guises, such as a splash page that prevents website entry until contact details are submitted, or urging site visitors to add their name to a petition. The many mechanisms for collecting email addresses include passing sign-in sheets at party meetings, providing mail-back forms in parliamentary newsletters, and recording electors' contact with party or

Parliament offices. The information is added to the Liberalist, NDP Populus (see Chapter 8 by David McGrane), or Conservative Constituent Information Management System databases. Emails flow soon afterwards. They start with a warm salutation – the recipient's first name, or simply "Friend." Messages are customized; thus, someone who expresses interest in a particular policy issue is emailed additional information about that issue. As is common in fundraising, anyone who donates is moved into another category and is urged to donate more next time. This includes encouragement to get involved as a means of moving up the so-called ladder of engagement. Jeremy Broadhurst, the Liberal Party's national director who was subsequently appointed as Prime Minister Trudeau's deputy chief of staff, explained:

> We've seen that once a person has donated once, they are far more likely to further engage with the party, sometimes by donating again but also by becoming a member, participating in the party's open nomination process or volunteering for the party. If we were setting the bar too high on that initial ask, we could risk losing that ongoing engagement before it even gets started. (quoted in Bryden 2014)

But not everyone in the party's database is a supporter; periodically, a spy sweep is conducted to expunge undesirables and potential saboteurs (McLean 2012, 11).

More broadly, we know little about the dynamics of permanent campaigning and fundraising during by-elections. If everything in the permanent campaign environment and political fundraising is geared towards optimizing votes and seats and using all available public resources at a party's disposal, then by-elections deserve special attention. These mini-contests operate in somewhat of a vacuum given the absence of a national campaign (Flanagan 2014, 203–10; Loewen and Bastien 2010). As with the party fundraising reports, they too are treated by the media and punditry as an inter-election proxy for the party's election readiness and momentum. Studying political emails is an opportunity to extract some information about how national-level permanent campaigning activity changes when a by-election campaign is under way. By-elections are also a laboratory for political parties to test-run their email communication as they enter a heightened state of election readiness.

The civic education function of political emails matters in an environment of fluctuating election turnout and declining party membership. In theory, this constant campaigning should result in a more informed and engaged citizenry. For many people, listserv emails are the only regular unmediated interaction that they have with a political institution. Subscribers receive information that increases their awareness of select public policy issues, or at least how a party frames those issues. Political participation is stimulated by encouraging a donation, signing a petition, attending an event, discussing topical issues with peers, and canvassing. In short, fundraising by email and by other electronic means has become one of the most common forms of civic outreach by political parties.

Case Study

To shed light on this stealth campaigning, we study the content of messages sent by the Conservatives, Liberals, and New Democrats during the first year of the second session of the 41st Canadian Parliament (October 16, 2013, to October 15, 2014). Over time, the parties have been gravitating towards more visual email communication that uses embedded HTML to display emoticons, graphic design, animation, photographs, and sometimes video. During the period of our study, the norm was more likely to be written messages that were accompanied by stylized fonts, the party logo, website addresses, and perhaps a banner.

METHOD

The name of one of the study authors, a university email account, and the Memorial University civic address were submitted to each of the three parties' websites in mid-2013.[2] The name and email are not associated with any record of party affiliation or financial support. All messages were opened; if the Obama campaign is any indication, this signals that the email address should not be purged for inactivity. We did not respond to any email appeals or donate. We are aware of some limitations of this data collection method. It is likely that another email account and acting on requests would receive a different quantity of messages and different subject matter. Had we submitted multiple email addresses with different postal codes, we would have collected useful comparative data to judge how messages vary, particularly during by-election campaigns. Nevertheless all things being equal, we possess the full universe of messages sent to a general user. We collected 522 emails during the study period, meaning that the parties each sent, on average, approximately one email every two days.

Each email was abstracted using a data entry form in Microsoft Access database management software. We coded the following variables: email subject line, email personalization (i.e., salutation), political party, email date, email time, first and second stated purposes of the email, donation amount(s) requested, name of the sender, stated occupation of the sender, gender of the sender, call to action, and nature of the message. To develop the abstraction form, we reviewed twenty randomly selected emails for common features and reoccurring themes, which were then codified into the variables listed above. Open-ended variables (e.g., email, subject line, name of sender) were copied and entered directly. Categories for closed-ended emails (e.g., first stated purpose of email) were determined a priori. The abstraction form was pretested on rounds of twenty emails to ensure that data were available and that the coding scheme captured all possibilities. A coding manual was developed to enhance the coding consistency.

A research assistant coded the emails in the date order in which they were received. To assess inter-rater reliability, a second research assistant coded a 10 percent random sample of the emails. Kappa scores ranged from a low of 0.714 for nature of the message to 1.00 for the email subject line, for the political party, and for the donation amount requested. A kappa score of 0.61 to 0.80 is considered substantial agreement and 0.81 to 1.00 is considered almost perfect agreement.

RESULTS

Canadian political parties' email appeals followed a common structure during the study period. Information was offered about a public policy issue, a bill before the legislature, a wayward remark made by an opponent, or an upcoming event. There were one or more calls to action, which is a standard marketing technique that urges the recipient to respond immediately. There tended to be one or more links to external content and possibly an embedded gif animation or video. One noticeable difference between the parties' emails was that, at the time, only Liberal emails included a French translation after the English message. The substantive parts of other parties' messages were unilingual.

Figure 5.1 is an example of a call to civic engagement, sent by the NDP. The party periodically urges participation in a weekend "day of action," a countrywide door-to-door canvassing day. This is a contrast with the negative emails

Figure 5.1

Call to action email, NDP

From: *Name removed* <info@ndp.ca>
Sent: February 26, 2014
Subject: Reporting back: The NDP's National Day of Action

NDP National Day of Action:
The numbers say it all

Friend,

2,172 grassroots activists in 141 communities hit the doorsteps for our first National Day of Action on Saturday. First-time volunteers got a taste of organizing on the ground and essential training ahead of next year's election. Supporters braved the cold temperatures in Edmonton and the snow in Surrey. All that work paid off. Check out these numbers:

- 141 teams across the country knocked on 112,453 doors to share the NDP's practical plan to make life more affordable.
- Hundreds more shared content online to reach as many Canadians as possible.
- In one day alone, 28,298 new supporters joined our affordability campaign.

That's an impressive start, and a strong sign of what's possible when we organize neighbour-to-neighbour. That's why we're planning four more National Days of Action in 2014. It's days like Saturday, when thousands of New Democrats take action together, that will make all the difference in 2015. But this kind of organizing requires a steady stream of resources – for clipboards, walk-sheets, pens, leaflets, coffee, and lunch for hungry canvassers. It's going to take all of us pitching in what we can. Donate now, or forward this email to five friends, and ask them to join the NDP:

Donate: www.ndp.ca/donate
Join: www.ndp.ca/join

Thanks again for making the first National Day of Action a great success. Whether you shared content online or knocked on your neighbour's door, you're part of the movement that will elect the first ever NDP government.

Thanks,

Name removed
National Director
Canada's New Democrats

P.S. As our movement grows, so does the need for resources on the ground. Our team leaders and volunteers will need a new supply of materials for the next National Day of Action. Help out with a donation today: www.ndp.ca/donate

----

FOLLOW TOM ON FACEBOOK   FOLLOW TOM ON TWITTER
SUBSCRIBE   UNSUBSCRIBE   MODIFICATION DE LANGUE   UPDATE YOUR PROFILE

New Democratic Party of Canada, 300-279 Laurier West, Ottawa ON K1P 5J9
1-800-555-5555

NOTE: Party emails increasingly include colourful graphics such as the party logo, stylized fonts, emoticons, photos and/or embedded video. They are not reproduced here for copyright reasons.
SOURCE: Rotman (2014)

Figure 5.2

Status report email, Conservative Party

From: *Name removed* <info@conservative.ca>
Sent: January 22, 2014
Subject: Is this a mistake?

[Conservative party logo]

Friend,

I just checked our records, and it doesn't look like you've added your name to our list of supporters yet.

Don't forget to add your name now to show you're with us:
http://www.conservative.ca/start-2014-strong

We're counting on your support. The stakes in the next election couldn't possibly be higher.

In 2015, Canadians will have the opportunity to choose between the strong, stable leadership of Stephen Harper and the poor judgment of Justin Trudeau.

Our economy has the best economy in the G7 – and if we want to keep it on track, we need to re-elect our Prime Minister.

Are you with us? *[links to http://conservative.us5.list-manage.com/track/click]*

Sincerely,

Name removed
MP, Vancouver Island North

P.S. You can also follow our campaign on Facebook and Twitter –
and please share this with your friends once you've added your name.
[hidden link to http://conservative.us5.list-manage.com/track/click]

We believe email is an important way to stay in touch with Canadians.
If you no longer wish to receive email updates from us, click here to unsubscribe.

If you wish to update your profile or change your preferred language, click here.
Si vous voulez metre votre profil à jour ou changer la langue préférée, cliquez ici.

Email communications from:
Conservative Party of Canada 1204-130 Albert St Ottawa, ON KIP 5G4 Canada

SOURCE: Duncan (2014)

sent by all parties that seek to provoke an emotional response and are information subsidies for media (e.g., Naumetz 2014). The regular volley of messages is interspersed with efforts to encourage non-responders to engage. An example of a negative email, sent by the Conservative Party, is presented as Figure 5.2. Negativity is not inherent, however: at some undetermined point, the Liberal Party decided to counter negativity with positive messaging. We generally observed that the positive email tone used by Trudeau's team throughout the 2015 campaign persisted when the party was in power.

December 31 offers an excellent example of the nature of email-based fundraising in Canadian party politics. This is the last day of the tax year and the final opportunity for donors to maximize their charitable donation receipts. The media report on the flurry of end-of-year emails and the sense of urgency communicated by the political parties (e.g., Bryden 2014). Three Liberal emails were collected on December 31, 2013. One with the subject line "At my computer" was signed by the party's senior director of fundraising and urged a donation so that Liberals could celebrate out-fundraising the Conservatives. Another titled "2014" from Trudeau extended New Year's greetings with a family photo before asking for a three-dollar donation. The final email, called "The last email you'll get," was from that party's national campaign co-chair, who reasoned that "Maybe you're getting ready to go out tonight, so I'm going to keep this simple and easy: If you donate $3 right now, there's a good chance we'll be able to ring in the New Year by out-raising Stephen Harper."

Two emails were received from each of the New Democrats and Conservatives. NDP leader Tom Mulcair supposedly authored one titled "Can I count on you?", a subject line the party has used repeatedly on the last day of a quarter. The message pleaded for a five-dollar donation ("That's just $1.25 after tax credits," he added) to top off the party's fundraising campaign. Exactly a year later, a nearly identical email was repeated word-for-word, using the same subject line and the same remark from Mulcair that "My team called first thing this morning with an exciting update." The content of "Last chance – NDP Boxing Day sale" urged a donation to help the party meet a fundraising target while there was still time. The Conservatives asked for considerably more and said much less. In "Meeting with Stephen Harper," the president of the Conservative Party reported that he would be providing the prime minister with an update and encouraged a donation of "$25 or whatever you can afford." In a subsequent December 31 missive, using the subject line "Last chance," he relayed that the party was close to meeting its fundraising target and asked for "$25 or more." It is unclear whether suggested amounts were related to the party's standing in the House of Commons or public opinion polls. Our impression is that a party in government is prone to leverage its status and to suggest a higher donation than is a fringe party. Perhaps a governing party has more expertise with database marketing or deploys market research resources to pinpoint optimal amounts to request from potential donors.

During the year of emails that we studied, the most prevalent characteristic that we coded was a request that the recipient complete a task. As shown in Table 5.1, a call to action was found in 97 percent of the emails, of which by far the most common was a plea to make a donation (63 percent). At times, this constitutes a branded fundraising initiative, such as the Conservative Party's so-called "seize the moment" campaign to raise $2 million or the Liberals' limited-time "win dinner with Justin" contest. This was followed by asking the recipient to provide contact information to signal concern about a specific issue (nearly 16 percent) or to watch or share videos or media content (9 percent). The clustered variety of other calls to action (12 percent) provide some evidence of building a relationship and engagement. This includes completing opinion surveys; signing up for party updates; following the party on social media; forwarding emails to friends; submitting questions, feedback, or comments; signing up for party membership or to volunteer; donating to an organization or charity other than the party; clicking on a URL link to view information, ideas, photos, or speeches; and so on.

The emails were often personalized. Over half (58 percent) used the salutation "friend" or an equivalent, and a third (33 percent) addressed the recipient by name. Only 9 percent of the studied messages were not personalized. If the informal nature of subject lines is designed to prompt the reader to click on a link, then the same must hold for selecting how to identify the sender. For this reason, the party name did not typically appear in the "from" area of a receiver's email inbox. Half the time (nearly 50 percent), the message indicated that the author was a senior party staffer. About 17 percent of emails were from the party leader, and a fifth (20 percent) were from other elected officials. On occasion (roughly 12 percent of the time), the email was signed with nothing more than the general party name. Occasionally emails were sent by others: the winners of marketing contests, retired politicians (including former prime ministers), or the president of a

Table 5.1

Comparison of email characteristics, by political party

Variable	All emails %	(n)	Conservative emails %	(n)	Liberal emails %	(n)	NDP emails %	(n)	p value
Party logo present in email									.000
Yes	89.3	(466)	94.4	(136)	94.8	(182)	79.6	(148)	
No	10.7	(56)	5.6	(8)	5.2	(10)	20.4	(38)	
Email personalization									.000
Yes: "friend" or equivalent used	58.4	(305)	88.2	(127)	90.1	(173)	2.7	(5)	
Yes: recipient's name used	32.6	(170)	5.6	(8)	0	(0)	87.1	(162)	
No	9.0	(47)	6.3	(9)	9.9	(19)	10.2	(19)	
Email author									.000
Party staff	49.5	(253)	54.5	(78)	37.2	(71)	58.8	(104)	
Party leader	17.2	(88)	0.7	(1)	34.6	(66)	11.9	(21)	
Other politician	20.2	(103)	37.1	(53)	14.1	(27)	13.0	(23)	
General party name	11.7	(60)	7.0	(10)	11.0	(21)	16.4	(29)	
Other	1.4	(7)	0.7	(1)	3.1	(6)	0	(0)	
Call to action									.047
Yes	97.1	(503)	96.5	(136)	95.3	(182)	99.5	(185)	
No	2.9	(15)	3.5	(5)	4.7	(9)	0.5	(1)	
Description of main action									.000
Donate	63.4	(319)	51.5	(70)	62.6	(114)	73.0	(135)	
Add name to signify support/ concern	15.7	(79)	27.2	(37)	8.8	(16)	14.1	(26)	
Watch/share videos or media	8.9	(45)	9.6	(13)	11.0	(20)	6.5	(12)	
Other	11.9	(60)	11.8	(16)	17.6	(32)	6.5	(12)	
Total number of emails sent	522	(100)	144	(27.6)	192	(35.6)	186	(38.6)	

NOTE: Totals may not add up to 100 percent due to rounded data nor add up to 522 cases due to missing data.

political support group. Messages tended to include the party logo (89 percent of the time).

Thus, the typical political email message uses a personalized salutation, contains the party logo, is from a party staffer or elected official, and asks for money. Based on this, we can cautiously confirm that Canada's three major political parties use email communication primarily for fundraising purposes, as Giasson and Small suggest in Chapter 6. However, we must not lose sight of the role of email communication in permanent campaigning and relationship building. Listserv recipients are provided with political information from party insiders about what the party and its chief opponent(s) are up to. The colloquial nature of some email subject lines (e.g., "Bumping this"), the intimate style of salutations, and the variety of signatories convey a camaraderie with political parties that most Canadians never experience outside of general election campaigns, if ever. Messages to donate are crafted in a cause-oriented manner. The governing party seeks funds to carry on its work and prevent the latest scheme of its opponents from becoming reality. Opposition parties claim that they need money to replace the government and introduce different policies. More concrete reasons are specified for election readiness, such as money to pay for food and supplies needed to carry out a day of campaigning in between elections. In this way, a steady stream of emails is the basis for civic education and engagement. However, there are far more calls to donate than to become a party member, and offering information about how to get involved with a local electoral district association or become a candidate is rare. In the emails that we studied, the parties expressed no desire to add to their workload by encouraging people to contact their local MP for assistance with government services or for help with an issue of concern. Perhaps they do so when people respond to calls to action. Nevertheless, all indications are that the civic virtue of political emails, such as stimulating a culture of democratic civility, is more theory than reality.

As Table 5.1 indicates, the nature of email content varied somewhat by political party. During the studied period, the Liberal Party (nearly 36 percent of all emails) and NDP (nearly 39 percent) communicated more often than did the Conservative Party (nearly 28 percent). Suffice it to say that all political parties promoted uplifting information about what they were doing and/or expressed alarm or outrage about their main opponent's latest initiative. Compared with the other two parties, the Conservatives were more willing to send messages from politicians other than the leader, usually from their MPs. Conservative emails tended to build the precision of the party's database by urging the recipient to signify support or concern for an issue, such as by adding one's name to a petition. A larger proportion of Liberal Party emails were sent from the leader, and less likely from staff.

During the timeframe that we collected data, this no doubt reflected a desire to capitalize on Trudeau's popularity and his recent ascendency to the party mantle, a style that persisted into governance. The party also occasionally sent emails from past Liberal prime ministers. Its calls to action personalized the leader in innovative ways, such as offering videos of Trudeau speaking to the viewer, or encouraging the recipient to share a December "holiday card" digital photograph of the leader and his wife and children. Trudeau was commodified through inducements such as donors being entered into contests to win dinner with the leader and to win Trudeau-labelled merchandise, or being informed that they might receive a personal phone call from him if they were to contribute. A listserv message with the subject line "I never thought I would win," which was presented as authored by one of the Liberal contest winners, illustrates the fusion of personalization, fundraising, loyalty marketing, and political engagement:

> Friend: When I donated to the last Win Dinner with Justin Contest back in September, I thought, "There's no way I'm going to win this!" And yet, on November 22, there I was, sitting across the dinner table from Justin Trudeau, with the chance to ask him anything. In a grassroots movement like ours, it's crucial we create opportunities like the one I had to engage with our leader. If you give, you'll be automatically entered for the chance to win dinner with Justin and four friends in your town, like I did. You could also win one of twelve limited-edition Justin Trudeau scarves. Just give $3 – seriously, that's just 75 cents – to show your support for Justin and help take us to $1 million. (Corbeil 2013)

This trend continued, including after the 2015 election. For instance, on the day that he was sworn in as prime minister, Trudeau quipped that the reason there was gender parity in his cabinet was simply "because it's 2015." Five days later, the Liberal Party email machine was offering "limited-edition" t-shirts with the phrase. Anyone donating $100 or more would receive the t-shirt. Email recipients were urged to hurry to take advantage of the limited-time offer.

For reasons unknown to us, the Liberal emails that we compiled opted almost exclusively for the salutation "friend." Conversely, NDP messages routinely used the recipient's name. Compared with the other parties, the NDP tended to include a party logo and to identify a party staff member as the author. Almost every NDP message contained a call to action.

As mentioned, the study of political party email communication is an opportunity to explore how permanent campaigning occurs during the special circumstance of a by-election campaign. During the studied period, there were two sets of by-elections. On October 20, 2013, four by-elections were announced for November 25, 2013, in the ridings of Bourassa, Brandon–Souris, Provencher, and Toronto Centre. On May 11, 2014, another group of four by-elections was announced for June 30, 2014, in Fort McMurray–Athabasca, Macleod, Scarborough, Agincourt, and Trinity, Spadina. We need not get into the dynamics of the races, other than to say that all three parties were experiencing ebbs and flows in national public opinion polls, and the media used the by-elections as proxies for permanent campaigning momentum. Four of the seats were vacated by Conservative MPs, three by Liberals, and one by an NDP member. Only one seat changed hands, when Trinity–Spadina switched from NDP to Liberal.

We wanted to see whether the intensity of political parties' email communication fluctuated during by-elections for a general national audience; that is, for someone who submitted a postal code in a seat that was not being vacated. In an even distribution, the mean of 1.43 total emails sent per day would normally accumulate to 123 messages over the course of the eighty-six days of by-election campaigning. We found that during this period, the overall pace of emails that we received slowed down, with 92 messages received rather than the expected 123 (Table 5.2). The New Democrats and to a lesser extent the Liberal Party were noticeably more active on a national level than the governing Conservative Party. This contrasts with the week prior to Prime Minister Harper announcing the by-elections, when the governing Conservatives sent more pan-Canadian messages than their two main opponents combined. It appears that the Conservatives emphasized pre-writ electioneering with respect to by-elections. By comparison, the writ drop activated the opposition parties. They treated the local events as an opportunity to rally the troops nationwide and to pull funds from Canadians elsewhere who wanted to influence the outcome. At times, by-elections were cited as a reason to donate, regardless of which electoral district the donor

Table 5.2

Frequency of emails during by-election campaigns, by political party

When email was sent	Total all emails		By political party						p value
			Conservative		Liberal		NDP		
	%	(n)	%	(n)	%	(n)	%	(n)	
During by-election campaign	17.6	(92)	11.8	(17)	17.7	(34)	22.0	(41)	.050
One week before by-election called	1.7	(9)	3.5	(5)	1.6	(3)	0.5	(1)	
Other time period	80.7	(421)	84.7	(122)	80.7	(155)	77.4	(144)	
Total	100	(522)	100	(144)	100	(192)	100	(186)	

lived in. For instance, in an email titled "Breaking: By-election alert," the NDP's national director wrote:

> Moments ago, we got news that Stephen Harper officially called all four by-elections ... We've got teams hard at work, now we have to get them the resources they need. Your urgent donation will go directly toward renting out a local campaign office, running phone banks and canvasses, and arming volunteers with door-knocking materials. We'll have to buy lawn signs, leaflets and advertising space in local papers. *Make a special donation of $5 or more to our New Democrat by-election fund today.*[3] (Rotman 2013)

During the by-elections, all three parties used email to introduce their candidates to supporters across Canada, which included a request for a donation to support the party's efforts. For instance, in an email titled "Have you met these four Canadians?," the Conservative Party similarly mentioned that campaigning is considerable work and identified the Conservative candidates' names and electoral districts. "We need to run fully-funded campaigns in these ridings if we want to be competitive," wrote the party's director of political operations. "Will you chip in $5 or whatever you can afford to support the Conservative Party and these four outstanding Canadians in these by-elections?" (DeLorey 2014). The June by-elections were held at the end of a fiscal quarter, meaning that this coincided with the regular stream of quarterly pleas. For example, as the by-election campaigns were climaxing, a Liberal Party email titled "Our fundraising quarter is at stake" advised that just 100 hours remained to meet their $269,038 fundraising goal to "close the gap on Q2 2013" and that the "donation will go directly toward 2015 election readiness. The election could be called as early as next spring – and we want to ensure that our team has everything it needs to win" (Topp 2014). All of this illustrates that party operations are interloped as they prepare for an official campaign that is months or years away.

Some limited comparative data are helpful to further situate these findings. We continued to collect messages in the same manner during the seventy-eight-day official campaign period and after the government changed. From August 4, 2015, when the writ of election was signed, through to election day on October 19, 2015, we compiled considerably more from the NDP (n = 225) than from the Liberals ($n = 141$) or Conservatives ($n = 70$), possibly explained by the postal code associated with the email address in what was an NDP stronghold but ultimately went Liberal. Email communication during the remainder of the year saw a proportional increase in messages from the Liberals ($n = 50$) compared with those received from the NDP ($n = 49$) or the Conservatives ($n = 37$). This seems to reflect that the winning party continues its campaign messaging while defeated parties recalibrate, and we suspect that the opposition parties' communication will ramp up as leadership matters are settled, as by-elections are called, and as the next general election approaches. Further research is needed to understand how this varies across the country and over time. Thus, we are unable to ascertain whether opposition parties are likely to communicate more often as a rule or whether the volume of communication depends on what the party database identifies as the location of the recipient. One thing is constant irrespective of party, leader, or frequency of email messages: a steady tempo of asking recipients for money, particularly at the end of a fiscal quarter.

Permanent Campaigning in Canada

This chapter set out to establish the extent to which the use of emails in the permanent campaign constitutes an ongoing fundraising tool and whether this potentially performs a democratic information service. We knew that political parties are turning to email communication for fundraising. We did not know, however, that their continual requests for money are so blatant and so frequent. During the most intense periods at the end of a quarter, the parties come across as spammers. We suspect that this has more to do with organizational ethos than it does position in power. It certainly appears to be a formative element of the drumbeat of perpetual campaigning. Whether this offers anything to constructive democratic engagement is another matter.

Digital fundraising of this sort has fundamentally reshaped party finance. We are unable to ascertain how this behaviour changes if someone responds to a call to action, or how it varies in an election campaign. Our analysis is limited to data collected during a one-year, inter-election period. Another limitation is that the per-vote subsidy formula came to an end in early 2015 while this research was being conducted. Without that stream of quarterly revenues, and due to the $1,500 individual donation maximum at each of the national and riding levels, political parties have greater incentive than ever to generate a series of repeated small donations from individuals. Money is needed to pay for staff, advertising, offices, and all manner of political party life. This need builds as an election campaign approaches. The data collected here suggest that the repeated email interactions could be considered as steps in a political party's attempt to cultivate a lasting and meaningful connection, one that will shift from the permanent campaign to the official campaign.

It is a reasonable hypothesis that the distribution of party emails results in a more informed and more engaged citizenry. Issues and perspectives, as well as engagement opportunities, are shared directly with supporters who may otherwise not be aware of such information. The emails likely act as a strategic cue for the media and hold promise as a vehicle for civic literacy, despite the narrowcast nature of the practice. With some exceptions, the encouragement of offline civic engagement is rare, given that scant information is offered about contacting an MP, getting involved in a local electoral district association, participating in canvassing activities, and so on. We suspect that the tone of email messages may, however, contribute to a more polarized citizenry, given that most recipients are exposed to emails from one party only. The more that people receive negative information about other political options, the more that they are likely to become partisan and hostile to alternatives. The implications of all forms of digital communication on hyper-partisanship need monitoring.

The democratic implications of this aspect of the permanent campaign are mixed. Political parties have financial and organizational incentives to engage directly and repeatedly with Canadians for whom they have an email address. Financial regulations mean that the parties must repeatedly fundraise from a broad array of Canadians. The competitive nature of permanent campaigning and election readiness leads to what some may interpret as overly eager calls to chip in. Political parties have at their disposal a low-cost and reliable mechanism to communicate slanted information with target markets. An email listserv is the epitome of political marketing insofar as it embodies the practice of segmenting electors and sending messages in a cost-efficient manner to presumed supporters. Software programs allow them to segment audiences and test messages. They may also frame debate knowing that journalists are paying attention. A reduced role for the fourth estate means that Canadians receive more partisan and biased information that lacks important context.

This assessment leads to a conclusion that political email distribution in the permanent campaign is foremost a sales volley that benefits the party more than the citizenry. Those who are not on a party email list, or who are excluded by software rules, are not privy to the same communication as other citizens. There are indications of some difference in message tone and content between the parties, with, for example, the Liberal Party commodifying the celebrity of their leader. Further data collection is needed to analyze the two-way nature of direct voter contact and to identify whether different forms of responses result in a more meaningful relationship with Canada's political parties. As well, comparative analysis of party emails during an election campaign may identify variations; for instance, the frequency of emails increased when the 2015 election was called, and the Conservatives and New Democrats sent a message encouraging listserv members to sign up to volunteer with their local candidate. We are cognizant of the changing nature of institutional conditions – such as the provision in the *Fair Elections Act* (2014) that all political parties are provided with Elections Canada data identifying which electors voted – and the privacy implications of party databases, as elucidated by Steve Patten in Chapter 3. Even in an age of social media and texting, the data presented here signal that the importance of studying email communication and perpetual fundraising by Canadian political parties should increase in value.

NOTES

1 See www.campaignmonitor.com and http://mailchimp.com.
2 It is possible that a greater number of NDP emails were received because the university is located in the riding of St. John's East, where the previous federal election

result was 70.7 percent NDP, 20.5 percent Conservative, 7.8 percent Liberal, and 1 percent Green. We cannot discount the possibility that a small number of emails were caught by the university's spam filters.

3 Link to NDP donation page is not shown because, as with the other parties', an embedded link leads to a specialized URL that is lengthy and temporary. This allows a party to monitor the click-through success of its emails.

REFERENCES

Agariya, Arun Kumar, and Deepali Singh. 2011. "What Really Defines Relationship Marketing? A Review of Definitions and General and Sector-Specific Defining Constructs." *Journal of Relationship Marketing* 10 (4): 203–37. http://dx.doi.org/10.1080/15332667.2011.624905.

Bryden, Joan. 2014. "Political Parties in a Fundraising Frenzy as Year Draws to a Close." *CBC News*, December 30. http://www.cbc.ca/news/politics/political-parties-in-a-fundraising-frenzy-as-year-draws-to-a-close-1.2886299.

Chase, Steven. 2008. "Tories Toe Harper Government's Line." *Globe and Mail*, November 16. http://www.theglobeandmail.com/news/national/tories-toe-harper-governments-line/article1066007/.

Corbeil, Dorothy. 2013. "I never thought I would win." Liberal Party listserv email, December 4.

DeLorey, Fred. 2014. "Have you met these four Canadians?" Conservative Party listserv email, May 21.

Duncan, John. 2014. "Is this a mistake?" Conservative Party listserv email, January 22.

El Akkad, Omar, and Josh Kerr. 2013. "Beyond Loyalty: Why Retailers Track Your Every Purchase." *Globe and Mail*, July 19. http://www.theglobeandmail.com/report-on-business/industry-news/marketing/beyond-loyalty-why-retailers-track-your-every-purchase/article13329311/.

Flanagan, Tom. 2009. *Harper's Team: Behind the Scenes in the Conservative Rise to Power*, 2nd ed. Montreal/Kingston: McGill-Queen's University Press.

–. 2014. *Winning Power: Canadian Campaigning in the Twenty-First Century*. Montreal/Kingston: McGill-Queen's University Press.

Flanagan, Tom, and Harold Jansen. 2009. "Election Campaigns under Canada's Party Finance Laws." In *The Canadian Federal Election of 2008*, edited by Jon H. Pammett and Christopher Dornan, 194–216. Toronto: Dundurn Press.

Green, Joshua. 2012. "The Science behind Those Obama Campaign Emails." *Bloomberg*, November 29. http://www.bloomberg.com/news/articles/2012-11-29/the-science-behind-those-obama-campaign-e-mails.

Harfoush, Rahaf. 2009. *Yes We Did! An Inside Look at How Social Media Built the Obama Brand*. Berkeley: New Riders.

Jackson, Nigel A. 2005. "Vote Winner or a Nuisance: Email and Elected Politicians' Relationship with Their Constituents." *Journal of Nonprofit & Public Sector Marketing* 14 (1–2): 91–108. http://dx.doi.org/10.1300/J054v14n01_06.

–. 2006. "An MP's Role in the Internet Era: The Impact of e-Newsletters." *Journal of Legislative Studies* 12 (2): 223–42. http://dx.doi.org/10.1080/13572330600739561.

Loewen, Peter John, and Frédérick Bastien. 2010. "(In)significant Elections? Federal By-Elections in Canada, 1963–2008." *Canadian Journal of Political Science* 43 (1): 87–105. http://dx.doi.org/10.1017/S000842390999076X.

Marland, Alex. 2016. *Brand Command: Canadian Politics and Democracy in the Age of Message Control*. Vancouver: UBC Press.

McLean, James S. 2012. *Inside the NDP War Room: Competing for Credibility in a Federal Election*. Montreal/Kingston: McGill-Queen's University Press.

Naumetz, Tim. 2014. "Conservative Party Uses Trudeau's 'Juvenile' CF-18 Remark to Fundraise." *Hill Times*, October 6. http://www.hilltimes.com/2014/10/06/conservative-party-uses-trudeaus-juvenile-cf-18-remark-to-fundraise-whip-out-our-cf-18s-and-show-them-how-big-they-are/29873/39873.

Nielsen, Rasmus Kleis. 2012. *Ground Wars: Personalized Communication in Political Campaigns*. Princeton, NJ: Princeton University Press. http://dx.doi.org/10.1515/978140 0840441.

O'Malley, Kady. 2015. "Conservatives Still on Top as Parties Report Latest Fundraising Totals." *CBC News*, May 1. http://www.cbc.ca/news/politics/conservatives-still-on-top-as-parties-report-latest-fundraising-totals-1.3057522.

Rotman, Nathan. 2013. "Breaking: By-election alert." NDP listserv email, October 20.

–. 2014. "Reporting back: The NDP's national day of action." NDP listserv email, February 26.

Sherman, Elaine. 1999. "Direct Marketing: How Does It Work for Political Campaigns?" In *Handbook of Political Marketing*, edited by Bruce I. Newman, 365–88. Thousand Oaks, CA: SAGE Publications.

Sheth, Jagdish N., and Atul Parvatiyar. 1995. "Relationship Marketing in Consumer Markets: Antecedents and Consequences." *Journal of the Academy of Marketing Science* 23 (4): 255–71. http://dx.doi.org/10.1177/009207039502300405.

Topp, Brian. 2010. *How We Almost Gave the Tories the Boot: The Inside Story behind the Coaltion*. Toronto: Lorimer & Company.

Topp, Christina. 2014. "Our fundraising quarter is at stake." Liberal Party listserv email, June 26.

6

Online, All the Time: The Strategic Objectives of Canadian Opposition Parties

Thierry Giasson and Tamara A. Small

When it comes to Internet politics, the 2008 American presidential campaign is often presented as a turning point in how digital media have become fundamental tools for postmodern campaigning. Much has been written about the transformative aspect of the Obama campaign's prototypical use of social media and of its online mobilization platform, My.BarackObama.com, commonly referred to as MyBO (Chadwick 2013; Kreiss 2012, 2016; Nielsen 2012; Vaccari 2010). These tools allowed the campaign to mobilize supporters for on- and offline activities, collect donations, and create an impressive database of socio-demographic and political information from site visitors. However, other researchers indicate that the much-hyped MyBO may be more of an outlier in digital politics (Vaccari 2013, 135). Online communications tools developed for the American presidential system, with its dual contest of candidates fighting for independent voters in a relatively limited regulatory framework where technological innovation is facilitated by access to massive resources, are seen as not generalizable to many other electoral contexts. These academics are calling for investigations to be carried out on "less obvious cases" (Enli and Moe 2013, 641) of multiparty systems and parliamentary elections, such as Canada, where partisan identification and electoral regulations remain strong. Such research is needed to better understand the similarities and differences in the roles that institutional, social, and cultural factors may play in why and how political parties adopt or resist technological innovations (Gibson 2013).

Moreover, the 2008 Obama campaign tells us very little about the inter-election period. While there are some significant past contributions looking at online practices beyond elections (see Foot and Schneider 2006; Gibson and Römmele 2001; Greffet 2011; Howard 2006; Kreiss 2012; Römmele 2003), less is known about the ways in which parties continue to engage with digital technologies in the context of the permanent campaign. This inter-election period is important to consider. Unlike television or radio adver-tisements, which typically wane between elections, websites, social media sites, and email create a permanent presence twenty-four hours a day, seven days a week, all year long. According to Kristen Foot and Steven Schneider (2006, 204), digital technologies enable political organizations "to engage in the same practices that its electoral incarnations had established, and to build on the databases cataloguing transactional relationships previously established with voters, supporters, contributors, journalists and other pol-itical actors."

From this, we believe that digital technologies have the capacity to support permanent campaigning in Canada (Small 2012). Anna Lennox Esselment's (2014) contribution on the permanent-campaign ethos of the Harper Con-servatives' successive minority governments provides some insights. She notes that digital platforms offer parties the ability to target and direct com-munication to Canadians. In his book *Winning Power*, Flanagan (2014) re-minds readers of the pervasive nature of digital technologies in Canada's permanent campaigning. Referring specifically to Naheed Nenshi's active use of social media prior to and during his victorious campaign for mayor of Calgary in 2010, Flanagan concludes that Canadian political parties, as control-obsessed organizations, have to innovate on these platforms to win elections. Finally, a recent contribution from Thierry Giasson and his col-laborators on the strategic objectives guiding online campaigning during the Quebec 2012 elections (Giasson, Greffet, and Chacon 2014) reveals how hybridity and digital technologies impact electoral preparedness and imple-mentation in Canadian parties. It shows that opposition and left-leaning parties were more actively engaged online than governing and right-leaning formations.

This chapter focuses on a less obvious case in the inter-election period. Here, we explore how Canadian political parties conceptualize digital tech-nologies between elections as part of the permanent campaign. Our analysis differs significantly from other Canadian studies. In Canada, political sci-ence research on digital politics has focused mostly on how parties and pol-iticians communicate with voters and citizens on different websites and social media platforms, such as blogs, Twitter, or Facebook (for instance, see Bastien and Greffet 2009; Small 2014; Smith and Chen 2009). Most of these studies highlight the difficulty parties have in using social media in an interactive way and state that they therefore carry "not-so-social" campaigning online. These content analyses of communication activities on digital platforms show that elite-based governing parties and right-of-centre organizations engage in less interaction and dialogue than do opposition, membership-based, and left-of-centre parties (Giasson et al. 2013; Giasson and Small 2014). Apprehensions over loss of message control are commonly presented in the literature as explanations for the reticence of parties to be more open to retroaction, dialogue, and co-production on social media.

Instead of examining the supply of online content produced by parties, we consider the intersection of partisan politics and digital technologies in a strategic perspective. That is, we explore the strategic objectives of parties when using and producing digital political content in the context of the permanent campaign. To the best of our knowledge, there is no work on Canadian federal parties that has investigated directly the strategic objectives on which online practices rely. Furthermore, no research looks at these questions in the perspective of the permanent campaign, and none focuses precisely on how opposition parties deal with web-based innovation in this novel context of continuous campaigning.

Case Study

This study investigates the strategic objectives underlying the use of online technologies, and social media platforms specifically, by the three national federal opposition parties in Canada in 2015. For what purposes are they maintaining an online presence between elections? What are the strategic goals guiding their use of emails, party websites, social networking sites (Facebook), microblogging (Twitter), and file-sharing sites (YouTube)? As past research indicates, there is a theoretical rationale for exploring opposition parties. The outparty innovation incentive hypothesis suggests that challengers are generally more likely than incumbents to adopt technological innovations (Karpf 2012). Opposition political formations are more likely to take risks than are governing parties who cling to power and carry out more prudent and disciplined communications, both online and offline. Opposition parties are consistently depicted in previous research as less risk-averse than governing parties when it comes to online campaigning initiatives (see Giasson, Greffet, and Chacon 2014; Giasson and Small 2014). As challengers prepare for an election, they may be more open to using digital technologies in more innovative ways.

As noted, we are less concerned with the online content produced by Canadian parties than their strategic considerations when using digital technologies. The literature on electoral use of digital technologies indicates that political parties follow three broad categories of strategic goals in their online presences: communication goals, political goals, and marketing goals. These objectives are not mutually exclusive, as parties often aim to achieve all three categories simultaneously during an online campaign. Communication objectives refer to a party's will to broadcast its partisan messages, to personalize its leader and team, to correct or spin media coverage of its actions, and to attack its opponents' campaigns (Bor 2013; Karlsen 2009; Vaccari 2010). Political goals are associated with winning the election, mobilizing supporters, getting out the vote, gaining visibility, generating resources (such as donations and volunteers), and promoting an ideology or political project (the core political values of the party, not its electoral platform) (Bor 2013; Karlsen 2009; Vaccari 2010). Finally, parties use social media and other Internet tools for marketing purposes such as collecting voter information data, creating a relationship with voters by managing a community, or microtargeting voters (Chadwick 2013; Kreiss 2012).

Method

To assess the strategic objectives of Canadian opposition parties, we conducted three semi-structured interviews with key informants who are involved in the design and implementation of the three major opposition parties' online strategies.[1] Qualitative interviews are rarely conducted when researching digital politics in Canada, which is usually content-analysis-based. In early 2015, we interviewed the communications directors or digital strategists of the Green Party of Canada, the Liberal Party of Canada, and the New Democratic Party of Canada (NDP). At the time this chapter was written, there were five parties seated in opposition benches, with the NDP as the official opposition. To ensure a more valid comparison between organizations, we chose to investigate the three federal opposition parties who run candidates in all provinces of Canada, rather than just in Quebec. This national status imposes specific organizational challenges, such as in fundraising or regional accommodation. Such challenges may impact how permanent campaigning is carried out, including how online technologies are used. As our research is qualitative and investigates the understudied world of strategic decision making regarding Internet campaigning, which is carried out by a very limited number of individuals within Canadian political parties, we have a small number of interviews.

Each interview covered seven topics dealing with the organization of online communication in the inter-election context, including strategic goals, target audiences, e-political marketing practices, budgets and personnel, and management of Internet user-generated content. The content of the transcripts was analyzed using QDA Miner, a deductive text analysis software, to identify the dominant strategic objectives of each party, based on a similar study on the Quebec provincial election of 2012 (Giasson, Greffet, and Chacon 2014).[2] As will be shown, the data produced from the text analysis highlight recurrent themes in our informants' accounts. We used them as illustrative conceptual tools rather than as quantitative measures of strategic decision-making expression.

Findings

We began by asking the party strategists to state what role they thought digital platforms played in the inter-election period for their party. Table 6.1 presents a detailed outline of the central strategic objectives mentioned by respondents regarding different digital platforms. First, they all stated that online technologies allow them to talk directly, and quickly, to Canadians who use these tools in growing numbers to access political and partisan information. This answer from our Liberal Party informant summarizes this conception: "Well, for us, it plays a significant role. Part of it is using it as an opportunity to bypass traditional media and go directly to audiences, as well as speaking to our base and quickly communicating a message that the base of our party needs to understand." It is hardly surprising that communication objectives dominate our interviewees' narratives. According to them, communication goals guide the use of digital platforms in the inter-election period, especially as a way to broadcast messages to audiences. The Liberal interviewee pressed communication objectives as more central to the party's permanent campaign in her responses. The election of Justin Trudeau as Liberal leader in 2013 and the decision of the party establishment to use online platforms to define and diffuse his image through personalization may explain why communication objectives were so dominantly expressed in the Liberal strategist's narrative.

However, political goals top strategic priorities for permanent campaigning for the NDP and the Greens, especially the importance of generating

TABLE 6.1

Strategic objectives associated with digital technologies

Digital media	Shared objectives
Facebook	Broadcast messages Personalize the leader
Twitter	Broadcast daily messages of the party Target groups (journalists, party supporters)
YouTube	Broadcast party messages Broadcast party events (live or not)
Emails	Generate resources Broadcast messages to the community Mobilize through calls to action (online and offline)
Party website	Broadcast messages (ideas, electoral platform) Mobilize through calls to action

NOTE: The table lists for each digital platform the strategic objectives most frequently mentioned in the experts' interviews.

resources and mobilizing supporters for actions. Our NDP informant expressed his organization's preoccupation with mobilization as a core goal of their digital permanent campaign:

> I guess it's basically urgency and volume in terms of the difference. But the reality is that with increasing partisanship between elections, we're sort of campaigning more than we have before. Obviously the non-campaign period doesn't get the sort of media attention, close scrutiny, but we use issue campaigns, leader-focused campaigns to bring supporters on board to ultimately influence supporters for our opponents and ourselves.

All three party insiders also expressed how important permanent campaigning on digital platforms is in helping to achieve political marketing goals, such as collecting voter information through email and social media analytics, targeting more effectively message audiences, and building online communities of supporters. The interviews therefore revealed interesting differences in the types of communication objectives parties have expressed and in the relative importance of political and marketing goals in their online permanent campaigning.

Strategists mentioned a range of communication objectives. Unsurprisingly, broadcasting partisan messages to audiences was at the top of their lists. When it came to online permanent campaigning, especially when talking about party websites, email, and social media, all three digital strategists kept coming back to the central importance of having their organizations' messages available online and sent to their targeted publics. Our Liberal interviewee summed up the paramount importance of persuasive communication in the permanent campaign: "We are using all of those channels [social media and website] as methods of persuasion ... So bringing people along, talking to them about the issues that they care about, so that maybe they'll be interested in giving us their email address so that we can continue to communicate with them about that." Hence, online platforms are seen as integrated communication tools that help disseminate messages effectively and bring in Internet users to the party website so that they will provide their email addresses. They are an integral part of a cohesive plan of permanent persuasive communication geared at establishing and maintaining contact between the party and its targeted constituencies.

All three interviewees mentioned on numerous occasions the importance of maintaining email databases that better communicate targeted messages to different constituencies of the party but also to achieve political goals such as levying financial contributions or mobilizing supporters for specific tasks. Current research on electoral web politics and online campaigning focuses a lot on the use of social media and much less on the use of emails. Our interviews could serve as reminders of the continued relevance if not centrality of those Web 1.0 devices in political communication. As the previous chapter in this volume discussed, emails are a core component of permanent campaigning in Canada. According to our NDP interviewee, online permanent campaigning depends on an integrated approach to digital communication:

> At the end of the day, social media drives web content and, particularly when you tie in that, part of our objectives are getting people who support us through support for an issue, support for an MP, whatever, to sign up to be on our email list which is how we continue to engage them. A good social media program can't be driven on witty tweets alone; you need content, you need videos, you need infographics, you need landing pages with interesting information.

Over the years, a party's email list becomes a strategic weapon for permanent campaigning. Mobilization, fundraising and persuasion are goals that are met through the use of targeted email campaigns – a position also expressed very clearly by our Green informant speaking of his party's strategic conception of Facebook:

> You want to articulate a certain message in the lead-up stages to the campaign, or during the campaign. You're trying to use it to build followers, increase your visibility, enhance your profile, articulate your message on certain policies or issues, current issues, while at the same time, you use it as a fundraising tool. That's another one and it's huge.

Our informants also mentioned the personalization of their leaders as another important communication objective associated with online permanent campaigning, especially on social networking sites such as Facebook. All three parties have Twitter and Facebook accounts dedicated to their leaders. Green leader Elizabeth May is known for her active use of microblogging (Small 2012), and Justin Trudeau and NDP leader Thomas Mulcair tweet regularly. Following the 2011 federal election, both the Liberals and NDP elected new leaders. Strategists from these organizations mentioned how social media are used to define their leaders' prime ministerial image, to provide them with additional visibility, or to help create a relationship with Canadians. New leaders must establish their reputation and their credibility. Working in Parliament from opposition benches does not always provide them with the visibility needed to present their image to citizens. In addition, Mulcair and Trudeau became leaders of their parties with little experience in federal politics. This may explain why objectives of image building and personalization through social media were often mentioned in our interviewees' narratives:

> For the leader too, it's a great way for us to show his personality and there really aren't very many other outlets to do that unless you meet him in person, or ... you see a clip on the news ... It might give you a great sense of his values, but not who he is. So we use it a lot for that, and to show people he's a father, kind of a nerd, he's a Quebecer, to show those kinds of things about him that you wouldn't necessarily know. (Liberal respondent)

When it came to political objectives, our interviews revealed a central strategic preoccupation for resource collection. As mentioned in Chapter 1, as of April 2015 political parties in Canada no longer receive per-vote public subsidies, so they therefore rely on donations from individual Canadians. This puts additional pressure on partisan organizations to find alternative sources of funding. According to our respondents, online technologies (particularly social media and emails) are used between elections specifically for this purpose of raising financial contributions. When asked to explain the role of digital technologies in the changing party financing regulatory context, the Liberal informant stated that "it accounts for about a third of our fundraising, and it is the channel that's growing the fastest ... I think that's where we're able to move ... online, asking for more small donations. Which I don't think that's how our fundraising worked in the past." The interviewee described online fundraising as her party's "fastest-growing channel" and explained that the Liberal organization was finding more innovative ways to stimulate this "most important route" for financial donations.

We also asked the strategists why parties keep using emails in this social media–obsessed era. When stating their objectives for communicating to citizens via email, all our interviewees referred to fundraising as the leading factor. The following quote from our NDP interviewee summarizes the narratives of all three respondents on the matter:

> Fundraising is huge ... The fundraising is important all the time so ultimately we grow our email list and use it to fundraise and all of the other activity. Although there is a certain political value around engaging Canadians, providing high-quality, rich content, speaking to the issues people care about, there is sort of a reality of "we have to fundraise to survive," and email is increasingly an important part of that.

This also speaks of another important political objective that parties try to achieve online in their permanent-campaign efforts: to mobilize supporters for political activities through what they refer to as calls for action.

The strategists indicated that party communication to citizens during the inter-election period focuses more on issue-based debates, such as public policies being debated in Parliament. Parties use online technologies to bring those debates directly to Canadians by introducing them to their partisan positions on the issues of the day. Making information available to citizens is often mentioned as a key strategic objective; however, mobilizing supporters to carry actions such as signing petitions, sharing videos, posting content on social media, writing emails to elected officials, or canvassing in specific ridings are also dominant goals for permanent online campaigning. Often, online mobilization is stimulated for offline actions. This is in line with Andrew Chadwick's (2013) model of hybrid campaigns, which depicts the integration of online and offline communication channels and the more novel compromise of grassroots activism and elite control in the organization and implementation of electoral strategies. Our Liberal informant revealed this notion of hybridity in calls for engagement: "One thing that we're looking at are 'days of action,' which will centre around getting ready on an online presence and then moving to door knocking in communities, but it'll be started on an online presence. Again we ask people on our various issues-based posts, we ask them to share, "do you agree?" We'll also ask people if they'll sign up for petitions for those issues posted. We do encourage people to engage more." Fundraising, mobilization, and calls for action on issue-based policy debates are key political objectives that our interviewees all agreed on regarding online permanent campaigning. Furthermore, they all mentioned the central role that email plays as an instrument of communication with Canadians to achieve those goals. Our interviews indicated that all parties maintain elaborate email list systems that allow them to not only reach large pools of like-minded citizens, but also target subsamples of them regarding specific issues. For instance, our Green respondent highlighted in his answers the importance of measuring the reactions to different messages sent to the varying segments of subscribers of party email databases: "It's language, age, location, and then you're testing it, like A-B testing in marketing, right. You could be saying 'this message works in this region but it doesn't work in this region,' so you could test the same message in two regions or you can change one message a little and begin your next test to see what the difference was." Parties use these message-testing procedures, mostly done via emails, as a way to ensure their subscribers are exposed to call for actions related to issues they strongly care about, therefore increasing the probability they will either engage in offline actions or send donations to the party.

Our informants frequently mentioned message targeting as a marketing goal in permanent campaigning. All three digital strategists also had a lot to say about collecting (through online means) voter information into databases and using them to send targeted issue-specific messages and calls for action to subsamples of supporters or potential supporters. Data collection, voter targeting, and community building were recurrent themes in the informants' narratives regarding marketing objectives.

On data collection, the three interviewees explained how their organizations obtain personal information that is provided online by citizens themselves. Some parties collect this through their websites, others via social media. As mentioned in past Canadian contributions (see, for instance, Delacourt 2013; Flanagan 2014; Marland, Giasson, and Small 2014) and in Steve Patten's chapter in this volume, federal parties collect, on an ongoing basis, numerous types of voter information that are integrated in databases. They use these information systems for message distribution, fundraising, voter segmentation, or riding targeting during the permanent campaign and for electoral preparedness. Some of these tools, such as the Conservative Party's Constituent Information Management System (CIMS), have been developed in-house, while others, such as Liberalist or NDP Vote (recently remodelled into Populus), were created for the parties by private American firms (respectively, Blue State Digital and 270 Strategies). The NDP has maintained an ongoing collaboration with Democratic strategist Jeremy Bird's 270 Strategies to inform its strategies for digital campaigning, fundraising, and field organizing. As the following comments from the NDP strategist reveal, innovation is a necessity for online campaigning, as sometimes, outside perspectives are warranted: "I think it was that we wanted to modernize the field, we wanted to figure out what was next. We've been doing a lot of the same things the same way and we wanted somebody to challenge us, and we wanted to aggressively grow our online fundraising program because public financing was being removed and we wanted support." Expertise on digital marketing therefore exists within parties, who invest important resources – both human and financial – dedicated directly to online campaigning, especially for message production, online platform monitoring, and managing interactions with Internet users. Yet our interviews indicated that the organizations also willingly contract outside firms to help expand their practices, such as the 270 Strategies association with the NDP and the Blue State Digital partnership with the Liberal Party.

The informants also mentioned using social media analytics for message targeting purposes as a strong strategic advantage of online permanent campaigning. Google, Twitter, Facebook, and most other social media companies provide their clients, including political parties, with strategic advice to develop efficient campaigns on their platforms as well as in-depth metrics profiling the members, followers, or friends of their respective networks or communities. These detailed profiles, assembled by algorithms, help parties to engage in precise and microtargeted messaging or advertising distribution on each platform. Along with their own email databases, these social media metrics present another online feature that partisan organizations use to communicate with different subgroups of voters according to their age, gender, location, or consumer interests. Data collected through social media can also be included in parties' databases. As the Green Party strategist stated, targeting is used for communication purposes and ultimately to contribute to fundraising:

> Age, demographics, gender, likes, what they like; we can measure who's following us, or donating to us by their interests, by their education, by their income ... I mean on Facebook we're using their metrics, but as you buy some of their ad work, you're getting into deeper metrics. On our donor base, they're collecting that information as it's coming in and they're filling it off to fields. They're asking very specific questions to try to get a demographic profile of who's voting for us, but not only, who's donating to us and who's supporting us. And so you build that supporter base. Does that translate into votes? Potentially, but it tells you who is actually willing to support and take that next step.

Finally, our respondents mentioned relationship and online community building as a goal of their online permanent campaigning efforts. Commercial organizations engaging in marketing activities on social media try to maintain strong bonds with their social media followers, to engage with them regularly, and even to ask for their participation in marketing activities of products and services. Followers and supporters of companies and organizations should then be considered as potential promotional agents or part-time marketers for brands on social media platforms. Our respondents seemed to adhere to this principle. All three mentioned that their parties understood the importance of online brand ambassadors; two said that their organizations had created actual communities of Internet and social media supporters who were tasked with defending the party message by sharing, blogging, posting, and tweeting it online. These communities are usually assembled through private Facebook groups or limited email lists and are composed of very active party supporters or members. The Liberal strategist described these communities as follows:

> So there are two groups that were created. The first is that social media engagement group with people that were volunteers for the party, and were asked, "would you be interested in joining that?" And then the other group is actually something that's very new for us, which is more of an ambassadors group. We looked at people who were engaging most with our posts or were influencers within our spheres and we reached them and said, "would you like to join our rapid response team?" You know there might be an issue that breaks out during the day and we need you to spread the Liberal position or the Liberal message on this issue, or to hit back frankly against an unfair attack.

Here again, hybridity expresses itself as "newer" online technologies, and marketing logics help federal parties to engage in traditional political activities such as fundraising, message distribution, field organization, and spin control. In permanent campaigning, digital innovations cohabit with older forms of electioneering.

Permanent Campaigning in Canada

The narratives of our key informants told the story of three actively engaged opposition parties online, using the entire scope of digital technologies to achieve communication, political, and marketing goals. Respondents from all parties indicated that the permanent campaign in Canada is a hybrid process combining integrated conventional and digital communication technologies and approaches. They all expressed their growing interest in the political marketing potential associated with social media campaigning, especially in regard to voter data collection and targeting.

However, hybridity took different forms and reached varied levels within the party system. All three opposition parties are running fully integrated online campaigns, with social media being their central drivers. But two of them, the NDP and the Liberals, are bringing the notion of Internet parties to another level by having teams of online supporters organized in private Facebook groups mobilized and tasked with disseminating messages of the day and protecting the party brand online. All three digital strategists claimed that engaging in a permanent campaign online was unavoidable not only since increasing numbers of Canadians use the Internet to access political information or engage in political actions, but also because social media, especially Twitter, force parties to deal with a hyperreactive political and media environment. In addition, in light of the abolition of government per-vote financial subsidies to political parties, respondents from the three opposition parties said that their organizations were faced with financing challenges that email or social media fundraising campaigns were helping them to meet.

The literature on web campaigning during elections indicates that strong contenders positioned to win an election and form government, as is the case for the NDP and the Liberals, are usually more risk-averse and more prone to running cautious, controlled, and cohesive social media strategies. However, these two parties are running innovative online permanent campaigns with surprisingly high levels of hybridity and openness to interactive and dialogic principles in their strategic objectives and tactical actions. Most of their digital initiatives and innovations are following rather traditional strategic communication objectives: getting the message out, making information available, or personalizing their leaders. Nevertheless, they are organized or implemented in hybrid forms, mixing old and new media or involving citizens as active marketing agents.

Our interviews revealed hybridity in the permanent campaigning of all three federal opposition parties. Fundraising, message broadcasting, issue mobilization, and data collection were all mentioned as key aspects of maintaining an active presence online between elections. The representatives of the three opposition parties alike may have mentioned that they welcome citizen-initiated actions, but they also mentioned the paramount importance of constantly monitoring what is going on online, whether it comes from within the party, from opponents, from Internet users, or from the news media. In this context of obsessive scrutiny and instantaneous reaction, public message cohesiveness is as important for parties in the inter-election period as it is in an electoral campaign. Actually, as the permanent-campaign hypothesis posits, the electoral campaign never ends, both offline and online. The narratives of the three strategists indicated that digital technologies are now mobilized and fully integrated in this ongoing effort. As previous research has stated, hybridity never equates to being off message. In their analysis of social media use in British politics, Nigel Jackson and Darren Lilleker (2009) spoke of Web 1.5 campaigns, where parties gave the impression of openness and dialogue in social media when they actually were engaging in traditional top-down, hierarchical electoral communication. With its presentation of increased levels of hybridity in operational management and marketing practices in the permanent campaign of three opposition parties, our study seems to indicate an evolution from that model.

The election of Justin Trudeau and the Liberals in the 2015 election raises some interesting questions for the role of digital technology and its place in permanent campaigning. Popular accounts laud the Liberals' use of social media in the 2015 campaign (Jeanes 2015), suggesting it was essential to the party's success with young Canadians. The party's access to power now questions the outparty innovation hypothesis. As noted, we did find evidence that the Liberals had actively engaged online in the run-up to the 2015 election. It could then be argued that the party's success may have been a continuation of that active online engagement. Now that they are the incumbent party, will the Liberals modify their innovative approach and revert to a more risk-averse style of online campaigning, or will they carry on their strategy of openness, dialogue, and creativity developed in opposition? The first few months of their tenure in power seem to indicate a will to take some (calculated?) risks and keep a very active presence online. The prime minister, known the world over for his appreciation of selfies (self-portrait photographs) widely distributed online, remains an avid Twitter user, and many members of his cabinet regularly express their opinions on social media. The new Liberal administration may very well have decided to carry over their strategy for online permanent campaigning within government, since the strategic goals of fundraising, data collection, issue mobilization, and partisan message broadcasting do remain as fundamental to an incumbent party as they are to opposition parties. The big difference for Liberal online strategists now rest with the new playing field from which they can operate, which mostly means access to government resources and its communications machine to carry their ongoing campaign efforts. Hence, the online battle goes on.

NOTES

1 Our interview guide contained twenty-nine questions and forty-six potential follow-up questions, all open-ended. The interviews took a conversational approach, which meant that in addition to the core research questions, some unscripted questions may have been asked. We interviewed two national communications directors who were in charge of online strategies in their parties, as well as the director for digital

strategy of another party who developed and supervised all Internet campaigning and strategy for his organization. These party insiders are all directly involved in the development, implementation, and supervision of their respective organization's online strategies. The strategists were referred to us following requests for interviews that were submitted to the parties themselves. They answered our questions at length during interviews that ran an average of seventy-five minutes. Respondents were assured anonymity to help them respond more openly to our questions. Interviews were conducted in person or over the phone. The conversations were transcribed in text format to facilitate content analysis.

2 The detailed coding grid and results are available on request. We list here the categories associated with each of the three types of objectives: (1) communication objectives: broadcast a message, advertise party events and leader activities, attack opponents, control/spin the message, broadcast media content, personalize the leader; (2) political objectives: generate resources, promote an ideology, get known/ increase notoriety, get votes/get out the vote, achieve online mobilization, achieve offline mobilization, achieve mobilization in general; (3) marketing objectives: collect voter data, collect market intelligence, target, build relationship/community, modify the strategy, build the brand, manage databases.

REFERENCES

Bastien, Frédérick, and Fabienne Greffet. 2009. "Les campagnes électorales sur Internet: Une comparaison entre France et Québec." *Hermès* 54: 211–19.

Bor, Stephanie E. 2013. "Using Social Networking Sites to Improve Communication between Political Campaigns and Citizens in the 2012 Election." *American Behavioral Scientist*, June 7: 1–19. http://dx.doi.org/10.1177/0002764213490698.

Chadwick, Andrew. 2013. *The Hybrid Media System: Politics and Power*. Oxford: Oxford University Press. http://dx.doi.org/10.1093/acprof:oso/9780199759477.001.0001.

Delacourt, Susan. 2013. *Shopping for Votes: How Politicians Choose Us and We Choose Them*. Madeira Park, BC: Douglas and McIntyre.

Enli, Gunn, and Hallvard Moe. 2013. "Introduction to Special Issue: Social Media and Election Campaigns – Key Tendencies and Ways Forward." *Information, Communication and Society* 16 (5): 637–45. http://dx.doi.org/10.1080/1369118X.2013.784795.

Esselment, Anna. 2014. "The Governing Party and the Permanent Campaign." In *Political Communication in Canada: Meet the Press and Tweet the Rest*, edited by A. Marland, T. Giasson, and T. A. Small, 24–38. Vancouver: UBC Press.

Flanagan, Thomas. 2014. *Winning Power: Canadian Campaigning in the Twenty-First Century*. Montreal/Kingston: McGill-Queen's University Press.

Foot, Kristen, and Steven M. Schneider. 2006. *Web Campaigning*. Cambridge, MA: MIT Press.

Giasson, Thierry, Fabienne Greffet, and Geneviève Chacon. 2014. "Digital Campaigning in a Comparative Perspective: Online Strategies in the 2012 Elections in France and Québec." Paper presented at the World Congress of the International Political Science Association. Montreal, July 19–24, 2014.

Giasson, Thierry, Gildas Le Bars, Frédérick Bastien, and Mélanie Verville. 2013. "QC2012: l'utilisation de Twitter par les parti." In *Les Québécois aux urnes. Les partis, les médias et les citoyens en campagne*, edited by F. Bastien, E. Bélanger, and F. Gélineau, 133–48. Montreal: Les Presses de l'Université de Montréal.

Giasson, Thierry, and Tamara A. Small. 2014. "#elections: The Use of Twitter by Provincial Parties in Canada." Paper presented at the Annual Meeting of the British Association for Canadian Studies. London, UK, April 25–26, 2014.

Gibson, Rachel K. 2013. "Party Change, Social Media and the Rise of 'Citizen-Initiated' Campaigning." *Party Politics*, January 30: 1–15. doi: 10.1177/1354068812472575.

Gibson, Rachel K., and Andrea Römmele. 2001. "A Party Centered Theory of Professionalized Campaigning." *International Journal of Press/Politics* 6 (4): 31–44. http://dx.doi.org/10.1177/108118001129172323.

Greffet, Fabienne. 2011. *Continuerlalutte.com: Les partis politiques sur le web*. Paris: Presses de la Fondation nationale des sciences politiques.

Howard, Philip. 2006. *New Media Campaigns and the Managed Citizen*. New York: Cambridge University Press.

Jackson, Nigel, and Darren Lilleker. 2009. "Building an Architecture of Participation? Political Parties and Web 2.0 in Britain." *Journal of Information Technology & Politics* 6 (3–4): 232–50. http://dx.doi.org/10.1080/19331680903028438.

Jeanes, Katie. 2015. "5 ways Justin Trudeau's Social Media Game Trumped Other Leaders." *Huffington Post Canada*, October 22. http://www.huffingtonpost.ca/katie-jeanes/justin-trudeau-social-media_b_8362414.html.

Karlsen, Rune. 2009. "Campaign Communication and the Internet: Party Strategy in the 2005 Norwegian Election Campaign." *Journal of Elections, Public Opinion, and Parties* 19 (2): 183–202. http://dx.doi.org/10.1080/17457280902799030.

Karpf, David. 2012. *The MoveOn effect: The Unexpected Transformation of American Political Advocacy*. Oxford: Oxford University Press. http://dx.doi.org/10.1093/acprof:oso/9780199898367.001.0001.

Kreiss, Daniel. 2012. *Taking Our Country Back: The Crafting of Networked Politics from Howard Dean to Barack Obama*. Oxford: Oxford University Press. http://dx.doi.org/10.1093/acprof:oso/9780199782536.001.0001.

–. 2016. *Prototype Politics. Technology-Intensive Campaigning and the Data of Democracy*. Oxford: Oxford University Press.

Marland, Alex, Thierry Giasson, and Tamara A. Small. 2014. "Political Communication and Marketing in Canada: Challenges for Democracy." In *Political Communication in Canada: Meet the Press and Tweet the Rest*, edited by A. Marland, T. Giasson, and T.A. Small, 229–46. Vancouver: UBC Press.

Nielsen, Rasmus Kleis. 2012. *Ground Wars. Personalized Communication in Political Campaigns*. Princeton: Princeton University Press.

Römmele, Andrea. 2003. "Political Parties, Party Communication and New Information and Communication Technologies." *Party Politics* 9 (1): 7–20. http://dx.doi.org/10.1177/135406880391002.

Small, Tamara A. 2012. "Are We Friends Yet? Relationship Marketing on the Internet." In *Political Marketing in Canada*, edited by A. Marland, T. Giasson and J. Lees-Marshment., 193–208. Vancouver: UBC Press.

Small, Tamara A. 2014. "The Not-So Social Network: The Use of Twitter by Canada's Party Leaders." In *Political Communication in Canada: Meet the Press and Tweet the*

Rest, edited by A. Marland, T. Giasson, and T.A. Small, 92–126. Vancouver: UBC Press.

Smith, Peter, and Peter John Chen. 2009. "A Canadian E-lection 2008? Online Media and Political Competition." Paper presented at the Annual Meeting of the Canadian Political Science Association. Ottawa, May 27–29, 2009.

Vaccari, Cristian. 2010. "Technology Is a Commodity: The Internet in the 2008 United States Presidential Election." *Journal of Information Technology & Politics* 7 (4): 318–39. http://dx.doi.org/10.1080/19331681003656664.

–. 2013. *Digital Politics in Western Democracies: A Comparative Study*. Baltimore: Johns Hopkins University Press.

7
Permanent Polling and Governance

André Turcotte and Simon Vodrey

In Chapter 1, the editors mention that American pollster Patrick Caddell is generally credited – or blamed – for coining the expression "permanent campaign." But whatever Caddell was describing in the late 1970s has little affinity with today's reality. One of the unforeseen developments is the extent to which opinion polling has emerged as the essential building block of permanent-campaign activity. Without polling, permanent campaigning is impossible, since it depends on a constant stream of data for validation and evaluation. The marriage between permanent campaigning activities and public opinion polling has been so close that polling is now described more adequately as market intelligence. Jennifer Lees-Marshment (2012) explains how different types of political parties use market intelligence in modern campaigning. While the details are peripheral to this discussion, it is clear from her description that the use of polling data has gone through an important transformation over the last few decades: from a general information-gathering function to strategic marketing and communication applications. The practical repercussions of this transformation have been given little academic attention, an issue that this chapter attempts to address.

Initially, we should clarify the terminology we will use. Generally speaking, polling falls within the larger field of quantitative analysis: it is one form of survey research. As such, it relies on probability and aims at inference. The main distinction between "polling" and the more general "survey research" is that polling implies a regular monitoring of opinion focused on change and trends, while survey research tends to be more in-depth and less focused on longitudinal patterns (see Erikson and Tedin 2011 for a fuller discussion). The literature about polling and its different applications is vast and varied. In broad terms, polling has been examined from four different perspectives. First, numerous authors have looked at the technical aspects of conducting public opinion polling. This perspective is situated within the broader field of survey research and dates back to Emile Durkheim's (1951) seminal study on suicide. Paul F. Lazarsfeld and Morris Rosenberg's (1962) *The Language of Social Research* established most tenets of the discipline. Recently, attention has been directed towards the methodological challenges generated by the emergence of the Internet as the most efficient way to collect survey data (see, for example, Callegaro, Manfreda, and Vehovar 2015; Tourangeau, Conrad, and Couper 2013).

A second well-developed perspective is the publication and discussion of polling results by both academics and practitioners. George Gallup began this tradition with his *America Speaks* and *The Gallup Poll* in the 1940s and 1950s, and many have followed suit. A recent Canadian example of this approach is Darrell Bricker and John Ibbitson's (2013) *The Big Shift*.

A third perspective focuses on the potential negative impact of polling on democracy. Michael Wheeler created a stir when he published *Lies, Damn Lies, and Statistics* in 1976. In his book, Wheeler described the close relationship between politicians and pollsters and how they collaborate to manipulate public opinion. As with the previous two perspectives, numerous works followed from academics (Lewis 2001), international scholars (Blondiaux 1998; Lech 2001), and self-promoting practitioners (Moore 2008; Morris 1998; Plouffe 2009; Rollins 1996). While revealing and interesting, those books tend to suffer from specific shortcomings. They are either written from the viewpoint of academics with little practical understanding or from that of practitioners with little propensity to reflect critically on the consequences of their craft.

The fourth perspective is more limited in scope but purports to examine and reflect on the inner workings of polling in democracy. Some authors have focused on polling in government (Butler 2007; Page 2006), while most have looked at how practitioners use their expertise to serve their political clients. In some ways, this fourth perspective is related to the previous one, since it aims to exhibit an important aspect of governing and campaigning. The limited literature on the link between the permanent campaign and polling generally falls within this perspective and is beginning to isolate signposts to measure the increasing reliance on opinion research within the permanent campaign. One key indicator is the amount spent on polls while a party is in office (Murray and Howard 2002; Page 2006; Tenpas and

McCann 2007). While indicative of the volume of polling activity, such a measure gives an incomplete picture of the impact of the research efforts. It does not suggest how (or if) the findings were used to influence the strategic directions of the government, how any given polls were linked (or not) with electoral considerations, or who was involved in the process. Furthermore, if polling becomes an in-house function as it has with the federal Conservatives since 2006 (and with their Liberal counterparts following suit), the cost of polling is reduced, thus allowing greater efficiency in its use for strategic purposes. Looking at sheer volume does not account for that situation. One of our assertions is that recent developments at the provincial level and within the federal Liberal organization mean that the same person – or group of people – is likely to conduct public opinion polling and to participate directly in informing the strategic directions of the party organization (or government if they happen to be in power at the time). The merging of the roles of pollster (campaign function) and advisor (government function) is a better indication of the extent to which electoral and government polling have become intertwined. There is no clear demarcation between political insights – derived for electoral purposes – and governing insights – garnered to support policy development.

A second signpost in the literature monitors the extent to which market research techniques – such as focus groups, perception analyzers, and branding surveys – are making their way into the practice of political polling (see, for example, Sparrow and Turner 2001). Such an examination is entrenched in the literature by Lees-Marshment (2012), whose work we referred to earlier and is in line with the approach we are pursuing in this chapter. Through our interviews, we are able to provide more recent developments on how political polling is borrowing from other approaches to allow for the constant monitoring of opinion well beyond the writ period.

But getting current and insightful information about the practice of polling is difficult. Practitioners are reluctant to divulge their secrets, and scholars must examine the issue from the sidelines. We will rely on interviews with current Canadian pollsters to address this weakness in the literature, but we will look to some previous works to guide our analysis. In the American context, Joe Trippi's (2005) *The Revolution Will Not Be Televised* is a good example of a campaign director explaining how his campaign innovations had an impact on both electioneering and democracy. To understand the emergence of permanent polling in Canada, we can draw on two specific works published fifteen years apart. The first was co-authored by a practitioner and a journalist and reveals the evolution of polling in Canadian elections and its transformation into market intelligence. In this work, unlike other similar books, the authors reflect on the consequences of their craft. The second was written by an academic who found himself in the unprecedented situation of running an election campaign.

The first of these two contributions is *Leaders and Lesser Mortals*, published in 1992 by John Laschinger and Geoffrey Stevens. Its authors recount how Laschinger and researcher Allan Gregg went to meet Nova Scotia Progressive Conservative leader John Buchanan in 1977 to tell him everything he "would have to do during the next year if he wanted to be premier" (Laschinger and Stevens 1992, 3). The brazenness, the long outlook, the kind of advice, and the trip itself epitomized the relationship between polling and campaigning at that time. Pollsters would be brought in a few months before the beginning of the election campaign to gauge the mood of the public and help map out the election strategy. The implementation of that strategy was left to others. The party pollster would stay involved throughout the pre-writ and writ periods, but would be kept at arm's length. Moreover, little attention was given to incorporating polling into the workings of the government or to how policy making could be leveraged for targeted electoral gains. This structure would remain in place until the polling function morphed into the more permanent process we are describing in this chapter.

Martin Goldfarb and Gregg were this country's first homegrown party pollsters, and both greatly influenced the development of the practice of polling in Canada. Goldfarb once said that "like any seer or oracle, the pollster plays a role that is viewed with a combination of respect, fear, intrigue, and controversy" (quoted in Laschinger and Stevens 1992, 55). Starting back with George Gallup and the earliest days of scientific public opinion research, pollsters developed an aura of detachment and objectivity. Gallup often remarked that he never voted, and he used that fact as a badge of his impartiality. Michael Marzolini, who succeeded Martin Goldfarb as Liberal pollster in 1993, would echo this mantra several years later. The pollster's role was to bring the voice of the people into the political process.

Gregg and Goldfarb were opposites in style and personality. As Laschinger and Stevens (1992, 71) put it, "Where Goldfarb is a missionary, Gregg is a mercenary." When it came to polling, Goldfarb was an anthropologist and sociologist. His approach focused on his aptitude for grasping the general mood of the electorate and his ability to interpret the trends. He was solidly in the tradition of the "one person, one vote" interpretation of public opinion espoused by the early polling pioneers (Turcotte 2010, 208). In contrast, Allan Gregg was a rock star. He had long hair, leather jackets, and, more importantly, a rigorous background in quantitative analysis, not to mention a devotion to precise methodology. Nevertheless, both epitomized the detached seer and the from-the-outside-looking-in relationship that first developed between pollsters and their political clients. If they were fortunate enough to provide advice to the winning party, government contracts would follow. However, they remained outside of the intricacies of governing, something that would change with the new generation of pollsters.

This is not to say that Goldfarb and Gregg did not leave their imprints on political polling. More than most, Goldfarb introduced psychographics to Canadian politics. Broadly defined, psychographics focuses on values, beliefs, and lifestyles to understand the behaviour of consumers or, in this instance, voters. Goldfarb was able to provide a precise understanding of the Liberal voter and, in doing so, was able to guide the numerous Trudeau re-election campaigns. For his part, Gregg introduced methodological rigour to political analysis. Because of his academic background as a doctoral student in political science at Carleton University – as well as the time he spent in the United States with experts such as Peter Hart, Pat Caddell, Lance Tarrance, Stu Spencer, and, more importantly, Richard Wirthlin – Gregg was then unrivalled as a methodologist in political polling in Canada (Sawatsky 1987, 109). Wirthlin, who became famous for his role in the election of Ronald Reagan as president of the United States in 1980 (see Perry 1991), had a particularly strong influence on Gregg. For instance, Wirthlin believed in large-scale tracking surveys and precise segmentation of the electorate. Gregg quickly demonstrated the usefulness of those American-learned lessons by facilitating majorities for Bill Davis in Ontario's 1981 provincial election and for Brian Mulroney in the 1984 and 1988 federal elections (Turcotte 2010, 208).

Future generations of political pollsters in Canada would learn from Gregg's contributions. Across the aisle, Michael Marzolini would also rely on tracking and, with the help of technology, was able to monitor voter preferences on a daily basis during the 1993 Canadian federal election. He would continue to do so until he was replaced as Liberal Party pollster in 2004. This focus on the daily examination of Canadians became one of the essential building blocks of what we now describe as permanent polling. The importance of segmentation was to be fully exploited many years later.

The victory by Prime Minister Paul Martin and his Liberals in the 2004 election is largely responsible for opening a new chapter in political polling in Canada. Although they lost their majority status in the House of Commons, the Liberals held onto power despite being ensnared in a series of scandals. In fact, the 2004 results were as much a Conservative defeat as they were a Liberal victory. The Harper Conservatives were confident that their time had come and that they were ready to defeat the scandal-plagued Liberals. However, their inability to do so led to a complete rethinking of their campaign approaches. These developments are chronicled in *Harper's Team* (Flanagan 2007), the second contribution of note detailing political polling's evolution into a permanent practice.

Much has been written about the Conservative victory that Stephen Harper spearheaded in 2006. Several factors contributed to the Conservative resurrection. In *Harper's Team*, Tom Flanagan highlights the recruiting of Patrick Muttart as an important development in the preparations leading up to the 2006 election. Muttart brought marketing insight through his previous work for a hotel chain and political acumen through his apprenticeship at Navigator, a consulting firm led by veteran political operative Jaime Watt (Flanagan 2007, 219). As noted in a previous study, "The most important change that Conservative strategists made after the 2004 election was to bring all market intelligence in-house" (Turcotte 2012, 83). By hiring an insider like Muttart, whose role extended far beyond polling, Harper's strategists and advisors moved away from the practice of hiring a pollster of record. Muttart was part of the decision-making process when it came to policy priorities, campaign strategy, and communication imperatives. The change proved effective: the Conservatives won the 2006 election. Once in power, the Harper Conservatives fully integrated polling activities within the PMO, thereby blurring the lines between governing and electioneering. As we noted previously, when it came to polling, there was no longer a separation between the extra-parliamentary wing of the party and the government because the person in charge of Conservative polling was at the same time a government employee. Polling thus became an ongoing practice for parties in the inter-election context and the foundation of permanent campaigning. This approach had been tried before – albeit unsuccessfully – by Mackenzie King (Robinson 1999) and to some extent by the federal Progressive Conservative Party in the 1993 federal election (McLaughlin 1994). On the other hand, the Parti Québécois adopted a similar structure successfully in the 1970s and 1980s.

While the second major change is technological rather than structural, it is no less important. The Harper strategists combined polling with new technology in voter identification (voter ID) and developed an extremely granular understanding of voting intentions. Their large-scale voter ID efforts allowed them to segment the electorate into highly targeted groups and to use polling data to make sure that they clearly understood the issue priorities of those groups (Flanagan 2007, 223–24). Although focusing on key voters is not new, the Conservatives were able to do this with greater efficiency and sophistication than ever before.

Scholars have since begun to reflect on the importance and consequences of these new developments in polling. Dennis Johnson's works in political management, most notably *No Place for Amateurs* (2007) and *The Routledge Handbook of Political Management* (2009), explore the applications and consequences of the emerging interactions between polling and the permanent campaign. For her part, Susan Delacourt (2013) positions her analysis within the political marketing literature and draws some important conclusions. Her main argument focuses on how the relationship between voters and politicians can be better understood through the lens of marketing than that of political science. Consequently, she argues that voters are essentially choosing their elected officials in the same way that they choose consumer products, while politicians look at the electorate as market segments instead of as citizens. Although we do not question the validity of those conclusions, we suggest that the literature so far reflects just part of the story. Also of note is Tom Flanagan's *Winning Power* (2014), which expands on his previous book discussed above and explores the transferability of the lessons from the Harper years to Alberta politics. We too will turn our attention to provincial politics.

Case Study

Four broad objectives guided the design of our research for this chapter. First, one of the main arguments herein is that while the Harper Conservatives made an important contribution to our current understanding of how polling is conducted in Canadian politics, the glory of victory led to a situation where other developments have been ignored. While not dismissing the Harper approach to permanent polling, we examine innovations made by others that have been, to date, simply overlooked. More specifically, we turn to the Liberals, who have been in a position to more readily embrace the latest changes in the conduct of opinion polling than have the NDP, simply because the Liberals have been in the fortunate position to be in government in the two provinces large enough to have the resources to implement permanent polling activities. Second, as with many things in Canadian politics, the provinces often serve as a testing ground for new approaches but fail to generate the appropriate level of academic recognition. To address this situation, we examine two recent electoral contests: the 2013 British Columbia Liberal campaign and the 2014 Ontario Liberal campaign. As we just pointed out, while other provincial elections have been held recently, only Ontario, British Columbia, and possibly Quebec can reasonably be considered as potential cases, and it would appear that the developments we are discussing here have not yet been implemented in Quebec. The selection of the 2014 Ontario Liberal campaign as one of our cases was particularly fortuitous, since the strategist interviewed – David Herle – subsequently joined the Trudeau campaign in the 2015 federal election and "used provincial campaigns as a road map for Trudeau's" (McGregor 2015). Third, we wanted to depart from the existing literature on the link between the permanent campaign and polling to provide a more practical look at the changes that are currently happening. Fourth, as stated previously, it is challenging to get up-to-date and revealing information about the practice of polling, since those involved are reluctant to divulge their secrets. This has led to a situation where practitioners discuss their craft either too late or in a self-serving manner, while scholars have a superficial understanding of the practical consequences of the innovations. For this study, we secured the participation of three of the handful of people who currently conduct political polling in Canada. Every year, fewer than ten people can reasonably claim to be called a party pollster in Canada, so the participation of three of these key practitioners will yield invaluable insights into the current practice of polling.

METHOD
We first chose to interview strategists who are in charge of conducting public opinion research for two provincial governments. In British Columbia, we interviewed Dimitri Pantazopoulos and, in Ontario, we turned to Herle, who is leading the research efforts for the Kathleen Wynne government. Finally, to gain an understanding of the current federal Liberal approach, we interviewed Dan Arnold, who took over the federal Liberals' internal polling operations as lead research strategist, a newly created position signalling a new approach to opinion research. The three practitioners were

first contacted by telephone (Pantazopoulos) or in person (Herle and Arnold) and asked to share their perspective on the current practice of polling. Given options of the interviewing method, they chose a semi-structured secured online questionnaire. The questionnaires were sent on March 2, 2015, and the data collection was completed by April 10, 2015. The interviewing instrument can be found in this chapter's appendix. The direct references and quotes that follow are gleaned from the interviews.

In the review above of the sparse literature on the link between polling and the permanent campaign, we identified two signposts. We offer three additional signposts in this chapter. They are to some extent interrelated and focus on the practical execution of polling. Specifically, we focus on:

1 the in-house integration and the resulting blurring of responsibilities
2 the disappearance of the pre-writ period
3 hypersegmentation.

Our interviewees' specific insights about each of these signposts will be reviewed in the next section.

FINDINGS

We first turn our attention to the in-house integration of polling activities and the resulting blurred lines between partisan and government responsibilities. The decision by Harper's team of strategists and advisors to bring the polling function in-house has been discussed above. We also mentioned that, after the 2006 election, the Conservatives went one step further and created a staff position within the PMO in charge of polling activities. The more recent experiences in British Columbia, in Ontario, and with the federal Liberals point to a further integration of polling within government activities.

Dimitri Pantazopoulos had been a member of Harper's team of strategists and was part of both the 2000 Alliance and 2004 Conservative campaigns. Not surprisingly, his answers revealed that he built on the lessons learned from that period, and we see a further blurring of the lines between campaigning and governing in British Columbia. After leaving the Harper strategists, Pantazopoulos acted as chief of staff and principal secretary in the Christy Clark BC Liberal government. Later he became Premier Clark's assistant deputy minister of international relations and trade. He exercised those functions until it was time to take the helm of Clark's re-election preparations. Unlike Patrick Muttart, who was an outsider brought inside the party to direct Conservative polling activities, Pantazopoulos was already a government official when he was asked to take over the polling function for the BC Liberals. While the Conservatives fully integrated all polling activities within the PMO after their 2006 electoral victory, Pantazopoulos was in charge of the Premier's Office well ahead of the 2013 election campaign and directed government polling with electoral objectives in mind. More than most, he epitomizes the new breed of pollsters: one with a deep understanding of government policy and how this can help win elections.

While not as much of an insider as Pantazopoulos, David Herle too had occupied institutional positions within the Liberal Party before he was brought in to lead the research efforts for the Wynne government. In one of his answers, he also mentioned the extent to which "research [is] at the centre of decision making ... And this seems like it was a key difference in Ontario [in] 2014."

The appointment of Dan Arnold opened a new chapter in the institutionalization of the polling function at the centre of strategic decision making in the Liberal Party of Canada. As their lead research strategist, Arnold made the transition from being outside to inside the Liberal political machine. But even before he assumed this position, Arnold was no stranger to the Liberal Party. He already had substantial experience using his research and data analytics knowledge to campaign for the Liberals, but he did so from outside the political machine. For instance, prior to the spring of 2014, he was an associate vice president at Pollara Strategic Insights, immersed in the world of political consulting, but at arm's length.

In the spring of 2014, Arnold crossed the threshold. As he put it, "The big change for me has therefore been moving from an external to an in-house relationship with political parties." And it would seem there are no regrets. For example, as he explained, "The largest benefit of the in-house approach is that I can live and breathe political research 24/7, without having to answer to corporate clients who pay the bills." His statement signified that "when we're not fielding national studies, I can update seat projections, prepare regional reports, or work with local candidates on riding surveys." In essence, moving in-house lubricated the party machine and therefore increased its rhythm and efficiency to a previously unattainable standard. This breaks with the business-as-usual model of political polling and creates a new realm of possibilities. Pulling back the curtain on one of these new possibilities by contrasting it to the past, Arnold explained that "research has traditionally been kept in a vault at the national office guarded by a three-headed dog, but if we can show our candidates that the research says a certain line is effective at breaking down [opposition] support, they're a lot more likely to use that line than if we just force feed it to them without explanation." But these decisions must come from inside the party machine, which, unlike before, is where Arnold now sits.

The second signpost of permanent polling activity identified in our respondents' narratives is the disappearance of the pre-writ period. When Prime Minister Harper dropped the writ on August 2, 2015, beginning the longest continuous campaign in over a century, he may just have acknowledged that there is no longer such a thing as a pre-writ period. Of course, electoral rules are different once the writ is dropped, but in practical terms, politicians never leave the campaign trail and polling never stops informing their decisions.

For instance, when we interviewed Dan Arnold in March 2015, he mentioned that he had completed a large survey of 15,000 Canadians in fall 2014 to build the Liberal Party's predictive models. This was done a full year before the election and was used to guide the parliamentary priorities of the Liberal leader and his caucus. The same information also guided the Liberal election strategy. In British Columbia, Pantazopoulos was the premier's chief of staff for two years before he officially took charge of party polling. In the Premier's Office, he controlled the research conducted for the BC government, and, as he mentioned in his interview, he "transferred those insights seamlessly" when focusing fully on Clark's re-election campaign. The events in Ontario had some similarities with the BC experience and borrowed from the innovations brought in by the Harper Conservatives. Research was conducted from the inside by David Herle. The focus was on a few key segments of the electorate, and polling was fully integrated within the government communications and strategic functions. Herle's efforts preceded the official launch of the 2014 campaign and continued well after Kathleen Wynne's election on June 12, 2014.

The final indicator of continuous polling highlighted in our informants' narratives relates to the practice of hypersegmentation. One of the main lessons from Flanagan's (2007) *Harper's Team* was the extent to which the Conservatives' electoral success was the result of a disciplined approach to segmenting the electorate and developing policies that would specifically cater to those segments. Targeting voters is nothing new in politics, but the Harper Conservatives took the practice to such a level of sophistication that their approach has been labelled as hypersegmentation (Turcotte 2012, 85). Those lessons were not lost on the current group of pollsters.

In early May 2013, all looked lost for BC premier Christy Clark and her Liberal colleagues. The majority of media polls pointed to an inevitable defeat. It appeared that Clark, who had been the leader of the governing Liberals since winning her party's nomination in February 2011, was not going to remain as premier. Internal turmoil coupled with political scandals had been steadily eroding Liberal support (Hutchinson 2013). Yet when the final votes were tallied, the Liberals received 44 percent of the vote, ahead of the NDP at 39 percent (Hutchinson 2013). More importantly, the Liberals won forty-nine seats in the Legislative Assembly and formed another majority government. What happened?

Unlike many of the media organizations and traditional polling firms, which largely relied on web-based surveys to predict the supposed NDP landslide, Dimitri Pantazopoulos was conducting surgical telephone-based interviews that proved far more accurate (Hutchinson 2013). The BC Liberals began conducting internal polls more than a year before the election at a very granular, riding-by-riding level (Hutchinson 2013). Pantazopoulos and his "survey team gathered responses to specific issues and fed them to Liberal party headquarters. Riding candidates were made aware of key subjects to raise when out door-knocking" (Hutchinson 2013). As Pantazopoulos mentioned in our interview, "We used polling to determine where to call, and the message. In other campaigns, there is a lot of tension between the two areas, but as this was all directed in one spot – by me – it was easier to manage." Pantazopoulos added that this allowed the Liberals to "focus the campaign on the correct 'group' of ridings" and choose strategically among the list of government policy priorities. He observed that polling between elections has become much more in-depth and richer in analytical insights. Campaign polling can build on the knowledge acquired between elections and be more nimble by concentrating on key messages and target audiences.

The federal Liberals also understand the potential of hypersegmentation and the link with policy development. Arnold explained in one of his answers:

> By working closely with the analytics team, we've been able to develop a greater understanding of the relationship between target voter groups and target ridings. I can tell you with great precision

how many more seats we'd win if we increased our support or turn-out by 10 percent with any one of 30 demographic groups. It was in doing this research that we recognized how important indigenous voters are to us electorally – they're a growing population segment with Liberal leanings who are found disproportionately in swing ridings. So by combining our polling and analytics, we've been able to come up with a list of ridings where outreach efforts to indigen-ous voters carry the largest electoral impact for us. That's an exer-cise we've repeated with several key populations. Similarly, when deciding the specific income cut-offs for the fairness tax changes we rolled out this spring [2015], we were able to run the analytics to fully understand how many "winners" and "losers" there would be under our plan in each riding.

The comment about fairness tax changes is important, since it shows the impact of having an insider directing campaign research efforts. Very quickly, the lines between policy-making decisions and campaign strategy simply disappear. Linking hypersegmentation and policy development is made possible by the permanent campaign and is functionally feasible because of the new in-house integration of the polling function, the disappearance of the pre-writ period, and hypersegmentation, which are currently considered as essential to electoral victory.

Permanent Campaigning in Canada

The relationship between the public, polling, politics, and leadership has always been a complicated one. From the time that George Gallup, Archibald Crossley, and Elmo Roper founded the polling industry in the 1930s, recon-ciling the importance of giving a voice to voters and the need for leaders to do more than simply pander to polls has been the subject of much academic discussion. Ideally, politicians would try to achieve a balance between their public policy responsibilities and their instinct for political survival. But as V.O. Key suggested back in 1961, "We have practically no systematic infor-mation about what goes on in the minds of public men as they ruminate about the weight to be given to public opinion in governmental decision" (490). Politicians are constantly trying to reconcile the need to win elections with their role as policy makers. Those two realities are not necessarily mu-tually exclusive, but the effectiveness of the techniques associated with permanent polling renders the decision arguably more difficult. More money spent on polling, the introduction of market research techniques in polling practices, the in-house integration of the polling function, and hyper-segmentation are currently associated with electoral victory. And the emerging innovations are likely to tilt the balance even more towards political survival.

Our interviews have revealed that, since political parties no longer rely on external polling input, the lines are blurred between pre-writ activities and campaign planning. Moreover, the type of data used to supplement public opinion data, specifically voter ID but more broadly data analytics, means that parties are in a position to constantly update their voting models regardless of the electoral cycle. Those models are not limited to campaign tactics but inform public policy making. In short, we have permanent polling activity at work. And more changes are under way.

For three elections from 2006 to 2011, the federal Liberals bore the brunt of the innovations effected by the Harper Conservatives. They rectified this situation before the 2015 election. When the Conservative Party hired Muttart, he consulted Australia's John Howard and was inspired by the way that Howard's Liberal–National coalition used segmentation to win in 1996. From that emerged the much-discussed development of fictional characters to focus the Conservative efforts towards winnable voters. Muttart created Dougie, Rick, Brenda, and others as representations of the campaign's strategic imperatives (Flanagan 2007, 223–24). For the 2015 election, the Liberals hired Dan Arnold. Arnold and the Liberals were intrigued by the methodological breakthroughs of the Obama campaign. Of particular interest was the reliance on data analytics – or big data – as a way to get more value out of opinion data. Advisors from the Obama team helped Arnold move the Liberal research abilities on par with, if not ahead of, the Conservatives. As he explained:

> At [the] LPC, we've moved to integrate research and analytics as much as possible. The party has taken great steps forward when it comes to predictive modelling, and we've made sure this is done in lockstep with regular polling. This provided us with a better sense of our support and growth potential at a very localized level ... We've been running large-sample weekly IVR [Interactive Voice Response] tracking throughout 2015, which will give us a sample size of 100,000 cases by the time the election hits.

With such a large database, the capacity to isolate the impact of policy options on electoral outcomes expands exponentially. The federal Liberal victory in 2015 has given Dan Arnold and his team the ability to fully explore the potential of a full integration between policy development, data analytics, and opinion data. Because of their electoral success, the Liberal approach will be put under great scrutiny and will influence further development in the practice of polling. Arnold mused about the future in stating that,

> from a political perspective, the largest change will no doubt be the gradual merger of "big data" and polling. The Conservatives had a head start, but the Liberal Party has taken great strides to catch up in recent years. Polling data can be used to strengthen predictive voter models, and analytics can help with the implementation of policy decisions that flow from polling.

In tangible terms, this means that we know not only about Dougie, Rick, and Brenda, but also about what they are doing at any given time. The ultimate objective is to try to find out what they will do next if presented with different policy alternatives. In the first section of this chapter, we mentioned that polling has evolved into what Lees-Marshment (2012) describes as market intelligence. However, the potential of emerging developments may mean that market intelligence may be on the verge of turning into something closer to market surveillance.

APPENDIX: INTERVIEW QUESTIONS

1   How did your approach to conducting political polling change over the last ten years or so? I mean "approach" either from a very narrow sense (methodology, design, analysis) and/or from a broad sense (client relationship, role within a campaign, etc.).

2   And from a broader perspective, thinking about the practice of political polling in general, what do you think have been the three most important changes over the last ten years or so?

3   Thinking about the last election campaign you were involved in, which specific innovations did you introduce in how you structured your polling program?

4 How were your results used within the broader campaign?

5 How would you compare the way you conduct polling between elections with polling during an election campaign? Discuss similarities and differences.

6 Are you familiar with the changes made by the Harper campaign team – especially in the 2006 election – with regards to polling? Those changes have been documented in several sources including Tom Flanagan's *Harper's Team* and Susan Delacourt's *Shopping for Votes*.

6A (IF FAMILIAR at Q6) What do you think of these innovations? Discuss strengths and weaknesses.

6B (IF FAMILIAR at Q6) To what extent do you think they were actual innovations?

6C (IF FAMILIAR at Q6) Did they influence in any way your approach to conducting polling?

7 What influences (people, practitioners, books, etc.) had an impact on your approach to conducting polling?

8 Finally, now thinking about the future of polling, how do you see things changing, if at all, in the next five years or so?

Thank you for your cooperation.

REFERENCES

Blondiaux, Loïc. 1998. *La Fabrique de l'opinion*. Paris: Seuil.

Bricker, Darrell, and John Ibbitson. 2013. *The Big Shift*. Toronto: HarperCollins.

Butler, Peter M. 2007. *Polling and Public Opinion: A Canadian Perspective*. Toronto: University of Toronto Press.

Callegaro, M., K.L. Manfreda, and V. Vehovar. 2015. *Web Survey Methodology*. London: SAGE Publications.

Delacourt, Susan. 2013. *Shopping for Votes: How Politicians Choose Us and We Choose Them*. Madeira Park, BC: Douglas and McIntyre.

Durkheim, Emile. 1951. *Suicide: A Study in Sociology*. Glencoe, IL: The Free Press.

Erikson, Robert S., and Kent L. Tedin. 2011. *American Public Opinion*, 8th ed. Boston: Longman.

Flanagan, Tom. 2007. *Harper's Team: Behind the Scenes in the Conservative Rise to Power*. Montreal/Kingston: McGill-Queens University Press.

–. 2014. *Winning Power: Canadian Campaigning in the Twenty-First Century*. Montreal/Kingston: McGill-Queens University Press.

Hutchinson, Brian. 2013. "Why the Liberals Were Able to Predict Their Victory in B.C. While Public Election Polls Missed the Mark." *National Post*, May 18. http://news.nationalpost.com/news/canada/canadian-politics/why-the-liberals-were-able-to-predict-their-victory-in-b-c-while-public-election-polls-missed-the-mark.

Johnson, Dennis. 2007. *No Place for Amateurs: How Political Consultants Are Reshaping American Democracy*, 2nd ed. New York: Routledge.

–, ed. 2009. *The Routledge Handbook of Political Management*. New York: Routledge.

Key, V.O. 1961. "Public Opinion and the Decay of Democracy." *Virginia Quarterly Review* 37: 481–91.

Laschinger, John, and Geoffery Stevens. 1992. *Leaders & Lesser Mortals: Backroom Politics in Canada*. Toronto: Key Porter Books.

Lazarsfeld, Paul, and Morris Rosenberg. 1962. *The Language of Social Research*. Glencoe, IL: The Free Press.

Lech, Jean-Marc. 2001. *Sondages privés*. Paris: Stock.

Lees-Marshment, Jennifer. 2012. "The Impact of Market Research on Political Decisions and Leadership: Practitioners' Perspectives." In *Political Marketing in Canada*, edited by A. Marland, T. Giasson, and J. Lees-Marshment, 91–106. Vancouver: UBC Press.

Lewis, Justin. 2001. *Constructing Public Opinion*. New York: Columbia University Press.

McGregor, G. 2015. "Former Martin Aide Used Provincial Campaigns to Lay Out the Road Map to Trudeau's Victory." *Ottawa Citizen*, October 23. http://ottawacitizen.com/news/politics/former-martin-aide-used-provincial-campaigns-to-lay-out-the-road-map-to-trudeaus-victory.

McLaughlin, David. 1994. *Poisoned Chalice: The Last Campaigns of the Progressive Conservative Party?* Toronto: Dundurn Press.

Moore, David W. 2008. *The Opinion Makers*. Boston: Beacon Press.

Morris, Dick. 1998. *Behind the Oval Office*. New York: Renaissance Books.

Murray, Shoon Kathleen, and Peter Howard. 2002. "Variation in White House Polling Operations: Carter to Clinton." *Public Opinion Quarterly* 66 (4) 527–58.

Page, Christopher. 2006. *The Role of Public Opinion Research in Canadian Government*. Toronto: University of Toronto Press.

Perry, Roland. 1991. *Hidden Power: The Programming of a President*. New York: Beaufort Books.

Plouffe, David. 2009. *The Audacity to Win*. New York: Viking.

Robinson, Daniel J. 1999. *The Measures of Democracy*. Toronto: University of Toronto Press.

Rollins, Ed. 1996. *Bare Knuckles and Backrooms*. New York: Broadway Books.

Sawatsky, John. 1987. *The Insiders: Government, Business, and the Lobbyists*. Toronto: McClelland and Stewart.

Sparrow, Nick, and John Turner. 2001. "The Permanent Campaign: The Integration of Market Research Techniques in Developing Strategies in a More Uncertain Political Climate." *European Journal of Marketing* 35 (9/10): 984–1002. http://dx.doi.org/10.1108/03090560110400605.

Tenpas, Kathryn Dunn, and James A. McCann. 2007. "Testing the Permanence of the Permanent Campaign: An Analysis of Presidential Polling Expenditures 1977–2002." *Public Opinion Quarterly* 71 (3): 349–66. http://dx.doi.org/10.1093/poq/nfm020.

Tourangeau, Roger, Frederick Conrad, and Mick Couper. 2013. *The Science of Web Surveys*. New York: Oxford University Press.

Trippi, Joe. 2005. *The Revolution Will Not Be Televised*. New York: Harper Books.

Turcotte, André. 2010. "Polling as Modern Alchemy: Measuring Public Opinion in Canadian Elections." In *Election*, edited by H. MacIvor, 199–217. Toronto: Emond Montgomery.

–. 2012. "Under New Management: Market Intelligence and the Conservative Party's Resurrection." In *Political Marketing in Canada*, edited by A. Marland, T. Giasson, and J. Lees-Marshment, 76–90. Vancouver: UBC Press.

Wheeler, Michael. 1976. *Lies, Damn Lies, and Statistics*. New York: Dell Publishing.

8

Election Preparation in the Federal NDP: The Next Campaign Starts the Day after the Last One Ends

David McGrane

Since elections are at the heart of a campaign, the permanent campaign undoubtedly includes long-range preparations for elections. However, what does it take for political parties to prepare for elections? Has the process of election preparation changed in recent times? How does election preparation relate to the permanent campaign? Interestingly, political scientists have yet to explore these questions in a systematic and theoretical manner. Indeed, there is no precise definition of the concept of election preparation in either Canadian or international political science.

The preparations that Canadian federal parties have gone through are detailed in portions of the chapters on each political party contained in the *Canadian Federal Election* series (see for example McGrane, 2011). However, these sections are often preambles to the chapters' main arguments about the parties' strategies during the campaigns and assessments of their electoral performances. From a practitioner's point of view, Brad Lavigne (2013) and Tom Flanagan (2014) provide valuable insights into election preparation by outlining the steps that their respective parties took to prepare for recent Canadian federal elections. Nonetheless, neither author offers a systematic and comprehensive definition of the concept of election preparation.

Recent international political marketing research argues that there was a modernization of campaigning during the twentieth and early twenty-first centuries as it passed from a premodern to a modern to a postmodern phase (Farrell and Webb 2000; Marland 2012; Norris 2000; Plasser and Plasser 2002; Strömbäck 2009). The premodern era stretched from the beginning of the twentieth century into the 1960s. It was an era of local party men leaning on their friends and neighbours to vote for their party, newspaper advertisements, and rallies held as leaders passed through small towns on trains or buses. The modern era of campaigning began in the late 1960s and early 1970s. It was characterized by reliance on sound bites by leaders on the national news, national television advertisements, mass direct mail, centralized phone banks, and local foot canvassers to blanket neighbourhoods. Finally, the postmodern phase gradually emerged in the early twenty-first century and concentrates on online campaigning, multimedia advertising, microtargeting, data collection, and narrowcasting messages.

The international research on campaign modernization also contains no precise definition of the concept of election preparation. Its basic argument is that the length of time devoted to preparing for elections increases as campaigns modernize. Preparation for premodern campaigning was either non-existent or ad hoc and done at the last minute. Modern campaigning features longer preparatory periods making use of a specialist committee struck by the party several months to a year prior to an election. In postmodern campaigning, election preparation is constant: parties start planning for the next campaign shortly after the previous one is finished. The primary shortcoming of campaign modernization literature is that it discusses the length of the preparatory period for an election but not the nature of the preparation itself.

Given that the concept of election preparation lacks definition, the starting point for this chapter is to provide one. A generic meaning would be that election preparation encompasses the activity prior to the start of the official campaign period that focuses on getting a political party ready to fight an election. Such a definition is insufficient, as it does not differentiate between the types of activities that include election preparation and the types of activities that are part of normal party life between elections.

What is needed is a conceptual framework to summarize the key activities that parties undertake to prepare for elections and to understand how these activities have changed in recent years. To this end, I have devised two models of election preparation, outlined in Table 8.1.

These models represent ideal types gleaned from the practice of contemporary Canadian political parties outlined by authors like Lavigne (2013) and Flanagan (2014), as well as from a reading of the broader international literature on campaign modernization. The key idea behind the models is that election preparation not only takes a longer time as campaigning enters the postmodern era, but also is a much more meticulous and elaborate process. It is not just the length of the preparatory period that is different; it is the nature of the preparation itself.

This chapter tests whether this definition of election preparation, based on these two models, can be applied to the federal New Democratic Party (NDP). The federal NDP was chosen because it was much less professionalized in the early 2000s than other major political parties (Marland 2012) when the movement towards a permanent campaign in Canadian politics began. As such, the contrast between the professionalization that characterizes perpetual election preparation and the amateurism that characterizes traditional election preparation is very immediate, direct, and easy to discern within the NDP. Due to the federal NDP's rapid modernization, testing these two models on this party is a good starting point for developing a systematic and cohesive definition of election preparation for contemporary political parties. Nonetheless, the applicability of these two models to other Canadian political parties and political parties in other parts of the world remains unscrutinized and is an avenue for future research.

The contention here is that the activities identified in Table 8.1 as "perpetual election preparation" should be seen as essential components of the permanent campaign in Canada. As outlined in Chapter 1, the permanent campaign is a broader concept that encompasses a new mode of politics adopted by governments, political parties, politicians, and civil society stakeholders. Perpetual election preparation is a narrower concept that applies only to examining the activities of professionals employed by political parties between election periods. Indeed, the extent to which operatives from all political parties have adopted the perpetual election preparation model is a good measuring stick to gauge how entrenched the permanent campaign has become within Canadian politics.

The last piece of this theoretical puzzle is political market orientation. As a key concept within political marketing literature, the definition and operationalization of political market orientation have been the subjects of considerable debate (Ormrod, Henneberg, and O'Shaughnessy 2013, 145–57). The commonality among theories of political market orientation is that they have at their root the idea of market orientation, as it applied to private business, that was first articulated in the 1960s by scholars such as Theodore Levitt. Levitt (1960) persuasively argued that businesses that single-mindedly fashion their organizations around creating the best products will fail, and businesses that understand the structure of the markets they are serving by focusing on the needs and desires of their customers will succeed. From Levitt's work, a whole literature has emerged that debates

TABLE 8.1

Traditional election preparation versus perpetual election preparation

	Traditional election preparation	Perpetual election preparation
Evaluation of previous campaign	Informal, minimal, and impressionistic	Formal, extensive, and scientific
Nomination process	Locally controlled and completed close to the beginning of the campaign period	Centrally controlled, extensive vetting, and candidates in place long in advance of the beginning of the campaign period
Volunteer mobilization and training	Localized campaign training that is run by volunteers and takes place close to the beginning of the campaign period	Regularly incorporating activist training into party gatherings, centrally organized training efforts with a standardized curriculum, professional trainers
Voter contact	Preparation of local databases or a paper system to be used for canvassing during the campaign period	Ongoing data collection from canvassing outside of the election period; live telephone calls are supplemented with robocalls and data are inputted at the doorstep, eliminating need for paper; all data are fed into a national database
Personnel	Volunteers and central campaign staff hired on short-term contracts in the months leading up to the election	Permanent staff at party headquarters
Organization of leader's tour	Campaign-style rallies and events are confined to the campaign period, as are platform announcements	Leader constantly holding campaign-style events, including the announcements of platform planks prior to start of campaign period

Research	Emphasis on researching background on current issues that could arise during the campaign; leader's speeches and news releases created during the campaign period	Emphasis on opposition research to throw competitors off message; leader's speeches and news releases can be devised prior to the start of the campaign
Platform development	Volunteer activists working with party staff devise the platform from existing party policy passed at policy conventions	Policy department at party headquarters and leader's office responsible for long-term visioning and platform development using existing party policy passed at conventions as well as original research
Legislative activity	Separation of the activities of the party's legislative caucus and election preparation at party headquarters	Activities of party's legislative caucus and party headquarters are closely coordinated and legislative activities structured in accordance with emerging election themes
Outreach to civil society	Reliance on traditional allies such as unions, businesses, churches, or ethnic groups	Ongoing relationship building with traditional allies as well as outreach to various civil society actors for use as third-party validators
Financing and fundraising	Fundraising intensifies as campaign period approaches	Fundraising is constantly at a high intensity
Advertising and polling	Polling and focus groups close to the start of the campaign period and advertising done only during the campaign	Constant polling, focus groups, and branding exercises along with substantial pre-campaign advertising

how to measure the levels of market orientation of firms and connect levels of market orientation to profitability (see Kohli and Jaworski 1990; Narver and Slater 1990). All definitions of political market orientation are based on this conceptual foundation borrowed from business marketing literature. Political parties achieve a political market orientation through structuring their organizations in ways that prioritize the goal of becoming responsive to the needs and desires of voters. They still concentrate on making the best political products (i.e., policies and solutions to societal problems), but their broader focus hinges on understanding how the political products they create meet the needs and desires of their targeted voters.

In addition to defining the concept of election preparation, a further theoretical argument advanced here is that the adoption of perpetual election preparation should be appreciated as one factor that leads political parties towards a higher level of political market orientation. Such a conclusion makes intuitive sense. If a party is constantly preparing for an election, it is constantly thinking about the wants and desires of voters, and its behaviour centres on discovering ways to be responsive to voter concerns. A party that adopts the traditional model of election preparation is more likely to become occupied with internal matters between elections and to debate its own ideology with only tangential reference to what voters want and desire.

Case Study

Based on this theoretical framework, the following case study is intended to test the hypotheses that (1) the federal NDP gradually shifted from a traditional to a perpetual model of election preparation from 2000 to 2015, and (2) the adoption of perpetual election preparation by the federal NDP increased its political market orientation. The 2000 election was chosen as the starting point for the analysis because it represented an electoral low point for the federal NDP and it was the last election of the pre–Jack Layton era.[1] Given the electoral success and changes that Layton's leadership brought to the federal NDP, the party's preparation for the 2000 federal election offers an excellent contrast to the preparation that the party undertook in subsequent elections.

Method

To test these hypotheses, eighteen semi-structured elite interviews with open-ended questions (Kvale and Brinkmann 2009) were held with political operatives for the NDP from October 2014 to April 2015. Some of the interviews were conducted in person and others took place by telephone. Each interview lasted approximately one hour. A funnel interview protocol was employed (Harrell and Bradley 2009, 50–55) that moved from broad to specific questions to ensure consistency across the interviews. As opposed to making recordings, handwritten notes were taken during the interviews. The interview sample was selected by choosing a key informant for each election and then producing a snowball sample using suggestions of potential interviewees from that key informant. Efforts were made to ensure that all elections during the 2000 to 2015 period were equally represented, and several of the interviewees worked in multiple elections, enabling them to make comparisons across time. Some of the interviewees were employed at the time by the federal NDP and in the midst of preparing for the 2015 federal election, while other interviewees had been employed by the party during the preparations for previous elections and had moved on to other employment (see the appendix to this chapter for a list of the interviewees).

There are advantages and disadvantages to this research design. There were no memory lapses for interviewees who were involved in the 2015 federal election preparations, but they may have been less open to disclosing all of their preparatory activities. Interviewees discussing elections previous to 2015 may have had difficulty recalling the details of their activities during those periods, but they felt freer to reveal sensitive information. While snowball sampling procedures can be criticized for creating a sample that skewed towards the key informants' closest friends and coworkers, the small number of operatives involved in the preparations examined here limited this possibility. Given the small number of people at the apex of the party's election preparations and their clearly defined roles, it was difficult for key informants to neglect to mention significant people to the researcher. For instance, if asked about fundraising for the 2004 election, there was only one person who had led this activity, and the key informant had to identify that person. Certainly, handwritten notes lack the exactitude of recorded interview data. However, several interviewees indicated that they would not participate in the project if discussions were recorded. Further, the absence of a recorder undoubtedly made the interviewees more comfortable and open. Ultimately, the imperatives of guaranteeing an appropriate level of participation of research subjects to carry out the project and ensuring that interviews remained candid were judged to be more important than improving the precision of data by recording the interviews.

Results

The interview data confirmed that the federal NDP gradually moved away from a traditional model of election preparation to perpetual election preparation during the period under scrutiny. For the 2000 and 2004 elections, the federal NDP followed the traditional model of election preparation. The three federal elections of 2006, 2008, and 2011 occurred during a transition phase in which the federal NDP mixed elements of both the traditional and perpetual models of election preparation. It was not until the lead-up to the 2015 federal election that the federal NDP fully embraced perpetual election preparation.

After the 1997 federal election, the NDP did little in terms of a campaign post-mortem analysis. Nothing was formally passed on to operatives preparing for the 2000 election regarding campaign operations and plans that were either more or less successful (Fraser interview 2014). In May 2002, one month before resigning as leader, Alexa McDonough appointed a blue-ribbon committee of veteran NDP operatives to assess the party's past election performances (Whitehorn 2004, 109). However, interviewees from the core campaign team of the 2004 election did not recall this report being influential in their decision making (Hébert-Daly interview 2014; Chris Watson interview 2015). Brian Topp, co-chair of the 2006 and 2008 campaigns, introduced the idea of a formal election post-mortem as a reflection on what went well and what went poorly in the previous campaign (Topp interview 2015). These post-mortem exercises became more elaborate following the 2008 and 2011 elections to include polling and other quantitative measurements of the effectiveness of the party's performance and were used to inform the decision-making process for the next election (Rotman interview 2015). Indeed, one of NDP leader Tom Mulcair's first moves following the party's disappointing showing in the 2015 federal election was to establish a working group to perform a formal post-mortem on the party's performance.

At the same time as post-campaign debriefs were more usefully employed, the NDP slowly moved away from its tradition of giving responsibility for election preparation to volunteers and staff on short-term contracts. The reliance on professionals in permanent positions at party headquarters to drive election preparation is a key development in the move to a permanent campaign. Volunteers are unable to devote the time necessary for preparatory activities that take three or four years, and short-term contracts are put in place only when an election is imminent. In short, without permanent employees at party headquarters, there is no permanent campaign and no perpetual election preparation. For the 2000 and 2004 elections, the NDP campaign director and staff who were needed to run the campaign were hired approximately eight to twelve months prior to the election. Many short-term staffers came from the pool of employees working in national union offices headquartered in Ottawa who were either seconded to the party or given vacation time to facilitate their hiring by the campaign. As was normal practice for NDP campaigns at the time, an election planning committee (EPC) was gradually put into place that included the volunteer members of the federal executive as well as the federal secretary, assistant federal secretary, and union representatives.

For the 2006 and 2008 elections, this structure shifted slightly. In the aftermath of the 2004 election, Brian Topp and Sue Milling were appointed campaign co-chairs. Although both were volunteers, the co-chairs worked with staff at party headquarters, staff in the leader's office, and short-term staff within the EPC working group, with only periodic breaks during the four-year period from 2004 to 2008 (Topp interview 2015). The EPC working group was a semi-permanent entity tasked with running and preparing campaigns and reporting their progress to the larger EPC. Following the 2008 election, the NDP federal council passed a motion to make the federal executive the permanent EPC, and Brad Lavigne, as a permanent employee, was named both national director of the NDP and national campaign director for the next election. From this point onwards, permanent staff at party headquarters became solely responsible for election preparation and reported to the federal executive on their progress. While the labour movement maintained an influence on election preparations through their representatives on the federal executive, the previously important role played by the influx of union activists coming into election preparations just prior to the start of the campaign was diminished.

In the 2000 and 2004 elections, the NDP left training of campaign activists up to volunteers in local riding associations and staff in the provincial NDP offices, who organized what were referred to as campaign schools (Fraser interview 2014). At campaign school, volunteers and new candidates were taught the basic requirements to perform their duties in the upcoming election (e.g., how to foot-canvass, how to organize a leaflet drop, etc.). When Anne McGrath became party president in 2005, one of her priorities was to use conventions and federal councils as opportunities for more intensive activist training that went beyond the basics of campaign organizing

(McGrath interview 2014). Following the 2011 election, NDP activist training became far more professionalized. In the lead-up to the 2015 election, the party developed a curriculum that was taught face to face as employees from party headquarters either travelled across Canada or gave the training virtually through video conferencing (Sampson interview 2015). The curriculum allowed for the acquisition of both basic and more advanced campaigning skills.

Professionals at NDP headquarters have also taken a much greater role in the nominations process and platform development. For the 2000 election, nomination processes were almost entirely the purview of local riding associations, and the party headquarters' role was limited to telephoning local activists to implore them to move faster on nominating their candidates (Fraser interview 2014). For the 2004 and 2006 elections, a process was put into place by which candidates were required to disclose potentially embarrassing facets of their personal lives so that the party could prepare a response (Peel interview 2015). After the past digressions of certain NDP candidates made national news during the 2008 election following the release of video footage of their drug use (Lavigne 2013, 156–58), the party implemented a stricter vetting process that could disallow candidacies that staff at party headquarters determine are potentially problematic during an election campaign (Lavigne interview 2014).

The 2000 and 2004 election platforms were written by a group of volunteers using policy passed at NDP conventions and were coordinated by a staff person on a short-term contract (Smallman interview 2014). The platform was subsequently approved by the federal council, a body made up of volunteer activists elected by party members of their province. In the 2006 and 2008 elections, the NDP platform was drafted by key staffers and circulated to the EPC, which at the time was a mix of volunteer activists and personnel from party headquarters (Topp interview 2015). In 2011 and 2015, the federal platform was drafted by the policy department at party headquarters and the leader's office based on their research and consultation with MPs, the federal executive, and other member-controlled bodies such as the women's, youth, and Aboriginal commissions. The final approval of the platform rested with the leader (Lucy Watson interview 2015).

Much like nominations and platform development, methods of voter contact have also been professionalized over the past fifteen years. In the 2000 campaign, most ridings were keeping track of voter contact information on paper that was then stored at the homes of volunteers between elections. In the 2004 and 2006 campaigns, the federal NDP introduced a computer platform called NDP Vote (Fraser interview 2014), which allowed each constituency to build its own voter contact database using templates and conventions that were standardized across the party. There was still no Canada-wide NDP voter contact database for use in the 2011 federal election. In preparation for the 2015 election, one of the party's priorities was the creation of a single national voter contact database called Populus, which is accessible through a web portal (Pratt interview 2015). The creation of Populus has been accompanied by an emphasis on periodic foot and phone canvassing prior to the writ being dropped. In the lead-up to the 2015 federal election, the party held a number of "days of action" on specific issues, with its activists going door to door gathering data on voter intention to feed into Populus.

Whereas the Conservative Party of Canada has no formal association with provincial parties and the Liberal Party of Canada is integrated with provincial Liberal parties in only select provinces, federal and provincial NDP wings are integrated with each other in every province except Quebec, where a provincial NDP wing does not exist. Due to this structure, all fundraising initiatives had to go through the provincial wings of the party, and by the 2000 and 2004 elections, the practice had developed that the federal party would do rounds of direct mailing close to federal election campaigns (Fraser interview 2014). New party financing rules established in 2004 gradually forced the financial separation of the federal NDP from its provincial wings, giving the federal party unfettered access to membership lists (Pilon, Ross, and Savage 2011). Initially, the federal party adopted a more aggressive year-round fundraising strategy, but it continued to ramp up the intensity of fundraising as an election approached. However, with a string of minority Parliaments in the 2000s, the timing of elections became unpredictable and the intensity of the NDP's fundraising was constantly maintained at a high level. Following the election of the majority Conservative government in 2011, the NDP continued to make daily fundraising appeals to its donors (McGrath interview 2014). Instead of looming elections, other deadlines were used to create a sense of urgency for donors, such as reporting for Elections Canada's quarterly party financing reports that are routinely covered in the media, eligibility for tax credits at the end of the year, or even contests to go to a hockey game with Mulcair (Roy interview 2015).

Transformation has also occurred in the outreach and research that the federal NDP headquarters performs in the lead-up to an election. While the

NDP's small parliamentary caucus did do outreach to civil society groups in their critic areas in the early 2000s, staff at party headquarters generally did not perform outreach activities, with the exception of consultation with affiliated unions. On becoming leader, Layton directed party headquarters to make a more concerted effort to reach out to social movements (e.g., Greenpeace) and involve them within the structures of the party. His outreach coordinator, Franz Hartmann, made limited progress on this front (Hartmann interview 2015). In preparation for the 2011 and 2015 elections, the federal NDP rethought its approach to stakeholder outreach. While continuing to rely on traditional allies such as the labour movement and social movements, it expanded its outreach to build relationships with a wide array of actors from the business community and civil society (Watkins interview 2015). It was hoped that these groups, some of whom may not be perceived as NDP-friendly, would validate NDP policy positions during election campaigns (Watkins interview 2015).

In 2000, the federal NDP party headquarters had almost no research capacity beyond gathering analyses of issues that may become important during a campaign from sources like national unions, think-tanks, and academic writings (Moran interview 2014). As the federal NDP gradually adopted a model of perpetual election preparation during the 2000s, the research capacity of the party's headquarters increased and the type of research undertaken was altered. Conducting opposition research took on a higher priority in preparation for an election. This research was saved and used at strategically opportune times to destabilize the campaigns of other parties during the 2008 and 2011 elections.

In 2000 and 2004, polling, focus groups, and branding exercises were completed just prior to the election to craft the party's messaging (Fraser interview 2014; Hébert-Daly interview 2014). Starting in the lead-up to the 2006 election, this formal market intelligence gathering became a constant activity for party headquarters as it formulated electoral strategy well in advance of the election being called. During the periods between the 2006, 2008, and 2011 federal elections, party operatives used this research to focus on the party's messages on modest and practical policy proposals and to emphasize Jack Layton's leadership (Wesley and Moyes 2014, 86–88). Part of the NDP's broader electoral strategy became pre-election campaigns to position the party in a certain manner for the upcoming election. Heather Fraser (interview 2014) recalled that in 2000 there was a "pre-election panic as opposed to a pre-election campaign." However, starting in 2004 with the creation of the "fly our flag" website and the subsequent media relations campaign that sought to embarrass Paul Martin for flying flags from developing countries on the vessels of his shipping line for tax advantages, pre-election campaigns became part of the federal NDP's strategy. In the lead-up to the 2015 election, these pre-election campaigns evolved into announcing platform planks at campaign-style events featuring Mulcair.

Finally, one of the most striking changes made by the NDP is the extent to which it has begun to leverage state resources for election preparation and merge its legislative activity with its election preparations. In the early 2000s, party headquarters and the activity of the NDP parliamentary caucus were quite separate (Fraser interview 2014). A major change during the Layton years was that staff members employed within party headquarters changed jobs to become employed by NDP offices on Parliament Hill, and vice versa. This crossover of personnel was accompanied by a synchronization of House of Commons strategy and election preparation. For instance, several of the commitments contained in the 2008 NDP platform were first proposed as opposition bills in the House of Commons (Erickson and Laycock 2009, 112). From the end of the 2008 election until the writ was dropped for the 2011 election, a senior campaign team composed of top campaign officials from party headquarters and staff from the leader's office met weekly to assess election readiness and coordinate the NDP's question period and legislative strategy with emerging campaign themes (McGrane 2011, 94).

The NDP's historic breakthrough in the 2011 election meant a dramatic increase in state resources for the party as it took up the helm of official opposition. The Office of the Leader of the Official Opposition (OLO) emerged as a powerful and well-resourced entity whose activity was coordinated with party headquarters. There continued to be considerable crossover of personnel between the OLO and party headquarters and harmonization of the party's parliamentary activity and election preparation. Research done by the OLO on business before Parliament was rolled over for use by the party. For example, communications plans and materials devised for the party's business in the House of Commons or householders mailed out by MPs were reused by the party in its online advertising and appeals for fundraising (Roy interview 2015; Watkins interview 2015).

Controversially, sixty-eight NDP MPs pooled their House of Commons office budgets to pay the salaries of twenty-eight staff working in satellite party offices in Montreal, Quebec City, and Toronto in 2012 and 2013. With Liberal and Conservative MPs voting in favour of the motion and NDP MPs opposing it, the House of Commons' Board of Internal Economy ruled that these satellite offices were doing partisan work, constituting an improper use of parliamentary resources, and demanded that these MPs personally pay back $2.75 million. The NDP maintained that when the satellite offices were opened, there were no rules against this type of use of parliamentary resources and that the party was open and transparent about the tasks of the offices, which were to gather information and perform outreach in three cities to help MPs better do their jobs in Ottawa (Fortin interview 2015). While the offices were quickly shuttered, the party denied any wrongdoing and took the matter to the Federal Court of Canada.

A recent global survey of political marketing practices holds that a party's level of political market orientation can be understood using qualitative methods such as interview data and observation of party practice (Lees-Marshment, Strömbäck, and Rudd 2010, 4–11). Many of the participants in this interview sample stressed that the late 1990s and early 2000s were a time of considerable internal debate within the NDP. Prior to the 2000 election, there was fierce discussion over whether the party should moderate its ideology and adopt a Tony Blair New Labour–type "third way" model of social democracy. After disappointing results in the 2000 election, a group of left-wing party members – called the New Politics Initiative – proposed disbanding the NDP and creating a party built on alliances with social movements, such as those at the forefront of antiglobalization protests. While their resolution for a refounding of the party was rejected at the NDP's federal convention in 2001, discussions of the party's ideology and tactics dominated the leadership race that Layton won in early 2003.

Given the prevalence of these internal debates, it is clear that the federal NDP of the early 2000s had a relatively low level of political market orientation. As opposed to concentrating on the needs and desires of voters, the party spent a great deal of energy debating how their policies, strategies, and behaviours connected to the their ideological principles. Interviewees working for the party during this period confirmed that the volunteers and short-term staff who wrote the NDP's election platform would start from existing party policy as opposed to market intelligence about what voters wanted. Market intelligence was used to craft ways to sell the NDP's ideas as opposed to finding out what voters wanted first and then devising corresponding policies afterwards.

Layton's election as leader coincided with a string of minority Parliaments from 2004 to 2011. As we have seen, the NDP slowly moved towards perpetual election preparation during this period, as an election could be called at any time. Interviewees reported that this perpetual election preparation led to a greater professionalization of the party and changed the way it used market intelligence. As monitoring of public opinion and focus groups became a continuous activity of the party, staff began to track and model changes in the party's support and the leader's branding (Anderson interview 2014). They started to research the types of policies and leadership attributes that could convince soft Liberal and soft Bloc Québécois voters to switch to the NDP (Lavigne interview 2014). As platform development shifted away from volunteers and Parliament Hill staff began to work more closely with party headquarters, market intelligence shaped the commitments made during elections, the types of bills that the NDP introduced in the House of Commons, and the questions that NDP MPs asked during question period. After a majority government was elected in 2011, the fixed election date legislation passed by the Harper government furthered permanent-campaign thinking within the NDP. Knowing that the election was to be held on October 19, 2015, gave NDP operatives a target date on which to base their preparation. In fact, they were fully prepared to fight the election in April 2015 in case Harper called the election early (Lucy Watson interview 2015). Interviews confirmed that little changed in the lead-up to the 2015 election, and market intelligence to discern voters' needs and desires continued to play a predominant role in the NDP's platform development, legislative activity, and pre-electoral strategy.

The distinct increase in the political market orientation of the federal NDP is intimately related to the way that the party uses market intelligence within its election preparation. The example of the federal NDP illustrates the confluence of the concepts of political market orientation and election preparation. Shifting to a model of perpetual election preparation encouraged a change in the role of market intelligence, from informing the party on how to sell its ideas to understanding the desires and needs of voters, particularly Liberal/NDP switchers and Bloc/NDP switchers. In this way, perpetual election preparation helped to stimulate the NDP's move to a higher level of political market orientation. But this was not the only factor. Other factors included the string of minority Parliaments, the adoption of the permanent campaign by the Harper government, the agency of Layton and his team, and increased state funding to the party following the 2004 party financing reforms. Nonetheless, it is interesting that in a global survey of the barriers to and facilitators of moving towards a higher level of political orientation, alterations in the way that parties approach election preparation is not mentioned (Lees-Marshment, Strömbäck, and Rudd 2010, 279–89). Perhaps future empirical research and theory building employing the concept of political market orientation could take election preparation strategies into greater consideration.

Permanent Campaigning in Canada

The implications of adopting perpetual election preparation for the federal NDP are clear, in that the party increased its political market orientation. However, there are broader implications for governance and democracy that should be considered when discussing how political parties have moved towards perpetual election preparation as part of the wider entrenchment of the permanent campaign within Canadian politics.

Perpetual election preparation means that the activity of the parliamentary caucuses and their staff has become increasingly intertwined with the activity of party headquarters. Using parliamentary resources for partisan purposes has been the subject of extensive debate in the House of Commons during recent parliamentary sessions, with the controversy over partisan activities by Conservative senators as a prime example. This case study shows that the line between parliamentary activity and campaigning is blurred for both the governing party and opposition parties alike. The federal NDP now see their activity in the House of Commons as a critical part of their electoral strategy in terms of positioning themselves for the upcoming election. The NDP are governing in the House of Commons by debating and voting on bills, but they are also campaigning. Prior to the 2015 election, the NDP were convinced that the Conservatives under Stephen Harper routinely used taxpayer-funded government advertising and the government communications budget for partisan purposes. In retaliation, they were intent on pushing the boundaries of using state resources for their own election preparation, as illustrated by their satellite offices.

Another effect of perpetual election preparation has been the professionalization of the party and a corresponding reduction of the power of volunteer activists within the NDP. Election preparation takes years as opposed to weeks, and it involves specific skill sets such as online campaigning and the use of market intelligence. As such, party staff in permanent positions, as opposed to grassroots local NDP activists, are inevitably taking the leading role. Local NDP activists have not disappeared; they just take more direction from the professionals in Ottawa and exercise less independence over local organizing. This situation has been at the forefront of debates surrounding the future of the party following its disappointing 2015 election outcome. The official post-mortem on the 2015 NDP campaign found that rank-and-file activists were critical of the professionals within the central campaign for their reliance on polling and lack of communication with local campaigns, leading to an overcautious strategy (NDP 2016). The balance of power between the professionals at party headquarters and grassroots activists promises to be a continuing source of internal debate under a new leader heading into the next federal election.

At the same time, while the lack of clarity about using state resources for partisan purposes and the reduced independence of grassroots activists are potentially negative side effects of perpetual election preparation, there may be more positive aspects. A more professionalized approach to campaigning has given the NDP more presence in the media at the local and national levels, leading to greater voter awareness of the party's policy offerings. Such awareness can only be good for Canadian democracy. In addition, and in spite of the caution raised above, one of the primary tasks of professional organizers is now to mobilize local volunteers. The adoption of perpetual election preparation has meant the NDP is engaging more citizens through its canvassing efforts outside of the election period than ever before. It created what it calls the neighbourhood teams model to encourage the development of canvassing teams of local volunteers to talk directly to their neighbours about current political issues. This model is possible only because the professionals at party headquarters provide local activists with the training and digital infrastructure required to create these neighbourhood teams.

It appears that perpetual election preparation has become an enduring feature of Canadian politics as the shift towards the permanent campaign becomes more established. There may be some potentially negative aspects like unclear boundaries around the partisan use of state resources and the reduction of the power of grassroots party activists. On the other hand, perpetual election preparation could lead to more opportunities to develop linkages between citizens and political parties as the latter strive to better engage voters through frequent canvassing and teams of local activists dedicated to talking to their neighbours. As a result, any normative declarations about the implications of perpetual election preparedness are, for now, elusive. What can be said is that, in the era of permanent campaigning, the degree to which parties constantly prepare for campaigns, and how this is undertaken, remains ripe for further research.

Appendix: List of Interviews

Drew Anderson, director of communications (2010–11), October 30, 2014

Karine Fortin, deputy national director (2014–15), April 2, 2015

Heather Fraser, director of organization (2000–2008), October 27, 2014

Franz Hartmann, social movement outreach coordinator (2004–6), March 20, 2015

Éric Hébert-Daly, federal secretary (2004–8), October 30, 2014

Brad Lavigne, national director (2008–11), October 31, 2014

Anne McGrath, NDP president (2006–8), national director (2014–15), October 27, 2014

Steve Moran, deputy chief of staff to the leader (2012–15), October 31, 2014

Tara Peel, candidate search coordinator (2004–8), March 24, 2015

James Pratt, director of field organization (2014–15), March 25, 2015

Nathan Rotman, national director (2012–14), March 24, 2015

Michael Roy, digital director (2014–15), March 23, 2015

Danielle Sampson, deputy director of organization and associate director of training and development (2013–15), March 26, 2015

Vicky Smallman, co-chair of policy committee of federal council (2000–2006), October 27, 2014

Brian Topp, campaign co-chair (2004–8), March 26, 2015

Emily Watkins, director of outreach and stakeholder relations (2014–15), April 13, 2015

Chris Watson, federal secretary (2002–4), March 20, 2015

Lucy Watson, election readiness coordinator (2014–15), March 25, 2015

NOTE

1 Jack Layton was the popular and dynamic leader of the NDP from 2003 until his early death from cancer in 2011, not long after leading the party to official opposition status in the federal election.

REFERENCES

Erickson, Lynda, and David Laycock. 2009. "Modernization, Incremental Progress, and the Challenge of Relevance: The NDP's 2008 Campaign." In *The Canadian General Election of 2008*, edited by C. Dornan and J. Pammett, 98–135. Toronto: Dundurn Press.

Farrell, David, and Paul Webb. 2000. "Political Parties as Campaign Organisations." In *Parties without Partisans: Political Change in Advanced Industrial Democracies*, edited by R. Dalton and M. Wattenberg, 124–46. Oxford: Oxford University Press.

Flanagan, Tom. 2014. *Winning Power: Canadian Campaigning in the Twenty-First Century*. Montreal/Kingston: McGill-Queens University Press.

Harrell, Margaret, and Melissa Bradley. 2009. *Data Collection Methods: Semi-Structured Interviews and Focus Groups*. Santa Monica: RAND Corporation.

Kohli, Ajay, and Bernard Jaworski. 1990. "Market Orientation: The Construct, Research Propositions, and Managerial Expectations." *Journal of Marketing* 54 (2): 1–18. http://dx.doi.org/10.2307/1251866.

Kvale, Stienar, and Svend Brinkmann. 2009. *Interviews: Learning the Craft of Qualitative Research Interviewing*. London: SAGE Publications.

Lavigne, Brad. 2013. *Building the Orange Wave*. Madeira Park, BC: Douglas and McIntyre.

Lees-Marshment, Jennifer, Jesper Strömbäck, and Chris Rudd, eds. 2010. *Global Political Marketing*. New York: Routledge.

Levitt, Theodore. 1960. "Marketing Myopia." *Harvard Business Review* 38 (4): 45–57.

Marland, Alex. 2012. "Amateurs versus Professionals: The 1993 and 2006 Canadian Federal Elections." In *Political Marketing in Canada*, edited by A. Marland, T. Giasson, and J. Lees-Marshment, 44–61. Vancouver: UBC Press.

McGrane, David. 2011. "Political Marketing and the NDP's Historic Breakthrough." In *The Canadian Federal Election of 2011*, edited by C. Doran and J. Pammett, 77–110. Toronto: Dundurn Press.

Narver, John, and Stanley Slater. 1990. "The Effect of Market Orientation on Business Profitability." *Journal of Marketing* 54 (4): 20–35. http://dx.doi.org/10.2307/1251757.

NDP. 2016. *Campaign 2015 Review: Working Group Report*. Ottawa: NDP.

Norris, Pippa. 2000. *The Virtuous Circle: Political Communication in Post-Industrial Societies*. Cambridge: Cambridge University Press. http://dx.doi.org/10.1017/CBO 9780511609343.

Ormrod, Robert, Stephen Henneberg, and Nicholas O'Shaughnessy. 2013. *Political Marketing: Theory and Concepts*. London: SAGE Publications. http://dx.doi.org/10. 4135/9781473914827.

Pilon, Dennis, Stephanie Ross, and Larry Savage. 2011. "Solidarity Revisited: Organized Labour and the New Democratic Party." *Canadian Political Science Review* 5 (1): 20–37.

Plasser, Fritz, and Gunda Plasser. 2002. *Global Political Campaigning: A Worldwide Analysis of Campaign Professionals and Their Practices*. Westport, CT: Praeger.

Strömbäck, Jesper. 2009. "Political Marketing and Professionalized Campaigning." *Journal of Political Marketing* 6 (2): 49–67.

Wesley, Jared, and Mike Moyes. 2014. "Selling Social Democracy: Branding the Political Left in Canada." In *Political Communication in Canada: Meet the Press and Tweet the Rest*, edited by A. Marland, T. Giasson, and T.A. Small, 74–91. Vancouver: UBC Press.

Whitehorn, Alan. 2004. "Jack Layton and the NDP: Gains but No Breakthrough." In *The Canadian General Election of 2004*, edited by C. Dornan and J. Pammett, 106–38. Toronto: Dundurn Press.

PART 3

Governance ....

9

Institutional Change, Permanent Campaigning, and Canada's Fixed Election Date Law

Philippe Lagassé

Fixed election dates are closely linked to the permanent campaign.[1] Commentators have blamed the fixed-date election legislation for extending the 2015 electoral campaign beyond the formal writ period. Since the date of the election was known well in advance, political parties had an incentive to begin campaigning months ahead of time. Critics charge that this represents the importation of an American campaign cycle into Canadian politics (Smith 2015a). The chief electoral officer has also stated that the fixed-date election legislation undermines electoral finance laws, notably by encouraging third-party advocacy groups to engage in campaign-style advertising before the writ (Hall 2015). According to defenders of this electoral reform, however, the institution of a fixed election date has benefited Canadian democracy by discouraging opportunistic election calls by the prime minister (Knopff 2015; Neudorf 2014). Moreover, the causal connections between fixed election dates and the permanent campaign are not easily discerned. Permanent campaigning predates the fixed-date election law, and campaign finance loopholes are not a product of having a fixed election date per se.

Caution is therefore needed when examining the relationship between fixed-date election legislation and permanent campaigning. There is no straight line between the introduction of a fixed election date and the rise of permanent campaigning in Canada. But there is evidence that the law has amplified the permanent campaign. To explain the relationship between this electoral reform and permanent campaigning, it is necessary to examine what kind of institutional change the fixed-date election law represents and how it has been approached by political and media actors in Canada.

The power to dissolve Parliament is a prerogative of the Crown. Prerogative powers are discretionary authorities of the Crown that are exercised on the advice of the political executive – the prime minister and cabinet (Bolt 2008). Unlike statutory authorities, which are bestowed on the executive by

Parliament, prerogatives belong to the Crown in its own right as recognized by common law or the Constitution. While Parliament determines the scope and existence of prerogatives by statute, the legislature is not formally involved in exercises of these powers or in the advice that ministers give the Crown when they are employed. In addition to parliamentary dissolution, contemporary Crown prerogatives include the authority to prorogue Parliament, deploy the armed forces, ratify treaties, and grant passports and mercy.

Owing to significant discretion they afford the prime minister and cabinet, and their historical roots in monarchical government, prerogative powers have been attractive targets for reform across Westminster states (Rhodes, Wanna, and Weller 2011; UK HoC 2004). These calls for reform are motivated by a desire to rebalance the relationship between the executive and the legislature. Thus, prerogative reforms have sought to prevent the executive from deploying armed forces overseas or ratifying treaties without first consulting Parliament. Efforts have also been made to involve parliamentarians in appointments made under prerogative authority, notably judicial nominations. Regarding the dissolution prerogative specifically, the argument for reform holds that the duration and sittings of Parliament should not be decided by the executive. Instead, the life of a Parliament should be determined by the elected house of a legislature (Aucoin, Jarvis, and Turnbull 2011).

Calls for prerogative reform implicitly assume that changes will benefit the legislature over the executive and that democratization will push parties towards greater cooperation (UK HoC 2007). These assumptions rely on a linear understanding of institutional change. This linear understanding downplays the various motives that can bring about reforms. It also neglects the unanticipated consequences of reforming isolated parts of complex political systems. To arrive at a stronger explanation and understanding of how prerogative reforms have proceeded and the impact of these reforms, this analysis relies on the theory of gradual institutional change proposed by James Mahoney and Kathleen Thelen (2010). This theory sheds light on how prerogative reforms can contribute to or be guided by the permanent campaign. Their theory highlights how prerogative reform can lead to what the editors of this volume describe as "attempts made by political elites to circumvent or change rules and norms to accommodate the practice of permanent campaigning." Specifically, the categories provided by Mahoney and Thelen can be applied to identify institutional changes that are directly driven by the permanent campaign. Equally important, their categories can identify which types of institutional change are not necessarily motivated by the permanent campaign but can nonetheless amplify permanent campaigning.

Mahoney and Thelen (2010) identify four types of gradual institutional change and four types of change agents associated with them. The first, displacement, occurs when "existing rules are replaced by new ones" (16). The second type of change, layering, "occurs when new rules are attached to existing ones, thereby changing the ways in which the original rules structure behaviour" (16). Rather than introducing "wholly new institutions or rules," layering "involves amendments, revisions, or additions" (16), usually because existing rules and norms cannot be wholly displaced. The third type of change, drift, "occurs when rules remain the same but their impact changes as a result of shifts in external conditions" (17). The fourth type of institutional change is conversion. Under conversion, "rules remain formally the same but are interpreted and enacted in new ways" (17). This type of change exploits ambiguities surrounding rules and norms to alter institutions, rather than relying on more overt efforts to replace or add to rules or allow existing rules to slip.

According to Mahoney and Thelen (2010), the type of change that will be pursued will be influenced by the veto possibilities of those supporting the status quo. Veto possibilities can come in many forms, such as codified constitutions that limit the scope of reforms that rely on ordinary laws. When these veto possibilities are weak, displacement and conversion are more likely, whereas strong veto possibilities tend to encourage layering and drift. Discretion in interpreting or enforcing rules and norms affects change types as well. Drift and conversion are unlikely to occur when the interpretation and enforcement of rules and norms are highly discretionary. Layering and displacement, on the other hand, are likelier when interpretations and enforcement are less discretionary.

Mahoney and Thelen (2010) further identify four types of change agents. The first type, insurrectionaries, "consciously seek to eliminate existing institutions or rules, and they do so by actively and visibly mobilizing against them" (23). Insurrectionaries will therefore be linked with efforts to displace existing rules and norms. A second type of change agent are symbionists, who "exploit an institution for private gain," but "carry out actions that contradict the 'spirit' or purpose of the institution" (24). In so doing, they undermine the institution over the long term and are thus associated with drift, as the institution remains but rules are neglected. Subversives are the third type of change agent. They do not seek to preserve existing institutions, yet they respect institutional rules as they attempt to bring about change. As their name suggests, their respect of the rules gives the impression that they are favourable to the status quo, though their hidden aim is to undermine it. Subversives will therefore be drawn to layering. Finally, the fourth type of change agents are opportunists. These actors are ambivalent about institutional change and existing rules. Their principal concern is advancing their political interests, and they "exploit whatever possibilities with the prevailing system to achieve their ends" (26). Accordingly, opportunists tend to support the status quo and "can be a major source of institutional inertia" (26). Yet when existing institutions present an obstacle to achieving their ends, opportunists will gravitate towards conversion, reinterpreting rules and norms as needed to "suit their interests" (27).

In light of Mahoney and Thelen (2010), institutional changes can be connected to permanent campaigning in various ways. Insurrectionary displacements and subversive layerings that extend the campaign period or loosen electoral finance regulations in law would be changes that directly contribute to the permanent campaign. Symbonist drift would not normally be directly associated with permanent campaigning, unless there is a rule or norm that fuels permanent campaigning by not being updated. Opportunistic conversion, on the other hand, would be associated with indirect contributions to permanent campaigning. Under this institutional change, rules and norms can be deployed or interpreted to accommodate permanent-campaigning practices. This type of change can also foster institutional ambiguities that motivate permanent campaigning.

Case Study

Method

The question asked here is whether the federal regulation on fixed election dates – legislated in 2007 – has contributed to the permanent campaign in Canada, and if so, how it has done so. The methodology that guided the analysis was process tracing (Vennesson 2008). Process tracing establishes and evaluates links between factors and seeks to explain and understand how the factors are connected. By analyzing the actions and declarations of political actors, process tracing was applied to make abductive inferences (Douven 2011) about the motives and aims of these actors, using the categories and causal claims set forth in Mahoney and Thelen (2010).

The analysis relied on qualitative data. To establish the motive behind the fixed-date election law, the statute was placed in its proper historical and political contexts. This was done by looking at parliamentary reform efforts since the formation of the Special Joint Committee on the Constitution of Canada in 1970; previous fixed-date election bills; Liberal Party, New Democratic Party, and Conservative Party electoral platforms; and parliamentary studies.[2] Next, statements made by ministers and members of the House of Commons when the legislation was proposed in November 2006 were assessed to establish how the government presented the purpose and functioning of the bill. This was buttressed by a reading of the legislation and constitutional provisions that shaped how it was drafted. To understand how the legislation operated and affected political decision making, political statements and behaviours from 2006 to the summer of 2015 were examined. The statements were drawn from the Hansard database and political behaviours were traced based on media reporting of party activities. The wider effects of the legislation on the permanent campaign were assessed through a qualitative, interpretive analysis (Fairclough and Fairclough 2012) of media reports, commentaries, and the opinions of subject matter experts during this same period. A total of twenty-two media reports, commentaries, and opinion pieces were collected and analyzed from the *Toronto Star*, the *Toronto Sun*, the *Globe and Mail*, the *National Post*, the *Ottawa Citizen*, the *Hill Times*, *Loonie Politics*, *La Presse*, and *CBC.ca*.

Findings

Calls for fixed federal election dates have been heard for several decades in Canada. The first private member's bill to abolish the dissolution prerogative was tabled in 1970. The explanatory note to the bill highlighted its intent: "To abolish the Royal Power of Dissolution with a view to reducing the arbitrary power of the Prime Minister and enhancing the independence of the private Member of Parliament" (quoted in Robertson 2007, 12) Although the bill did not pass and fixed-term Parliaments were not a high priority for parliamentary reformers at the federal level over the next two decades, there remained lingering concerns with the prime minister's discretionary authority over the life of a Parliament. These concerns became more pronounced with the formation of the Reform Party in the late 1980s. Fixed-date elections became a pillar of the democratic reform agendas of the Reform Party, the Canadian Alliance, and the Conservative Party. The

Canadian Alliance, for instance, included a pledge to introduce fixed-date election legislation in its 2000 electoral platform, where it stated that it would "set fixed election dates every four years, to remove from the Prime Minister the discretionary power to call an early snap election or hold onto office late" (Canadian Alliance 2000, 20). Outside of Ottawa, provincial legislatures moved forward with fixed-date election legislation. British Columbia established fixed election dates with a 2001 statute. Newfoundland and Labrador followed suit in 2004, as did Ontario in 2005. The reform was gaining momentum.

In 2004, Stephen Harper, the leader of the newly formed Conservative Party of Canada, tabled a private member's bill that would have introduced a fixed election date. The bill explicitly referenced the "concentration of power in the Office of the Prime Minister, and the unnecessary domination of the executive over the House of Commons," (Bill C-512, 2004) as its rationale. Harper's bill was defeated, but the Conservatives promises to introduce fixed election dates in their 2006 electoral platform. Drawing on the provincial efforts, the platform pledged that a Conservative government would "introduce legislation modelled on the BC and Ontario laws requiring fixed election dates every four years, except when a government loses the confidence of the House (in which case an election would be held immediately, and the subsequent election would follow four years later)" (Conservative Party 2006, 44). The Conservatives were quick to follow through with this pledge when they formed the government in 2006.

Bill C-16, *An Act to Amend the Canada Elections Act*, was presented in November 2006. It eschewed the bold language of Harper's private member's bill, but it retained its key feature. The bill set a fixed date for federal elections every four years. But rather than seeking to remove the prerogative power over dissolution, the bill preserved the governor general's authority to dissolve Parliament and hence the prime minister's ability to advise dissolution at a date other than the one set in the bill. The bill thus appeared to represent change by layering, with the Conservative government being motivated by subversion; namely, a desire to establish fixed election dates while accepting the need to preserve the prerogative of dissolution.

Two factors support the idea that the reform was a form of subversive layering. First, the prerogative of dissolution would arguably have required a unanimous constitutional amendment to abolish. Paragraph 41(a) of the *Constitution Act, 1982* requires the unanimous consent of Parliament and the provincial legislatures to alter the offices of the Queen, governor general, and lieutenant-governor of a province. Jurisprudence suggests that the dissolution prerogative would fall under the governor general's office, making paragraph 41(a) a strong veto possibility for attempts to abolish that power (Lagassé and Baud 2016). Faced with these strong veto possibilities, layering was a preferable avenue for institutional change. In fact, all provincial fixed-date election laws contained a provision preserving the lieutenant-governor's prerogative to dissolve the legislature. This commonality reinforces the strength of the veto possibility involved. In light of this constitutional veto, displacement was not a realistic path for instituting a fixed election date.

Second, the government's initial statements regarding the bill suggested a subversive intent. Justice Minister Rob Nicholson assured members that the bill aimed to limit the prime minister's discretion and provide for veritable fixed election dates. Yet he further noted that the preservation of the governor general's authority to dissolve Parliament allowed for an election when a government lost the confidence of the Commons, an essential constitutional convention of responsible government. When asked what would stop prime ministers from using this provision to call an election when it suits them, Conservative MP Jay Hill argued that a prime minister who did so would "be held accountable by the people, because of their expectation, though the legislation itself, would be that the date was off into the future."[3] These comments indicate a subversive effort to introduce fixed election dates while accommodating constitutional rules surrounding losses of confidence. Considering that the Conservatives were governing during a minority Parliament at the time, the need to accommodate losses of confidence would have been evident. Indeed, their 2006 electoral platform demonstrates that this factor was part of their thinking. As formulated, the law allowed for dissolution if a government lost a confidence vote, while encouraging majority governments, and minority governments that retained confidence, to respect the fixed election date (Knopff 2015).

Bill C-16 was granted royal assent in May 2007. A little over a year later, Prime Minister Harper advised the governor general to dissolve Parliament on September 7, 2008, without losing a vote of confidence in the House of Commons. Shortly before, Harper explained the legislature was effectively dysfunctional, with chaotic committees hampering the Commons' work and the majority Liberal Senate stalling government legislation (CBC News 2008). This justification was at odds with Nicholson's claim that the retention of the prime minister's discretion was meant for losses of confidence. Minority Parliaments where government initiatives were being undermined were now upheld as reasons why the fixed election date might not be respected. Tom Flanagan (2014, 140) further notes that the decision to call the election prior to the fixed date was driven by the Conservatives' belief that the conditions were ripe to win a majority of seats in the Commons. The fact that Harper could do so in spite of the fixed-date election law suggests that the legislation did not alter political norms surrounding the exercise of prime ministerial discretion over the timing of an election. That said, the 2006–8 minority Parliament had lasted for a relatively long time and the prime minister's claim that voters should be called on to express themselves in light of the parliamentary logjam has value. But it remains that Harper's justification for the 2008 dissolution did not accord with the stated intent of the law.

The federal fixed-date election law, therefore, appears to have been a form of opportunistic conversion, rather than subversive layering. As the letter of the statute indicates, the law did not affect the prerogative. But the justice minister's statement leading up to the passage of the bill indicated that the statute was meant to bring about a normative change regarding the exercise of the dissolution prerogative. That did not occur either. This was made clear by a court challenge to the 2008 dissolution. Launched by the advocacy group Democracy Watch, the challenge failed to prove that the law had established a constitutional convention limiting exercises of the dissolution prerogative. According to Judge Shore of the Federal Court, the fixed-date election law:

> did not create a new constitutional convention because the three-question test adopted by the Supreme Court of Canada ... for determining the existence of a convention was not met. Particularly, there were no precedents with respect to the existence of a convention from the relevant actors, and those actors (the Prime Minister and the Governor General) clearly did not recognize the existence of such precedent. In addition, there was no evidence of an explicit agreement between the political actors of their intent to create a new convention.[4]

Furthermore, Judge Shore backed the prime minister's view that the dissolution prerogative could be exercised if the government felt unduly stifled by Parliament. "Votes of non-confidence," he noted, "are political in nature and lack legal aspects. It should be left to the Prime Minister to determine when the government has lost the confidence of the House of Commons."[5] Save for establishing a date when an election will occur unless it happens earlier, the law left the formal rules in place.

Yet the legislation did create ambiguities. In particular, the law was vague about when the prime minister could advise dissolution prior to the fixed election date. A generous reading would say that an early dissolution can be advised when the prime minister no longer feels that Parliament is allowing the government to govern. A more cynical view would say that the law allows dissolution whenever it suits the prime minister. These ambiguities continue to surround the law and its meaning.

Insofar as the prerogative of dissolution was unaffected by the fixed-date election law, it is difficult to draw a direct connection between the statute and the permanent campaign. The legislation effectively retained an institutional structure that had been in place and exploited by prime ministers before permanent campaigning fully emerged in Canadian politics. However, the ambiguity fostered by the law about the timing of elections did interact with and encourage a permanent campaigning mentality leading up to the fixed election date of October 19, 2015. From late 2014 to the spring of 2015, speculation that the prime minister might trigger an election prior to October 2015 was rampant (see, for instance, Ivison 2015; Kinsella 2014; Martin 2014; Reid 2015; Warren 2014). Ironically, the fact that there was a fixed election date but that Harper could advise dissolution when he pleased fuelled significant interest in the upcoming campaign, despite the reality that the prime minister had always had the discretion to advise dissolution. The fixed election date made an earlier election a bigger story, as it were. For a few months at least, the timing of the election became fodder for pundits.

Indeed, the speculation that the fixed-date election law created about the timing of the election is arguably the legislation's strongest contribution to permanent campaigning. Once the fixed date was a year away, the possibility that the prime minister might dissolve Parliament earlier became a focal point of media discussion. The fact that the fixed-date election law was a form of opportunistic conversion, moreover, amplified discussions of an earlier dissolution. Although prime ministers had always had the ability to dissolve Parliament at a time when it best suited their political interests, the fixed election date made the opportunism of an earlier election particularly evident. In turn, the reasons why the prime minister might seize this opportunity, or why he might not, became fodder for columnists and political panels. The effect of this speculation was to introduce regular discussions of the election into media analyses several months prior to the actual dropping of the writ. In this sense, it is possible to draw a connection between the ambiguity of the fixed-date election law and the prevalence of election date speculation.

The fixed election date helped extend the campaign period in other ways, too. Party platforms and positions began to appear early in 2015, months before the election was held. Jockeying over these platforms, particularly economic policies, effectively began in the early spring. Although an extended campaigning season would likely have occurred without a fixed election date, the predetermined date established a frame within which permanent campaigning was normalized and structured. Since the election was known to be taking place in October 2015, it encouraged the governing party to treat the spring 2015 budget as an electoral platform. The opposition parties, in turn, used their critiques of the budget to lay out elements of their own electoral platforms. Parliament's sittings in the months prior to the election were increasingly dominated by a campaign mindset. Electoral debates were even planned for the summer of 2015, months before the election would actually take place. Governing and opposing in their traditional parliamentary sense, wherein the government governs and the opposition is focused on holding them to account as opposed to presenting its own policy proposals, were no longer the main concern (Dale Smith 2015b; David Smith 2013).

Writing in favour of this development, *National Post* comment editor Andrew Coyne (2015) noted that "the endless campaign has actually made room for some pretty good policy discussion ... The result: a long, leisurely rollout of policies in the months before the election, eventually pulled together into complete platforms in time for the writ drop – with perhaps a few surprises saved for the official campaign." Coyne further noted that "to the average voter, it's a godsend ... by the time the election rolls around, they will have caught enough glimpses of what the parties have on offer to be able to make a halfway informed decision." Taking a negative view and writing about eight months earlier, *Toronto Star* columnist Tim Harper (2014) lamented that "whether we like it or not, we're beginning a 399-day federal election campaign." He further argued that the fixed election date could be used to benefit the government, despite its supposed intent to end the incumbent's advantage: "The fixed election date has allowed the government to manipulate the calendar in a different way, artificially waiting for the final year of the mandate to ensure a surplus which will allow it to offer tax breaks and new programs in a re-election bid." Jean-Pierre Kingsley, a former chief electoral officer, sided with critics of the longer campaign and fixed election date. He blamed the fixed date for helping to erode campaign spending and advertising rules. Accordingly to Kingsley, "When we lose the financial controls, we lose the ability to maintain what we call the level playing field, which is at the very core of our electoral act" (quoted in CBC News 2015). Kingsley's concerns were echoed by Marc Mayrand, the current chief electoral officer, who noted that Canada's campaign finance laws should have been reformed alongside the fixed election date (Marquis 2015). Whether one agrees with Coyne or these critics, the effects they describe, both positive and negative, were facilitated by the appearance of a fixed election date, however unbinding it may be.

Looking beyond how the legislation has affected campaigning, however, *Toronto Star* columnist Chantal Hébert argued that the fixed-date election law had served its underlying purpose. Although the Conservative Party would likely have benefited from an earlier election, Harper's decision to respect the spirit of his government's own law "boxed him in" (Hébert 2015). Hébert's point, furthermore, reinforces arguments that have long been made in favour of fixed election dates. In choosing to respect the fixed election date, Harper gave up the advantages that might have been gained by advising a dissolution earlier. Polls in early 2015 indicated that the Conservatives were well placed to carry an election (Abacus Data 2015). It is possible that the Conservatives might have fared better at the polls had an election been held at this time. Similarly, had Harper kept the writ short when calling an earlier election, which would have made sense if the aim was to take advantage of a resurgence in support for the Conservatives, it is possible that Justin Trudeau's Liberal Party would not have had the chance to surge as it did in October 2015. Suffice to say, this would probably have benefited the Conservatives as well. In both these senses, Harper's respecting of the fixed election date can be said to have weakened the incumbent prime minister's ability to use the timing of an election to his or her advantage. It further suggests that a longer election period or extended writ may not necessarily offer the incumbent an alternative means of securing an advantage while still respecting the fixed date.

While this was bad for Harper and the Conservatives, the law arguably succeeded in discouraging a baldly partisan exercise of the dissolution prerogative in 2015. A question that remains is whether Prime Minister Justin Trudeau and his successors will also respect the date set by the fixed-date election law. Trudeau has been largely silent about the law and the timing of the next election, and the Liberals' electoral reform efforts do not appear to foreshadow any intent to reconsider the fixed-date election law. At this stage, it is impossible to predict whether Trudeau will respect the fixed date. Significant events or crises could warrant an early election, even under a majority government. Political expediency could also trump other considerations, compelling Trudeau to dissolve Parliament at an opportune time. On the other hand, calling an early election would result in unfavourable comparisons with Harper and be an easy target for opposition attacks. As well, Trudeau stressed that his government will respect Parliament, which would discourage calling an election before the date mandated by parliamentary statute. As part of larger electoral reform efforts, the Liberal government could choose to reinforce the fixed election date through a cabinet manual or other document codifying the conventions that surround the dissolution of Parliament. This would be especially worthwhile if a new electoral system produces more minority Parliaments or coalition governments.

If the Trudeau government respects the fixed election date and future majority governments do as well, a custom may develop such that majority governments should adhere to the legislated election date. If this occurs, the fixed election date would achieve the institutional change by subversive layering, as the Harper government originally presented it. Likewise, if norms surrounding an adherence to the fixed date were strengthened through a cabinet manual, a prime minister's ability to call an earlier election would remain, but there would be additional pressure not to do so. Were the fixed election date to become more certain, it could reduce some of the amplifying effects that the legislation has had on permanent campaigning. Talk of an earlier election would presumably be quieted under majority governments. However, it would not diminish the elongation of the campaign preparation period that the fixed-date election law has encouraged. The fixed date will continue to normalize campaign preparation and campaign-like activities months, if not a year or more, before the actual writ.

Permanent Campaigning in Canada

Prerogative power reform is supposed to reduce executive discretion in favour of legislative deliberation, end advantages the governing party enjoys over the opposition, and encourage greater cooperation and less partisanship between parties. As with other forms of institutional change, however, prerogative reform has not been linear and has produced unanticipated consequences. One of these consequences has been to amplify the permanent campaign.

The introduction of a fixed election date was meant to ensure greater predictability and fairness between parties. Yet the fixed date has also facilitated campaigning well before the writ. Fixed election dates cannot be said to have caused the permanent campaign, nor would permanent campaigning cease to exist without them. Fixed election dates are neither a necessary nor sufficient condition for permanent campaigning. Yet it is possible to infer that fixed election dates have encouraged permanent campaigning and helped its practices appear more normal and mundane. Indeed, the ambiguity of the fixed-date election law has a doubly amplifying effect. Because the law does not actually prevent the prime minister from advising the Crown to hold an election when he or she chooses, opposition parties have an incentive to prepare for an election at any time, lest the fixed election date lull them into a false sense of certainty about the timing of the next writ. Media commentators fuel this need to prepare for an earlier election, since the possibility of a prime minister advising the dissolution of Parliament now has an air of impropriety, making this possibility an attractive topic of punditry. Greater speculation about an early election, even under a majority Parliament, makes pre-writ campaigning seem logical and prudent. When it becomes clear that the prime minister will respect the fixed election date, the second amplifying effect is felt: the permanent campaigning practices that were deployed in anticipation of an early election are reinforced and redoubled in preparation for the predetermined date, even if the election is many months away. Here again, the establishment of a fixed election date helps the extended campaign period appear logical and even desirable. There is no need to justify or explain the longer campaigns, given that the fixed election date provides a point of reference for these efforts.

As noted, the fixed-date election law's amplification of the permanent campaign may become less pronounced if it becomes customary for prime ministers to respect the set date. Were such a custom to take root, there would likely be less media speculation about early dissolutions and fewer incentives for opposition parties to prepare themselves for an election well in advance. However, the incentives to begin campaigning long before the writ would not disappear. Evidence for this claim is seen in the United Kingdom. Unlike the Canadian law, the British *Fixed-term Parliaments Act*

2011 displaced the dissolution prerogative (Gardner 2015). The British Parliament is dissolved and an election held on a fixed date, unless the House of Commons agrees or there is no government that can hold confidence. The British law thus avoids the ambiguity of the Canadian legislation. Nonetheless, British politicians have argued that the law encourages pre-writ campaigning (Zurcher 2015). Labour MP Austin Mitchell stated that the law led to parliamentarians "pretending to do things when we are just electioneering and throwing custard pies at each other" (quoted in Nelson 2015). Former Conservative cabinet ministers have attempted to repeal the law on the grounds that it creates "zombie" Parliaments (Hope 2015). Hence, the amplification of the permanent campaign would not entirely cease if Canada's legislation was less ambiguous and less susceptible to opportunistic conversion.

The fixed-date election law's impact on Canada's parliamentary democracy remains unclear and may be inherently a question of trade-offs. On the one hand, the law may discourage snap elections and level the playing field between political parties. The legislation may also bring greater certainty to the electoral cycle. The extended campaign period encouraged by the law, furthermore, can lead to better policy debates. And this can presumably lead to a more knowledgeable and informed voting public. On the other hand, the fixed election date can create periods when the House of Commons focuses less on holding the government to account and becomes a prolonged electoral debating club. This, in turn, can further reduce the time and effort spent on governing versus campaigning. In the lead-up to the fixed date, the Commons' consideration of government policy will be increasingly filtered through a campaigning lens.

As Dale Smith (2015b) has observed, moreover, as campaigning begins to trump governing and opposing in the year and months leading up to the fixed election date, party leaders spend increasingly less time in question period. Parliament's status as the centre of federal political affairs is further diminished as a result. While there is no question that Parliament's decline is a long-standing problem, the fixed election date may be yet another factor that will contribute to the diminishment of the institution. In conclusion, it is safe to say that the effects of the fixed-date election law on Canadian politics and democracy are much like the legislation itself: ambiguous.

10

Preaching to the Choir in Case It Is Losing Faith: Government Advertising's Direct Electoral Consequences

Denver McNeney and David Coletto

While the public debate regarding the substance and style of government advertising has shifted over the past decades, government advertising is by no means a new phenomenon in Canada. Indeed, governments have employed extensive advertising for a variety of goals across Canada's history, including settling the west, recruiting for wars, and, perhaps most importantly, community- and nation-building activities (Rose 2000). Like all government communication, its advertising is purposive – designed to change attitudes or behaviours among some or all of the public. As Jonathan Rose (2000, 21) argues, government advertising is "never 'innocent' in the sense of merely providing information or respondent to public demand"; its function is to persuade, not merely inform.

It is surprising, then, that little work has been done to uncover the electoral and perceptive consequences of government advertising in Canada today (though see Dougan 2007; Nesbitt-Larking and Rose 2004; Rose 2001, 2003; Rutherford 2000) or the role it might play in the permanent campaign. This lack of attention is particularly egregious given the obvious importance of government communication in fostering an engaged, informed, and critical electorate. Though the bulk of this literature focuses on citizens as *consumers* of political information, the government's role as a *producer* of political communication is of substantive importance in its own right. In fact, by effectively bathing the public with information regarding policies, programs, and other government activities, public advertising may supply an otherwise disengaged and apathetic citizenry with the information required to competently wield the levers of democratic accountability. Of course, if the majority of content produced by the government of the day is less informative than it is outwardly partisan in nature, any normatively appealing account of government advertising ultimately splinters. Especially

NOTES

1 The author acknowledges the financial support of the Social Sciences and Humanities Research Council of Canada.

2 Previous fixed-date election bills were found on Parliament's LEGISinfo website, http://www.parl.gc.ca/LegisInfo/; party platforms were found at http://www.poltext.org/en/part-1-electronic-political-texts/electronic-manifestos-canada; and parliamentary studies were found at the Library of Parliament website, http://www.parl.gc.ca/About/Library/VirtualLibrary/index-e.asp.

3 *House of Commons Debates*, 39th Parliament, 1st Session, No. 077 (November 6, 2006), 1210–1345.

4 Conacher v. Canada (Prime Minister), 2009 FC 920, [2010] 3 FCR 411, paragraph 2.

5 Ibid., paragraph 3.

REFERENCES

Abacus Data. 2015. "Budget Propels Conservatives to 8 Point Lead." http://abacusdata.ca/wp-content/uploads/2015/04/Abacus-Release-Headline-Political-Data_April2015.pdf.

Aucoin, Peter, Mark D. Jarvis, and Lori Turnbull. 2011. *Democratizing the Constitution*. Toronto: Emond Montgomery.

Bill C-512. 2004. *An Act to Provide Fixed Dates for the Election to the House of Commons and to Amend the Constitution Act, 1867*, 3rd Session, 37th Parliament, clause 52–53.

Bolt, Major Alexander. 2008. *The Crown Prerogative as Applied to Military Operations*. Ottawa: Office of the Judge Advocate General, Strategic Legal Paper Series.

Canadian Alliance. 2000. "A Time for Change: An Agenda of Respect for all Canadians." http://www.poltext.org/sites/poltext.org/files/plateformes/can2000all_plt_en._14112008_173717.pdf.

CBC News. 2008. "Harper Hints at Triggering Election." August 14. http://www.cbc.ca/news/canada/harper-hints-at-triggering-election-1.745252.

–. 2015. "Fixed Election Date Eroding Campaign Rules, Ex-Elections Chief Says." May 23. http://www.cbc.ca/news/politics/fixed-election-date-eroding-campaign-rules-ex-elections-chief-says-1.3084146.

Conservative Party. 2006. "Stand Up for Canada." http://www.poltext.org/sites/poltext.org/files/plateformes/can2006pc_plt_en._14112008_165519.pdf.

Coyne, Andrew. 2015. "In Praise of the Endless Election Campaign." *National Post*, May 16. http://news.nationalpost.com/full-comment/andrew-coyne-in-praise-of-the-endless-election-campaign.

Douven, Igor. 2011. "Abduction." In *Stanford Encyclopedia of Philosophy*, edited by Edward N. Zalta. http://plato.stanford.edu/archives/spr2011/entries/abduction/.

Fairclough, Isabela, and Norman Fairclough. 2012. *Political Discourse Analysis: A Method for Advanced Students*. London: Routledge.

Flanagan, Tom. 2014. *Winning Power: Canadian Campaigning in the Twenty-First Century*. Montreal/Kingston: McGill-Queen's University Press.

Gardner, Carl. 2015. *What a Fix-Up! The Fixed-term Parliaments Act 2011.* n.p.: Carl Gardner. Kindle edition. http://www.headoflegal.com/2015/05/06/what-a-fix-up-my -e-book-on-the-fixed-term-parliaments-act/.

Hall, Chris. 2015. "HarperPAC, Engage Canada Highlight Confusion over 3rd-Party Ads." *CBC.ca*, June 27. http://www.cbc.ca/news/politics/harperpac-engage-canada -highlight-confusion-over-3rd-party-ads-1.3129882.

Harper, Tim. 2014. "Ready for a Year-Long Campaign? Didn't Think So." *Toronto Star*, September 14. https://www.thestar.com/news/canada/2014/09/14/ready_for_a_ yearlong_campaign_didnt_think_so_tim_harper.html.http://www.thestar.com/ news/canada/2014/09/14/ready_for_a_yearlong_campaign_didnt_think_so_tim_ harper.html

Hébert, Chantal. 2015. "Fixed-Date Election Comes back to Bite Harper." *Toronto Star*, June 26. https://www.thestar.com/news/canada/2015/06/26/fixed-date-election -comes-back-to-bite-stephen-harper-hbert.html.

Hope, Christopher. 2015. "Axe 'Zombie' Parliaments Law, Say Former Cabinet Ministers." *Telegraph*, January 16. http://www.telegraph.co.uk/news/general-election-2015/ 11348786/Axe-zombie-Parliaments-law-say-former-Cabinet-ministers.html.

Ivison, John. 2015. "Why Current Events Are Making It Seem Increasingly Likely Harper Will Call an Early Election." *National Post*, January 13. http://news.national post.com/full-comment/john-ivison-why-current-events-are-making-it-seem -increasingly-likely-harper-will-call-an-early-election.

Kinsella, Warren. 2014. "Will Harper Call Early Election?" *Toronto Sun*, May15. http:// www.torontosun.com/2014/05/15/will-harper-call-early-election.

Knopff, Rainer. 2015. "Did the 2015 Alberta and PEI Elections Kill Fixed Election Dates?" 6 July. https://rainerknopff.ca/2015/12/10/did-the-2015-alberta-and-pei-elections -kill-fixed-election-dates-2/.

Lagassé, Philippe, and Patrick Baud. 2016. "The Crown and Constitutional Amendment after the *Senate Reform* and *Supreme Court* References." In *Constitutional Amendment in Canada*, edited by Emmett Macfarlane, 248–70. Toronto: University of Toronto Press.

Mahoney, James, and Kathleen Thelen. 2010. "A Theory of Gradual Institutional Change." In *Explaining Institutional Change: Ambiguity, Agency, and Power*, edited by James Mahoney and Kathleen Thelen, 1–37. Cambridge: Cambridge University Press.

Marquis, Melanie. 2015. "Fixed-Election Comes with Concerns, Say Observers." *Canadian Press*, July 5. http://www.nationalnewswatch.com/2015/07/05/fixed-date- election-comes-with-concerns-observers-say/#.WDX36LIrKUk.

Martin, Lawrence. 2014. "Harper's Election Timing? Expect the Unexpected." *Globe and Mail*, September 30. http://www.huffingtonpost.ca/2014/09/30/harpers-election- timing-e_n_5907860.html.

Nelson, Fraser. 2015. "This Act of Folly Has Condemned Us to Five Years of Political Torment." *Telegraph*, January 2. http://www.telegraph.co.uk/news/general-election -2015/11320637/This-Act-of-folly-has-condemned-us-to-five-years-of-political -torment.html.

Neudorf, Lorne. 2014. "In Defence of Fixed-Election Dates." *National Post*, October 8. http://news.nationalpost.com/full-comment/lorne-neudorf-in-defence-of -fixed-election-dates.

Reid, Scott. 2015. "The Case for a Spring Election." *Ottawa Citizen*, February 20. http:// ottawacitizen.com/opinion/columnists/reid-the-case-for-a-spring-election.

Rhodes, R.A.W., John Wanna, and Patrick Weller. 2011. *Comparing Westminster*. Oxford: Oxford University Press.

Robertson, James R. 2007. *Bill C-16: An Act to Amend the Canada Elections Act*. Library of Parliament, Parliamentary Information and Research Service, Legislative Summary, LS-530E.

Smith, Dale. 2015a. "No More Year-Long Elections, Please." *Loonie Politics*, January 13. http://looniepolitics.com/year-long-elections-please/.

–. 2015b. "Who Killed Question Period?" *National Post*, May 28. http://news.national post.com/full-comment/dale-smith-who-killed-question-period.

Smith, David E. 2013. *Across the Aisle: Opposition in Canadian Politics*. Toronto: University of Toronto Press.

UK HoC (United Kingdom House of Commons). 2004. *Taming the Prerogative: Strengthening Ministerial Accountability to Parliament*. Public Administration Select Committee, Fourth Report of Session 2003–4.

–. 2007. *The Governance of Britain Green Paper*. House of Commons Library, Research Paper 07/72.

Vennesson, Pascale. 2008. "Case Studies and Process Tracing: Theories and Practice." In *Approaches and Methodologies in the Social Sciences*, edited by Donatella Della Porta and Michael Keating, 223–39. Cambridge: Cambridge University Press. http:// dx.doi.org/10.1017/CBO9780511801938.013.

Warren, R. Michael. 2014. "Why Stephen Harper Will Call an Early Election." *Toronto Star*, November 9. https://www.thestar.com/opinion/commentary/2014/11/09/ stephen_harper_will_call_an_early_election.html.

Zurcher, Anthony. 2015. "Election 2015: The Americanisation of the UK Election." *BBC News Magazine*, April 1. http://www.bbc.com/news/magazine-32156264.

relating government advertising to the growing literature on the permanent campaign and the obvious incumbency advantages of using state resources to partisan ends, one must question whether partisan-tinged government advertising differs from normal partisan ads in its effects on the electorate. It is this topic of government partisan advertising that this chapter takes up directly.

Perhaps one of the most difficult aspects of the study of ostensibly partisan government advertising has been the basic task of definition. Indeed, the great majority of this work appears to follow former United States Supreme Court justice Potter Stewart's proclamation that "I shall not today attempt further to define the kinds of material I understand to be embraced within that shorthand description, and perhaps I could never succeed in intelligibly doing so. But I know it when I see it."[1] That said, however, the Ontario provincial government's *Government Advertising Act* of 2004 is a helpful guide. In it, government advertising is agreed to be partisan in nature if it contravenes any of the following conditions:

(a) it includes the name, voice or image of a member of the Executive Council or of a member of the Assembly, unless the item's primary target audience is located outside of Ontario;

(b) it includes the name or logo of a recognized party, within the meaning of subsection 62 (5) of the *Legislative Assembly Act*;

(c) it directly identifies and criticizes a recognized party or a member of the Assembly; or

(d) it includes, to a significant degree, a colour associated with the governing party.

While this definition is no doubt subject to interpretation, it provides a helpful benchmark from which we can proceed in understanding the substantive implications of such partisan works.

Government advertising over longer periods using extensive advertising buys can build a foundation and set the agenda for an upcoming election campaign (van Onselen and Errington 2007). In a sense, this is the basic foundation of the permanent campaign – constant messaging from governments hoping to secure another election win. The question is whether governments are cognizant of this fact and are spending state resources accordingly. Patterns of government spending on advertising here are highly suggestive.

From fiscal years 2002–3 to 2013–14, the Government of Canada spent
$1.074 billion (in 2015 dollars) on advertising, averaging $89.5 million per
year. In comparison, during that period the Office of the Auditor General of
Canada spent $100 million to fulfill its mandate (Office of the Auditor
General 2014), MPs spent $123.6 million on salaries, travel, and office ex-
penses (CBC News 2013), and the Canada Student Grants program spent
$50 million on grants for students with permanent disabilities (Employment
and Social Development Canada 2014). The progression of advertising
spending – spanning two political parties over a decade – can be seen in
Figure 10.1. As seen, the most spent in one year over this period was in
2009–10 ($148.9 million; Conservative government) followed by 2002–3
($136 million; Liberal government). In the most recent fiscal year for which
data were available at the time of writing (2013–14), the Government of
Canada spent $76.1 million. The objectives of the 2013–14 advertising cam-
paigns included efforts "to inform newcomers about the steps the Government of Canada is taking to create a fast and flexible immigration system"
($1.8 million), to "encourage taxpayers to claim the tax relief measures to

FIGURE 10.1

Government of Canada annual spending on advertising (2015, $million)

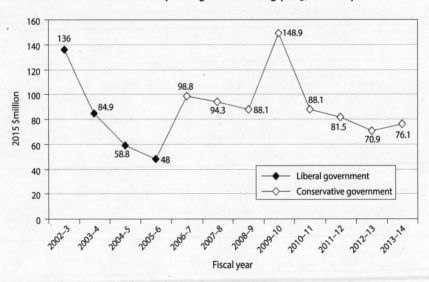

Fiscal year

SOURCE: Public Works and Government Services Canada 2015.

which they are entitled" ($5.7 million), "to inform Canadians of the tangible programs and benefits available to them through the Economic Action Plan" ($10.5 million), and "to encourage youth to pursue education in high demand fields and to inform Canadians of programs to support training and skills development to succeed in today's job market" ($11.3 million). In addition, there was also a campaign to "provide facts about Government of Canada telecommunications policy and measures to improve services and costs for consumers" at $7.6 million (Public Works and Government Services Canada 2015). Other advertising during this period promoted the government's efforts to increase competition in the wireless sector, to encourage youth to pursue skilled jobs, to recruit for the Canadian Armed Forces, and to raise awareness of the consequences of bullying.

As seen, actors in government from the two ruling parties over the past decade have routinely raided the coffers of the state to promote their own party. Not all of this government advertising is partisan in nature, of course, but politicians have strong incentives to align their official government communication with their ongoing campaign work. While the direct magnitude of this incumbency advantage is investigated in the following pages, it is important to place this government spending in perspective of the broader theme of the permanent campaign. As mentioned in Chapter 1, partisan use of government funds for campaigning purposes between elections is a particularly obvious manifestation of the permanent campaign in Canada. While the kinds of advertising employed by governments still differ from the kinds of advertising used directly by parties during official election periods – in particular, governments appear fairly cognizant of the potential public opinion backlash of including *overt* partisan signals in government advertising – the hope of partisans is that the same electoral effects of party advertisements can be replicated in more subtle government iterations.

Of course, the use of government advertising to promote policy changes or programs is not unique to Canada. In Australia, for instance, while governments have historically used advertising to communicate with the public, the coalition government led by John Howard became known for its increased use of government advertising. Spending increased from $61 million (in 2004 dollars) in 1991–92 to $240 million in 1999–2000 when the government introduced a national goods and services tax and employed extensive advertising to promote the tax change (van Onselen and Errington 2007). Moreover, the Howard government was heavily criticized for its use of government advertising in the lead-up to the 2004 Australian election because "the messages in that advertising were clearly coordinated with the Coalition's own campaign messages" (van Onselen and Errington 2007, 83).

Furthermore, Sally Young (2006) finds that in Australia there is a convergence between government and political advertising when it comes to spending, regulation, timing, content, media placement, and audiences. In doing so, political parties in power are increasingly coordinating their extra-parliamentary activities with the activities of government. This is the most visible and contentious manifestation of the permanent campaign: the use of public resources to partisan ends. Indeed, a similar pattern can be found in the circumstances that led Ontario to adopt the *Government Advertising Act* referenced above. In short, the Mike Harris Tories employed extensive partisan advertising while in power to bolster their party's communications strategy (Rose 2000, 3). The *Government Advertising Act* was brought in by Dalton McGuinty's Liberal government, though his Liberal successor Kathleen Wynne sought to water down the legislation's provisions.

The primary question here is whether citizens respond to government advertising that is ostensibly partisan, and if so, whether such advertisements are more effective than party messaging. There are compelling reasons to assume this may be the case. For one, government advertising could effectively avoid the tendency of citizens to selectively consume political media that are friendly to their existing predispositions (Prior 2007; Sears and Freedman 1967). This is a potentially powerful advantage harnessed exclusively by governments. As noted by early works documenting the surprisingly minimal effects of political party advertising, even the most influential ads are muted in their effect due to the propensity of a voter to "expose himself to the propaganda with which he already agrees, and to seal himself off from the propaganda with which he might disagree" (Lazarsfeld, Berelson, and Gaudet 1944, 1). If, however, government advertising *avoids* the kinds of party cues that alert voters to the partisan nature of advertising content (Iyengar and Valentino 2000), government advertisements may have significant effects across the entire ideological spectrum. Second, the Government of Canada is generally perceived to be a highly credible source of information, and decades of work in social psychology suggest that messages from such a source have powerful persuasive effects (e.g., Heesacker, Petty, and Cacioppo 1983; Hovland and Weiss 1951; Lupia and McCubbins 1998; Pornpitakpan 2004). This is especially true for those citizens who are unlikely to expend much cognitive effort processing the content of messages; the credibility of the source of information can significantly increase the likelihood of message acceptance *independent of the content of the message itself.*

To this end, before examining the impact of government advertising, we must first consider the theoretical mechanisms that inform our understanding of the interaction between source credibility and persuasion (see Druckman 2001b; Petty and Wegener 1998). On the one hand, there is near unanimity in social psychology research suggesting that, all else being equal, messaging from a high-credibility source is simply more persuasive than the same messaging from a low-credibility source (for a review, see Pornpitakpan 2004). On the other hand, social-psychological models of information processing suggest that not all people are equally likely to be swayed by the credibility of the source alone. Of note here is the elaboration likelihood model of persuasion effects developed by Richard Petty and John Cacioppo (1981).

In brief, the elaboration likelihood model asserts that there are two modes of information processing when one encounters a novel piece of information. The first, central route processing, is a high-effort and time-consuming mode of information processing whereby each message-relevant consideration in memory is brought to bear on the content of the message at hand. For those people employing this mode of cognition, the primary determinants of political persuasion will be the quality of the argument at hand and their pre-existing opinions. While the credibility of the source still influences persuasion here, its primary effect is to simply increase the amount of scrutiny one affords to the message (Petty and Wegener 1998).

For those at the other end of the elaboration continuum, however, we expect to see a mode of information processing known as peripheral route cognition (Petty and Cacioppo 1981). This mode of cognition, as compared to central route processing, tends to focus more on heuristic qualities of the communication rather than the content of the communication itself (on heuristics, see Popkin 1994). That is to say, rather than spend the time and effort dissecting the qualities of the argument at hand, peripheral route cognition instead focuses attention on simple rules of thumb that suggest whether the message ought to be accepted or not. With regard to source credibility, the heuristic here is that highly credible sources can be trusted and, as such, any message coming from such sources ought to be accepted without much consideration as to what that message may be.

Given the variable consequences of source credibility for those using central or peripheral route processing, the next logical step is to investigate whether there is a systematic pattern of use for each of these modes of cognition. While a variety of source, message, and communications mode effects exist that help determine the mode of information processing (see Petty and Wegener 1998 for an exhaustive review), the primary focus here is respondents' levels of education. While this will be fleshed out in greater detail in the next section, the crux of this argument is that highly educated respondents are most likely to systematically engage in high-effort central route cognition. In this sense, we ought to expect highly educated citizens to more actively lean on their existing opinions about the party in power when processing partisan government advertising as compared to less-educated citizens, who are likely swayed by the credibility of the source independent of their existing partisanship.

Put together, the above furnishes a number of expectations that will inform the empirical presentation of our case study. While the exact details will be fleshed out alongside a more in-depth presentation of the empirical strategies employed, the basic questions here are whether (1) citizens respond to partisan government advertisements differently than non-partisan government advertisements and (2) whether citizens of different levels of education lean on their existing attitudes towards the government of the day in differing magnitudes. Put formally, we test the following two hypotheses:

H1: Support for all forms of government advertising (partisan-leaning and information-leaning) will be correlated with the typical socio-demographic characteristics that are associated with support for the government of the day.

H2: Respondents of high education will respond to partisan government advertising as a greater function of their existing attitudes towards the government of the day as compared to respondents of lower education.

Case Study

METHOD

Survey data from public opinion research firm Abacus Data were used in this observational study. A total of 1,172 adult English-speaking Canadians (eighteen years of age or older) participated in the study as part of Abacus Data's April 2015 monthly omnibus survey. Participants were recruited randomly from Research Now, a national online panel provider. The sample was stratified and weighted to ensure that it was representative of the Canadian population.

The online survey was designed to show respondents two advertisements. Half of the group was randomly first shown a Government of Canada advertisement produced by the Canada Revenue Agency (CRA) to promote new tax measures implemented or proposed by the Government of Canada. In particular, the advertisement highlighted tax credits and benefits for "hard-working families," including the children's arts tax credit, the doubling of the children's fitness tax credit, and the new family tax cut, an income-splitting scheme targeted towards households with two parents and children under eighteen. The CRA advertisement also promoted the family caregiver tax credit that provides tax relief to those who provide care for aging family members. The other half of respondents was first shown a simple Canadian Armed Forces recruitment advertisement produced by the Department of National Defence (DND). Importantly, the DND advertisement did not concern partisan-leaning material, nor did it act as a framing attempt by the Conservatives to refocus attention towards favourable issue areas. In short, while the DND advertisement was obviously non-partisan, the CRA ad was tinged with partisan colouration for the ruling Conservative Party. In this way, the selection of the two advertisements provides us with a nice contrast between two kinds of government advertising: ads that may increase partisan support and non-partisan ads that serve government services. As the taxation information – income splitting in particular – would go on to be a central feature of the Conservative's re-election campaign, this partisan material clearly differs from the DND ad content. We thus label these advertisements as "partisan-leaning" and "information-leaning."

After being exposed to the first advertisement, respondents were asked a series of questions. They were then presented with the second advertisements (the DND advertisement for the first half of the sample and the CRA advertisement for the second half).

The variation in the subject matter of government advertising shown here is vitally important to separate respondents' general attitudes towards government advertising as opposed to their specific attitudes and responses to *partisan* government advertising. Recall that respondents were shown both a DND recruitment advertisement and a CRA advertisement promoting new tax measures – a core component of the Conservative government's re-election bid. Of note, the DND advertisement had very little partisan colouration or references to partisan material. Instead, the advertisement served to attract new recruits to the Canadian Forces. The CRA advertisement, on the other hand, was tinged with partisan material and positive affect towards the Conservative Party. While the advertisement was clearly a vehicle to inform citizens about existing tax policies of which they could take advantage, some of the content of the advertisement was, at the time of broadcast, still under consideration by Parliament and subject to its approval. In this sense, the advertisement appears to have been designed to champion the tax policies implemented or proposed by the Conservative government.

For each advertisement, respondents were asked whether they recalled seeing the ad (to check for respondent engagement with the survey) and their overall reaction to it (positive, neutral, or negative). A final question queried which of two statements came closest to their view about the ad they had just reviewed: "It is a legitimate use of public money to raise awareness about the [Canadian Forces/Tax Reform]" or "It is an effort by the Conservatives to use public money for their advantage," with an additional category of "Unsure."

FINDINGS

To begin, we investigate the socio-demographic characteristics associated with support for each of the two video advertisements shown to respondents. This will allow us to understand the socio-demographic foundations of support for government advertising *writ large* as well as specific support for partisan-leaning government ads. If there is no difference between the two patterns of support, then it would appear as though partisan-leaning government advertising does not effectively move the needle any more than strictly factual government ads do. The dependent variable here for each advertisement is respondents' summary reaction to each ad, measured via a simple five-point scale (*Very Positive / Positive / Neutral / Negative / Very Negative*) that has been recoded to the (0,1) interval such that *Very Positive* is (1) and *Very Negative* is (0). Ultimately, a paired *t*-test reveals that the DND advertisement elicited a more positive reaction ($M = 0.65$; $SD = 0.24$) than the CRA advertisement ($M = 0.58$; $SD = 0.64$; $t(1293) = -9.19$, $p < .01$). Delving deeper, Table 10.1 highlights some of the socio-demographic characteristics associated with support or disapproval of each advertisement.

Looking first at the reactions to the partisan-leaning CRA advertisement, we see that the effect appears to be concentrated in the Conservative Party's

Table 10.1

Who responds to government advertising

	(1) CRA ad		(2) DND ad	
Female	0.018	(0.01)	0.001	(0.01)
Retired	0.030*	(0.02)	−0.018	(0.02)
Age	−0.002***	(0.00)	0.002***	(0.00)
Female with children	0.064***	(0.02)	−0.009	(0.02)
Male with children	−0.001	(0.02)	0.033	(0.02)
Education	−0.012*	(0.01)	−0.022***	(0.01)
Taxes most important issue	−0.019	(0.01)	0.022	(0.01)
Job creation most important issue	0.024**	(0.01)	0.012	(0.01)
Approval of government	0.044***	(0.01)	0.016	(0.01)
Impression of Harper	0.009	(0.01)	0.026***	(0.01)
Economic evaluations	0.025**	(0.01)	0.018	(0.01)
Next six months' economy	0.054***	(0.01)	0.048***	(0.01)
Tax change ad viewed second	0.001	(0.01)	0.030**	(0.01)
Constant	0.319***	(0.04)	0.255***	(0.05)
R^2	0.257		0.148	
Degrees of freedom	1279		1279	
N	1293		1293	

NOTE: Standard error in parentheses; * $p < .10$; ** $p < .05$; *** $p < .01$.

usual support groups. That is, less educated and retired individuals were more likely to have positive reactions to the advertisement. Likewise, the usual metrics indicating government approval – positive retrospective and prospective economic evaluations and government approval – also tabbed higher support for the CRA advertisement. Finally, those respondents who believed job creation to be the most important political issue – a recent Conservative area of issue ownership – also rated the advertisement more highly than those whose priorities lay elsewhere. Interesting to note, however, that respondents' impressions of Prime Minister Stephen Harper do not appear to have influenced reactions to the advertisement and, perhaps most interesting, younger respondents were more likely to support the tax advertisement than older respondents, who tend to be the Conservative Party's usual base of support. While this may be particular to the specific measures introduced in the taxation advertisement, it is a hint that perhaps there are some cross-cutting effects of partisan government advertising, limited though they may be.

But along with a more positive reaction from those who had a favourable disposition towards the federal government, the CRA tax change advertisement also scored positively with mothers of children under fifteen years of age. In fact, the coefficient estimate is largest with this group. Women with children are an important constituency for the Conservative Party. According to the 2011 Canadian Election Study (CES) (Fournier, Cutler, Soroka, and Stolle 2011), 35 percent of women with children under eighteen years of age in the household voted Conservative in 2011, the same percentage who reported voting Conservative in the full CES sample. In the Abacus Data survey, on the other hand, support for the Conservatives among decided female respondents with children is approximately 19 percent.[2] If the Conservative Party felt they were losing support among this key group, this might explain the advertisement's focus on tax measures designed to appeal to this voter subset. The focus of the advertisement on family-friendly policies would appeal the most to those with children, particularly women. That said, this is speculative on our part, as our data can illuminate only the broad correlates of support and not the specific reasons for those patterns or the strategic reasoning behind the advertisement's design.

Further, the CRA advertisement also promoted the family caregiver tax credit, which provides tax relief to those who provide care for aging family members, no doubt something that appeals to those caring for aging parents, mostly women, but also those who are retired and require care or may require care in the future. This might explain why retired respondents reacted more positively to the advertisement.

Though the findings here are interesting in their own right – indicating that government partisan advertising that has become synonymous with the permanent campaign impacts those people already predisposed to support the present government, as well as, it seems, key voter targets for the incumbent political party – it is worthwhile to investigate whether such patterns of support are ubiquitous across *all* government advertising. To this end, Model 2 in Table 10.1 analyzes patterns of support for the information-leaning Canadian Armed Forces recruitment advertisement. However, as comparing coefficients across models can be difficult, Figure 10.2 graphically plots the coefficients alongside their respective confidence intervals (CIs) to investigate whether the various government ads captured the support of different segments of the population.

FIGURE 10.2

OLS regression estimates for government advertisements

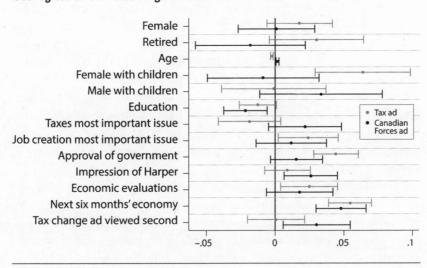

As seen in Figure 10.2 and broadly hinted in Table 10.1, the two advertisements appear to roughly correspond in their respective favourable audiences. While we may be capturing some overlapping dynamics of support between the Canadian Forces and the ruling Conservative Party (i.e., that people that most support the Canadian Forces may also be most apt to find the Conservative advertising favourable as well), the patterns here strongly suggest that government advertising of all types is mostly directed towards in-group partisans. However, the significant effect on women with children and retired respondents that exists in the CRA advertisement model disappears in the model testing reaction to the Canadian Forces recruitment advertisement – though the difference between the coefficient estimates is not significant at the $p < .05$ level.

To sum up, it appears that both partisan-leaning and information-leaning government advertising tend to find traction with roughly the same constituencies, but politically targeted advertising that promotes policies directed at specific groups can perhaps reactivate patterns of support for waning subpopulations. That said, and similar to the minimal effects literature (e.g., Berelson, Lazarsfeld, and McPhee 1954; Campbell et al. 1960; Patterson and McClure 1976), the patterns of support suggested in Table 10.1

strongly suggest that support for government advertisements are endogenous to support for the government party itself. While we cannot investigate whether such advertisements are effectively priming or framing other groups to think more deeply about Conservative Party issues, the direct effect of these ads appears to concentrate on traditional support groups for that party (on framing, see Chong and Druckman 2007; Druckman 2001a; Iyengar 1991; on priming, see Iyengar and Kinder 1987; Krosnick and Kinder 1990; Tversky and Kahneman 1981). Notably, the results also suggest that government advertising that is targeted towards particular voter groups (as the CRA advertisement was to women with children) may positively influence perceptions about government policy and the incumbent political party in those groups.

To recall the theoretical discussion, we ought to expect the most powerful effects of advertisements to be concentrated among those citizens engaging in peripheral route cognition. It is these voters who will defer to the apparent expertise of the Government of Canada while ignoring the substantive content of the messaging and, in particular, whether it contradicts their existing attitudes. For those engaged in central route cognition, on the other hand, we should see the content of the advertisement weigh more heavily on their subsequent information processing, and, most importantly, their prior attitudes should cast a significantly long shadow on their developing attitudes towards the advertisements.

To help systematically separate those who are most likely to use central route cognition from those who will defer to the heuristics cues of peripheral route cognitive processes, the present study uses respondents' levels of education. While a direct battery measuring respondents' level of need for cognition would be theoretically ideal (on need for cognition, see Cacioppo and Petty 1982), level of formal education is a compelling proxy in its own right. For one, education, especially post-secondary education, endows citizens with the kinds of cognitive resources and political engagement necessary to think deeply about political issues (on the relationship between education and politics, see Verba, Schlozman, and Brady 1995). Put in the terminology of social psychology, such resources and engagement give respondents the motivation and ability to thoughtfully process message argumentation, carefully weighing each consideration against their bank of considerations that exist in short- and long-term memory (see Petty and Wegener 1998). Second, direct tests of the relationship between education and need for cognition reveal that the association is "reliable and in the expected direction" (Cacioppo et al. 1996, 217). Need for cognition, in sum, is a general dispositional trait that certain individuals possess that makes them more likely to use central route cognition. In this sense, education is a theoretically convincing mechanism to tab respondents' use of central route cognition. For the present study, we ought to expect the effect of prior attitudes to weigh much more heavily for highly educated respondents in response to partisan government advertising than for less educated respondents.

To come to a measure of education, all respondents with a high school education or less ($n = 539$) were given a score of (0), while those with at least some post-secondary schooling were given a score of (1) ($n = 961$). To gauge a more nuanced reaction to the partisan advertisement of the CRA, respondents were asked whether they believed the ad that they watched was "a legitimate use of public money to raise awareness about Tax Reform" (1) or "an effort by the Conservatives to use public money for their advantage" (0), or whether they were "unsure" (0.5). The summary measure has a mean of 0.47 and a standard deviation of 0.45, indicating that, in general, all respondents did see the ad as roughly partisan-leaning. Finally, to get a sense of respondents' prior attitudes, a general question was administered prior to the advertisements that asked about their approval of the Consertive government, using a five-point scale (*Strongly Disapprove / Somewhat Disapprove / Neither Approve nor Disapprove / Somewhat Approve / Strongly Approve*). After recoding to the (0,1) interval, this measure has a mean of 0.45 and a standard deviation of 0.32.

To probe the influence of source credibility on the different segments of the population of interest, we employed an ordered-logit regression equation (reporting odds ratios) with a simple interaction between levels of education and respondents' attitudes towards the Harper government. If the proposed hypothesis regarding the interaction between source credibility and central route cognition holds, we should expect this interactive term to be statistically significant and have an odds ratio larger than one.

Looking at Table 10.2, it appears as though respondents of high education did indeed respond to the partisan-leaning government ad as a function of their prior opinion about the government. In short, the effect of prior attitudes on respondents' feelings about the legitimacy of the advertisement was significantly more powerful for those respondents who are highly educated. This significant increase in the overall impact of prior attitudes again suggests that those who attended more actively towards the content of the

Table 10.2

The effect of education and prior attitudes on advertising support

	(1) CRA ad	
Education	0.599**	(0.13)
Government approval	11.556***	(3.56)
Education x Government approval	2.625**	(1.01)
R^2	0.03	
N	1,292	

NOTE: Ordered-logit regression reporting odds ratios; * $p < .10$; ** $p < .05$; *** $p < .01$.

message were more powerfully swayed by their pre-existing attitudes than the highly credible government advertisement. However, respondents' feelings towards the Conservative government also mattered a great deal for those with low education. The more that respondents with low education liked the Harper government, the more likely they were to be higher on the response scale measuring their attitudes towards the specific advertisement. Again, this was a substantial effect of prior attitudes that was even more powerful for the highly educated.

This case study yields a set of results that, taken together, are broadly consistent with the existing literature on party advertising. Despite compelling theoretical expectations that government advertising may be more cross-cutting and effective in its direct persuasive results, the evidence here suggests a more mundane and partisan explanation: the advertisements were best received by those who were predisposed to accept them. In a sense, this is unsurprising. After all, decades of research into political persuasion suggests that citizens are either aware enough to reject counterattitudinal messaging or so tuned out from politics as to miss the signal of advertisements altogether (see Zaller 1992 for an in-depth treatment). Along this vein, the results presented above fit neatly into an existing literature that has long espoused the role of pre-existing attitudes rather than direct persuasion of television advertisements. While this does not discount the ability of television ads to effectively frame public opinion (Iyengar 1991), it does suggest that worries about the nefarious use of government resources for partisan ends to persuade citizens to support the incumbent party ought to be refocused more intently on the normative debate about the use of state resources in this manner in the first place, rather than the apparent power of these ads to sway large segments of the population.

Going further, the above results suggest that well-targeted advertisements can perhaps bring sagging partisans back into the fold by bundling micro-targeted government activities in neat advertising packages. In particular, women with children under the age of fifteen – a constituency that appears in our data to have moved away from the Conservative Party – may have been reactivated by the CRA advertisement. While it is difficult to say what the direct effect of the advertisement might have been on their vote intentions, we can clearly see the enthusiastic response of this subpopulation to this particular facet of the permanent campaign.

Permanent Campaigning in Canada

Government advertising is neither new nor likely to disappear. Though the tone of these advertisements may shift with the incoming Liberal government – though that remains to be seen – it is unlikely they will disappear altogether. What is new, however, is the more overt use of government resources for partisan ends in advertising. Whether through framing, priming, or direct persuasive effects, the worry here is that incumbents enjoy an electoral advantage far beyond what we might consider reasonable. They do this by harnessing the power of the state to saturate the population with government promotional messaging. What our case study suggests is that while government advertising is more positively received by those who have a favourable predisposition to the government and party in power, well-targeted advertisements can potentially stoke the flames of support from groups whose approval of the incumbent party had begun to fade.

Still, what this research suggests is that this incumbency advantage is concentrated on subpopulations of citizens who are already likely to vote for the ruling party. While there is no doubt an advantage to effectively rallying the base or reactivating certain partisans, fears that the permanent government advertisement campaign may sway large tracts of the population do not appear to be particularly well founded. Of course, this is not to downplay the normative and substantive objections to the use of state resources for partisan means, but it ought to focus our thinking more clearly on the kinds of citizens that are likely to accept the messaging contained in these ads and their potential impact on citizens and voters. Moreover, we might question whether a governing party recognizes that such advertising has a limited effect.

In particular, our research suggests that the direct effect of the government partisan ads may be larger for respondents who do not expend a great deal of cognitive effort thinking about political matters. While the above study shows that these voters do respond to advertising as a function of their prior attitudes, the more educated and engaged respondents were able to connect their existing opinions of the Harper government with their responses to the partisan advertising in a much more substantive manner. The worry here, then, is that the increased reach of government advertising – during prime-time television hours and major sporting events, for example – may more effectively command the attention of Canadians who are not usually exposed to partisan advertising. Less able to recognize the partisan colouration of these ads, such voters may simply respond to the high credibility of the messages' source rather than attempt to connect implicitly partisan advertising with their existing opinions about the government of the day. Though the above research makes clear that these citizens still attend to their existing opinions, even small changes in the balance of their considerations about the government can have large perceptive effects that, alongside the cumulative effects of repeated advertising campaigns, could sway public opinion. In this sense, the implications of the permanent campaign are clear: despite murky evidence about its broad effectiveness, the risk/reward ratio for governments is too lopsided to ignore the potential for these ads to court voters.

What's more, as the present research is mainly concerned with citizens' *direct* responses to advertisements, we cannot say whether the true effect of government campaigns was in framing and priming the electorate to think about issue areas dominated by the Conservative Party (Iyengar 1991). In fact, the bulk of the literature on political advertising suggests this may in fact be the primary mechanism of influence for such public opinion campaigns. Rather than directly change voters' minds about the Conservative government, this literature suggests that television ads were particularly effective at changing the cognitive foundations of voters' decision-making criteria. By thus bathing the public in information about economic policies – a recent area of strength for the Conservative Party – the permanent campaign may gradually shift the voting calculus of the public to weigh economic considerations more heavily in their final vote choice. By effectively leveraging the built-in incumbency advantages of media support, ruling parties are no doubt given much better access to framing and agenda-setting mechanisms.

Still, without direct evidence of such framing and priming effects, we are left with a conclusion that perhaps sits uneasily with the ongoing narrative regarding the permanent campaign in government: such advertisements are largely preaching to the choir. While this may be particularly effective when some members of the choir are losing faith, the overall results here suggest that there are few direct cross-cutting effects for government partisan advertisements.

NOTES

1 Jacobellis v. Ohio, 378 U.S. 184 (1964), 197.
2 Considering the sample size ($n = 138$), the estimate ranges from 11 percent to 28 percent.

REFERENCES

Berelson, Bernard R., Paul F. Lazarsfeld, and William N. McPhee. 1954. *Voting: A Study of Opinion Formation in a Presidential Campaign.* Chicago: University of Chicago Press.

Cacioppo, John T., and Richard E. Petty. 1982. "The Need for Cognition." *Journal of Personality and Social Psychology* 42 (1): 116–31. http://dx.doi.org/10.1037/0022-3514.42.1.116.

Cacioppo, John T., Richard E. Petty, Jeffrey A. Feinstein, and W. Blair G. Jarvis. 1996. "Dispositional Differences in Cognitive Motivation: The Life and Times of Individuals Varying in Need for Cognition." *Psychological Bulletin* 119 (2): 197–253. http://dx.doi.org/10.1037/0033-2909.119.2.197.

Campbell, Angus, Philip Converse, Warren Miller, and Donald Stokes. 1960. *The American Voter.* New York: Wiley.

CBC News. 2013. "MPs Spend over $123.6M in Office and Other Expenses." September 30. http://www.cbc.ca/news/politics/mps-spend-over-123-6m-in-office-and-other-expenses-1.1873801.

Chong, Dennis, and James Druckman. 2007. "Framing Public Opinion in Competitive Democracies." *American Political Science Review* 101 (4): 637–55. http://dx.doi.org/10.1017/S0003055407070554.

Dougan, Laura. 2007. "What Does It Really Mean to Be Partisan? An Analysis of Government Advertising in Ontario." Paper presented at the Annual Meeting of the Canadian Political Science Association. Saskatoon, June 1.

Druckman, James N. 2001a. "The Implications of Framing Effects for Citizen Competence." *Political Behavior* 23 (3): 225–56. http://dx.doi.org/10.1023/A:1015006907312.

–. 2001b. "Using Credible Advice to Overcome Framing Effects." *Journal of Law Economics and Organization* 17 (1): 62–82. http://dx.doi.org/10.1093/jleo/17.1.62.

Employment and Social Development Canada. 2014. *Canada Student Loans Program Annual Report 2012–2013.* Ottawa: Government of Canada.

Fournier, Patrick, Fred Cutler, Stuart Soroka, and Dietlind Stolle. 2011. The 2011 Canadian Election Study. [dataset]. http://ces-eec.arts.ubc.ca/english-section/surveys/.

Government Advertising Act, S.O. 2004, C 20.

Heesacker, Martin, Richard E. Petty, and John T. Cacioppo. 1983. "Field Dependence and Attitude Change: Source Credibility Can Alter Persuasion by Affecting Message-Relevant Thinking." Journal of Personality 51 (4): 653–66. http://dx.doi.org/10.1111/j.1467-6494.1983.tb00872.x.

Hovland, Carl I., and Walter Weiss. 1951. "The Influence of Source Credibility on Communication Effectiveness." Public Opinion Quarterly 15 (4): 635–50. http://dx.doi.org/10.1086/266350.

Iyengar, Shanto. 1991. Is Anyone Responsible? How Television Frames Political Issues. Chicago: University of Chicago Press. http://dx.doi.org/10.7208/chicago/9780226388533.001.0001.

Iyengar, Shanto, and Donald Kinder. 1987. News That Matters: Television and American Opinion. Chicago: University of Chicago Press.

Iyengar, Shanto, and Nicholas Valentino. 2000. "Who Says What? Source Credibility as a Mediator of Campaign Advertising." In Elements of Reason: Cognition, Choice, and the Bounds of Rationality, edited by A. Lupia, M.D. McCubbins, and S.L. Popkin, 108–29. New York: Cambridge University Press. http://dx.doi.org/10.1017/CBO9780511805813.006.

Krosnick, Jon A., and Donald Kinder. 1990. "Altering the Foundations of Support for the President through Priming." American Political Science Review 84 (2): 497–512. http://dx.doi.org/10.2307/1963531.

Lazarsfeld, Paul F., Bernard Berelson, and Hazel Gaudet. 1944. The People's Choice. New York: Duell, Sloan and Pearce.

Lupia, Arthur, and Matthew McCubbins. 1998. The Democratic Dilemma: Can Citizens Learn What They Need to Know? New York: Cambridge University Press.

Nesbitt-Larking, Paul, and Jonathan Rose. 2004. "Political Advertising in Canada." In Lights, Camera, Campaign! Media, Politics, and Political Advertising, edited by D.A. Schultz, 273–99. New York: Peter Lang.

Office of the Auditor General of Canada. 2014. Performance Report of the Office of the Auditor General of Canada. Ottawa: Government of Canada.

Patterson, Thomas E., and Robert D. McClure. 1976. The Unseeing Eye: The Myth of Television Power in National Elections. New York: G.P. Putnam's Sons.

Petty, Richard E., and John T. Cacioppo. 1981. Attitudes and Persuasion: Classic and Contemporary Approaches. Dubuque, IA: Wm. C. Brown.

Petty, Richard E., and Duane T. Wegener. 1998. "Attitude Change: Multiple Roles for Persuasion Variables." In The Handbook of Social Psychology, vol. 1, edited by D.T. Gilbert, S.T. Fiske, and G. Lindzey, 323–90. Boston: McGraw-Hill.

Popkin, Samuel. 1994. The Reasoning Voter: Communication and Persuasion in Presidential Campaigns. Chicago: University of Chicago Press.

Pornpitakpan, Chanthika. 2004. "The Persuasiveness of Source Credibility: A Critical Review of Five Decades' Evidence." Journal of Applied Social Psychology 34 (2): 243–81. http://dx.doi.org/10.1111/j.1559-1816.2004.tb02547.x.

Prior, Markus. 2007. *Post-Broadcast Democracy: How Media Choice Increases Inequality in Political Involvement and Polarizes Elections*. New York: Cambridge University Press. http://dx.doi.org/10.1017/CBO9781139878425.

Public Works and Government Services Canada. 2015. *2013–2014 Annual Report on Government of Canada Advertising Activities*. Ottawa: Government of Canada.

Rose, Jonathan. 2000. *Making "Pictures in Our Heads": Government Advertising in Canada*. Westport, CT: Praeger.

–. 2001. "The Advertising of Politics and the Politics of Advertising." In *Communication in Canadian Society*, edited by B. Singer and C. McKie. Toronto: Nelson. 151–64.

–. 2003. "Government Advertising and the creation of National Myths: The Canadian Case." *International Journal of Nonprofit and Voluntary Sector Marketing* 8 (2): 153–65. http://dx.doi.org/10.1002/nvsm.209.

Rutherford, Paul. 2000. *Endless Propaganda: The Advertising of Public Goods*. Toronto: University of Toronto Press.

Sears, David O., and Jonathan Freedman. 1967. "Selective Exposure to Information: A Critical Review." *Public Opinion Quarterly* 31 (2): 194–213. http://dx.doi.org/10.1086/267513.

Tversky, Amos, and Daniel Kahneman. 1981. "The Framing of Decisions and the Psychology of Choice." *Science* 211 (4481): 453–58. http://dx.doi.org/10.1126/science.7455683.

van Onselen, Peter, and Wayne Errington. 2007. "The Democratic State as a Marketing Tool: The Permanent Campaign in Australia." *Commonwealth & Comparative Studies* 45: 78–94.

Verba, Sidney, Kay Lehman Schlozman, and Henry Brady. 1995. *Voice and Equality: Civic Voluntarism in American Politics*. Cambridge: Harvard University Press.

Young, Sally. 2006. "The Convergence of Political and Government Advertising: Theory versus Practice." *Media International: Australia Culture and Policy* 119: 99–111.

Zaller, John. 1992. *The Nature and Origins of Mass Opinion*. Cambridge: Cambridge University Press. http://dx.doi.org/10.1017/CBO9780511818691.

11

The Obama Approach in Canada: Lessons in Leadership Branding

J.P. Lewis and Kenneth Cosgrove

This chapter examines political branding and the permanent campaign in Canada, with special attention to developments in the United States. With Canada and the United States having different political, government, and party systems, comparing the two countries provides a unique examination of how political branding and the permanent campaign affect political institutions. This chapter considers the uses of pre-branding by US president Barack Obama and, in a longer case study, by Canadian prime minister Stephen Harper in the 2011 and 2015 campaigns. Both the Obama and Harper cases demonstrate the accelerated and sweeping adoption of political branding and the concomitant use of pre-branding against opponents. The two countries have developed a political marketing and branding orientation in their politics and, specifically in Canada, in government (Cormack 2012; Cosgrove 2007; Marland 2014; Marland and Flanagan 2013). As well, the two countries have been the focus of numerous comparative political studies, including notable work by political scientist Seymour Lipset (1990).

The brand can be summed up as the total user experience with the product (Zyman and Brott 2003) and has been used in American politics at least since the Reagan years (Cosgrove 2007). Parties and governments build brands to give voters visual and emotive cues that shape a properly positioned identity. A political brand can be applied to policies, parties, and individual candidates and lets a party present itself to either the whole electorate or targeted segments. A political brand is a powerful tool, but its impact is influenced by conditions in the country in which it is being presented and by the construction of that country's political and party systems. For example, the Republican brand worked in the United States in the 2000s but is struggling at present because of changing audiences and issue challenges. Political brands resemble commercial brands in how they define the product for the customer. As Volvo came to be connected to safety (Newman 1999), Bill Clinton came to articulate a new kind of Democrat.

A political brand helps to produce the kind of single ballot-box question that often confronts Canadian voters. The Canadian ballot-box question centres on the branded leader, their policies, and their personal traits. For example, former Conservative prime minister Stephen Harper's opponents insisted for years that he had a hidden agenda to transform the country. For their part, in the 2015 campaign, much of the Conservative effort was dedicated to presenting Justin Trudeau as being "just not ready." By others' making and their own, Canadian politicians' fates are bound together in a single party brand and by a single party platform (for an in-depth description of Canadian parties and their ability to discipline members, see Cross 2004).

A brand is an emotive tool that fits with the human experience of politics (Westen 2008). Brands are flexible and can be adjusted to fit the product of the moment, a long-term building plan, or a personality; a brand can be employed to build lasting relationships in politics. The brand can adjust to new actors, policies, or changes in strategic circumstances. Brands provide the pictures in our head and emotions to sum up a product. Branding exercises help to produce consistent political messaging and a common political product. Thus, they offer politicians an opportunity to sell themselves efficiently to voters. Recent work has started to make the connection between branding and changing political environments, particularly as a response to communications technologies. Crowdsourcing has been employed in both the United States and Canada as part of the brand-creation and -dissemination processes. Joseph Trippi (2004) writes extensively about crowdsourcing in the 2004 Howard Dean campaign, and Brad Lavigne (2014) does the same regarding the NDP's use of crowdsourcing to build success in Quebec in the 2011 federal election and the so-called Orange Wave. Crowdsourcing is an innovation that has made the public feel that they are co-creators of brands and products (Tapscott and Williams 2010). Social media are conduits for co-creation and customer evangelism through shares or likes or favourites on Facebook and Twitter. Such amplification gives the brand more credibility than it would have were its message coming from a stranger, an advertisement, or earned media, and it offers the potential to get the brand out to more people at a lower cost than through traditional media. Social media and co-creation of content have democratized brands and encouraged political marketers to provide customers with actual or potential experiences with their brands. Such experiential marketing is frequently part of an effort to attract low-dollar donors by holding online raffles that require a small donation in exchange for a chance at winning special perks, such as lunch with a candidate (see Chapter 5). The trend in both the United States and Canada of co-opting the creation of a political brand with a partisan base makes the articulation and execution of a brand even more crucial.

Still, while common political branding and communication trends persist, there are effects from different political systems. American parties are more ideological than they used to be, but they still have a long way to go before they approach the strong party system in Canada. The difference in party strength is reflected in the coherence of party brands. Canadian party brands are more coherent than American party brands. American parties face the problem of candidates adopting an unfocused and varied approach to the party brand or developing personal brands – traits that would not be tolerated in the strong party leader–centric context of Canadian political branding. In the United States, the tendency towards individual entrepreneurship and personal branding is accentuated because of the three-tiered system of presidential, Senate, and House elections, in which each office has its own electoral constituency. Canadian candidates are locked into the party brand and the brand is built around the leader.

The notion of divided government is relatively common in the United States (Mayhew 1991). While it offers brand-building opportunities, it also threatens brand coherence. Given that a Speaker of the House functions as leader of the opposition during times when the presidency is controlled by one party and the House by the other (Peters 1997) and party caucuses brand themselves (Rosenthal and Peters 2010), when a candidate like Barack Obama in 2008 comes along saying something different from the party brand, the emphasis on the candidate will increase and the party brand can lose coherence and relevance. On the upside, American parties gain a built-in excuse for their delivery and performance failures, as these can be explained away as the fault of the party in charge of another branch. Further, proposals can be made that, while popular with target audiences, have no real hope of legislative success, and investigations can be initiated that are partly aimed at brand building.

A method to corral the ideas of the de facto government or opposition is the use of platform brands. In the United States, platform or single-use brands have been used recently by the party that does not control the White

House. This party's purpose is to win back or maintain control of Congress; the goal of the effort is to thwart the incumbent president's policy agenda. Examples include the *Contract with America* from the Republicans, *6 for '06* by the Democrats, and the negative branding built for use in 2010 and 2014 by the Republicans around specific aspects of Barack Obama. In each of these cases, the party that did not control the White House was seeking to negatively define the party that did control it. This activity differs from what opposition parties do in Canada, because it has electoral and policy consequences that do not entail an incumbent president losing his position, as would happen if a governing party lost an election in Canada. The difference is one of political system. American House elections take place every two years, one-third of the Senate is up for election every two years, and the president is up once every four years. Thus, every president will be in office during a House and Senate election that does not also feature a presidential contest. Congressional incumbents tied to an unpopular president stress their personal brands by pointing out the benefits they have brought and their personal ties to the district (Fenno 1978). This individualistic orientation is not found in Canada's strong party system, which makes parliamentarians an afterthought in the overall campaign, often only newsworthy for embarrassing actions.

Canada's party brands are adjusted to fit the leader. Individual candidates do not deviate from the party brand. Canada normally has a longer period between the time the leader is picked and the writ dropping than what takes place in the United States, and this too encourages brand coherence. Both NDP leader Tom Mulcair and Liberal leader Justin Trudeau were party leaders for more than two years before the start of the 2015 federal election. Thus, the NDP and the Liberal Party of Canada had time to develop their brands during the permanent campaign. This long brand-building window is important, because the Canadian selling period is shorter than that in the United States. The difference in duration is shown by the reaction to the unusually long eleven-week Canadian federal election campaign in 2015, which was well above the country's average of fifty days (Deachman 2015), though still much shorter than the American experience of an almost year-long nomination and general election period.

In both countries, a party's brand is disseminated through paid advertising, earned media events, and social media. All three generate buzz about and impressions for the party's brand, leader, and products. Earned and social media are quite important in the Canadian system given the restrictions on campaign spending (for more on this, see Chapter 6 by Thierry Giasson and Tamara Small). In Canada, events like budget day and the opening session of Parliament can provide earned media and social media brand-building opportunities. Both countries give significant advantage to incumbents because they control the institutions of government and symbols of officialdom and can decide which issues, individuals, and regions are the focus of their earned media efforts, all of which are key parts of signalling audiences and teaching them about the brand. Before a fixed-date election law came to Canada, the party that formed the government had control over when an election was contested, unlike in the fixed-calendar American system.

The calendar matters a great deal in mid-term elections in the United States, because only one-third of the Senate stands for election in a given cycle. The way in which state legislatures have drawn congressional districts can go a long way towards shaping the competitive environment in which an election occurs. For example, during the 2008 and 2012 elections, Obama was the strongest aspect of the brand on which Democrats ran. These presidential elections had high voter turnout, something that presently rewards Democrats (Hacker 2014) and mutes the impact of Republican dominance of state legislatures and therefore the way in which House districts are drawn (Issenberg 2014; Liptak 2012). Obama's brand was at least as strong as the Democratic Party's brand by the time he won the election, but he was not on the ballot in the 2010 and 2014 mid-terms, meaning that many of his best customers had little incentive to participate in these elections. The power of the Obama brand was further limited as Republicans specifically set out to create a large number of favourable House districts by capturing as many state legislatures as they could after 2008 (state legislatures draw House districts) (Rove 2010). Further, in 2014, many of the Senate seats that were up were in states that were not favourable for Democrats. There are many explanations for the surge and decline phenomenon in Democratic mid-term turnout. Jacob Hacker (2014) points to voter identification and registration requirements, while the Democrats' own post-mortem argued that it was a result of campaign finance rules, the lack of a party-based brand narrative, and the resulting failure to develop strong customer relationships (Knickerbocker 2015). Republicans used the platform brand strategy to tie Democratic congressional candidates to an unpopular Obama, and the Democrats responded with no consistent brand. Add this to the unfavourable markets and it is clear why the Democrats have struggled in elections when Barack Obama and his strong personal brand were not directly on the ballot. The inability of the Democrats to translate the strong Obama personal brand onto their congressional candidates nicely illustrates the problems of meshing personal and political brands in the United States, a situation that does not exist in Canada.

Barack Obama has a strong personal brand. He was able to use it in 2012 to win re-election in what appeared to be a difficult market for an incumbent. As an incumbent, he did not have to campaign to win the nomination, but instead could use the primary process to reinforce the positive parts of his brand while negatively branding his likely general election opponent, Republican candidate Mitt Romney. Obama's campaign kicked off in April 2011 by releasing a new logo for 2012 that featured the stylized letter "O" used in the 2008 logo, this time part of the year 2012 (Thrush and Epstein 2011). A year later, Obama's team again used a video to release what would be its general election logo, "Forward," to supporters (James 2012). Released at the end of the primary season, the "Forward" logo kept with the concept of the one-word brand articulated by Saatchi.[1]

Contrasting his brand with that of his Republican opponent, Obama argued that voting for Romney would be a return to a dark past, either that of the previous Bush administration or as an out-of-touch plutocrat (Heilemann 2012). As Mark Penn (2011) notes, Labour leader Tony Blair did something similar in the UK. To avoid making the 2005 campaign into a referendum on his own leadership, Blair and his party used the theme of "Forward, Not Back" to create an electoral choice between the Labour Party or a return to failed Conservative policies (Penn 2011). The logo and slogan "Forward" offered a way for Obama to change the public perception of weak leadership and build up his positive brand equity during the Republican nomination process (Penn 2011).

The permanent campaign was at work during the lengthy period when the Democrats could brand Mitt Romney. The Obama campaign portrayed a specific version of Romney during the long Republican primary that saw Romney fending off a series of well-financed conservative challengers who were kept viable by the proportional delegate-allocation system (Schlesinger 2012). Conservatives were not happy with Romney, because he had been the governor of a liberal state and had a strong personal brand as a pragmatic leader. Both of these traits differed significantly from the conservatism at the core of the Republican house brand (Cosgrove 2014). Thus, he made claims to being "severely conservative" (O'Brien 2012) during the primary to solve his conservative base problem, but doing so raised charges that he was an opportunist lacking core convictions. The Obama campaign was happy to help that impression develop as part of its negative branding strategy (Schlesinger 2012). Romney's time spent shoring up his right flank shows the need to build a strong brand from which a campaign does not deviate.

Divided government helped Obama with his use of branding against Romney and the Grand Old Party (GOP). The president issued executive orders popular with his target audiences. The Democrats, who controlled the Senate, passed bills sure to be popular with targeted audiences that had no chance of passing the Republican-dominated House, which for its part did the same with bills popular with GOP targets. The Democrats used their Senate majority to express views about Mitt Romney that could have been the subject of litigation off the Senate floor, where senatorial speech is legally protected. Senator Harry Reid (D-Nevada), who was majority leader in 2012, justified his dishonest statements about Romney's tax returns in 2015 by citing the Obama victory (Olugbemiga 2015). The House Republicans, taking control of the institution in 2011, launched a series of investigations of the Obama Administration (Newsmax 2011). One result of these investigations was the Hillary Clinton email scandal that began as part of an investigation into events in Benghazi, Libya (Bade 2015). This situation is much different than the one facing Canadians who vote for members of Parliament in an election in which all candidates stand for election simultaneously. The early and consistent branding of political opponents has been a common trait of the American permanent campaign and is a practice that has been adopted by Canadian political actors. The race to brand one's opponent before they can brand themselves is becoming more sophisticated and strategic than previous efforts. Pre-branding an opponent can enhance the probability of victory and can reduce the cost of campaigning. Building brand loyalty towards a party's candidate and negative brand identity towards the opposition party can encourage significant parts of the audience to make decisions well before election day. The following case will show that pre-branding, both positive and negative, occurs in Canada. The case is focused on the leader, using the Conservative Party and Stephen Harper. The CPC built a positive brand around Harper and negative brands around its rivals, and led a successful election campaign as a result.

Case Study

This case study examines how political branding has been used in Canada in light of the above American experience and asks, how does the recent adoption of permanent campaigning in Canada compare to the American experience? We focus on recent elections and the Conservative Party of Canada (CPC).

METHOD

Some of the evidence comes from five confidential and semi-structured interviews with Liberal ministerial staff, Conservative ministers, and Conservative prime ministerial and ministerial staff from August 2013 to October 2014 (from a set of forty-five who were interviewed on cabinet decision making for another project). The interview questions focused on decision making in cabinet, relations between the prime minister and ministers, and communications strategy. Individuals were recruited using the Canadian parliamentary information website and the Ottawa political periodical the *Hill Times*. Participants were contacted by email and interviews lasted between thirty and forty-five minutes. The interviews were conducted by phone, audio-recorded, and transcribed verbatim. To preserve interviewee anonymity, respondents are cited as R1, R2, and so on.

FINDINGS

The contemporary experiences of the CPC and Stephen Harper demonstrate similarities to political brand creation in the United States. While the CPC has been branding since its inception in 2003, the approach was solidified once it formed the government in 2006 and was able to benefit from all the powers that come with this position (Marland and Flanagan 2013). Discussed at length in other chapters of this collection, the Conservatives quickly used the levers of government to change the colour of the Government of Canada's websites and outdoor signage from the traditional red (not coincidentally the shade long associated with the Liberal Party) to the Conservatives' official colour, blue. Furthermore, and reflective of the Conservative attachment to the monarchy, the word "Royal" was reinserted to the names of the Canadian Air Force (Royal Canadian Air Force) and Canadian Navy (Royal Canadian Navy).

The CPC consciously worked to move the country away from a perception that the Liberals were its traditional governing party in order to encourage voters to consider a different, Conservative future rooted in established traditions. This was much like what the American conservative movement had done in taking over the Republican Party to sell its policy innovations: brand them with an aura of tradition. In the Canadian case, the importance of branding and strategic communications is found in comments from a former staffer of the Conservative leader's office: "[A government communications strategy] was motivated not at all by message control or anything like that. It was motivated by the fact that it is stupid to have ministers going out, making great big national announcements without any planning and without any spacing between them. So that's why we created that capability" (R1). This interpretation of branding communications approaches is notable considering the common link between strategy and message control.

In the aftermath of the 2008–9 global recession, Stephen Harper presented himself and the Conservative government as offering steady leadership in troubled times. In 2009, the Conservatives branded the new Liberal leader Michael Ignatieff as out of touch and barely Canadian, given his decades living outside the country. The Conservatives repeatedly labelled Ignatieff as "just visiting" in both television advertisements and web videos. The party used paid advertising to quickly introduce its version of Ignatieff to the public and define him before he could define himself. Meanwhile, the Conservatives presented Harper as being Mr. Canada, a man who loves hockey and Tim Hortons (Cormack 2012; Cormack and Cosgrave 2012), and offered a different regional vision of Canada that included the West and the Arctic (Bricker and Ibbitson 2013). The Conservative branding campaign employed market research and microtargeting to find its audiences, with the goal of winning just enough specific niche audiences, like South Asian immigrants, to tip the result in ridings with high populations of these targeted groups (Friesen 2011). Such targeting and segmentation are commonly used in American marketing of all sorts and are often based on postal codes (Turow 1997). The idea is to target very specific voters at a level sufficient to mobilize focused constituencies, as Steve Patten observes in Chapter 3.

Political actors of all party stripes understand the importance of having a consistent, coherent brand that can be applied quickly to any situation. Such situations include negative news coverage and the efforts opponents make to develop negative brands around a candidate. As a former staffer of a cabinet minister in Paul Martin's Liberal government noted, there is significant incentive to respond quickly to negative assertions lest they become part of a negative brand: "I think it's the degree to which substantive issues versus, you know, the need to drive a twenty-four-hour news cycle. So, in fact, an allegation becomes news and you have to respond to the allegation [that has] completely warped political behaviours" (R2). Branding is a constant activity because the political news cycle now spans the clock and social media have sped it up. Thus, two of the staffers we interviewed cited strategic responses to the political environment as the rationale for branding.

To reinforce its paid media messaging, the CPC made extensive use of the earned media opportunities that being in government affords. An example of an official document that generated a lot of earned media for the campaign's branding was the 2011 federal budget. The budget was an official government document, but it moonlighted as a campaign document because it contained Harper's brand narrative and a specific platform brand: Canada's Economic Action Plan (EAP). The plan was developed in response to the global economic crisis. Compared to similar programs the United States and Australia and consistent with a branding-oriented party, the EAP was more dependent on government advertising and less transparent and less accountable (Stoney and Krawchenko 2012), but it was very successful in building Harper's and the CPC's brands.

The use of government advertising to promote the policies of a sitting government was not new in Canada. Further, many observers have written about the very tightly disciplined group of people who built the Conservative brand, meaning that the EAP's lack of transparency was equally the CPC's and the Government of Canada's transparency problem as well. The presentation of the budget just before the writ dropped was an effort to build synergy between government advertising, legislative activity, and paid advertising. Such synergy amplifies the brand through the generation of a large number of impressions and, given that it shows the political candidate keeping promises in office, can be a way to build brand credibility. The Government of Canada press release announcing the budget employed action verbiage to make its four points: (1) supporting job creation, (2) supporting families and communities, (3) investing in innovation and education, and (4) preserving Canada's fiscal advantage (Government of Canada 2011). It offered a positive vision and showed how past promises had been kept while directly linking new pledges with the kept promises.

The ensuing party platform also fit this messaging. Harper was pictured in the party-appropriate blue business suit and blue-and-red-striped tie, the red invoking Canada. He also wore a Canadian flag lapel pin. This visual was backdropped by a Canadian flag, and the words "Here for Canada" appeared above the CPC logo. Just in front of Harper was the title "Stephen Harper's Low Tax Plan for Economic Growth." The CPC pitched its policies as being prudent low-tax plans to protect and create jobs by completing Canada's recovery from the global economic recession (Conservative Party of Canada 2011). The supporting media package argued that Harper had more work to do and that, given the global instability facing the country, changing leaders was not prudent, as Harper's plans were working and the opponents might engage in reckless, opportunistic experiments if elected. The plan showed how the promise of stability for Canada was kept and was very much in keeping with what was in the budget documents. Thus, party and government documents – paid and earned media – were combined to build a positive brand around Harper that was consistent with his past efforts and cast a negative impression of his opponents.

Once the brand was in place, the CPC kept its team on message at all times to maintain brand coherence during the permanent campaign. As one former Harper minister recalls, "The Prime Minister's Office controls everything that you do. You do a press conference tomorrow, you have to send them the text. You know they control the text and what you will say" (R3). The Conservatives embraced the permanent campaign as a result of their two minority governments, which kept them in virtually constant campaign mode from 2006 to 2011. The permanent campaign and brand strategy thus became key parts of the CPC organizational culture. As one former ministerial staff member noted, "At the beginning of a new government and especially with a minority government, you really want to stay on message ... the government had five priorities to deliver ... [if] it wasn't one of the priorities of [the government] it made it very, very difficult on messaging" (R4). Communication control within a permanent campaign was helped by the acceptance of Conservative political staff. With political actors supportive of political branding, strategic communications, and the reality of existing in constant campaign mode, message discipline is easier to enforce (see Anna Lennox Esselment and Paul Wilson on political staff, Chapter 12). As another staffer noted, "I really believe in message discipline ... I believe in focused communications, in getting out there and saying what you have to say and not saying a whole lot of other things, you know. Let's give the media one thing to choose from in terms of what our message is going to be today, and not sixteen things. And that means not every minister should be out making any announcements she wants on any given day" (R5).

The significance of political marketing and branding is clear to those in-volved, as a ministerial staffer noted: "We all need to realize that when you do your polling and you do your research, if we can get the public talking and thinking about it [a very small number of issues], we are likely to come out on top with public opinion on those issues" (R5). Again, the political actors' perceptions are less about the strategies' effect on democracy and more on commonly accepted political communication strategy.

The official and partisan governing and campaigning blend is evident in the advertising done by the Harper government, which was crafted in ways that supported the partisan brand. One can argue that this was the case with the EAP throughout its existence. The Harper government used the EAP platform brand in earned media, in official advertising, and in party messaging to show that it was dealing with a global economic crisis in a strong, steady way that served Canadian interests.

In 2015, the federal budget was once again central to the branding and communications strategies. It was released as Canada's Economic Action Plan 2015 on a government website that featured photographs of Conserv-ative audience targets. These included a family next to the tag line "balan-cing the budget"; a hockey mom and her daughter at the rink next to the tag "making ends meet"; a worker and a military officer next to the tag "pro-tecting Canadians"; and two blue-collar workers, one a visible minority next to the tag "creating and protecting jobs and economic growth," and the other next to the tag "training a highly skilled workforce" (Government of Canada 2015).

Consistent with the rise of microtargeting and the CPC's interest in di-versifying its customer base, the budget was offered online in twenty differ-ent languages. It specifically contained Harper's core brand proposition of "strong leadership," a contrast to the aforementioned Trudeau, and offered a "balanced budget, low tax plan for jobs, growth and security" (Government of Canada 2015). The selling points dovetailed with the overall Conserva-tive brand and what Harper and the CPC had campaigned on in 2011. Thus, as they did in 2011, the Conservatives in 2015 showed an ability to campaign within media and within government, and in doing so, to blend both into the permanent campaign.

Branding is a continuous activity. The results of elections are the product of performance in office, the strength of the opposition, and environmental factors. In terms of communicating, while the CPC may have mechanically done the same things as a majority government as it did in other situations, the results were different, because the performance in office was different. Harper promised Canadians steady leadership, honest government, and a stable economy. And compared to his earlier rivals, he appeared to be keeping these brand promises. The problem that he had going into the 2015 campaign was that the results did not seem to support the brand promises. Harper did not get a deal with the United States on the Keystone XL pipeline, and his government was able to balance the budget only by tapping into the country's reserve funds. Thus, when it came time to campaign, Harper had to spend a great deal of effort defending visible weaknesses in his record that were not apparent in 2011. Meanwhile, the Liberals and NDP had an opportunity to unveil their contrasting brands in the same high-profile setting.

Contrast this situation with the one Barack Obama faced in 2012. Obama could credibly claim that his administration had accomplished big-ticket items. It had passed the *Affordable Care Act*, had bailed out the auto industry, had dealt with the financial crisis, and had brought American troops home from Iraq and was in the process of doing the same in Afghanistan. Thus, Obama's brand had considerable validity during the 2012 campaign season. Further, Romney made a series of statements like "binders full of women" and asserted that about 47 percent of the electorate was opposed to him; Obama's team capitalized on these missteps, proving the validity of negative branding. Harper was similarly situated as Obama in 2011 and was similarly rewarded, but given the CPC's brand problems and the strength of the opposition's brands, the same strategy did not produce the same results in 2015, and the Liberals won enough seats to form a majority government.

Permanent Campaigning in Canada

The permanent campaign blurs the distinction between campaigning and governing. Instead of an artificial division between the two activities, there is much more of a blended continuous effort that becomes more focused on campaigning as the election nears. Branding is but one tool aimed at trying to educate, inform, and ultimately encourage the voter/consumer to make a specific voting/purchasing decision. Ideally, brands can help a party build a lifetime relationship with a voter that moves through an entire partisan product line. The brand's power depends on the party's performance and its ability to keep its promises, and those things are dependent on environmental conditions. Brand promises must be kept or the brand's credibility drops. Parties that do not keep brand promises and do not deliver see their brand's power decline, as the post–George W. Bush Republican Party has shown. As noted above, Harper had his share of difficulties keeping his brand promises because of factors in and out of his control. Not surprisingly, his opponents presented his problems as proof that his brand lacked validity overall and that change was necessary.

The biggest lessons that political parties, especially those in opposition, should take away regarding the rise of the permanent campaign are that it is generally better to have a known face as the leader and that political marketing is a multifaceted activity in which opposition party leaders must be able to present themselves as credible alternatives to the incumbent prime minister. From 2011 to 2015, the incumbent Conservatives attacked Liberal challengers on their ability to understand the concerns of average Canadians and on their fitness for office, and they did so far in advance of the elections. Media and citizens need to be more aware of the way in which campaigning and governing have melded. Politically marketed leaders frequently make decisions based not only on what it is good policy, but also on what is good politics and what is good for their brand. Media and citizens should understand that politicians and political marketers always believe the next election could be right around the corner. Branded politicians try to keep their promises once in office to facilitate the task of winning the next electoral contest.

The United States and Canada have a unique relationship when it comes to political marketing and branding due to the sharing of political consultants (Cosgrove 2012; Marland, Giasson, and Lees-Marshment 2012) in a common market approach to politics (Lees-Marshment 2004). The permanent campaign in both the United States and Canada gives incumbents opportunities to brand their opponents long before election day. Such negative branding campaigns can be effective if the incumbent does not have brand problems, the opponent is not well known or is divided, and exogenous conditions such as the economy are favourable. Especially in the United States, where branding is tied up with money and the way money is used, the brand is heavily dependent on smart decision making. Mitt Romney had a lot of cash, but first had to spend it on primary contests and then did not spend it as wisely in the general election as Barack Obama did. Obama's task of negatively branding Romney was greatly facilitated by Romney's bad choices with resources.

Such was the case for Stephen Harper in 2011, but not in 2015. In both cases, he used a similarly timed pre-writ advertising campaign. The media coverage of his position as prime minister afforded him an opportunity to present a similarly themed Government of Canada advertising campaign to positively brand his government and negatively brand his opponents. Roughly two years out from voting day, the party's negative branding advertising campaign was launched. In 2009, Liberal leader Michael Ignatieff was described as "just visiting," and in 2014, Justin Trudeau was branded as "just not ready." These initial messages were cemented a few months before the election with official Government of Canada advertising that dovetailed into partisan messaging. In the interim, the Harper government used earned media to solidify the branding message. Still, the branding exercise had more impact on Harper's approval ratings in 2011 than 2015 because of (1) changes in environmental conditions, (2) changes in perceived performance, and (3) changes in relative evaluation of opponents. Harper in 2011 and Obama in 2012 were situated as incumbents and thus able to disqualify their challengers well in advance of the election. Both challengers, the Liberals and Republicans, were parties that had recently struggled through intra-party strife (Jeffery 2010), and both chose leaders who had to introduce themselves to the voters, thus opening the door to negative branding.

Harper had an easier time in 2011 than in 2015 because he was operating in a more favourable environment. He could brand his opponent in 2011 as being unacceptable because his own brand appeared to be working well, and his claims about his opponent being out of touch with Canadians were credible. In 2015, the political landscape had changed, and the popular perception of Harper's brand was therefore very different and his efforts did not yield the same results. A political brand gives voters a ready basis for comparison that enhances their ability to make a decision rather than detracting from it. Even though Harper may have branded Justin Trudeau as the unacceptable alternative, as he did to Michael Ignatieff in 2011, his marketing problem was more complicated in 2015 because the NDP alternative was better known and had served in Parliament as the official opposition for four years. Incumbents can brand their opponents as unacceptable provided that environmental conditions are favourable. Political leaders, like any product, grow stale over time and lose their rationale for office because the problems that they were elected to solve have been solved. New offerings more relevant to the times emerge, and the incumbent's own failings may be more obvious than they once were.

NOTE

1   Saatchi is a one-word brand approach popularized by advertising firm Saatchi and Saatchi.

REFERENCES

Bade, Rachael. 2015. "Congress: Clinton versus Gowdy." *Politico*, July 8. http://www.politico.com/story/2015/07/hillary-clinton-trey-gowdy-benghazi-committee-119864.

Bricker, Darrell, and John Ibbitson. 2013. *The Big Shift*. Toronto: HarperCollins.

Conservative Party of Canada. 2011. "Here for Canada." Federal Election Platform. https://www.poltext.org/sites/poltext.org/files/plateformes/can2011pc_plt_en_12072011_114959.pdf.

Cormack, Patricia. 2012. "Double-Double: Branding, Tim Hortons, and the Public Sphere." In *Political Marketing in Canada*, edited by A. Marland, T. Giasson, and J. Lees-Marshment, 209–23. Vancouver: UBC Press.

Cormack, Patricia, and James Cosgrave. 2012. *Desiring Canada*. Toronto: University of Toronto Press.

Cosgrove, Kenneth Mark. 2007. *Branded Conservatives: How the Brand Brought the American Right from the Periphery to the Center of American Politics*. New York: Peter Lang.

–. 2012. "Political Branding in the Modern Age: Effective Strategies, Tools and Techniques." In *The Routledge Handbook of Political Marketing*, edited by J. Lees-Marshment, 107–23. New York: Routledge.

–. 2014. "Personal Political Branding at the State Level." In *Political Marketing in the United States*, edited by J. Lees-Marshment, B. Conley, and K. Cosgrove, 148–64. New York: Routledge.

Cross, William. 2004. *Political Parties*. Vancouver: UBC Press.

Deachman, Bruce. 2015. "78 Days? The Long and the Short of Canadian Campaigns." *Ottawa Citizen*, August 3. http://ottawacitizen.com/news/politics/two-down-76-to-go-the-longest-election-campaign-since-we-first-re-elected-john-a.

Fenno, Richard. 1978. *Homestyle*. New York: Little Brown.

Friesen, Joe. 2011. "'Micro-Targeting' Lets Parties Conquer Ridings, One Tiny Group at a Time." *Globe and Mail*, April 22. http://www.theglobeandmail.com/news/politics/micro-targeting-lets-parties-conquer.

Government of Canada. 2011. "Government of Canada Reintroduces the Next Phase of Canada's Economic Action Plan – A Low-Tax Plan for Jobs and Growth." Press release, June 6. http://www.budget.gc.ca/2011/nrc/nrc-eng.html.

–. 2015. "Minister Oliver Tables Balanced-Budget, Low-Tax Plan for Jobs, Growth and Security." Press release, April 21. http://www.budget.gc.ca/2015/docs/nrc/2015-04-21-e.pdf.

Hacker, Jacob. 2014. "The Two Electorates." *Scholar Strategy Network*. http://www.scholarsstrategynetwork.org/page/two-electorates.

Heilemann, John. 2012. "Hope: The Sequel." *New York Magazine*, May 27. http://nymag.com/news/features/barack-obama-2012-6/.

Issenberg, Sasha. 2014. "How the Democrats Can Avoid Going Down This November." *New Republic*, April 27. https://newrepublic.com/article/117520/howdemocrats-can-avoid-going-down-2014-midterm-election.

James, Frank. 2012. "Obama 'Forward' Video: President's Case for Re-Election in a Nutshell." *NPR: It's All Politics*, April 30. http://www.npr.org/sections/itsallpolitics/2012/04/30/151719139/obama-forward-video-presidents-re-election-argument-in-nutshell.http://www.npr.org/sections/itsallpolitics/2012/04/30/151719139/obama-forward-videopresidents-re-election-argument-in-nutshell.

Jeffery, Brooke. 2010. *Divided Loyalties: The Liberal Party of Canada: 1984–2008*. Toronto: University of Toronto Press.

Knickerbocker, Brad. 2015. "Democrats: Why We Got Shellacked in the 2014 Elections." *Christian Science Monitor*, February 2. http://www.csmonitor.com/USA/Politics/DC-Decoder/2015/0221/Democrats-Why-we-got-shellacked-in-the-2014-elections.

Lavigne, Brad. 2014. *Building the Orange Wave: The Inside Story behind the Historic Rise of Jack Layton and the NDP*. Madeira Park, BC: Douglas & McIntyre.

Lees-Marshment, Jennifer. 2004. *The Political Marketing Revolution: Transforming the Government of the United Kingdom*. Manchester: Manchester University Press.

Lipset, Seymour. 1990. *Continental Divide: The Values and Institutions of the United States and Canada*. New York, London: Routledge.

Liptak, Kevin. 2012. "Reports Show Turnout Lower than 2008, 2004." *Political Ticker*, November 8, http://politicalticker.blogs.cnn.com/2012/11/08/report-shows-turnout-lower-than-2008-and-2004/.

Marland, Alex. 2014. "The Branding of a Prime Minister: Digital Information Subsidies and the Image Management of Stephen Harper." In *Political Communication in Canada: Meet the Press and Tweet the Rest*, edited by A. Marland, T. Giasson, and T.A. Small, 55–73. Vancouver: UBC Press.

Marland, Alex, and Tom Flanagan. 2013. "Brand New Party: Political Branding and the Conservative Party of Canada." *Canadian Journal of Political Science* 46 (4): 951–72. http://dx.doi.org/10.1017/S0008423913001108.

Marland, Alex, Thierry Giasson, and Jennifer Lees-Marshment. 2012. *Political Marketing in Canada*. Vancouver: UBC Press.

Mayhew, David R. 1991. *Divided We Govern*. New Haven: Yale University Press.

Newman, Bruce. 1999. *The Mass Marketing of Politics: Democracy in the Age of Manufactured Images*. Thousand Oaks, CA: SAGE Publications.

Newsmax. 2011. "Issa, House GOP Preparing Major Investigations of Obama Administration." January 4. http://www.newsmax.com/Headline/issa-obama-investigations-post/2011/01/04/id/381829/.

O'Brien, Michael. 2012. "Romney Boasts of 'Severely Conservative' Record in CPAC Speech." *NBC News*, February 10. http://nbcpolitics.nbcnews.com/_news/2012/02/10/10375038-romney-boasts-of-severely-conservative-record-in-cpac-speech.

Olugbemiga, Ayobami. 2015. "Harry Reid Gives Shameful Response to His Attack on Mitt Romney's Taxes." *Huffington Post*, June 6. http://www.huffingtonpost.com/ayobami-olugbemiga/harry-reid-gives-shameful-response-to-his-attack-on-mitt-romneys-taxes_b_6999996.html.

Penn, Mark. 2011. "What Companies Can Learn from Political Campaigns." *Harvard Business Review*, December 21. https://hbr.org/2011/12/what-companies-can-learn -from.

Peters, Ronald M. 1997. *The American Speakership*. Baltimore: Johns Hopkins University Press.

Rosenthal, Cindy Simon, and Ronald M. Peters, Jr. 2010. *Speaker Nancy Pelosi and the New American Politics*. Oxford: Oxford University Press.

Rove, Karl. 2010. "The GOP Targets State Legislatures." *Wall Street Journal*, March 4. http://www.rove.com/articles/219.

Schlesinger, Robert. 2012. "Obama Operation Chaos: The Obama Campaign Quietly Pushed Romney's Flip-Flopping and Bain Record into Republican Nominating Race." *U.S. News & World Report*, December 5. http://www.usnews.com/opinion/ blogs/robert-schlesinger/2012/12/05/how-the-obama-campaign-sabotaged -romney-in-the-2012-gop-primary.

Stoney, Christopher, and Tamara Krawchenko. 2012. "Transparency and Accountability in Infrastructure Stimulus Spending: A Comparison of Canadian, Australian and U.S. Programs." *Canadian Public Administration* 55 (4): 481–503. http://dx.doi.org/ 10.1111/j.1754-7121.2012.00235.x.

Tapscott, Don, and Anthony Williams. 2010. *Wikinomics: How Collaboration Changes Everything*. London: Portfolio.

Thrush, Glenn, and Jennifer Epstein. 2011. "Obama Launches Reelection Campaign." *Politico*, April 4. http://www.politico.com/story/2011/04/obama-launches-reelection -campaign-052457.

Trippi, Joseph. 2004. *The Revolution Will Not Be Televised*. New York: William Morrow.

Turow, Joseph. 1997. *Breaking Up America: Advertisers and the New Media World*. Chicago: University of Chicago Press. http://dx.doi.org/10.7208/chicago/978022 6817514.001.0001.

Westen, Drew. 2008. *The Political Brain: The Role of Emotion in Deciding the Fate of the Nation*. New York: PublicAffairs.

Zyman, Sergio, and Armen Brott. 2003. *The End of Marketing as We Know It*. New York: HarperCollins.

12

Campaigning from the Centre

...... *Anna Lennox Esselment and Paul Wilson*

All governments control communication. Whether shaping headlines to fit their preferred narrative or responding to potentially damaging stories or information, governments prioritize message management. But recent scholarship on the operation of government in Canada, particularly the Prime Minister's Office (PMO), suggests that tighter political management over communications and issues and the use of marketing techniques accelerated under the government of Prime Minister Stephen Harper (Delacourt 2013; Kozolanka 2014). The intense focus on these areas by the party in power reflects a permanent campaign where the tactics and tools used by political parties to win elections are extended to the core executive and employed in a way to maintain public approval, attack the opposition, and secure partisan advantage.

If a permanent-campaign-like atmosphere has infiltrated the centre of government in Canada, then what – or who – is perpetuating this new mode of operation? The new media environment is likely a good answer to the "what" (Elmer, Langlois, and McKelvey 2012). Our focus in this chapter is the "who." Political staff (also called exempt staff, since they are not subject to the same employment provisions as public servants) are hired directly by ministers to provide political advice as a complement to expert but non-partisan advice from the permanent public service (Privy Council Office 2015). This overt political mandate makes them prime candidates in the search for the driving force behind permanent campaigning. This chapter examines the role of political staff, principally in the PMO, with regard to strategic communications and issues management. The former encompasses proactive strategies to highlight government accomplishments through long-term agenda planning; the latter involves identifying potentially harmful stories and rapidly developing politically sensitive messages to combat them.

NOTES

1 The author acknowledges the financial support of the Social Sciences and Humanities Research Council of Canada.

2 Previous fixed-date election bills were found on Parliament's LEGISinfo website, http://www.parl.gc.ca/LegisInfo/; party platforms were found at http://www.poltext. org/en/part-1-electronic-political-texts/electronic-manifestos-canada; and parliamentary studies were found at the Library of Parliament website, http://www.parl. gc.ca/About/Library/VirtualLibrary/index-e.asp.

3 *House of Commons Debates*, 39th Parliament, 1st Session, No. 077 (November 6, 2006), 1210–1345.

4 Conacher v. Canada (Prime Minister), 2009 FC 920, [2010] 3 FCR 411, paragraph 2.

5 Ibid., paragraph 3.

REFERENCES

Abacus Data. 2015. "Budget Propels Conservatives to 8 Point Lead." http://abacusdata. ca/wp-content/uploads/2015/04/Abacus-Release-Headline-Political-Data_April 2015.pdf.

Aucoin, Peter, Mark D. Jarvis, and Lori Turnbull. 2011. *Democratizing the Constitution*. Toronto: Emond Montgomery.

Bill C-512. 2004. *An Act to Provide Fixed Dates for the Election to the House of Commons and to Amend the Constitution Act, 1867*, 3rd Session, 37th Parliament, clause 52–53.

Bolt, Major Alexander. 2008. *The Crown Prerogative as Applied to Military Operations*. Ottawa: Office of the Judge Advocate General, Strategic Legal Paper Series.

Canadian Alliance. 2000. "A Time for Change: An Agenda of Respect for all Canadians." http://www.poltext.org/sites/poltext.org/files/plateformes/can2000all_plt_en._ 14112008_173717.pdf.

CBC News. 2008. "Harper Hints at Triggering Election." August 14. http://www.cbc.ca/ news/canada/harper-hints-at-triggering-election-1.745252.

–. 2015. "Fixed Election Date Eroding Campaign Rules, Ex-Elections Chief Says." May 23. http://www.cbc.ca/news/politics/fixed-election-date-eroding-campaign-rules-ex -elections-chief-says-1.3084146.

Conservative Party. 2006. "Stand Up for Canada." http://www.poltext.org/sites/poltext. org/files/plateformes/can2006pc_plt_en._14112008_165519.pdf.

Coyne, Andrew. 2015. "In Praise of the Endless Election Campaign." *National Post*, May 16. http://news.nationalpost.com/full-comment/andrew-coyne-in-praise-of-the -endless-election-campaign.

Douven, Igor. 2011. "Abduction." In *Stanford Encyclopedia of Philosophy*, edited by Edward N. Zalta. http://plato.stanford.edu/archives/spr2011/entries/abduction/.

Fairclough, Isabela, and Norman Fairclough. 2012. *Political Discourse Analysis: A Method for Advanced Students*. London: Routledge.

Flanagan, Tom. 2014. *Winning Power: Canadian Campaigning in the Twenty-First Century*. Montreal/Kingston: McGill-Queen's University Press.

Gardner, Carl. 2015. *What a Fix-Up! The Fixed-term Parliaments Act 2011.* n.p.: Carl Gardner. Kindle edition. http://www.headoflegal.com/2015/05/06/what-a-fix-up-my-e-book-on-the-fixed-term-parliaments-act/.

Hall, Chris. 2015. "HarperPAC, Engage Canada Highlight Confusion over 3rd-Party Ads." *CBC.ca*, June 27. http://www.cbc.ca/news/politics/harperpac-engage-canada-highlight-confusion-over-3rd-party-ads-1.3129882.

Harper, Tim. 2014. "Ready for a Year-Long Campaign? Didn't Think So." *Toronto Star*, September 14. https://www.thestar.com/news/canada/2014/09/14/ready_for_a_yearlong_campaign_didnt_think_so_tim_harper.html.http://www.thestar.com/news/canada/2014/09/14/ready_for_a_yearlong_campaign_didnt_think_so_tim_harper.html

Hébert, Chantal. 2015. "Fixed-Date Election Comes back to Bite Harper." *Toronto Star*, June 26. https://www.thestar.com/news/canada/2015/06/26/fixed-date-election-comes-back-to-bite-stephen-harper-hbert.html.

Hope, Christopher. 2015. "Axe 'Zombie' Parliaments Law, Say Former Cabinet Ministers." *Telegraph*, January 16. http://www.telegraph.co.uk/news/general-election-2015/11348786/Axe-zombie-Parliaments-law-say-former-Cabinet-ministers.html.

Ivison, John. 2015. "Why Current Events Are Making It Seem Increasingly Likely Harper Will Call an Early Election." *National Post*, January 13. http://news.nationalpost.com/full-comment/john-ivison-why-current-events-are-making-it-seem-increasingly-likely-harper-will-call-an-early-election.

Kinsella, Warren. 2014. "Will Harper Call Early Election?" *Toronto Sun*, May15. http://www.torontosun.com/2014/05/15/will-harper-call-early-election.

Knopff, Rainer. 2015. "Did the 2015 Alberta and PEI Elections Kill Fixed Election Dates?" 6 July. https://rainerknopff.ca/2015/12/10/did-the-2015-alberta-and-pei-elections-kill-fixed-election-dates-2/.

Lagassé, Philippe, and Patrick Baud. 2016. "The Crown and Constitutional Amendment after the *Senate Reform* and *Supreme Court* References." In *Constitutional Amendment in Canada*, edited by Emmett Macfarlane, 248–70. Toronto: University of Toronto Press.

Mahoney, James, and Kathleen Thelen. 2010. "A Theory of Gradual Institutional Change." In *Explaining Institutional Change: Ambiguity, Agency, and Power*, edited by James Mahoney and Kathleen Thelen, 1–37. Cambridge: Cambridge University Press.

Marquis, Melanie. 2015. "Fixed-Election Comes with Concerns, Say Observers." *Canadian Press*, July 5. http://www.nationalnewswatch.com/2015/07/05/fixed-date-election-comes-with-concerns-observers-say/#.WDX36LIrKUk.

Martin, Lawrence. 2014. "Harper's Election Timing? Expect the Unexpected." *Globe and Mail*, September 30. http://www.huffingtonpost.ca/2014/09/30/harpers-election-timing-e_n_5907860.html.

Nelson, Fraser. 2015. "This Act of Folly Has Condemned Us to Five Years of Political Torment." *Telegraph*, January 2. http://www.telegraph.co.uk/news/general-election-2015/11320637/This-Act-of-folly-has-condemned-us-to-five-years-of-political-torment.html.

Neudorf, Lorne. 2014. "In Defence of Fixed-Election Dates." *National Post*, October 8. http://news.nationalpost.com/full-comment/lorne-neudorf-in-defence-of-fixed-election-dates.

Reid, Scott. 2015. "The Case for a Spring Election." *Ottawa Citizen*, February 20. http://ottawacitizen.com/opinion/columnists/reid-the-case-for-a-spring-election.

Rhodes, R.A.W., John Wanna, and Patrick Weller. 2011. *Comparing Westminster*. Oxford: Oxford University Press.

Robertson, James R. 2007. *Bill C-16: An Act to Amend the Canada Elections Act*. Library of Parliament, Parliamentary Information and Research Service, Legislative Summary, LS-530E.

Smith, Dale. 2015a. "No More Year-Long Elections, Please." *Loonie Politics*, January 13. http://looniepolitics.com/year-long-elections-please/.

–. 2015b. "Who Killed Question Period?" *National Post*, May 28. http://news.national post.com/full-comment/dale-smith-who-killed-question-period.

Smith, David E. 2013. *Across the Aisle: Opposition in Canadian Politics*. Toronto: University of Toronto Press.

UK HoC (United Kingdom House of Commons). 2004. *Taming the Prerogative: Strengthening Ministerial Accountability to Parliament*. Public Administration Select Committee, Fourth Report of Session 2003–4.

–. 2007. *The Governance of Britain Green Paper*. House of Commons Library, Research Paper 07/72.

Vennesson, Pascale. 2008. "Case Studies and Process Tracing: Theories and Practices." In *Approaches and Methodologies in the Social Sciences*, edited by Donatella Della Porta and Michael Keating, 223–39. Cambridge: Cambridge University Press. http://dx.doi.org/10.1017/CBO9780511801938.013.

Warren, R. Michael. 2014. "Why Stephen Harper Will Call an Early Election." *Toronto Star*, November 9. https://www.thestar.com/opinion/commentary/2014/11/09/why_stephen_harper_will_call_an_early_election.html.

Zurcher, Anthony. 2015. "Election 2015: The Americanisation of the UK Election." *BBC News Magazine*, April 1. http://www.bbc.com/news/magazine-32156264.

10

Preaching to the Choir in Case It Is Losing Faith: Government Advertising's Direct Electoral Consequences

Denver McNeney and David Coletto

While the public debate regarding the substance and style of government advertising has shifted over the past decades, government advertising is by no means a new phenomenon in Canada. Indeed, governments have employed extensive advertising for a variety of goals across Canada's history, including settling the west, recruiting for wars, and, perhaps most importantly, community- and nation-building activities (Rose 2000). Like all government communication, its advertising is purposive – designed to change attitudes or behaviours among some or all of the public. As Jonathan Rose (2000, 21) argues, government advertising is "never 'innocent' in the sense of merely providing information or respondent to public demand"; its function is to persuade, not merely inform.

It is surprising, then, that little work has been done to uncover the electoral and perceptive consequences of government advertising in Canada today (though see Dougan 2007; Nesbitt-Larking and Rose 2004; Rose 2001, 2003; Rutherford 2000) or the role it might play in the permanent campaign. This lack of attention is particularly egregious given the obvious importance of government communication in fostering an engaged, informed, and critical electorate. Though the bulk of this literature focuses on citizens as *consumers* of political information, the government's role as a *producer* of political communication is of substantive importance in its own right. In fact, by effectively bathing the public with information regarding policies, programs, and other government activities, public advertising may supply an otherwise disengaged and apathetic citizenry with the information required to competently wield the levers of democratic accountability. Of course, if the majority of content produced by the government of the day is less informative than it is outwardly partisan in nature, any normatively appealing account of government advertising ultimately splinters. Especially

Both are essential election campaign techniques which have been firmly entrenched within the operations of government.

In recent decades, political staff within the core executive have grown in number and influence (Eichbaum and Shaw 2010; Savoie 1999; Zussman 2009) and gained increasing prominence in countries with Westminster-style governments, including Canada (Benoit 2006; Craft 2016), Australia, New Zealand, and the United Kingdom (Blick 2004; Eichbaum and Shaw 2010; Tiernan 2007; Yong and Hazell 2014). In all these countries, however, political staffers have found themselves the centre of media controversy. As identified in Chapter 1, according to Peter Aucoin (2012, 178), they have become primary contributors to the partisan excesses of New Political Governance (NPG) in which governments abuse public resources and the public service for their own partisan advantage. NPG results from new pressures, such as the intense media environment, that compel governments to conduct public business as though constantly engaged in an electoral campaign.

The prevailing stereotype characterizes ministerial staffers as "young, ambitious, and politically loyal operatives" who prioritize partisan politics above all other considerations (Benoit 2006, 146). Aucoin (2012) argues that this wreaks havoc on the traditional relationship between the political executive and non-partisan officials (see Jonathan Craft's chapter, this volume). But how does he know this to be true? Political staffers may be influential, but they remain understudied in the Canadian context. Much of the literature on political staffers in Canada is dated (Axworthy 1988; D'Aquino 1974; Lalonde 1971; Mallory 1967; Tellier 1968), including survey-based studies (Campbell and Szablowski 1979; Plasse 1994; Savoie 1983). There are recent exceptions, in particular Liane Benoit's 2006 study for the Gomery inquiry and Jonathan Craft's (2016) and Paul Wilson's (2015 and 2016) research into policy advisors in the Harper government. In general, however, we lack basic data on their composition, role, and relationships. While rare first-person accounts from former senior political staffers provide insightful anecdotes (Burney 2005; Goldenberg 2006), they do not provide systematic analysis. Most scholars, Aucoin included, do not differentiate between categories of staffers, which risks overlooking important distinctions in roles and behaviours. In particular, not all political staff transfer equally into a campaign setting (Esselment 2010), and insiders have observed differences of partisan intensity between staff roles (Rathgeber 2014, 125).

We contend that political staffers in the areas of strategic communications (including branding and marketing) and issues management – formal position titles that first emerged under the Harper government – facilitate the permanent campaign in government through the institutionalization of specific election campaign approaches. This is driven in large part by exogenous factors in the broader political environment, especially ubiquitous horse-race polling, "a priori adversarial" journalism (Alboim 2012, 47), and the hyperconnectivity of 24/7 news and social media (Flanagan 2014; Taras and Waddell 2012). However, the intensity of integration is also influenced by political circumstances such as the parliamentary context, a party's or leader's governing style, and even the personality of senior staffers themselves. Given the environment, governments, whether current or future, have little choice about whether to integrate campaigning with government, but they can choose how – and how intensely – they do so.

Case Study

Method

We employed two methods to assess the contributions of political staff to the permanent campaign. First, we used Government of Canada telephone directories from 1957 to 2015 to track the growth of particular political staff positions.[1] This unique source lists the names and job titles of political staff employees in all ministerial offices, including the PMO, permitting us to analyze the evolution of differentiated functions, such as directors of communications, strategic communications, and issues management.[2] Second, we complemented the historical data analysis with non-random, semi-structured interviews conducted between January 2015 and April 2015 with eighteen key informants, including current and former political staff from the Conservative Party of Canada (CPC) and/or the government under Stephen Harper ($n = 10$), former political staff from the Chrétien and Martin administrations ($n = 3$), and current and former public servants ($n = 5$). Participants were selected based on our personal knowledge of the political community. Interviews, some in person and some by phone, lasted between twenty and ninety minutes and were audio-recorded and transcribed (with the exception of two participants, who declined consent to record). One participant responded to questions only by email, and several others provided additional information through follow-up emails. While six participants agreed to be identified by name, others requested anonymity and so are not named but rather referenced in order of interview date as Respondent 1 (R1), Respondent (R2), and so on. For confidentiality reasons, personal details such as gender and exact job title may not be identified. These discussions allow us to explore how and to what extent the CPC transferred campaign attitudes and techniques into government, how issues management and strategic communications function within the Government of Canada, and how this has evolved over time.

FINDINGS

Proactive marketing-based strategic communications and reactive issues management are essential tools of government in the age of the permanent campaign. The Government of Canada directories illustrate the growth and heightened significance these two areas have acquired over time (Figure 12.1). Our broad conceptualization of communications staff identified any job title that indicated responsibility for press or media relations or other forms of communication, such as speech writing and photography.

The earliest PMO political staff titles that point to a specific function concern liaison with journalists; for example, news secretary in 1960 under John Diefenbaker, and press secretary under Lester Pearson in 1966. Multiple press assistants supporting the press secretary appeared in 1969, and a stand-alone Press Secretariat formed in 1974. The director of communications title emerged in 1985 and remains a permanent fixture. Pierre Trudeau enlarged his communications shop in 1982 to include two speechwriters and a photographer. The press office was pared back at the end of Brian Mulroney's tenure in power, but Jean Chrétien quickly rebuilt it when he became prime minister. In 2006, Stephen Harper had twenty-seven political staff devoted to handling communications. This went to a high of thirty-three in 2009, but trended back to twenty-seven in 2015, the most recent numbers available. Reasons for the ebbs and flows are beyond the scope of this chapter, but aside from a leader's personal style, they could include political optics (especially approaching an election year), fiscal austerity, important government initiatives (such as Pierre Trudeau's constitutional reform in 1980 and Harper's Economic Action Plan in 2009), and, vitally, new communications technologies that change expectations for how political offices engage journalists and the public. Figure 12.1 shows the growth of both communications staff and total PMO staff under each prime minister from 1957 onward. Due to their short tenures in power, the administrations of Joe Clark, John Turner, and Kim Campbell are not included.

Figure 12.1

Average number of PMO communications staff and total PMO staff, by prime minister

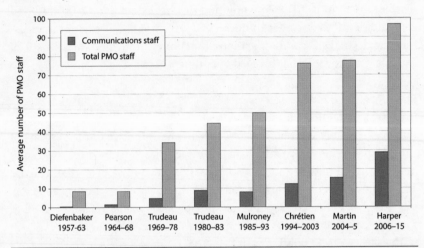

Our interview data suggest that the advent of Web 2.0 is an important factor in this expansion. Campaigns must communicate with voters – and with journalists – through a variety of platforms, many of which are now found online. The same is true in government. The most popular social media sites (e.g., Facebook, YouTube, Twitter, and Instagram) launched either shortly before or after Stephen Harper became prime minister, so his government had to wrestle with the impact and implications of governing in this changing context (see Marland, Giasson, and Small 2014). The continued focus on market research and regional communications in government became an important aspect of the PMO's communications that required the addition of political staff with that expertise.

All governments attempt to manage issues by identifying potentially harmful stories and developing politically sensitive messages to combat them. However, the government directories make no mention of any formal issues management unit or staff title until 2006. Previously, according to Chrétien PMO staffers Peter Donolo and John Milloy, the chief firefighting role was usually played by the political staffer responsible for legislative matters (such as briefing the prime minister for question period), with the support of about three people. In the Martin PMO, the deputy chief of staff for parliamentary affairs, assisted by a staff of six, handled responsibility for day-to-day issues, largely (as the title implies) focused on question period and the parliamentary context. It is therefore noteworthy that, in 2006, the Harper PMO created a dedicated unit with eleven political staff to manage issues for the new government. The issues management unit remained a key component in the Harper PMO from 2006 to 2015, averaging just over eight political staffers to handle its responsibilities.

Compared with previous administrations, then, the directory data show, under Harper, a notable increase in PMO staff charged with handling political communication and managing issues. It is evident that the Conservatives placed greater focus on these two areas, suggesting that they perceived them as crucial to how the government functions. But is that evidence of a permanent campaign? Did the Conservatives deliberately transfer best practices from their election war rooms into managing government? Telephone books do not tell the whole story, and so we turn to interview data to fill in the details.

The CPC was particularly susceptible to a permanent-campaign ethos, not only due to the emergence of Web 2.0 but also because years of internecine struggle to unite the right had conditioned the party and its activists to frenetic, constant campaigning. As Jim Armour, who spent three years as director of communications for Stephen Harper when he was the leader of the official opposition, observes, "For the longest time we *were* permanently campaigning."

The June 2004 election campaign exposed critical deficiencies in CPC preparation, especially issues management and incomplete message scripting (Flanagan 2007, 156, 197), attributable in no small part to the rapid transition for Harper's team from leadership campaign to general election. In the 2005–6 election campaign, these former weaknesses became CPC strengths, especially marketing to targeted demographic groups (Delacourt 2013, 213–14; Turcotte 2012, 84–85) and improved capacity to defend against attacks through stronger research and rapid response (Flanagan 2007, 240, 264–65). Recognizing that the new approach to strategic communications and issues management was essential to their electoral success, many key party operatives moved directly from the election war room into senior staff positions in the PMO. It is our purpose to show how these campaign techniques have been operationalized within government, especially with respect to the involvement of ministerial political exempt staff.

The new Conservative government consciously broke with the traditional PMO structure, which typically had a single communications branch, and created an institutional separation between the media relations/press office function and strategic communications. Press office tasks remained largely as before: handling journalists and their questions, providing briefings to the media, and, where required, speaking on behalf of the prime minister. Strategic communications, on the other hand, was a new unit, charged with proactively planning the government's communications. This improved the government's chances of following through on election promises. According to Ian Brodie, PMO chief of staff from 2006 to 2008, it was essential that "no matter how many day to day incoming missiles we had to defend ourselves against there was always someone preserved to be thinking ahead." As another former Conservative strategist (R12) explained, "None of us had ever worked in government. Our only point of reference was what we had done in the campaign and in opposition." So the strategic communications office was created to coordinate "all of the aspects of marketing communications," including government announcements, government advertising, speech writing, market research, ethnic outreach, and stakeholder relations. The means of coordination were imported from the campaign war room, including the integrated communications calendar and the system for planning and coordinating messaging at events. Another former senior PMO advisor (R11) agreed that strategic communications "bridges the divide between campaigning and governing ... You campaigned on an agenda, you got elected on that agenda, and strategic communication helps you to implement that agenda and keep the government focused on what got it elected in the first place." The branch existed to ensure consistent messaging that reinforced the government's key branding and reached target audiences. The Conservative PMO's approach to event "roll out" is a good illustration of the parallels between campaigning and governing.

The chief instrument for whole-of-government communications and management coordination was the weekly PMO roll-out meeting. Chaired by the director of strategic communications, the meeting was attended by all the strategic communications advisors as well as staff from other PMO departments such as issues management, media relations, and policy. According to a former senior PMO advisor (R11), the roll-out meeting allowed the PMO to consider all possible "announceables" from across the government and organize them to maximize the government's profile in the media. Broad thematic buckets contained subthemes to sustain a narrative over a longer period, supported by "messages of the day" that reinforced ministerial announcements. For example, an economic theme week might include sub-themes such as keeping taxes low, reducing red tape, and encouraging small-business growth. Themes frequently tied back to the election platform on which the government was first elected and ensured that, on a daily basis, it was talking about its preferred agenda.

The raw materials for this scripting exercise were message event proposals (MEPs).[3] While MEPs have been widely noted as a means of exercising control over the media (e.g., Blanchfield and Bronskill 2010; Thomas 2012), their two main purposes were, as Respondent 11 explained, first, to ensure that all announcements were carefully considered in terms of execution and message, and second, to provide sufficient information to the PMO to assess and organize announcements to maximize the impact of communications. MEPs were drafted by departmental communications officers in consultation with their minister's office and then circulated in two directions: by departmental officials to the Privy Council Office (PCO) and by the minister's office to PMO strategic communications advisors, who considered the political dimensions, consulted with PCO communications officials about the technical details, and brought forward the proposal for consideration at a weekly roll-out meeting. MEPs therefore resulted from collaboration between public servants, who ensured policy authority and factual accuracy, prepared materials, and handled event logistics, and political staffers, who advised their ministers with respect to timing, messaging, and overall event planning.

The Conservative PMO did not rely on MEPs alone in considering the forward-looking agenda. As a former senior staffer (R11) explained, the strategic communications unit searched across government to identify announcements that fit their thematic priorities in order to ensure an effective message each day. This included canvassing the agenda of cabinet policy committees and Treasury Board to anticipate announcements that might obtain policy authority in the near future.

Most announcements have potential political currency for the government, but only if (as in a campaign) they are properly managed. Using a central PMO perspective, the weekly strategic communications roll-out meeting scheduled these announcements and events to maximize their media impact, much in the same way a political party would strategically reveal elements of its platform in an election. It is counterproductive, for example, to table three major pieces of legislation on the same day or for two ministers to make announcements in the same city, because this dilutes their earned media coverage. The key central coordination method was the roll-out calendar, which mapped day by day all government-initiated activities as well as key external events. In the view of a former PMO advisor (R10), the calendar contained all the information necessary for the strategic communications unit to "micromanage" the government for several weeks out. Notably, the calendar also attempted to track upcoming appearances, announcements, and plans of the opposition parties, gleaned from news stories, party websites, or MP press releases. Incorporating the movements of the parliamentary opposition into a government strategy document is very much reflective of a campaign orientation.

The chief of staff to a minister (R4) explained that the PMO roll-out process grew out of a similar practice in the office of Ontario premier Mike Harris, and this is likely since Guy Giorno served as chief of staff to both Harris and Harper. But the strategic communications unit within Tony Blair's Labour government also used a grid system similar to Harper's PMO calendar (Kavanagh and Seldon 2000, 254–57). This underscores the extent to which the permanent campaign within government is a broad phenomenon and how practitioners in related circumstances employ similar solutions regardless of ideology.

While the roll-out exercise was largely about maximizing media attention for government announcements, PMO strategic communications staff also used new media technologies to bypass the national press gallery and deliver the government's message directly to voters. Examples in the Harper PMO included disseminating a "photo of the day" from the PMO photographic unit to regional media and through social media (Marland 2012) as well as instituting a weekly web video series, 24 Seven, which not only highlighted government announcements such as the budget, but also provided personal glimpses of Prime Minister Harper (see Chapter 14 by Mireille Lalancette and Sofia Tourigny-Koné). Such a dedicated web channel demonstrates that PMO strategic communications was trying to deliver its message straight to Canadian voters, in much the same way that a political party does during an election.

If strategic communications creates and advances the government's brand through proactive announcements and messaging, then issues management defends it against potential reputational risk. This involves obtaining accurate and timely information on issues in the media, including social media, to assess their political risk and to develop concise language (known as lines) that can be used in responding to the media and as a basis for ministers' answers in question period. William Stairs, former PMO issues management director, described issues management as a behind-the-scenes function providing "push-back against attacks or criticism" and coordinating and overseeing messaging across government. In his opinion, it is "very much a 100 percent partisan tool to get the government's communications out and make sure everyone is singing from the same song sheet."

Brodie explained that, after the 2006 election, when the campaign tool of issues management was first institutionalized within the PMO, the focus was on parliamentary affairs and, in particular, on preparing the prime minister for question period. PMO staffers began to hold a daily telephone conference call with representatives from all ministerial offices. This was useful for identifying issues and conveying information to the prime minister's issues management staff. However, as Respondent 10 recalled, the PMO issues management group at the time was reactive to the offices and not proactive in setting an agenda for response or establishing messages. Stairs, who was then chief of staff to a minister, agreed that the unit's function was more information gathering than dictating direction, whereas centralized messaging tended to come from PMO communications staff. By 2008, however, the pressures of a minority Parliament and, as Brodie remembered, the inexperience of many ministerial staffers and "responsiveness problems" with some departments, compelled the PMO issues management shop to take a more aggressive leadership role, and this approach has endured.

The daily 7:00 a.m. issues management meeting became a defining and continuing institutional feature of the Harper government. It was typically held over the phone, although sometimes in person at the PMO, and all ministers' offices had to be represented. As a former issues management director, Stairs saw three main purposes for the meeting. First, it required minister's offices to come prepared with context and facts on all possible media issues that posed political risk and gave them a chance to propose what the government's messaging should be. With this information, Stairs could then decide what lines to recommend to the prime minister ninety minutes later at the daily PMO senior staff meeting. As Respondent 10 explained, "Everyone in the system knew that these [lines] were going to be shared with the PM, so they were motivated to be responsive." Second, the meeting allowed the PMO to pass on direction – including the prime minister's perspective – to ministers' offices on pressing issues, and so it was an instrument for central messaging. As Stairs explained, "You can't have fifty-four offices coming up with different ideas. You need one idea. One set of messages." Ultimately, if ministers did not agree with lines suggested by the PMO, then they could argue their point with the prime minister when the full cabinet met each sitting day to rehearse for question period. Third, as Stairs explained, the morning issues meeting enabled the PMO to monitor the pulse of government by soliciting general feedback from offices, whether a heads-up on emerging issues, frustration with their departmental officials, or even frustration with the PMO. While the morning issues meeting was the main formal point of contact between ministers' offices and the PMO, informally, offices remained in close communication throughout the day.

As a minister's chief of staff (R4) explained, the issues management role was "absolutely critical" to an office. Issues managers required a mix of political and policy sense to develop strong communication messages early in the morning, "often before other staff are even awake," and the "gravitas" to defend the minister's handling of files and advocate for the minister's preferred messaging in cases when the PMO is pushing in a different direction. They had to work closely with departmental officials, not only to obtain the necessary information so that they could arrive prepared for the 7:00 a.m. meeting, but also to communicate decisions back to the department. Ultimately, their job required mitigating bad news on tight timelines, often with incomplete information. In Respondent 4's opinion, "It's very much the issues manager who gives your office a good name or a bad name first thing in the morning. If that person falters, the rest of your day is terrible and possibly your week." For Stairs, the issues management role requires "the most politically savvy people" who have "a very twitchy political nose" and who can "instinctively" anticipate political problems and quickly come up with lines to push back. "They just enjoy the game," he said. "They live and breathe politics."

There is no question that the growth of the formal issues management function represents the institutionalization of a campaign technique. While this began at the PMO in 2006, by November 2008 the Treasury Board's *Policies and Guidelines for Ministers' Offices* for the first time recognized issues management as a specific staff category equivalent to communications, policy, and parliamentary affairs (Treasury Board of Canada 2008, 6, 11). This title became entrenched within the Conservative government, although it did not displace parliamentary affairs as a political staff function. As an illustration, the federal government's online directory shows that on

July 29, 2015, nineteen ministers' offices had a director of parliamentary affairs and fourteen offices had a director of issues management. Ten offices had both positions, and in six of these, the two titles were held by a single individual. This growth of issues management was likely in part because chiefs of staff wished to emulate the PMO structure, and in part because it was a more accurate description of staff function. As a practical matter, having the option of an additional director-level position also gave chiefs of staff more flexibility in personnel management within the Treasury Board rules, since it came with higher status and a higher permissible salary, allowing them more opportunity to obtain, or retain, quality staff.

Permanent Campaigning in Canada

Does the institutionalization of strategic communications and issues management result in more informed and engaged citizens or more cynical ones? The strategic communications unit in the PMO was expressly created to improve the new Conservative government's ability to deliver on its election platform commitments, to increase its responsiveness to voters (at least to voter segments accessible to the CPC and necessary for its continued electoral success), and to ensure that the government could deliver clear and coordinated policy messages. These could be considered enhancements to Canadian democracy. However, central requirements for message discipline potentially constrain the conversation between citizens and their democratically elected representatives, especially if their MP sits in the government caucus.

One of the main casualties of the Conservative government's permanent campaign approach was its relationship with the national press gallery (Thomas 2012, 69). Strong central control over both proactive announcements and reactive issues messaging seeks to ensure that all ministers and MPs deliver a single approved message, to frustrate the media's natural inclination to highlight gaffes and dissent, and to ensure that a government spokesperson will be quoted on the government's desired message or not at all. This is a legitimate goal. But when discipline prevents public figures from commenting on public issues, especially when combined with restrictions on other sources of information, it then impairs the ability of journalists to do their job, which is an essential component in a democratic society.

Perhaps the most significant implications of the increased emphasis on strategic communications and issues management arise within government, in particular the challenge to avoid a short-term policy outlook and to maintain positive relations between the political executive and the public service.

Both public servants and political staffers expressed concern that campaigning in government detracts from longer-term policy making. One former senior PMO advisor conceded that issues management "sometimes (not infrequently) led to micro-policy decisions that themselves did not benefit from the scrutiny, analysis, and balancing of interests that typically was involved in the development of intentional and proactive policy" (R1). Media reports with negative implications for the government often precipitated rapid policy or legislative changes (eliminating old-age pensions for prisoners is just one example). A senior PCO official (R8), reflecting on his years of experience with multiple ministries, observed that there used to be a period, especially in a majority government, when government decision making was more about policy and less about electoral considerations. He now believes that "the system as a whole is twitchier, it's more reactive, it's shorter term," and that this leads to "unpredictability" and higher stress, upsets planning, and crowds out other work. He added, "I'm not saying we're on our way to hell in a hand basket, but there's a kind of risk that the longer term is sacrificed by perceived shorter-term gain that might not even be gain." Ian Brodie also expressed concern: "You're never going to do a 100 percent good job of issues management, ever ... And so if you are not making progress on what the government is actually trying to do in a policy sense and talking about it in a way that connects with people, you're never going to win a defensive war." Ultimately, the short-term horizon characteristic of an issues management culture impacts the government's ability to do longer-term strategic policy thinking, both in the public service and among political staff.

A further consideration is that campaigning in government affects relations with the public service. Undoubtedly, departmental officials have an important and appropriate role in supporting the communication efforts of ministers. They are well placed to anticipate issues within departments that are, as one deputy minister remarked, "a little bit subterranean for the political side" (R5). But the demand for speed in an issues management culture led by political staff leads to frustration and tension – frustration because the political side needs answers and wants to move much more quickly than the public service has traditionally been structured to accommodate, and tension because political demands can create an environment of pressure and stress in a context where, according to the same deputy minister, some relationships "are quite fine, but some of them are quite toxic" (R5).

Dangers on the strategic communications side are less about urgency and personality but more structurally challenging for keeping distinct lines between political and public service, as Peter Aucoin (2012) warned about in his NPG framework. One senior PCO official (R8) asked, "How do you distinguish between writing effective lines that communicate to the public what the government has done as opposed to advance the interests of the party in power?" Where should the line of propriety be drawn when it comes to the colour scheme on government websites or how much political perspective can be incorporated into departmental briefing materials? As a former PMO advisor observed, because "there's a political calculus to everything going forward ... the line between non-partisan public servants and the political side is being a little bit blurred" (R10).

Are these changes within the communications world here to stay, or might things be different under the Trudeau Liberal PMO and its successors? A senior PCO official noted that "for a variety of reasons political parties today – whoever's in power and those out of power – feel that all of their actions during their period in office need to be oriented, at least to some extent, towards the next election" (R8). The permanent campaign has become entrenched in many countries, and several political environmental factors suggest that it is the new normal in Canada regardless of the party in power.

Undoubtedly, the intensity of the permanent campaign depends greatly on the leadership style of the prime minister and, to a lesser but still significant extent, his or her political staff (Radwanski 2015), but it is also influenced by political realities. The governing style of the Conservative Party was shaped by the party's legacy, notably on the Reform Party side, of undisciplined and damaging statements that were amplified by eager media. One former senior PMO staffer suggested that this context explained Prime Minister Harper's "unshakeable" insistence on central message control, which was compounded by the fact that the Conservatives' governing style gelled in the instability of successive minority Parliaments (R1). Another former PMO advisor observed that the instinct to see every issue as life or death "became entrenched and ingrained in the staffers and in [the] PMO," such that now, even when the parliamentary pressure has dissipated, nothing has changed. "You don't need to strong-arm everything in a majority government, but," he concluded, "that's all I see" (R10).

At the same time, the permanent campaign is driven by forces that are bigger than any one party in government. In particular, two factors exogenous to political parties compel them to remain on a war footing all the time. The first is the ubiquity of published horse-race public opinion polling, including attempts at specific seat projections well outside any election period. The second is the ability of social media – particularly Twitter – to put issues, especially negative issues, on the national agenda. Twitter means that the government constantly risks losing control of specific stories, and it is impossible to overstate its impact within government. If a negative story is not defeated or denied, or no alternative version of events is provided, then it can take hold in the public's mind. While the Harper government paid "excruciating attention" to combatting reputational risk (R1), the need to do so was not unique to that government and is unlikely to disappear. Perhaps this explains why the Conservative issues management innovation remains embedded within the new Liberal government. As of July 2016, the government electronic directory showed that nine Liberal ministers had a director of issues management, including Prime Minister Trudeau, who had a dedicated four-person issues management unit in his office.

In summary, beginning in 2006, the Conservative government institutionalized its election war room priorities of strategic communications and issues management at the centre of government. The political staffers who assumed these roles were very familiar with electoral tactics and tools, and it was natural for them to transfer their formidable communications and management skills from the campaign to their new jobs in government. The media environment as well as the parliamentary minority context made it difficult for political staff to break from their campaign mindset. Consequently, campaigning and governing were, and remain, easily blended.

While it is clear that political staff are driving the permanent campaign, especially with respect to institutionalized campaign practices such as strategic communications and issues management, more robust empirical testing is needed to determine whether we have, in fact, entered an era of "new political governance." Public servants are concerned about coming too close to advancing the partisan interests of the governing party when developing their own communication material. Likewise, there is also some anxiety that strategic planning on the political communication side is not necessarily accompanied by long-term *policy* planning within government and that issues management imperatives sometimes precipitate hasty policy decisions. But the public servants we interviewed did not express concern that political

staffers, obviously engaged in aspects of the permanent campaign, were systematically threatening the non-partisan ethos of the public service. Certainly there are challenges. Normal tensions in personal relationships are
sometimes exacerbated by the stress of the 24/7 media environment. And
public servants are challenged to demarcate the appropriate boundary of
non-partisan service to ministers when it comes to new media. But such
things are part of legitimate democratic dialogue with respect to public service responsiveness to ministers and do not approach the "corrupt form of
politicization" feared by Aucoin (2012, 178). In other words, the distinction
between the political and the non-political in parliamentary government remains largely intact.

If we consider, however, our supposition that the permanent-campaign-
like atmosphere is here to stay – no matter the partisan stripe of the party
in power – then much more research and analysis on this subject are
required.

NOTES

1 Directories were obtained from Western University and Library and Archives
   Canada (LAC). We have been unable to find directories for the years 1959, 1965,
   1995, and 2003–4. According to LAC, no directory was published in 2003–4. The
   last paper directory was 2009–10; thereafter, information has been published online
   as the Government Electronic Directory Services (GEDS; http://sage-geds.tpsgc
   -pwgsc.gc.ca). No archive is available for GEDS. From 2010 on, data were derived
   either from GEDS records retained personally by the authors or from staff lists
   provided courtesy of the PMO.

2 Some caution is warranted since earlier directories may not include all PMO staff.
   For example, the 1970 and 1971 directories list thirty-three and thirty-five PMO
   staff, respectively. However, then PMO principal secretary Marc Lalonde reported
   a PMO staff complement of eighty-five in 1970–71 (Lalonde 1971, 532). This may
   reflect the absence of some administrative staff from the directory, or possibly the
   difference between a cumulative annual count and a point-in-time snapshot. All
   political staff are included in later directories.

3 Examples of MEPs can be found in Marland (2016), as can further detail about a
   number of concepts about the Harper PMO identified in this chapter.

REFERENCES

Alboim, Elly. 2012. "On the Verge of Total Dysfunction: Government, Media, and
    Communications." In *How Canadians Communicate IV: Media and Politics*, edited
    by D. Taras and C. Waddell, 45–53. Edmonton: Athabasca University Press.
Aucoin, Peter. 2012. "New Political Governance in Westminster Systems: Impartial
    Public Administration and Management Performance at Risk." *Governance: An*

International Journal of Policy, Administration and Institutions 25 (2): 177–99. http://dx.doi.org/10.1111/j.1468-0491.2012.01569.x.

Axworthy, Tom. 1988. "Of Secretaries to Princes." *Canadian Public Administration* 31 (2): 247–64. http://dx.doi.org/10.1111/j.1754-7121.1988.tb01316.x.

Benoit, Liane E. 2006. "Ministerial Staff: The Life and Times of Parliament's Statutory Orphans." In *Commission of Inquiry into the Sponsorship Program and Advertising Activities: Restoring Accountability*. Research Studies, vol. 1, 145–252. Ottawa: Public Works and Government Services Canada.

Blanchfield, Mike, and Jim Bronskill. 2010. "Harper's Message Control Is Unprecedented, Critics Say." *Globe and Mail*, June 6. http://www.theglobeandmail.com/news/politics/harpers-message-control-is-unprecedented-critics-say/article1375533/?page=all.

Blick, Andrew. 2004. *People Who Live in the Dark*. London: Politicos Publishing.

Burney, Derek. 2005. *Getting it Done: A Memoir*. Montreal/Kingston: McGill-Queen's University Press.

Campbell, Colin, and George Szablowski. 1979. *The Superbureaucrats: Structure and Behaviour in Central Agencies*. Toronto: Macmillan.

Craft, Jonathan. 2016. *Backrooms and Beyond: Partisan Advisers and the Politics of Policy Work in Canada*. Toronto: University of Toronto Press.

D'Aquino, Thomas. 1974. "The Prime Minister's Office: Catalyst or Cabal? Aspects of the Development of the Office in Canada and Some Thoughts about Its Future." *Canadian Public Administration* 17 (1): 55–79. http://dx.doi.org/10.1111/j.1754-7121.1974.tb01655.x.

Delacourt, Susan. 2013. *Shopping for Votes: How Politicians Choose Us and We Choose Them*. Madeira Park, BC: Douglas and McIntyre.

Eichbaum, Christopher, and Richard Shaw, eds. 2010. *Partisan Appointees and Public Servants: An International Analysis of the Role of Political Adviser*. Cheltenham, UK: Edward Elgar. http://dx.doi.org/10.4337/9781849803298.

Elmer, Greg, Ganalele Langlois, and Fenwick McKelvey. 2012. *The Permanent Campaign: New Media, New Politics*. New York: Peter Lang.

Esselment, Anna Lennox. 2010. "Fighting Elections: Cross-Level Political Party Integration in Ontario." *Canadian Journal of Political Science* 43 (4): 871–92. http://dx.doi.org/10.1017/S0008423910000727.

Flanagan, Tom. 2007. *Harper's Team: Behind the Scenes in the Conservative Rise to Power*. Montreal/Kingston: McGill-Queen's University Press.

–. 2014. *Winning Power: Canadian Campaigning in the Twenty-First Century*. Montreal/Kingston: McGill-Queen's University Press.

Goldenberg, Eddie. 2006. *The Way it Works: Inside Ottawa*. Toronto: McClelland & Stewart.

Kavanagh, Dennis, and Anthony Seldon. 2000. *The Powers behind the Prime Minister: The Hidden Influence of Number Ten*, 2nd ed. London: HarperCollins.

Kozolanka, Kirsten, ed. 2014. *Publicity and the Canadian State: Critical Communications Perspectives*. Toronto: University of Toronto Press.

Lalonde, Marc. 1971. "The Changing Role of the Prime Minister's Office." *Canadian Public Administration/ Administration publique du Canada* 14 (4): 509–37. http://dx.doi.org/10.1111/j.1754-7121.1971.tb00296.x.

Mallory, J.R. 1967. "The Minister's Office Staff: An Unreformed Part of the Public Service." *Canadian Public Administration* 10 (1): 25–34. http://dx.doi.org/10.1111/j.1754-7121.1967.tb00962.x.

Marland, Alex. 2012. "Political Photography, Journalism, and Framing in the Digital Age: The Management of Visual Media by the Prime Minister of Canada." *International Journal of Press/Politics* 17 (2): 214–33. http://dx.doi.org/10.1177/1940161211433838.

–. 2016 *Brand Command: Canadian Politics and Democracy in the Age of Message Control.* Vancouver: UBC Press.

Marland, Alex, Thierry Giasson, and Tamara A. Small, eds. 2014. *Political Communication in Canada: Meet the Press and Tweet the Rest.* Vancouver: UBC Press.

Plasse, Micheline. 1994. *Ministerial Chiefs of Staff in the Federal Government in 1990: Profiles, Recruitment, Duties and Relations with Senior Public Servants.* Ottawa: Canadian Centre for Management Development.

Privy Council Office. 2015. *Accountable Government: A Guide for Ministers and Ministers of State.* Ottawa: Her Majesty the Queen in Right of Canada.

Radwanski, Adam. 2015. "Harper's Enforcer: Meet Jenni Byrne, the Most Powerful Woman in Ottawa." *Globe and Mail,* May 29. http://www.theglobeandmail.com/news/politics/meet-the-woman-driving-harpers-re-election-campaign/article24699535.

Rathgeber, Brent. 2014. *Irresponsible Government: The Decline of Parliamentary Democracy in Canada.* Toronto: Dundurn Press.

Savoie, Donald. 1983. "The Minister's Staff: The Need for Reform." *Canadian Public Administration* 26 (4): 509–24. http://dx.doi.org/10.1111/j.1754-7121.1983.tb01042.x.

–. 1999. *Governing from the Centre: The Concentration of Power in Canadian Politics.* Toronto: University of Toronto Press.

Taras, David and Christopher Waddell, eds. 2012. *How Canadians Communicate IV: Media and Politcs.* Vancouver: UBC Press.

Tellier, Paul. 1968. "Pour une réforme des cabinets de ministres féderaux." *Canadian Public Administration* 11 (4): 414–27. http://dx.doi.org/10.1111/j.1754-7121.1968.tb00601.x.

Thomas, Paul G. 2012. "Communications and Prime Ministerial Power." In *Governing: Essays in Honour of Donald Savoie,* edited by J. Bickerton and B.G. Peters, 53–84. Montreal/Kingston: McGill-Queen's University Press.

Tiernan, Anne. 2007. *Power without Responsibility.* Sydney, Australia: UNSW Press.

Treasury Board of Canada. 2008. *Policies and Guidelines for Ministers' Offices.* Ottawa: Her Majesty the Queen in Right of Canada.

Turcotte, André. 2012. "Under New Management: Market Intelligence and the Conservative Party's Resurrection." In *Political Marketing in Canada,* edited by A. Marland, T. Giasson, and J. Lees-Marshment, 76–90. Vancouver: UBC Press.

Wilson, R. Paul. 2015. "A Profile of Ministerial Policy Staff in the Government of Canada." *Canadian Journal of Political Science* 48 (2): 455–71. http://dx.doi.org/10.1017/S0008423915000293.

–. 2016. "Trust but Verify: Ministerial Policy Advisors and Public Servants in the Government of Canada." *Canadian Public Administration* 59 (3): 337–56.

Yong, Ben, and Robert Hazell, eds. 2014. *Special Advisers: Who They Are, What They Do and Why They Matter*. Oxford: Hart Publishing.

Zussman, David. 2009. *Political Advisors. Expert Group on Conflict of Interest*. Paris: OECD.

13

Permanent Campaigning and Digital Government

Amanda Clarke and Mary Francoli

Internationally, governments are experimenting with a range of new digitally enabled policy instruments and have launched broader public management reform programs that centre on digital technologies (Government 2.0 Taskforce 2015; Orszag 2009). Authors exploring digital government (the application of digital technologies to the functions of the public sector) argue that the digital age will fuel more open and participatory governments and more effective and efficient policies and services (Dunleavy et al. 2005; Lathrop and Ruma 2010; Noveck 2009). By this perspective, digital technologies are vehicles of generally accepted principles of good governance. At the same time, the growth of digital government has coincided with another trend that authors have tied to public sector management, particularly in Westminster systems, in recent years – politicization of the professional, permanent, non-partisan public service, or what has been termed New Political Governance (NPG) (Aucoin 2012), a facet of the broader phenomenon of permanent campaigning. Albeit to a lesser extent than authors describing digital government, those exploring NPG also focus on the impact of digital technologies on the public sector, but draw very different conclusions than those found in the digital government literature. NPG asserts that digital technologies promote partisan communications in the public service and compel governments to become more secretive and resistant to consultation. By this view, the digital age incites and enables the public service to become a mechanism of the permanent campaign – a partisan resource wedded to securing the political fortunes of the governing party and, thus, an institution that betrays entrenched principles of good governance in Westminster systems.

This chapter considers these two contradictory narratives by exploring the following questions: Do trends in digital government compel the public service to become more politicized, as per the NPG narrative and, in turn, supporting the notion that the political system is now characterized as a permanent campaign? Alternatively, do digital technologies enable the public service to become more open, collaborative, and participatory, as is espoused in mainstream digital government literature? In posing these questions, we are not implying that these two outcomes are exhaustive of all potential influences of digital technologies on the public sector, or that these outcomes are mutually exclusive. Rather, we begin from the premise that it is possible that neither, or that both, of these trends are under way. We aim to consider these two perspectives on contemporary public sector govern-ance side by side to investigate if, and to what extent, the public sector's uptake of digital technologies affirms or contradicts the literatures on NPG (and broader theories of the permanent campaign) and digital government. We begin by detailing how these two literatures differ in their initial assump-tions about the role of digital technologies in government.

Peter Aucoin (2012) describes four core characteristics of NPG: the blend-ing of governance with campaign tactics; the growing influence of political staff in government ministries; the politicization of the senior public service; and the expectation that public servants engage in "promiscuous partisan-ship." This theory reflects the concerns of an existing literature on public sector politicization, which Chris Eichbaum and Richard Shaw (2008, 17) define "as an action or intervention which is contrary to the principle of an impartial and professional civil service." The principle to which they refer is part of the larger set of principles underpinning the institution of the public service within Westminster systems of government. This set of principles includes public service anonymity, ministerial accountability, and most rel-evant to public sector politicization (as reflected in Eichbaum and Shaw's definition), political neutrality and professionalism (Kernaghan and Langford 1990).

Recent literature on public sector politicization, especially works build-ing on Aucoin, argues that these principles are being abandoned via a ser-ies of trends that, while not completely new (see Kaufman 1956), have become more acute in certain Westminster governments in recent years (Savoie 2013; Shepherd, Stoney, and Turnbull 2014). This literature rarely focuses explicitly on the rise of digital technologies within society more generally and in the public sector specifically. However, in describing the pressures and trends that have propelled public sector politicization, the NPG literature does focus on activities and trends that have clear links to digital technologies. These include (1) the changing nature of public sector communications, (2) public sector transparency, and (3) growing demand for, and supply of, citizen engagement opportunities.[1]

Beginning with the changing nature of public sector communications, the literature on NPG emphasizes that the new media landscape, comprising traditional and new digital media, has hindered good governance practices. As this argument goes, the 24/7, rapid pace of this new media landscape amplifies the political pressures facing government. In turn, government communications officers are pulled into media management and advertising campaigns that serve partisan interests and that therefore betray their duty to direct government resources (here, official communications) to nonpartisan ends (Mulgan 2007). In addition, Aucoin (2012) posits that the growing emphasis on auditing in contemporary government compels defensive responses from government that are folded into official communications as part of tightly controlled public relations strategies, not open, engaging government-to-citizen dialogue facilitated by social media or other channels. Summarizing these claims, Aucoin (2012, 183) states that "the communications function of government has become the black hole of public service impartiality," an effect of the new "economic marketplace of the media" (181) that demands "virtual instantaneous response" (181).

Turning to the issue of public sector transparency and freedom of information specifically (as opposed to communications strategies that have the effect of reducing transparency), the NPG literature argues that the emergence of technologies that enable public disclosure of government information (such as open data portals, social media, and websites) compels governments to become more opaque for fear of the scrutiny invited by public disclosure of government information. Acknowledging the contrast between the interpretation of transparency reforms taken by digital government enthusiasts (discussed later in this chapter) and in the NPG literature, Richard Mulgan (2007, 585) writes:

> The greater transparency of the current era may be seen to cut both ways. On the one hand, it increases the likelihood that government deceptions will be uncovered and thus acts as a spur to government honesty. On the other hand, the fact that more public service advice may end up in the public arena places officials under greater pressure to compromise with the truth in the interests of not undermining the credibility of their political masters.

Adopting the latter interpretation expounded by Mulgan, and directly tying information and communications technologies to public sector politicization, Aucoin (2012, 182) argues that "the cumulative effects of the information and communications revolution ... have made even the most tightly controlled government operations at risk to leakage, intentional and otherwise." He argues that the potential for such leaks has induced public servants to avoid digital paper trails and recordkeeping to prevent unwanted public disclosures. Not only does this produce a public service that is more opaque, but it also allows for partisan interference in properly non-partisan policy work to continue without being documented and made open for scrutiny.

Finally, the NPG literature argues that digital technologies can expand the potential for citizen participation, and that this, paradoxically, reduces scope for a more collaborative, democratically responsive style of governance to emerge in the digital age. For example, in the face of increasing demand for "open consultative forums," Aucoin (2012, 182) argues that far from spurring genuine engagement with citizen demands "governments expect what they regard as *their* public servants to promote their agenda in the conduct of their activities, notwithstanding the fact that a government's agenda is necessarily a partisan agenda." In their study, Eichbaum and Shaw (2007, 628) explain that "a more demanding and discerning public were among the characteristics of a contemporary policy environment which – our respondents felt – places ministers under increasing pressure, in response to which they turn to political advisers for support and advice," as opposed to an active citizenry attempting to engage in government's work via the web.

While the NPG literature ties digital technologies to wholesale betrayals of core principles of good governance, as detailed through the three thematic areas outlined in this chapter (communications, transparency, and citizen engagement), with few exceptions (see Morozov 2013), mainstream digital government literature posits that digital technologies enable a more democratic, effective, and professional public service that is in tune with generally accepted principles of good governance (Borins 2007; Chadwick 2008; Dunleavy et al. 2005; Mergel 2014; Noveck 2009).

Beginning with the communications function, the digital government literature argues that digital technologies, especially social media, allow for more real-time, fluid, and interactive communication between government and outsiders (and internally, among public servants) via a range of platforms, including, among others, blogs, Facebook, and Twitter. In turn, authors argue that social media have the potential to improve the accessibility of government policies and services by making it easier for the public to directly interact with public servants (Mickoleit 2014; Tapscott, Williams, and Herman 2008).

In addition, strains of the digital government literature emphasize that open data (the release of raw, machine-readable government data) and the increased flow of information accompanying the digital age allow for unprecedented levels of transparency in the public sector, enabling citizens to assess the work of government and hold it to account, thus creating an "army of armchair auditors" (Davies 2012; Gov.UK 2010) from which government cannot hide its failings.

Finally, a third theme common to both the digital government and NPG literatures is citizen participation; again, the digital government literature offers an alternative, and more hopeful, interpretation of the effects of technology on this domain of government practice than that found in the NPG literature. Specifically, the digital government literature notes that technology allows for new models of consultation that can facilitate dialogue between citizens and government, allowing citizens a stronger and regularized role in policy making (Chadwick 2003; Lathrop and Ruma 2010; Noveck 2009).

These three information and communications technology–related trends – the changing nature of public sector communications, new forms of public sector transparency, and new opportunities for citizen participation – are common across both the NPG and digital government literatures. Yet authors exploring public sector politicization and those focused squarely on digital government reforms draw different conclusions about the effects of these trends on public sector governance. Do digital technologies, and the trends they generate in public sector bureaucracies, facilitate the emergence of NPG as part of the broader phenomenon of permanent campaigning, or do they support good governance, as per the digital government narrative? In response to this question, we next explore the impacts generated by digital technologies in these three areas in the Government of Canada.

Case Study

Method

Our case study of the Government of Canada is built on data culled from over fifty semi-structured key informant interviews that we conducted between 2010 and 2015, before the October 2015 election and subsequent

change of government, as part of a series of related research projects focused
on digital-era public management in the government. Those interviewed
primarily operate (or operated, in the case of former employees) at the centre of government, in the Treasury Board Secretariat (especially the Chief
Information Officer Branch). Interviewees also included officials in line departments and members of civil society (in particular, those advocating for
open government reforms in Canada). For the interviews with public servants, interviewees were selected to represent a range of authority levels
(from executive to junior official) within the following functional areas:
communications, information technology, information management, policy
advice, and program design and delivery. Interviewees from civil society
were selected based on their experience and knowledge of the three areas
related to open government: access to information, open data, and citizen
engagement. They included representatives from non-governmental organizations, access-to-information lawyers, journalists, data scientists, academics, and librarians. Interviews were transcribed in some, but not all, cases.
We analyzed interviews both thematically and as pieces of key informant
data; that is, as sources of insight to insiders' technical, procedural, and explanatory knowledge of internal organizational activities that would otherwise not be known (Van Audenhove 2007). For the thematic analysis, our
initial approach was primarily inductive, reflecting an exploratory approach
to the interviews, coupled with some deductive analysis (drawing on theories and concepts in the public administration and digital government literatures). For the purposes of this study specifically, the data were interpreted
deductively, with a view to assessing the extent to which they support the
theory of NPG or of digital government. When analyzing pieces of key informant data (e.g., information on how a particular process unfolded and
who was involved), we carefully considered respondents' potential biases
and errors and triangulated testimonies to check for their accuracy.
Interviewees were guaranteed anonymity; accordingly, data from interviews
are reported in this chapter without attribution. The interview data are supplemented and triangulated with data drawn from media reports, previous
studies of Canadian public management, and policy documents retrieved
from the Government of Canada website.

Findings

Beginning with the theme of public sector communications, we find some
evidence that government social media accounts have become components

of partisan campaigns, as claimed in the NPG literature. Most recently, in May 2015, then minister of Employment and Social Development Canada Pierre Poilievre faced criticism in the media for involving public servants in the preparation of a YouTube video that was deemed to be a promotional advertisement for the Conservative Party's platform on families, a key issue animating debate among federal parties in the run-up to the 2015 election. In another incident in November 2014, an assistant deputy minister at the Department of Finance was critiqued for soliciting retweets from other departments for a tweet to be published by the departmental Twitter account that was deemed to betray the non-partisan standards of public sector communication by including a hashtag – #StrongFamilies – that had been used in Conservative Party advertising (Canadian Press 2014b). In addition to these incidents of apparent social media politicization, both media reports (Canadian Press 2014a; Levesque 2013) and our interviews with communications officers in the federal government indicate that government social media accounts are often heavily controlled through many-layered approval processes, reflecting a commitment to message control that prevents the technology from supporting more fluid government-citizen interactions.

At the same time, we find evidence to suggest that in many ways, the digital age propels communications practices that respect the professionalism and non-partisanship proper to the tasks of the public service, thus betraying the NPG narrative. A series of Treasury Board policies introduced from 2009 onwards (Treasury Board of Canada Secretariat 2009, 2011, 2014b) encourage "the use of social media in communicating and engaging with the public and in delivering services" (Treasury Board of Canada Secretariat 2014b), but also elaborate in great detail the ethical and legal standards that must be upheld in their use, including those referenced in the *Values and Ethics Code for the Public Sector*.[2] One such policy explicitly identifies "attempts to engage in dialogue about political decisions or direction" as a "risk of use" that public servants should be conscious to avoid when using social media (Treasury Board of Canada Secretariat, 2011). Interviews consistently revealed that public servants are acutely aware that they must avoid engaging in partisan behaviour in their use of any communications channel, including social media. While there have been instances in which public servants have either not recognized that a communications activity was partisan or lacked the impetus or guidance to flag such an outcome to senior officials – as in the example of activities at Employment and Social

Development Canada and the Department of Finance discussed in this chapter – it is equally true that corporate policies and attitudes adopted by public servants suggest that the public service communications function has not been entirely co-opted by inappropriate partisan goals in the digital age.

On the issue of message control and communications centralization, we also find evidence to challenge the NPG narrative. Official departmental social media accounts are heavily managed, but this is a symptom of the long-standing tradition of risk-averse and controlled communication that has emerged from corporate policies and legal dictates, not partisan-political direction. Using social media in government demands adherence to a series of requirements, such as ensuring that all social media content is bilingual and accessible to those with disabilities. Other approvals emerge because public servants want to ensure that content does not betray standards in the *Values and Ethics Code for the Public Sector*, including that it avoids partisan messaging. Interviewees consistently explained that these concerns are the reason that social media channels have become heavily managed and often populated with prepared content (thus betraying the free-flowing, dialogic types of communication associated with social media more generally). In a context where multiple actors must approve content to meet legal and ethical standards, real-time interaction is difficult to achieve. This may warrant legitimate criticism for the opportunities lost through heavily controlled social media communication, but it is inaccurate to presume that the social media approval processes in the federal government are necessarily the product of partisan message control from political authorities, as opposed to a reflection of legal and ethical standards, and related corporate processes, at play in the public service.

In sum, while we find some evidence that digital technologies are facilitating NPG trends in communications, we find more evidence to suggest that the public service is aware of this potential and is attempting to counteract these trends through internal policies and procedures. Interestingly, in doing so, the public service renders itself less equipped to embrace the opportunity for open, real-time government–citizen communication advocated by digital government enthusiasts. On the digital communications file, then, the government offers neither evidence supporting the theory of NPG, nor evidence in favour of the promises made in the DG literature.

Turning from communications to transparency in the Government of Canada, our findings similarly indicate that neither theory fully captures the impact had by digital technologies on the federal public sector. We focus our analysis in this chapter on one particular program area in which digital technologies are shaping transparency in the government, and which is also a central preoccupation of the digital government literature: open data. In 2011, the government launched its open data portal (data.gc.ca – later rebranded open.canada.ca). The portal drew together a variety of federal data holdings and made them available in machine-readable formats so that they could be more easily analyzed and repurposed for other use by external actors. The digital, open, and reusable format is thought to allow those inside and outside of government to view and combine data, creating new insights into the functions of government, including expenditures and procurement. This in turn has the potential, among other things, to improve governance by compelling greater government accountability and better-informed public scrutiny of government operations.

Looking purely at the number of data sets made public via the portal, we see evidence that potentially disrupts the NPG narrative of information control. As of May 2015, there were 244,325 data sets on the open data portal. In June 2013, the federal government took steps to make the data easier to use by issuing an Open Government Licence. The licence allows users to freely "copy, modify, publish, translate, adapt, distribute or otherwise use the Information in any medium, mode or format for any lawful purpose."[3] Among other things, the government notes that the release of data in a machine-readable format with a licence for reuse will foster the sort of accountability and democratic reform espoused in the digital government literature. As explained on the Open Government website: "Increased access to government data and information provides the public with greater insight into government activities, service delivery, and use of tax dollars."[4]

However, while the federal government has constructed a narrative of increased transparency around its open data strategy that is consistent with normative theories of digital government, our analysis suggests that this narrative has some holes in practice. More data have been added to the portal, but much of the data are not new; that is, they were already publicly available prior to the portal's launch. The portal simply allowed for these data to be centralized. Other concerns have been raised about the quality of the data sets' metadata (i.e., how data are categorized and labelled), the lack of diversity in the data sets, and the fragmented nature of the data sets. As one civil society interviewee noted when commenting on the government's open data offerings, the "metadata and usability have a long way to go" (November 2013). Efforts to improve data quality are limited by a dearth of new resources for open data; the political rhetoric surrounding the initiative has not been met with a complementary envelope of funds to support the staffing and technological requirements that come with an open data program. A number of interviewees in line departments explained that, for them, efforts to improve open data releases were "corner-of-the-desk projects" – the product of their personal interest in the initiative, and not well-supported, top-down dictates. In short, the open data program faces significant challenges that limit its ability to further transparency and improve governance to the extent that the digital government literature, and the government's open data discourse, would have us believe.

In addition, others have noted that at the same time as information and communications technologies are being used to centralize federal data holdings, the government has discontinued a number of studies that were used to collect vital data, ensuring that even if data are made more open, there are other efforts under way to actually reduce the amount of data that government collects that could be opened to the public. Stakeholders in Canada's open data community interviewed as part of a major assessment of open government in Canada (Francoli 2014) viewed cuts to federal studies and data collection as part of the government's efforts to become more opaque, not more transparent. In addition, one interviewee from civil society who had previously worked in the federal government noted that there had "been meetings where government employees say that data sets have to be approved by the PMO" (November 2013), indicating that the flow of open data from the federal government to citizens is not strictly "open," but rather in some cases may be filtered through the partisan strategies of then prime minister Stephen Harper's staff. Together, these issues and concerns provide support for the notion that at least in the area of open data, theories of NPG provide a more accurate appraisal of the impact had by digital technologies on contemporary governance; the fact that the digital age in theory allows the government to be more transparent results in government practice that tightly controls the information it shares with the public. This outcome aligns with broader theories of the permanent campaign, which posit that the tight information and message control associated with electioneering now permeate the everyday activities of democratic institutions. But before drawing this conclusion, the testimonies of public servants tasked with the implementation of the open data initiative deserve consideration.

Interviews with members of the public service indicated that getting the data portal up and running, and making changes to improve its usability, is a complicated undertaking. It involves the creation of data management standards to which all departments and agencies must adhere. This necessitates a significant amount of stakeholder consultation, coordination, and approval processes. Another issue that muddies discussions and progress on open data relates to the division of power among levels of government in Canada. Interviews with members of the federal government, and documents such as *Canada's Action Plan on Open Government* (Treasury Board of Canada Secretariat 2014a) and the draft *Open Data Charter* (opendata charter.net), spearheaded by an open data working group led by the Government of Canada, indicate the importance of having open data standards and values that are inter-jurisdictional. This necessitates conversations between the federal government and other levels of government in Canada, a process that takes time to do well.

On the transparency file, then, there is some evidence of potential political interference that limits the free flow of open data and of deliberate efforts to reduce government data collection; these findings better support NPG's framing of digital-era public sector transparency. But complicating this conclusion, we see evidence supporting the transparency ideals found in the digital government literature, where government uses digital technology to provide information and data to its citizens. The number and types of data on the portal have bolstered transparency to a certain extent. In addition, our interviews suggest that rather than simply resulting from political interference, it is also the complex nature of open data initiatives in large federal bureaucracies that ensure open data has been difficult to implement. To be sure, those within the Government of Canada are aware that there is room for improvement and are working steadily towards it, by continuing to make and fulfill commitments related to open data within the framework of the Open Government Partnership. Indeed, even the most critical of civil society members indicated that open data is the one area of the open government initiative that has benefited from focused, substantial effort by the public service. Returning to the competing theories tested in this chapter, the theme of transparency, explored through the lens of the open data initiative, exposes some evidence that supports the theory of NPG. However, the results also echo what we find in the area of communications – bureaucrats themselves are eagerly working to realize the style of good governance espoused in the digital government literature, but face significant administrative and procedural barriers to doing so. Again, neither theory fully or accurately aligns with our evidence.

Finally, turning to the third theme, citizen participation, the federal government has undertaken a series of episodic departmental efforts to engage members of the public in policy development through online consultations. For example, the former Department of Foreign Affairs and International Trade completed a series of e-discussions (online consultations) with the public between 2007 and 2010. Industry Canada hosted online consultations on the issue of copyright reform in 2009 and on the digital economy in 2010. From 2011 onwards, the government also hosted a series of online consultations to develop its open government strategy. The open dialogue commitment of the first *Action Plan on Open Government* introduced in 2012, and the second introduced in 2014, represented a more systematic effort to promote online engagement with citizens using information and communications technologies (Treasury Board of Canada Secretariat 2012, 2014a). The first plan promised to promote "Web 2.0 and similar tools, such as crowdsourcing, to engage Canadians in a discussion on government policies and priorities" (Treasury Board of Canada Secretariat 2012). Specifically, under the open dialogue initiative, the government promised to replace the dated "Consulting with Canadians" website with "a new Web 2.0 citizen engagement platform that federal organizations can use to conduct public consultations" (Treasury Board of Canada Secretariat 2012). Under the open dialogue initiative, the government also promised that it would experiment with crowdsourcing as a new form of interactive citizen engagement.

The Government of Canada has made minimal progress on these commitments. Under an open regulation initiative, it introduced a website on which regulators could post information about regulatory changes, but a 2014 evaluation of the *Action Plan on Open Government* noted that while thirty-two regulators had posted information online, "it was not clear to stakeholders how open dialogue [was] achieved" by this one-way flow of information (Francoli 2014, 10). The government experimented with crowdsourcing via two tweet chats (consultations held on Twitter) hosted by the Treasury Board Secretariat,[5] but experimental forays into crowdsourcing via social media did not become common practice. The second *Action Plan on Open Government*, released in 2014, also discusses open dialogue and again committed to develop a new online consultation platform for the federal government. As was the case with the first action plan, the platform was not introduced.

While the open dialogue initiative has made slow progress to date, our analysis suggests that this has not resulted from a resistance to the more distributed forms of citizen participation facilitated by the Web, as per the NPG narrative. Rather, interviewees revealed that open dialogue has been difficult to implement because of the same technical and legal requirements that limit a more fluid use of social media for communication, as already discussed. For example, the common engagement platform has been difficult to develop because it must support bilingualism, meet accessibility standards, and be secure (to avoid data leaks and privacy infringements). While those seeking evidence of politicization effects might presume that weak progress on the open dialogue file reflects a government that is impervious to open, dialogic web-based citizen engagement, as per the NPG narrative, we find that the rules and procedures to ensure that public engagement exercises adhere to principles of good governance (e.g., ensuring all citizens have equal access to consultations) are what prevent the vision of web-based consultation proposed in the digital government literature from being realized.

Permanent Campaigning in Canada

The theory of NPG claims that core public sector principles are being displaced by a system in which the public service is merely a partisan tool employed by the governing party to further its electoral prospects as part of the permanent campaign. Within this theory of contemporary governance, digital technologies are cast as both driving and facilitating public sector politicization, a reading that contrasts sharply with mainstream theories of digital government. These theories contend that when the public sector adopts new digital technologies, governments and citizens communicate more fluidly, the public sector is more transparent, and policy processes become more participatory. If such trends are indeed taking hold, they would indicate that, at least in its uptake of digital technologies, the public service is in fact emboldening its commitment to core democratic principles, thus directly challenging the theory of NPG and the broader literature on the emergence of permanent campaigning.

What role do digital technologies play in contemporary government? This chapter has shown that in the case of the Government of Canada, social media are not being used to support more fluid interactions between government and citizens as per the digital government narrative. This is not to suggest that social media are solely employed as components of partisan message control in the public service either. Certainly a few key examples related to government advertising suggest that social media can be vehicles of partisan messaging, but we equally find compelling evidence indicating that social media–based communication is managed primarily through processes that seek to ensure that this communication aligns with core principles of good governance, including that it not support partisan goals. Similar findings emerged in our examination of web-enabled initiatives promoting citizen participation in the public sector. Rather than indicating that digital consultation efforts have been slowed by partisan-political efforts to tightly manage policy processes, our findings suggest that this outcome has resulted, in large part, from internal, corporate policies of the public service. In the case of technology and transparency, the open data strategy has made some strides towards increased transparency with the release and aggregation of data sets, as well as the establishment of the Open Government Licence, which facilitates the reuse of data. However, as we argue, cuts to federally funded studies used to collect data vital to good governance, and preliminary evidence that data releases are in some cases tightly controlled, suggest that the NPG's framing of digital-era transparency may hold some water. Nonetheless, such conclusions should ultimately be tempered by an appreciation for the legitimate challenges that accompany the implementation of an open data initiative across a large bureaucracy operating in a federal state.

In sum, our findings indicate that neither the theory of NPG nor the digital government literature accurately appraises the role that digital technologies have played in the Canadian federal government. We have not witnessed a digital government that has transformed to become supremely open, engaging, and participatory, but nor do we find that digital technologies are exclusively and systematically employed to politicize the work of the public service. More often, our analysis pointed to instances in which internal corporate policies and procedures marked the government's engagement with digital technologies, not partisan-political campaigns.

Our conclusions suggest that theories of digital government must better account for the ways in which digital technologies can challenge effective and democratic governance (as in certain instances of government advertising in Canada). But more fundamentally, our findings indicate that those advancing the theory of NPG will benefit by testing their propositions with more systematic and varied empirical inquiry. This chapter focused on one particular set of NPG claims – those related to digital technologies' effect on the public sector – and found, at first blush, what may appear to signal the politicization of the public service (e.g., social media message control, a slowly developing open data strategy, and weak efforts to deliver on promises of innovative online consultation). However, the study uncovered that NPG effects are not wholly or in certain cases even partially the cause of these outcomes. To be sure, our analysis does not indicate that NPG effects are not taking hold more generally in the Government of Canada, but rather that not all outcomes that appear to *signal* politicization are in fact truly the *result* of politicization. More precisely, our analysis suggests that at least in one of its assessments – the role of digital technologies in the public sector – the theory of NPG should be adjusted to appreciate the layered pressures shaping life in the contemporary public service. In turn, our findings point to the need for future research that probes unchecked assumptions currently at play in the literature on NPG and permanent campaigning. And in cases where the findings *do* align with assumptions in this literature, this chapter provides a cautionary check on the normative enthusiasm found in theories of digital government; evidently, these theories also suffer by ignoring the multiple competing pressures shaping government in the digital age, and in particular, the pressures that can arise from permanent campaigning.

Finally, this chapter sets the stage for studies that explore the influence of political leadership on digital government. Our study covered the period in which the Government of Canada was led by Stephen Harper, the first prime minister to govern in an age of social media, open data, crowdsourcing, and near ubiquitous Internet connectivity, but also a prime minister known for his sophisticated use of permanent campaigning tactics. Prime Minister Justin Trudeau has offered early signals that his administration will usher in a wholly different style of public management to the federal government, committing the public service to open engagement with Canadians, transparency, and experimentation with innovative digital models of policy development (Prime Minister of Canada 2015). Our analysis suggests that embracing social media, open data, and online citizen engagement is not simply a challenge in need of political leadership, but rather will require significant investments in the administrative apparatus and corporate policies that underpin these functions. As Canada's second digital-era prime minister, Trudeau's early commitment to open government and citizen engagement thus provides occasion to measure how much – or how little – political leadership matters in realizing the democratic renewal that theories of digital government promise, theories that offer distinctly more hopeful views of the institution of the public service than we receive in descriptions of the permanent campaign.

NOTES

1 This categorization scheme is imperfect, and there is some overlap between the three themes. However, the thematic identification provides a mechanism for thinking through different approaches and reactions to technology's place in the public sector and to the argument that Canada is engaged in a permanent-campaign style of governance.

2 See http://www.tbs-sct.gc.ca/pol/doc-eng.aspx?id=25049.

3 The terms of the licence are available at open.canada.ca.

4 "Open Government," open.canada.ca.

5 See http://open.canada.ca/en/consultations/transcript-tweet-chat and http://open.canada.ca/en/consultations/transcript-twitter-chat-about-open-government for full English-language transcripts of the tweet chats.

REFERENCES

Aucoin, Peter. 2012. "New Political Governance in Westminster Systems: Impartial Public Administration and Management Performance at Risk." *Governance: An International Journal of Policy, Administration and Institutions* 25 (2): 177–99. http://dx.doi.org/10.1111/j.1468-0491.2012.01569.x.

Borins, Sandford F., ed. 2007. *Digital State at the Leading Edge.* Toronto: University of Toronto Press.

Canadian Press. 2014a. "Government Tweets Sanitized through 'Super-Rigid Process.'" *CBC News,* February 2. http://www.cbc.ca/news/politics/government-tweets-sanitized-through-super-rigid-process-1.2520731.

–. 2014b. "Tories Turn to Public Servants for Twitter Pitch of Tax Proposals." *Toronto Star,* November 21. https://www.thestar.com/news/canada/2014/11/21/tories_turn_to_public_servants_for_twitter_pitch_of_tax_proposal.html.

Chadwick, Andrew. 2003. "Bringing e-Democracy Back In: Why It Matters for the Future Research on e-Governance." *Social Science Computer Review* 21 (4): 443–55. http://dx.doi.org/10.1177/0894439303256372.

–. 2008. "Web 2.0: New Challenges for the Study of e-Democracy in Era of Informational Exuberance." *I/S: A Journal of Law and Policy for the Information Society* 5 (1): 9–41.

Davies, Tim. 2012. "How Might Open Data Contribute to Good Governance?" In *Commonwealth Governance Handbook 2012/13.* Cambridge: Nexus Strategic Partnerships. http://www.opendataimpacts.net/2012/12/how-might-open-data-contribute-to-good-governance/.

Dunleavy, Patrick, Helen Margetts, Simon Bastow, and Jane Tinkler. 2005. "New Public Management Is Dead – Long Live Digital-Era Governance." *Journal of Public Administration: Research and Theory* 16 (3): 467–94. http://dx.doi.org/10.1093/jopart/mui057.

Eichbaum, Chris, and Richard Shaw. 2007. "Ministerial Advisers, Politicization and the Retreat from Westminster: The Case of New Zealand." *Public Administration* 85 (3): 609–40. http://dx.doi.org/10.1111/j.1467-9299.2007.00666.x.

–. 2008. "Revisiting Politicization: Political Advisers and Public Servants in Westminster Systems." *Governance: An International Journal of Policy, Administration and Institutions* 21 (3): 337–63. http://dx.doi.org/10.1111/j.1468-0491.2008.00403.x.

Francoli, M. 2014. *Independent Reporting Mechanism: Canada Progress Report 2012–13.* Washington, DC: Open Government Partnership. http://www.opengovpartnership. org/.

Government 2.0 Taskforce. 2015. "About." http://gov2.net.au/.

Gov.UK. 2010. "Eric Pickles 'Shows Us the Money'." August 12. https://www.gov.uk/ government/news/eric-pickles-shows-us-the-money-as-departmental-books -are-opened-to-an-army-of-armchair-auditors.

Kaufman, Herbert. 1956. "Emerging Conflicts in the Doctrines of Public Administration." *American Political Science Review* 50 (4): 1057–73. http://dx.doi.org/10.2307/ 1951335.

Kernaghan, Kenneth, and John W. Langford. 1990. *The Responsible Public Servant.* Halifax: Institute for Research on Public Policy and Institute of Public Administration of Canada.

Lathrop, Daniel, and Laurel Ruma, eds. 2010. *Open Government: Collaboration, Transparency, and Participation in Practice.* Sebastopol, CA: O'Reilly.

Levesque, Lisa. 2013. "Public Servant Use of Twitter Requires 9 Levels of Approval." *Canadian Government Executive,* February 28. http://www.canadiangovernment executive.com/management/business/item/1159-public-servant-use-of-twitter -requires-9-levels-of-approval.html.

Mergel, I. 2014. "Opening Government: Designing Open Innovation Processes to Collaborate with External Problem Solvers." *Social Science Computer Review.* http:// dx.doi.org/10.1177/0894439314560676.

Mickoleit, A. 2014. *Social Media Use by Governments: A Policy Primer to Discuss Trends, Identify Policy Opportunities and Guide Decision Makers.* OECD Working Papers on Public Governance No. 26.

Morozov, Evgeny. 2013. "The Meme Hustler: Tim O'Reilly's Crazy Talk." *The Baffler.* Number 22, http://thebaffler.com/articles/the-meme-hustler.

Mulgan, Richard. 2007. "Truth in Government and the Politicization of Public Service Advice." *Public Administration* 85 (3): 569–86. http://dx.doi.org/10.1111/j.1467 -9299.2007.00663.x.

Noveck, Beth Simone. 2009. *Wiki Government: How Technology Can Make Government Better, Democracy Stronger, and Citizens More Powerful.* Washington, DC: Brookings Institution Press.

Orszag, Peter R. 2009. "Open Government Directive." Memorandum for the Heads of Executive Departments and Agencies, December 8. https://www.whitehouse.gov/ open/documents/open-government-directive.

Prime Minister of Canada. 2015. "Ministerial Mandate Letters." http://pm.gc.ca/eng/ mandate-letters.

Savoie, Donald J. 2013. *Whatever Happened to the Music Teacher? How Government Decides and Why*. Montreal/Kingston: McGill-Queen's University Press.

Shepherd, Robert, Christopher Stoney, and Lori Turnbull. 2014. "Politicization: What, Why, How?" Paper presented at the National Annual Conference of the Institute of Public Administration of Canada. Edmonton, June 1–4.

Tapscott, Don, Anthony Williams, and Dan Herman. 2008. *Government 2.0: Transforming Government and Governance for the Twenty-First Century*. n.p.: nGenera Corporation. http://wiki.douglasbastien.com/images/a/aa/Transforming_govt.pdf.

Treasury Board of Canada Secretariat. 2009. "Guideline to Acceptable Use of Internal Wikis and Blogs within the Government of Canada." November 18. https://www.tbs-sct.gc.ca/pol/doc-eng.aspx?id=17555.

–. 2011. "Guideline for External Use of Web 2.0." November 21. http://www.tbs-sct.gc.ca/pol/doc-eng.aspx?id=24835.

–. 2012. "Canada's Action Plan on Open Government 2012–2014." http://www.opengov partnership.org/sites/default/files/legacy_files/country_action_plans/Canada%27s %20Action%20Plan%20on%20Open%20Government%20-%20Plan%20d% 27action%20du%20Canada%20sur%20le%20gouvernement%20ouvert_0.pdf.

–. 2014a. "Canada's Action Plan on Open Government 2014–2016." http://www.opengov partnership.org/sites/default/files/Canada%20Action%20Plan%20on%20Open %20Government%202014-16%20%28EN%29.pdf.

–. 2014b. "Guideline on Official Use of Social Media." March 4. http://www.tbs-sct.gc.ca/pol/doc-eng.aspx?id=27517&section=HTML..

Van Audenhove, Leo. 2007. *Expert Interviews and Techniques for Policy Analysis*. Cambridge, MA: MIT Studies on Media, Information and Telecommunication.

14

24 *Seven* Videostyle: Blurring the Lines and Building Strong Leadership

Mireille Lalancette and Sofia Tourigny-Koné

In an era of permanent campaigning, the communications strategies mobilized by the governing party play a central role in shaping perceptions of leadership, government, and political actors. Building on the assumption that permanent campaigning is the political practice of our age, we argue that image making becomes central and governments become instruments to support the elected official's popularity (Heclo 2000). In this context, the distinction between electoral and governing processes is blurred. Image and presentation outweigh performance, carefully crafted policies, and national and international comparisons (Sparrow and Turner 2001). Communications strategies are borrowed from commercial branding, and the expertise of pollsters, marketing researchers, and advertising firms is constantly mobilized during and between elections. Moreover, exercising tight control over the manner in which issues are presented is critical, as is crafting a clear and concise message that can be easily repeated on a loop, while neutralizing the strategy of other parties by using, for instance, negative advertising.

During the 2015 electoral campaign in Canada, despite the fact that negative attack ads were a feature that some parties used heavily, Justin Trudeau's Liberal Party opted for more positive messages. It turns out that optimistic messaging and positive images can be a boon for a party; image management is increasingly important in this respect. This is also true in government. Considering that former prime minister Stephen Harper has been a key player in defining the permanent-campaign context, this chapter investigates government video-style practices to understand how they contribute to constructing an image of strong leadership. We argue that it is crucial to better comprehend how video is being used as a means of image management. By using multiple web-based platforms, the Harper government (much like Trudeau in the 2015 campaign) strived to project a positive image, not only as a way to communicate, but also as a tool to create ways of seeing the world. Focusing our attention on image management and its impact on leadership is necessary, since leadership and image management are key aspects of politics. Rhetorical principles of managing the image of political figures (the *ethos*) and the uses of affective (*pathos*) and cognitive (*logos*) strategies for promoting politicians have been around for millennia and are still used today (Amossy 2010; Flanagan 2014).[1] The creative and insightful work of public relations expert Edward Bernays (1928) in the 1920s illustrates that image management was also a preoccupation in the early ages of mediated politics. The "presentation of self" (Goffman 1959) as a way to manage impressions remains a concern and is even more crucial in a 24/7 news environment where it is common to see a social media faux pas go viral. Moreover, in a context where celebrity and pop-culture practices rub off on political practices, style, character, and private life have become important elements in the assessment of political performance (Corner and Pels 2003; Van Zoonen 2006). Personality is considered a key feature of the modern election campaign. The role of the individual politician is often discussed using the concept of personalization of politics (Karvonen 2009; Lalancette with Lemarier-Saulnier and Drouin 2014), which is also presented as a form of "communication adaptation" from politicians to fit the process of mediatization (Strömbäck and Van Aelst 2013).

In this context, politicians and their advisors devote time, money, and energy to present candidates in the best possible light; they try to offer the electorate an appealing and carefully crafted package (Arbour 2014; Stanyer and Wring 2004). On the campaign trail, every detail is controlled, from the politician's clothes to the locations visited or the features of his/her private life shown to the public. Why devote all this energy to image management and "selling" the candidate? Because research shows that perceptions of image and personality traits are important determinants of individual voting preferences (Brown et al. 1988; Gidengil et al. 2012; Johnston 2002). Also significant are perceptions of competence and responsiveness (Bittner 2011). Voters want competent candidates for three reasons. They want office holders who (1) deliver policies that can be tailored to particular constituencies; (2) understand the issues of the country, have the knowledge and judgment to make good decisions, and can successfully manage the country; and (3) are able to deal with unanticipated problems (Arbour 2014). Voters' perceptions of characteristics such as leadership abilities, honesty, intelligence, friendliness, sincerity, and trustworthiness play a role at election time (King 2002). Image-management techniques are used to offer the impression that politicians possess these qualities (Mayer 2004). Picturing the candidate with his/her family often showcases reliability and trustworthiness. Abilities and intelligence are conveyed through the candidate's background in politics or in business. Friendliness is depicted through the candidate's interaction with multiple types of citizens: children, the elderly, the poor, the affluent, men and women (Grabe and Bucy 2009; Marshall 1997). In a context where we know that voters have specific expectations and images of the ideal candidate, this demands academic attention, and even more so since research shows that image-management techniques can affect and manipulate voters' perceptions of qualities like competence, integrity, likeability, and general fitness for political office (Rosenberg and McCafferty 1987).

Image-management techniques have now moved to the online sphere, and documenting the day or the week of the heads of government seems to be the norm (Marland 2012). The Government of Canada is no stranger to this trend and is increasingly moving towards digital-image management. The focus is now more on TV and the Internet than on print advertising, as these platforms are better suited for branding and can be consistently monitored (Burgess 2015). In this fast-paced context where images and information are abundant and competition for the public's attention is fierce, Harper's political advisors and marketing team devoted great effort to controlling the information process. Image-management techniques were used to frame him in a positive light. The websites of both the Conservative Party of Canada (CPC) and the Prime Minister of Canada frequently featured photographs of Harper during routine government business. Social media platforms like Twitter were also used to offer a friendly, approachable, and "feel-good" image of him (Boesveld 2013). To counter the impression of a serious ideologue, Stephen Harper's team tried to humanize him in various ways, including his love of hockey, cats, and Beatles songs. There were successful attempts to soften Harper's image and make him appear more approachable. For example, his playing piano and singing the Beatles' hit song "With a Little Help from My Friends" with celebrity cellist Yo-Yo Ma at the National Arts Centre generated 500,000 YouTube visits in a week (Rana 2009) and was widely discussed in the media. This "pseudo-event" (Boorstin 1992) was so popular that the prime minister played piano at numerous other occasions, and this event put pressure on his office to offer other entertaining content inspired by pop-culture practices (Marland 2016).

In Canada, research about the "photo of the day" has examined the use of digital photographs by the Prime Minister's Office (PMO) to manage

Harper's image (Marland 2012, 2014). The PMO's tight image management was inspired by Republican techniques under George W. Bush's presidency, but most directly by the regular use of a photo of the day by Barack Obama's White House. To prime and frame Harper in a strategic manner, image handlers strictly managed the visuals that were offered to the press. When news events were controversial, the public relations team used the image of the day to circumvent the events and offer a counternarrative. For example, with these pictures, the PMO tried to offset Harper's negative image by presenting him as an ordinary Canadian. The content analysis of a year's worth of PMO photos (227 photos published online in 2010) showed that the dominant visual framing was one of the prime minister as a hard-working head of government both in Ottawa and elsewhere in the world (Marland 2014). Fifty-seven inductive dichotomous coding categories were created to determine how the prime minister was visually branded. Harper was mostly showcased wearing business clothes (82.8 percent of photos) and occupied in different tasks – meetings, telephone conversations, document signing – in the Parliament buildings, while interactions with cabinet ministers showed them listening to the prime minister (46.3 percent). He was also often presented with international dignitaries and leaders, such as Queen Elizabeth II and other G20 representatives (9.7 percent). While it was the construction of Harper's personal brand that was most important, Conservative policy priorities were also conveyed through the photos. For instance, the CPC law-and-order message was showcased using military personnel, troops, veterans, and the minister of national defence (7.5 percent), while education was seldom pictured (1.3 percent). The images were a tool to personalize and humanize the prime minister; they presented Harper as head of a nuclear family and as a loving husband. Laureen Harper (11 percent) was featured more often than cabinet ministers (10.6 percent) and international leaders. Pop-culture celebrities were also shown (4.8 percent) as well as Stephen Harper wearing casual clothes (9.7 percent). Children (10.1 percent), non-Caucasians (7.5 percent), senior citizens (6.6 percent), and Aboriginals (0.4 percent) were also included in the images. Lastly, the prime minister's brand also revolved around being a patriotic Canadian sports fan, with hockey being the most popular sport (6.6 percent). This was evident from the prominent positioning of celebrities and pop-culture icons in many of the images. The use of hockey images could be part of larger promotional strategies to use this sport to signify a particular type of Canadianness and to present a political elite as an ordinary citizen (Scherer and

McDermott 2011). Similar strategies were employed to present George W. Bush as a common man, a leader in a time of war, and a big baseball fan (Mayer 2004).

In addition to the photo of the day, the PMO website also featured videos called *Stephen Harper: 24 Seven*, illustrative of the move into video image-management techniques. The videos offered a behind-the-scenes look at the prime minister's activities and personal life. The videos could be accessed through multiple entry points. Episodes could be viewed on the Prime Minister of Canada website and the Prime Minister of Canada YouTube channel, both bilingual sites.[2] Sometimes the videos were also promoted on the Government of Canada's website home page (www.canada.gc.ca). Citizens could sign up on the PMO website to be notified when there was a new video. The video magazine took the form of a weekly show. Each episode began and concluded with a refrain from "The Maple Leaf Forever," and the Canadian flag was overtly present. Every detail appeared scripted, and the narrative was thoroughly controlled. A crew of six followed the prime minister and helped put together a portrait of the week to offer insight on how the government operated (Simpson 2014). The PMO had a video and photography unit composed of three people. One photographer/videographer had backstage access to the prime minister. The target audience for the videos was unclear, but research suggests that the videos functioned as public relations information subsidies produced to control media content (Curtin 1999). In a continuous newscast and market-driven journalism era, these kinds of promotional political strategies are becoming more important (Strömbäck and Van Aelst 2013). From 2008 to 2015, under the Harper Conservative era, a team of communication bureaucrats working for Employment and Social Development Canada was tasked with finding "new ways to reach out to Canadians" (Galloway 2015). Many Conservative ministers were also using videos to promote their actions. Pierre Poilievre, former minister for employment and social development, did so when promoting how new measures adopted by his cabinet would benefit families.

The *24 Seven* video magazine grouped three types of videos. First, there were videos presenting "The Week of Stephen Harper," which usually had two parts: one showing Harper in task-oriented settings, and the other portraying his wife, Laureen, in more private settings or doing charitable work. These videos were often narrated by a female voice using a captivating style of speech. Second, there were thematic videos organized around news stories called "prime minister delivers remarks on ... " in which the prime minister addressed events like the Parliament Hill shootings, the death of Jim Flaherty, and the G20 summit, all of which were used to reinforce the government's views on issues like terrorism, economic decisions, and international relations.[3] Also in this category were the "24 Seven Exclusives," which showed the highlights of Stephen Harper's week and presented him performing different official functions, such as at honorific celebrations. Third, there were videos in which the prime minister spoke directly to the camera in a format similar to the one used when giving a televised address to the nation. One such video showed the prime minister offering an apology on behalf of Canadians for the Aboriginal residential school system; in others he conveyed positive wishes for religious occasions (e.g., Christmas, Hanukkah, and Diwali).

The 24 Seven videos acted as a permanent-campaign technique and are worth studying for many reasons. Videos offer the possibility of combining discourse and image management, and images are often more memorable than written or verbal content (Grabe and Bucy 2009). With carefully crafted images, political advisors and publicists can create emotion, use shared cultural values and patriotic themes, and showcase the political figure's character, qualities, and personality. Videos are a very visual medium that facilitates message adoption. Visuals are instrumental in shaping public opinion (Grabe and Bucy 2009). Social media simplify the act of sharing and posting on different platforms, so the potential impact of the videos and their messages can easily be multiplied. For example, the five-minute Poilievre video called "Strong Families Make a Strong Country" was posted on many Conservative MP websites, which effectively propagated the message (Galloway 2015). If we are witnessing the institutionalization of the permanent campaign, it is worth asking whether spending taxpayers' dollars to produce videos is an appropriate use of public money. In light of events where, in one episode of 24 Seven, security was breached when the faces of several Canadian special forces soldiers appeared on the video, leaving them vulnerable to physical attacks (Chase 2015; Puzic 2014), one could also question how far one should go to circumvent media coverage and build strong leadership.

To document how leadership was constructed using the 24 Seven videos, this study builds on Alex Marland's (2012, 2014) results on how the PMO tried to control Harper's leadership image using "photo of the day" images. Our analysis underlines the similarities in image-management techniques used for photos and for video and complements earlier studies by high-lighting other new features related to videos, such as storytelling style, use of appeals, and issues discussed.

Case Study

METHOD

To study how leadership is defined and projected by the PMO in the course of the permanent campaign, we analyzed archived videos available on the former prime minister's YouTube account.[4] To analyze videos that had a form of visibility in the public domain and that might have affected the political discourse and journalistic coverage, we first included all the videos on the site that had more than 10,000 views. Since there were only thirteen such videos in the summer of 2014, we added other videos that had between 1,000 and 10,000 views ($n = 57$), while trying to balance all three types of videos – "The Week of Stephen Harper," "prime minister delivers remarks on ... ", and direct addresses to citizens- randomly. With seventy videos, we reached a saturation point and stopped collecting data.

Using both an inductive and a deductive approach, we developed a coding grid to identify the actors represented in the storytelling and the issues discussed in the videos. We also adapted the storytelling and appeal coding grid of Bystrom et al. (2004)[5] to the context of the *24 Seven* videos. To prevent a subjective interpretation of the videos, indicators were developed for all the variables and given to the coders, who were instructed to code the presence or absence of the variables (inter-coder reliability: 91.7 percent). The coders simultaneously evaluated the images and narrator speech and/or discourse of the protagonists of the videos in an integrated process. For example, if a video portrayed Stephen and Laureen Harper attending a sporting event in a primary school, we coded the presence of three types of actors: the prime minister, the prime minister's wife, and children. When the narrator of the video made the connection between the sporting event and the new meas-ures for families, the issue, "economic assistance (for families, the elderly, and victims of criminal acts)" was coded as being present. If the prime min-ister included statistics in one of his discourses, we coded the use of the ap-peal, "use of facts, statistics, or concrete examples." For all the videos, we coded the presence of the different variables and transformed this into a percentage. These descriptive statistics helped us identify the characteristics of the videos and reflect on how leadership is presented in the videos.

FINDINGS

As we will see in the analysis, leadership is constructed using many communications strategies. The key concerns seem to be conveying a specific message, selling credibility, and offering a positive image of the prime minister. The *24 Seven* series was one of the tools used to promote government actions and that this was done using public resources, which is a significant component of permanent campaigning strategy.

As we can see in Table 14.1, in all the videos it was the prime minister who was centre stage performing official tasks. The prime minister was often shown interacting with citizens and electors when giving speeches or while in public settings or meetings. Harper's identity was also built on his international presence. He was portrayed giving official addresses and meeting other countries' leaders. CPC MPs and ministers were present in the videos, but they were most often secondary actors. In some cases, their names and titles were not publicized. Some appeared in the background during the debate period at the House of Commons. Military personnel, active-duty soldiers, and war veterans were represented during official events like ceremonies welcoming soldiers back home from conflict zones or official military celebrations such as Remembrance Day. Children and elderly people were

TABLE 14.1

Actors figuring in storytelling in PMO videos

Actors	Frequency of presence (%)
Prime Minister Stephen Harper	87
Citizens/electors	56
Other CPC MPs and ministers	41
International representatives	36
Laureen Harper	35
Children	24
Military personnel	21
Elderly people	7
Celebrities	6
Political opponents	0

NOTE: Percentages total more than 100 percent due to multiple actors in videos. The coding of frequency denotes the percentage of analyzed videos in which these actors appeared and does not reflect the duration of the appearances.

part of the stories showcasing the prime minister in his visits to residences for the elderly, carnivals and festivals, and, most often, sporting events. He was also shown in positive interactions with celebrities like Bill Gates and Wayne Gretzky.

The *24 Seven* depiction of actors appears to have followed the same image-management practices employed in the photo of the day part of the site and aligns with Marland's (2014) findings. In fact, the way Prime Minister Harper was pictured in the videos is strikingly similar to the photos of the day. The prime minister was still the central actor, and he was framed as a hard-working statesperson in a relationship with a loving and caring spouse. Laureen Harper was also an important figure in the videos, although she was a little less present in our sample of videos than in the sample of still images analyzed by Marland. Major events were also used as a stepping stone to frame Harper as a leader. International spokespeople, ministers, military personnel, and children were more important in videos than in the photo of the day analysis. These differences could be explained by the fact that more information can be offered in videos, thus boosting the presence of these actors in our analysis. The videos also showed the prime minister in different settings, showcasing his authority and his good nature. For example, in some videos he cracked a joke; this kind of interaction is more difficult to convey in a still image with no explanation. In line with Maria Grabe and Eric Bucy's (2009) analysis, images in the videos of Harper interacting with other cabinet members and the portrayal of the prime minister as an international actor could be seen as ways to visually project his statesmanship, power, and active leadership. In addition, and according to these researchers, qualities like compassion and empathy are exhibited through positive interactions with children and families. These exchanges could be viewed as a means to create a symbolic linkage with supporters. The prime minister's commonness was also shown by the regular display of him wearing casual clothes like khaki pants and a blue shirt with the sleeves rolled up or, when in athletic settings, Team Canada clothing (hockey was the most common, but volleyball and other sports were also featured). Following Grabe and Bucy's work (2009), this type of visual appearance is part of an effort to appear as an average citizen and, hopefully, relate to voters. This result is similar to the image constructed of George W. Bush as an everyman who shared American values. He was depicted as a sports fan, and events were carefully chosen to reinforce and associate the visuals with that characterization (Mayer 2004).

TABLE 14.2

Issues discussed in PMO videos

Type of issue	Frequency (%)
Economy	51
Cultural pluralism and immigration	43
Terrorism and national defence	29
Economic assistance (for families, the elderly, and victims of criminal acts)	19
Crime, justice, and civil rights	17
Taxes	13
Patriotism	7
Education	7
Environment	6
Health	6
Debt	1

NOTE: Percentages total more than 100 percent due to multiple issues in videos.

Another important actor was Laureen Harper, who brought a soft touch to the portrait. She appeared as a "First Lady of Canada," often shown at 24 Sussex Drive doing charitable work and supporting various causes such as wildlife preservation and breast-cancer prevention. She was repeatedly shown with other Canadians, and the emphasis was on her social and relational skills. For example, she was featured taking care of the family pets and attending her children's sporting events. She was also presented running a half-marathon in support of the military. This accent on motherhood and caring corresponds to what is expected of women in politics (Van Zoonen 2006). Together, Stephen and Laureen Harper offered a balanced picture of a task-oriented husband who was well matched with a compassionate and sensitive wife. This could have a significant impact, since the family is seen as a credibility-developing device (Arbour 2014) and a traditional nuclear family could invoke conservative values.

The prominence of a number of issues identified in the videos were consistent with the CPC topics put forward in other forums and on other platforms (Table 14.2). These included the economy; cultural pluralism and immigration; terrorism and the importance of national defence; economic

Table 14.3

Dominant storytelling format of PMO videos

Storytelling style	Frequency (%)
Journalistic style with narration	48
Direct address to citizens and electorate	34
Musical, with acknowledgments and testimonials of citizens and military personnel	9
Videos promoting values and ideas of the government	7

assistance for families, the elderly, and victims of criminal acts; crime, justice, and civil rights; taxes. In this line of thought, some issues were seldom discussed, most obviously the environment, health, education, and the country's debt. Often the message was simple to understand and conveyed with black-and-white thinking. The clear partisan angle could be seen as an effort to control the agenda and prime the CPC's core issues. Every topic and political event promoted a government position and could be considered hyperpartisan, which aligns directly with permanent-campaign principles (Esselment 2014).

In our analysis, we also focused attention on the style of storytelling used in the videos. The way a message is constructed and framed has an impact on its reception. The dominant storytelling style (Table 14.3) used in the videos was journalistic, most often with accompanying narration. The narrative was promotional and offered in a dramatized, spectacular tone; one could follow Harper's life like a television show with its intrigues and surprises. The prime minister and Laureen were centre stage in the videos, and their lives were often depicted aesthetically with polished images. Presented as a loving and ideal traditional couple, they were shown in the Canadian North walking along a lake holding hands and stopping for a kiss. They wore matching Canada Goose coats. On other occasions, they were shown snowmobiling and dog sledding in Canada's picture-perfect winter settings. Or, when attending Jim Flaherty's funeral, Laureen was shown as despondent and tearful. These videos embraced an emotional feel-good angle. The accent on *pathos* as a communication strategy was important, but was well-balanced with more serious (*logos*) themes, such as the business of managing the country, international relations, terrorism, patriotism, war, ethnic diversity, and family values. In this sense, the *24 Seven* videos could be seen as a way to present Harper as a hard-working leader whose priority was the Canadian economy. They also humanized the prime minister while increasing his credibility and legitimacy. When he was featured in the videos, Harper appeared in control. In speeches, he used both logical and emotional arguments. Local and international political events were all woven into the larger narrative and framed to emphasize Harper's leadership and his administration's values. This could be important, since charismatic leadership assessment revolves around qualities like being energetic, enthusiastic, and determined, as well as having a vision and clear sense of direction (Javidan and Waldman 2003).

The second most popular storytelling style was direct address to citizens and the electorate, with the prime minister speaking to the camera. Other formats were acknowledgments and testimonials of citizens and military personnel and videos promoting the values and ideas of Harper's government. The different storytelling strategies used in the videos were ways to circumvent the news media and speak directly to Canadians and to specific segments of the population. In fact, this strategy and the previous strategy could be considered as public relations information subsidies to construct a specific reality and offer a particular interpretation of events to journalists (Marland 2012).

Storytelling style is not the only interesting aspect of the *24 Seven* videos. Various types of appeals were also used in the videos and are worthy of analysis (Table 14.4). Highlighting the Harper government's position on specific issues was the most common type of appeal. It was achieved by using a news event to reinforce the message on issues like the economy and the prevention of terrorism. The next most popular appeal used facts, statistics, and concrete examples. A third type was the adoption of an intimate tone, usually in the videos where the prime minister addressed citizens directly. Fourth were appeals to highlight the prime minister's authority, which was accomplished by presenting him delivering speeches in an international context and by showing him taking a stand on different issues. The last prevalent appeal was using the endorsement of public and pop-culture personalities. These types of appeals are consistent with the storytelling styles most frequently used – journalistic and direct address – and fall in line with what Arbour (2014) calls candidate-centred communication strategies, where highlighting the candidate's character, reinforcing issue positions, and

Table 14.4

Appeals most frequently used in PMO videos

Type of appeal	Frequency (%)
Highlighting the Harper government's position on specific issues	46
Use of facts, statistics, or concrete examples	26
Adoption of an intimate tone (addressing the electorate like equals or peers)	24
Highlighting the prime minister's authority	20
Highlighting endorsements from public and pop-culture personalities	17
Adoption of an offensive position	0

NOTE: Percentages total more than 100 percent due to multiple actors in videos.

demonstrating competence is central tenets. The endorsement of pop-culture personalities could also be seen as an attempt to control the image of the prime minister and to create positive affect (Marland and Lalancette 2014). Offensive positions, like in attack ads, were not adopted in the *24 Seven* videos. Attack ads were transmitted using the CPC website and YouTube channel. In all of the *24 Seven* videos, images and clips were reused and repackaged.

Permanent Campaigning in Canada

During his time in office, Stephen Harper and his team made a concerted and continual effort to promote a precise image and political agenda. This occurred not just through photos and texts, but also through professionally produced videos available on various government websites and other online platforms. Using mostly a journalistic and therefore common style to frame Harper's leadership positively, the *24 Seven* videos helped establish his legitimacy and credibility. They were also a great tool to construct the leader's *ethos* and carefully balance informative facts (*logos*) and emotional cues (*pathos*). In this sense, and as presented in the introduction, this case study highlights three of the strategic objectives of permanent campaigning in Canada: resource exploitation, communication control, and the redefinition of norms.

A major difference exists between traditional electoral campaigning and the permanent campaigning approach put forward by the *24 Seven* videos in terms of resource exploitation: in the latter, the PMO was not compelled to respect electoral budgets for advertising, since these videos were not produced during the writ period. Ultimately, this raises ethical questions about the PMO channelling public resources for partisan purposes. Moreover, if government resources, time, and energy are used to promote re-election and partisan issues, it likely means that other pressing policy issues are left unaddressed. When electoral and governing processes are blurred in such a way, one can question the impact these practices have on democracy.

The communication control aspect looks more obvious. In a political system where leaders' personalities are becoming increasingly crucial and playing a larger role in voters' choice, it is important to point out that the videos under scrutiny strongly emphasized the prime minister's leadership style. Anna Lennox Esselment (2014), Tom Flanagan (2012), and Alex Marland (2014, 2016) have already illustrated aspects of the Harper team's desire to control the message and put the leader forward. With *24 Seven*, this practice appears to have been pushed to the limit, and one could wonder how it was possible for citizens to be more objectively informed, since the PMO was using, among other communications strategies, prepackaged information to control the press and build its own agenda. As a result, the use of permanent campaigning strategies raises serious questions about their impact on Canadian political practices and the perception of government actors. When does engaging in an ongoing process to woo public opinion go too far? In a time when voter turnout is falling, will permanent campaigning turn more citizens away from politics and increase cynicism?

Such tight control on the political message sent out through digital platforms and elsewhere limits citizens' and the media's capacity to understand, discuss, and assess the government's actions. Simultaneously, the same digital platforms used by the PMO to promote its agenda now offer a variety of information sources and are powerful tools to instantaneously share news, concerns, and ideas. Although mobilization will always depend on the people's will to actively engage with democracy, social media platforms, which can easily support homemade videos, have the potential to offer a wider diversity of viewpoints and to counterbalance, to a certain point, official and carefully staged discourses.

Permanent campaigning also has other important implications as they are redefining norms. First, communications strategies such as *24 Seven* could be interpreted as heralding a more acute era of presidentialization in Canadian political practices. Impression management is not a new feature of Canadian politics, and elections have always centred on leaders, from John A. Macdonald to Pierre Trudeau (Bakvis and Wolinetz 2009). However, with presidentialization comes the idea of a politicized leadership where the focus is on partisan politics and fundraising. Second, though personalization and advertisements are not new, there is now a plethora of tools that can be used to carefully craft the perception of the politician and make him/her appear to have requisite leadership skills. The *24 Seven* videos were made available online, facilitating the transmission of messages narrowly cast for specific segments of the electorate and providing a rapid response outlet in case of attacks. Third, all the online platforms (websites and YouTube channels) are direct ways to circumvent traditional news media discourses to speak directly to Canadians.

Now that the Conservatives are no longer in power, and with Justin Trudeau as prime minister of Canada, we will see a transformation of communication practices. Just days after the election, he began the process of re-engagement with journalists. From a broader perspective, he began reshaping how and to what extent the government communicates with the public and offered a renewed and positive message. The image of what a Canadian prime minister is has already begun to change. In the future, the Liberal PMO will most certainly use some of the same communications strategies to promote their leader as the Conservative PMO used to promote theirs. As was the case for Harper, family plays a central role in Justin Trudeau's image-making practices. His wife, Sophie Grégoire Trudeau, was on the cover of the French and English editions of *Chatelaine* magazine in 2016, and he often appears with his children in public. He also made other strategic moves to create a positive image, participating, for example, in the Toronto Pride parade in July 2016. Nevertheless, image-management techniques are still omnipresent; Trudeau's photographer, Adam Scotti, is a constant presence. These photos are posted on both Instagram accounts as well as on the Liberal Party and Trudeau PMO accounts and their Twitter feeds (Schmunk 2015). In sum, this recalibration of prime minister image-making strategies will offer more material that will lead to more reflections on the role of the contemporary permanent campaign in Canada.

NOTES

Acknowledgments: The first author would like to thank Alex Marland and Vincent Raynauld for their comments on a preliminary version of this paper, as well as research assistants at Université du Québec à Trois-Rivières, second author Sofia Tourigny-Koné, and Grégoire Boucher.

1 The *ethos, pathos,* and *logos* are Aristotle's three modes of persuasion. An orator must take all three aspects into consideration to properly convince his or her audience.

2 Though the sites were bilingual and the prime minister speaks both languages, in an official event, the French part is often subtitled in English, but the reverse was not true. In addition, sometimes the message was presented differently in French than in English.

3 This practice is also used by leaders elsewhere in the world. For example, President Obama delivers a weekly address on the White House YouTube channel, https://www.youtube.com/user/whitehouse.

4 https://www.youtube.com/user/pmocpm. The site is now about Trudeau and unfortunately the content of Harper era is now deleted from the site.

5 The Bystrom et al. (2004) analysis was of campaign ads in the United States, so some variables needed to be adapted for use with the *24 Seven* videos.

REFERENCES

Amossy, Ruth. 2010. *La présentation de soi. Ethos et identité verbale.* Paris: Presses Universitaires de France.

Arbour, Brian. 2014. *Candidate-Centered Campaigns. Political Messages, Winning Personalities, and Personal Appeals.* New York: Palgrave Macmillan.

Bakvis, Herman, and Steven B. Wolinetz. 2009. "Canada: Executive Dominance and Presidentialization." In *The Presidentialization of Politics. Comparative Study of Modern Democracies,* edited by T. Poguntke and P. Webb, 199–220. Oxford: Oxford University Press.

Bernays, Edward. 1928. *Propaganda.* New York: Liverlight.

Bittner, Amanda. 2011. *Platform or Personality? The Role of Party Leaders in Elections.* Oxford: Oxford University Press. http://dx.doi.org/10.1093/acprof:oso/9780199595365.001.0001.

Boesveld, Sarah. 2013. "#dayinthelife: Stephen Harper Tweets His Entire Day." *National Post,* January 28. http://news.nationalpost.com/news/canada/canadian-politics/dayinthelife-stephen-harper-tweets-his-day.

Boorstin, Daniel. 1992. *The Image: A Guide to Pseudo-Events in America.* New York: Vintage Books.

Brown, Steven D., Ronald D. Lambert, Barry J. Kay, and James E. Curtis. 1988. "In the Eye of the Beholder: Leader Images in Canada." *Canadian Journal of Political Science* 21 (4): 729–55. http://dx.doi.org/10.1017/S0008423900057425.

Burgess, Mark. 2015. "Feds' $75 Million in Ads Move Away from Print as "Branding" Better Suited to TV, Internet." *Hill Times,* April 13, 1, 21.

Bystrom, Diane G., Mary Christine Banwart, Linda Lee Kaid, and Terry A. Robertson. 2004. *Gender and Candidate Communication: VideoStyle, WebStyle, NewStyle*. New York: Routledge.

Chase, Steven. 2015. "Prime Minister's Office Admits to Security Breach in Posting Videos of Soldiers in Iraq." *Globe and Mail*, May 6. http://www.theglobeandmail.com/news/politics/pmo-yanks-promotional-videos-of-soldiers-in-iraq-kuwait/article24252442/.

Corner, John, and Dick Pels. 2003. *Media and the Restyling of Politics. Consumerism, Celebrity and Cynism*. London: SAGE Publications.

Curtin, Patricia A. 1999. "Reevaluating Public Relations Information Subsidies: Market-Driven Journalism and Agenda-Building Theory and Practice." *Journal of Public Relations Research* 11 (1): 53–90. http://dx.doi.org/10.1207/s1532754xjprr1101_03.

Esselment, Anna. 2014. "The Governing Party and the Permanent Campaign." In *Political Communication in Canada: Meet the Press and Tweet the Rest*, edited by A. Marland, T. Giasson, and T.A. Small, 24–38. Vancouver: UBC Press.

Flanagan, Tom. 2012. "Political Communication and the 'Permanent Campaign.'" In *How Canadians Communicate IV: Media and Politics*, edited by D. Taras and C. Waddell, 129–48. Edmonton: Athabasca University Press.

–. 2014. *Winning Power. Canadian Campaigning in the Twenty-First Century*. Montreal/Kingston: McGill-Queen's University Press.

Galloway, Gloria. 2015. "Poilievre Makes no Apologies for Tax-Paid Promotional Video." *Globe and Mail*, May 15. http://www.theglobeandmail.com/news/politics/poilievre-makes-no-apologies-for-child-care-benefit-promotional-video/article24456646/.

Gidengil, Elisabeth, Neil Nevitte, André Blais, Joanna Everitt, and Patrick Fournier. 2012. *Dominance and Decline. Making Sense of Recent Canadian Elections*. Toronto: University of Toronto Press.

Goffman, Erving. 1959. *Presentation of Self in Everyday Life*. New York: Doubleday Anchor Books.

Grabe, Maria Elizabeth, and Eric Page Bucy. 2009. *Image Bites Politics. News and the Visual Framing of Elections*. Oxford: Oxford University Press. http://dx.doi.org/10.1093/acprof:oso/9780195372076.001.0001.

Heclo, Hugh. 2000. "Campaigning and Governing: A Conspectus." In *The Permanent Campaign and Its Future*, edited by N. Ornstein and T. Mann, 1–37. Washington, DC: American Enterprise Institute.

Javidan, Mansour, and David A. Waldman. 2003. "Exploring Charismatic Leadership in the Public Sector: Measurement and Consequences." *Public Administration Review* 63 (2): 229–42. http://dx.doi.org/10.1111/1540-6210.00282.

Johnston, Richard. 2002. "Prime Ministerial Contenders in Canada." In *Leaders' Personalities and the Outcomes of Democratic Elections*, edited by A. King, 158–83. Oxford: Oxford University Press. http://dx.doi.org/10.1093/0199253137.003.0006.

Karvonen, Lauri. 2009. *The Personalization of Politics: A Study of Parliamentary Democracies*. Colchester: ECPR Press.

King, Anthony. 2002. "Do Leaders' Personalities Really Matter?" In *Leaders' Personalities and the Outcomes of Democratic Elections*, edited by Anthony King, 1–43. Oxford: Oxford University Press. http://dx.doi.org/10.1093/0199253137.003.0001.

Lalancette, Mireille, with Catherine Lemarier-Saulnier and Alex Drouin. 2014. "Playing along New Rules: Personalized Politics in a 24/7 Mediated World." In *Political Communication in Canada: Meet the Press and Tweet the Rest*, edited by A. Marland, T. Giasson, and T.A. Small, 144–59. Vancouver: UBC Press.

Marland, Alex. 2012. "Political Photography, Journalism and Framing in the Digital Age: The Management of Visual Media by the Prime Minister of Canada." *International Journal of Press/Politics* 17 (2): 214–33. http://dx.doi.org/10.1177/1940161211433838.

–. 2014. "The Branding of a Prime Minister: Digital Information Subsidies and the Image Management of Stephen Harper." In *Political Communication in Canada: Meet the Press and Tweet the Rest*, edited by A. Marland, T. Giasson, and T.A. Small, 55–73. Vancouver: UBC Press.

–. 2016. *Branding Command: Canadian Politics and Democracy in the Age of Message Control*. Vancouver: UBC Press.

Marland, Alex, and Mireille Lalancette. 2014. "Success Hollywood: Celebrity Endorsements in American Politics." In *Political Marketing in the US*, edited by J. Lees-Marshment, B. Conley, and K. Cosgrove, 130–47. New York: Routledge.

Marshall, David P. 1997. *Celebrity and Power*. Minneapolis: University of Minnesota Press.

Mayer, Jeremy D. 2004. "The Presidency and Image Management: Discipline in Pursuit of Illusion." *Presidential Studies Quarterly* 34 (3): 620–31. http://dx.doi.org/10.1111/j.1741-5705.2004.00215.x.

Puzic, Sonja. 2014. "PMO Apologizes for Showing Elite Soldiers' Faces in Promotional Videos." *CTV News*, May 5. http://www.ctvnews.ca/politics/pmo-apologizes-for-showing-elite-soldiers-faces-in-promotional-videos-1.2358990.

Rana, Abbas. 2009. "PM's Beatles Singing Gets Nearly 500,000 YouTube Views in One Week." *Hill Times*, October 12, 1.

Rosenberg, Shawn W., and Patrick McCafferty. 1987. "The Image and the Vote: Manipulating Voters' Preferences." *Public Opinion Quarterly* 51 (1): 31–47. http://dx.doi.org/10.1086/269012.

Scherer, Jay, and Lisa McDermott. 2011. "Playing Promotional Politics: Mythologizing Hockey and Manufacturing 'Ordinary' Canadians." *International Journal of Canadian Studies/Revue internationale d'études canadiennes* (43): 107–34. http://dx.doi.org/10.7202/1009457ar.

Schmunk, Rhianna. 2015. "Trudeau Sits Down for Heart-To-Heart with Boy Who Had a Tough Day." *Huffington Post Canada*, December 12. http://www.huffingtonpost.ca/2015/12/12/trudeau-heart-to-heart_n_8796426.html.

Simpson, Jeffrey. 2014. "A Government Obsessed with Image – 24 Seven." *Globe and Mail*, July 9. http://www.theglobeandmail.com/opinion/a-government-obsessed-with-image-24-seven/article19512158/.

Sparrow, Nick, and John Turner. 2001. "The Permanent Campaign - The Integration of Market Research Techniques in Developing Strategies in a More Uncertain Political Climate." *European Journal of Marketing* 35 (9/10): 984–1002. http://dx.doi.org/10.1108/03090560110400605.

Stanyer, James, and Dominic Wring. 2004. "Public Images, Private Lives: An Introduction." *Parliamentary Affairs* 57 (1): 1–8. http://dx.doi.org/10.1093/pa/gsh001.

Strömbäck, Jesper, and Peter Van Aelst. 2013. "Why Political Parties Adapt to the Media: Exploring the Fourth Dimension of Mediatization." *International Communication Gazette* 75 (4): 341–58. http://dx.doi.org/10.1177/1748048513482266.

Van Zoonen, Liesbet. 2006. "The Personal, the Political and the Popular. A Women's Guide to Celebrity Politics." *European Journal of Cultural Studies* 9 (3): 287–301. http://dx.doi.org/10.1177/1367549406066074.

15

Vulnerable Populations and the Permanent Campaign: Disability Organizations as Policy Entrepreneurs

•••••• *Mario Levesque*

The permanent campaign is now firmly established in Canadian federal politics (Flanagan 2010). Left unclear is its impact on interest groups in the policy process, where agendas are often predetermined. How have interest groups responded to ensure their members' interests are considered, and how have their responses changed during and between election campaigns? Interest groups are a vital part of a pluralistic society, representing large constituencies and a means of inclusion, representation, and participation (Meadowcroft 2004; see also Young and Everitt 2004). Yet they are increasingly marginalized in public policy processes for factors both external (e.g., governing party ideology, access) and internal (e.g., limited use of political marketing, poor communication and funding) (Foster and Lemieux 2012; Grosenick 2014). This is especially true of groups that represent vulnerable populations.

This is important, because one measure of a society is how it treats its most vulnerable people – the elderly, the young, the poor. Cutting across this vulnerable population are issues of disability. For example, the disability rate among seniors (sixty-five years of age or older) is three times that of non-seniors (fifteen to sixty-four years of age) (Statistics Canada 2012). Similarly, the disability rate for youth (five to fourteen years of age) is 5 percent, leaving them in a precarious position given that youth with disabilities are two and a half times more likely to experience violence and are more likely to live in low-income households (Human Resources and Skills Development Canada 2011; Public Safety Canada 2000). The effect of youths with disabilities on parental employment is considerable: 30 percent of parents work fewer hours, 17 percent quit working, and 21 percent decline employment in order to provide care for their child. Issues of poverty continue into adulthood; people with disabilities are employed at two-thirds the rate of people without disabilities (Turcotte 2014). Hence, how disability groups –

advocates of vulnerable people – have embraced the permanent campaign is significant given the dynamics of the neo-liberal agenda, which has facilitated its expansion. That is, state–society relations have been restructured from a collaborative to a competitive environment forcing disability groups into a situation where they now compete for the opportunity to partner with the state to deliver needed services, a situation largely foreign to them. For example, prior to the mid-1990s, disability groups were embedded in policy processes working with governments to advance their agenda, which typically had all-party support. The current situation is different, with disability groups much more focused on targeting specific times to engage with decision makers. Considering the changes to the environment within which they operate (e.g., funding structure, reporting, and auditing), this process underscores the fact that the permanent campaign is a relatively new phenomenon for disability groups. Consequently, examining how disability groups have adapted in this process provides us with one lens for how the treatment of our most vulnerable in society has changed. The results are not intended to be generalizable to other groups representing vulnerable populations; additional research examining other groups is required to make such claims.

For disability groups in this investigation, the question becomes, what to do? The term "disability" refers to physical, visual, hearing, mental health, intellectual, or learning disabilities. Little is known about disability organizations and the work they carry out in Canada (but see Chouinard and Crooks 2008; Levesque 2012). They are not mainstream, and the media pay little attention to them other than in high-profile situations, such as to address issues of discrimination and economic vulnerability; the federal government's decision to reinstate funding that supported fifty positions for developmentally disabled adults after significant public outcry is an example (Cobb 2015). However, disability organizations remain an important locus of activity for inclusion, sense of citizenship, and developing an understanding of relevant issues (Canadian Centre on Disability Studies 2002; Hendriks 2006; Prince 2010). Even so, interest groups representing vulnerable populations, such as people with disabilities, are seen by many government officials (including ministers) as corrosive forces in the policy process whose efforts need to be curtailed (Imagine Canada 2012). Disability issues are on neither political parties' nor the federal government's agendas, which is leading to few incremental policy changes. Leadership on the file is often non-existent at best, given that it is not "sexy" and involves small dollars (Graefe and

Levesque 2010). For example, Aldred H. Neufeldt (2003) reminds us that the Disabled Persons Secretariat within the Secretary of State, formed in the mid-1980s to be the lead on disability policy, was downgraded to the status of a unit during the late 1990s as part of federal restructuring to address budgetary issues, thus severely limiting its ability to move the file forward. Since 2008, the federal Office for Disability Issues (established in 1981) has been transformed into more of a service delivery entity (e.g., disability savings plans) and to act as a point of contact for people rather than its original conception of research and policy development functions (Employment and Social Development Canada 2013). This may be in the process of changing; in November 2015, Prime Minister Trudeau announced the new Ministry of Sport and Persons with Disabilities.

While the challenge of advocating for vulnerable populations is significant, several tools for activism are available to disability organizations. These include lobbying, consultations, election campaigning, demonstrations and protests, and litigation. Lobbying, which is communicating with decision makers, can take several forms. Organizations can work to meet privately with politicians and bureaucrats or capitalize on informal meetings at social events – something that is typically afforded to those with wealth or high social status. Alternatively, organizations can lobby indirectly through their members by educating them on the issues, capitalizing on their contacts, or facilitating meetings with officials. Organizations can also lobby the broader public to change public opinion on issues through the dissemination of research, public relations campaigns, and working with the media. A second tool at organizations' disposal is consultations with government via legislative or parliamentary hearings, task forces, and advisory committees. For governments, these are opportunities to gather relevant information and legitimize decisions while offering organizations an opportunity to educate decision makers on topics of importance to them. However, groups risk being dismissed if they feel outcomes are predetermined or co-opted with frequent lengthy consultations. Alternatively, a third option is for organizations to concentrate resources in the period leading up to and during elections. This could involve meeting with political party strategists to include favourable positions on issues in their campaign platforms, educating candidates on issues, asking parties to clarify their positions on issues, and broader public education campaigns through the media. Demonstrations and protests are a fourth activism tool. These have the advantage of drawing intensive media scrutiny to the issue, yet organizations run the risk of being dismissed as eccentric by decision makers and the public alike, and media attention is often short-lived. Used in conjunction with other tools, demonstrations and protests may be effective. Organizations may also pursue litigation as a strategy, either individually or as an intervener. Such was the case with the *Jodhan* case, which challenged the inaccessibility of federal government websites. Since losing this case, the federal government has invested significant resources to ensure its websites are accessible for persons with disabilities.[1] While expensive, the courts remain an important counterbalance to uphold the rights of vulnerable populations, including persons with disabilities, in a system of majoritarian rule. Cutting across these activism tools is the fact that organizations can act together through coalitions to maximize resources, provided issues are well defined and reflect, at least in part, an organization's goals (for an overview of these activism tools, see Berry and Wilcox 2009; Young and Everitt 2004).

Even with this array of activism tools, organizations may be limited in the amount of advocacy or political activities they can conduct. When we consider Canada Revenue Agency (CRA) regulations, this is especially true for registered charities. The CRA defines political activities as explicit calls to political action, explicit public communication of a position on a government law, policy or decision, or explicitly indicating intent to pressure officials to act on the organization's position (Canada Revenue Agency 2014). Depending on their annual revenues, the CRA limits the political activities of registered charities to 10 to 20 percent of their total activities; if they go beyond this, they face losing their charitable status and are therefore no longer able to issue tax receipts for donations (Canada Revenue Agency 2003). However, not all registered charities conduct political activities. For example, only two of the six charities studied here reported political activities, as shown in Table 15.1. Most of their political activities were print-based (Internet, media releases, publications, letter-writing campaigns) coupled with workshops and speeches, and were consistent with the CRA's guidelines and analysis (Blumberg 2015; Canada Revenue Agency 2015).

Disability organizations work within this limited advocacy role to put forth solutions to problems of interest to their members. Understanding the relationships between problems, policies, and politics remains crucial and is at the heart of John Kingdon's (1984) multiple streams framework of policy making, which is used below to assess how disability organizations have responded to a limited agenda-setting role. Kingdon's framework introduces randomness and ambiguity to the decision-making process to examine

TABLE 15.1

Political activities reported, select organizations

Type	Resources used		
	Staff	Volunteers	Financial
Media releases and advertisements	✓	✓	–
Conferences, workshops, speeches, or lectures	✓	✓	✓
Publications (printed or electronic)	✓	✓	✓
Rallies, demonstrations, or public meetings	–	–	✓
Petitions, boycotts (calls to action)	–	–	–
Letter-writing campaigns (printed or electronic)	✓	✓	✓
Internet (websites, social media such as Twitter, YouTube)	✓	✓	✓

SOURCE: Adapted from the "Registered Charity Information Return" (Canada Revenue Agency 2014).

which issues get addressed by decision makers. Given time constraints, few issues get their attention, and for those that do, accepted solutions are less than optimal. This should come as no surprise, as Kingdon notes that solutions and problems act independently. Multiple solutions and problems exist based on imperfect information held among a diverse set of stakeholders who find it increasingly difficult to agree on a path forward. The fragmented nature of the disability sector and their associated positions, as well as the nature of disability problems, which cross-cut numerous government departments – usually set up to work vertically rather than horizontally across departments – illustrates this nicely. Ambiguity remains prominent in the decision-making process.

Three processes are at the heart of the multiple streams framework. *Problems* are issues in need of attention. They come into focus based on indicators that measure conditions, due to focusing events, or through the study of issues. The impoverished economic condition of persons with disabilities is repeatedly revealed through income surveys and has increasingly been identified as a problem in need of attention. *Policies* are ideas for how to address identified problems. Ideas are plentiful and vary depending on the stakeholder, with few seriously considered by decision makers because of time and institutional constraints, among other things. Lastly, *politics* refers not only to the individuals involved in the policy process (and their turnover), but also to the broader set of groups exerting pressure for change as well as to the political climate within which they operate (i.e., ideology).

The key to policy making in the multiple streams process is the coupling of problems, policies, and politics. All three need to come together for an issue to be addressed, and this is where much of the randomness occurs. Problems and policies coming together in an inhospitable political climate will go nowhere. For the three streams to come together, a window of opportunity must open for coupling to occur. These can be random opportunities, such as a favourable minister or deputy minister entering the decision-making process or a change in societal attitudes to the inclusion of persons with disabilities. Alternatively, windows of opportunity can be regular, such as through yearly budget consultation processes or regular elections. The coupling of the streams also needs to be facilitated by policy entrepreneurs. These are highly skilled individuals attuned to the political climate and cognizant of existing problems and policies. With their substantial resources, they are able to bring the streams together by crafting an acceptable framework for stakeholders to support.

The multiple streams framework is useful for assessing decision making by considering the randomness and ambiguity involved in the process. It is used here to shed light on how the permanent campaign has affected the representatives of one subset of vulnerable populations – disability organizations – and calls into question the context within which they operate.

By the late 1990s, much hope existed in the disability community for significant changes in disability policy. This was the result of several reports since the early 1980s that culminated in the 1998 *In Unison* report, which elaborated the vision of full inclusion for persons with disabilities in all aspects of Canadian society based on a series of disability supports, employment preparation, and income supports (Human Resources Development Canada 1998; for a fuller discussion, see Graefe and Levesque 2010). To date, on-the-ground progress has been incremental at best (Levesque and Graefe 2013; Prince 2004). For example, voting rights for persons with disabilities – including those with intellectual disabilities – were finally achieved in 2002 when the last appeal to the 1993 legislative changes was exhausted.[2] In 2004, Steven Fletcher (C–Charleswood–St. James–Assiniboia) became the first quadriplegic to serve in the House of Commons and, in 2008, in cabinet. On forming government, Trudeau named two persons with disabilities, Kent Hehr and Carla Qualtrough, as ministers. A registered disability savings plan (RDSP) was introduced in 2007, and many smaller tax credit changes have been introduced in the last twenty years (e.g., Department of Finance 2007).

Yet these gains have been eroded by significant setbacks. This includes cancellation of the Participation and Activity Limitation Survey, which previously collected statistics on persons with disabilities every five years. This was eventually replaced with the Canadian Survey on Disability in 2012, but the latter is less informative and is based on answers from the voluntary National Household Survey that replaced the mandatory long-form census (Statistics Canada 2014), which has been reinstated for 2016 by the Trudeau government. The result is a lack of richness in survey data. Similarly, the Court Challenges Program, which persons with disabilities could, and did, use to challenge the federal government to either provide services or upgrade accessibility standards, was cancelled, again, in 2006, only to be reinstated by the new Trudeau Liberal government in 2015 (Brodie 2016; Kloegman 2007). In 2012, additional reporting, monitoring, and enforcement requirements were introduced for registered charities to help ensure charitable organizations work within the prescribed limits (Carter and Cooper 2012). These measures were controversial, especially the aggressive enforcement mechanisms from which the Trudeau Liberal government has indicated it is withdrawing (Goar 2016). Coupled with the elimination of direct federal funding of disability groups in the 2012–13 federal budget, disability organizations have been left in a precarious position, and progress on disability issues has been slow (Department of Finance 2012).

The Harper Conservative government was thus left with a small social policy role, especially in the disability sector. For example, it continued to transfer costs for persons with disabilities to themselves or their families through such mechanisms as the RDSP, noted above. With this plan, persons with disabilities or their families can contribute money to an RDSP account, which works like a regular Registered Retirement Savings Plan, so that money can be taken out at a later date, when needed, and often when parents have passed away. While helpful for some, the RDSP is problematic given that persons with disabilities and their families may be the *least* able to afford such a plan due to low incomes (Levesque 2012).

Matters have since changed with the election of the Trudeau Liberal government in 2015. It has sought an inclusionary social policy role. This includes symbolic measures such as forming a very diverse cabinet, which includes two persons with disabilities and a new cabinet portfolio devoted to sport and persons with disabilities. This is significant; issues of disability have been elevated to a junior cabinet post, and the minister, Carla Qualtrough, has been charged with engaging stakeholders prior to the passage of a *Canadians with Disabilities Act*. Such measures are a dramatic shift from the Harper Conservative era, leading to questions about the involvement of disability organizations in the permanent campaign.

Case Study

METHOD

We conducted semi-structured telephone interviews in the spring of 2015 with executive directors of national disability organizations in Canada. Twenty-two organizations were identified through Internet searches and a review of their "links" pages, and key documents revealed another thirty-nine organizations, for a total of sixty-one national disability organizations. From these, we selected a sample of sixteen (about 25 percent) for potential interviews, with the goal of conducting six to ten interviews. Organizations were selected based on their activities to ensure representation across different types of disabilities – physical ($n = 4$), visual and hearing ($n = 4$), mental health ($n = 2$), intellectual ($n = 1$), learning ($n = 1$) and umbrella/advocacy ($n = 4$) – and based on the size of their revenues to ensure a range of organizations. Interview requests were forwarded via email and included a cover letter that briefly explained the research and solicited their participation and an informed consent form. We received seven responses and completed six telephone interviews: two with organizations involving physical disabilities, two involving visual and hearing disabilities, one involving mental health, and one umbrella/advocacy disability organization. The seventh respondent initially accepted, only to later decline to be interviewed, citing fear of retribution given the then Conservative government's "unfriendly" view of and "chilly climate" towards non-economic groups. We re-sent interview requests to non-respondents two weeks after the initial request, but received no new responses. Overall, the response rate was 44 percent (seven of sixteen requests) and the completed interview request rate was 38 percent, which is considered strong (Klandermans and Staggenborg 2002). Even so, considering the small number of interviews completed, the findings should be considered preliminary and not generalizable to all disability organizations as a whole or to other types of groups representing vulnerable populations. Still, the interviews provided us with a view of the situation, and if there was one similarity among the representatives interviewed, it was that they were well experienced in the not-for-profit sector (not necessarily with the same organization).

Interviews lasted an average of forty-five minutes. Executive directors were asked a series of questions on three themes. The first theme probed the type and quantity of advocacy work currently undertaken by their organization and how this had changed over the last two decades. A second set of inquiries probed how they decided on the mix of advocacy strategies used in the permanent campaign (and why), including who they targeted (e.g., government MPs, opposition members, the bureaucracy, and other third parties). It also queried their experience with and assessment of various forms of advocacy. Lastly, a third set of questions delved into the opportunities and challenges they encountered in participating in the policy process. Executive directors were selected for the interviews given their position and knowledge of their organization. In all but one case, they were accompanied by another senior management person, such as their policy director or analyst, depending on their expertise or organizational memory. Accommodations (e.g., interpretation, alternative formats) were also made as required. To facilitate analysis, interviews were audio-recorded, transcribed, and reviewed for common themes. The narrative in the results section below was crafted based on a synthesis of the information provided by the interview respondents; that is, it is *their* narrative and includes many direct quotes to give voice to these individuals and to emphasize their experiences. To protect their identities, all names and other identifiable information are not provided; rather, interview respondents are referred to as R1, R2, R3, and so on when directly quoted.

Findings

Our first question explored changes in advocacy in the last three decades. All interview respondents noted the transformation in advocacy work in response to significant changes in the political climate and in technology (discussed below). This is a fundamental shift concerning the social policy role of the Canadian federal government. As was noted, we have gone from a period when policy development was a collaborative process, regardless of level of government, and the key for disability organizations was "simply finding a place at the table" (R1). Such were the times when large consultations were occurring about the Canadian Charter of Rights and Freedoms. Governments valued the input of organizations, fully expected them to participate in consultations, and provided mechanisms and tables for those consultations. Consultations also involved the bureaucracy, which was also heavily engaged in the process. As one interview respondent noted, "There were internal champions in the bureaucracy that had capacity to explore new ways of doing things that would take some initiative and some risk in trying out new models and new approaches to service delivery or enforcement mechanisms or whatever it was" (R5). Several developments were key in this process, including the work by David Smith, then chair of the House of Commons Special Committee on the Disabled and the Handicapped, to identify key obstacles faced by persons with disabilities (see Smith 1981) and the enshrinement of equality rights for people with disabilities in section 15(1) of the Charter. Similarly, it was the Brian Mulroney Conservative government (1984–93) that established the House of Commons Standing Committee on the Status of Disabled Persons (1987) and a five-year National Strategy for the Integration of Persons with Disabilities (1991). Note that these were broad framework initiatives aimed at all persons with disabilities. All interview respondents lamented the loss of this collaborative policy environment, which occurred in the mid-90s with the failure of the Lloyd Axworthy social security review (for an overview, see Battle and Torjman 1995), the move to deficit-reduction initiatives, and the ending of cost-shared programming.

The Harper Conservatives reinforced this shift. First, they adopted a narrow programmatic approach in the search for solutions given their preference for measurable results and to connect with citizens directly, bypassing the provinces in the process. Hence, we see targeted or boutique initiatives such as library services for people with vision impairments or the establishment of the Abilities Centre in former finance minister Jim Flaherty's riding. The problem with these boutique initiatives is that they lack an integrated approach (which is what is needed given the complexity of disability issues, which cut across government departments), divide the disability community by pitting disability organizations against each other in vying for government largesse, and reinforce incremental policy changes. As one interview respondent summarized, there are now "fewer openings for good public policy debate and discourse" (R6), with the debate quickly polarizing.

Second, clear political support is required for initiatives to move forward, which has affected the activism tools used by disability organizations. As characterized by one executive director (and reinforced by the others):

The bureaucracy can do very little to assist you and in fact the bureaucracy can do nothing to assist you in the last almost ten years. We used to spend hours with key bureaucrats – ADMs, DMs, directors general of programs; we no longer do that [other than to] keep some people informed, but they are unable to advance agendas. We spend all of our time now with elected officials or with their chiefs of staff, political staff in ministers' offices, or MP offices. To move anything in the current environment requires that political support and buy-in. It is a fundamentally different era; it isn't that we haven't been able to move [on issues, but in] the current political environment, it needs a signal before anything will move in the bureaucracy. (R5)

This characterization reinforces the importance of the permanent campaign. Yet engaging in it is challenging, since disability has become a partisan issue, which was not the case previously when all-party support was the norm (e.g., for Mulroney's five-year strategy). This can be seen in the fact that organizations now have to tailor their demands to fit the government's agenda. The result is that they move on aspects of files that are not necessarily what are most needed at the time but are what the opportunity affords them. This is tied to the fact that bureaucratic officials are "way less receptive" to meeting with a not-for-profit unless they think their department is somehow lined up with its goals (R6). For other officials, they have just "battened down the hatches and don't want to talk because they feel threatened [and are] very insecure in their positions" (R2). How to proceed in this new climate of permanent campaigning?

With political parties in constant electoral-preparedness mode, disability organizations have come to adopt a similar mindset, albeit within the prescribed allowable limits on political activities. The second set of questions broadly probed advocacy strategies used by disability organizations in the permanent campaign. All executive directors we interviewed noted the need for constant engagement and that this can be taxing on an organization's human and financial resources. Long gone are the days when one could make a presentation and have a fair expectation that action would follow. Most executive directors felt that presentations were largely useless and that emphasis should be placed on developing relationships with people. Whether the work is pre- or post-election matters little; rather, the key is to be in constant communication and to choose your time carefully to make your organization's demands. For example, as they explained, meetings with officials up to eight to ten months in advance of an election will be largely fruitless, though the ground may be more fertile for new ideas. While one may get lucky with a political party if it addresses the group's demands in its platform, as executive directors stressed, one must realize that the platform is a partisan document and means little; party officials will say almost anything, since they are not sure what they will do once they are elected (R4). This position stands somewhat in contrast to more recent political marketing research that emphasizes how important it is for parties forming government to deliver party manifestos and platforms to secure re-election (see, for instance, Esselment 2012). Rather, as another official explained, one should meet sixteen to twenty months ahead of an election and replicate the meetings every three months. To the interviewees, the replication of the meetings was important, as was making their pitch in a low-pressure environment, which as one moves closer to the election date does not exist. Furthermore, meeting in the twelve to fourteen months immediately following an election, other than to gently remind officials of their commitments, is largely futile given that a party forming a majority government will likely be implementing their electoral agenda closely.

Indeed, times have changed for disability organizations. No longer do they send out questionnaires to political parties to identify where they stand on issues. Rather, the real key in this, as one official explained, "is to be attentive to windows of opportunity; where they are, where they may crop up, so we tend to do a regular scan of the environment and to be very flexible in looking for these opportunities, to be mindful of them all the time" (R4). This includes being mindful of issues in the media, such as the incident at Nelson Mandela's memorial service in December 2013, when a man posing as a sign language interpreter provided incomprehensible interpretation as world leaders conveyed their condolences (see Associated Press 2013). Disability organizations in Canada used this opening to press for quality interpreters in Canada, which the federal government is examining.

Windows of opportunity also include researching the backgrounds of elected members who might be more receptive to an organization's interests. This can include a junior minister or rookie MP who wants to make a name for him or herself, or individuals who are truly interested in the issue and who may be true champions for the cause. Former finance minister Jim Flaherty was one such champion; he had a child with a disability and had firsthand experience with available services and challenges that remained.

All interview respondents noted Flaherty's leadership on the issue, stating that he was reasonable to talk to regardless of party stripe, and pointing to his leadership on the RDSP as one example – an initiative for which Flaherty took "a lot of heat" from then prime minister Harper, who questioned it on its inconsistency with his government's overall orientation and costs (R2). This stands in stark contrast, for example, to the leadership shown by the Trudeau Liberal government in pursuing a *Canadians with Disabilities Act*.

More broadly, advocacy work in a context of permanent campaigning consists of a wide range of initiatives, such as policy or position papers, meetings with officials, broader public education work, meetings with bureaucratic officials when possible, meetings with elected members and their staff, "days on the Hill," when they would try to meet with as many officials as possible, and email blitzes via members of the organization. Of these, days on the Hill were deemed challenging given logistics, access to elected and government officials, and costs. Interviewees also noted that it was hard to tell if these days were effective, with most feeling that they were of limited use other than to maintain a presence. One respondent recollected that while petitioning on the Hill to encourage the government to ratify the UN Convention on the Rights of Persons with Disabilities, two of the organization's members happened to meet Peter MacKay on the street, who promptly informed them that he was going to ratify it the following week (R2). One notices this opaque, haphazard decision-making process slowly changing under the Trudeau regime, given the planned consultations on a *Canadians with Disabilities Act* as announced in budget 2016 (Klingbeil 2016).

All interview respondents acknowledged the importance of digital communications tools, which are relatively new. Email blitzes to elected officials are regularly used to inform and influence them on key issues. Online communications tools have also greatly helped in organizing events, which can now be done more quickly and at a lower cost, especially when members are located across the country. This is especially helpful when working in coalitions, when there is often a need to swiftly distribute and solicit feedback on key documents. Similarly, online meetings reduce the need for costly travel and improve efficiency. Respondents also noted the ease of organizing attendance for all-candidates' meetings with digital tools. Even so, disability organizations conducted less advocacy overall given the recent chill in Ottawa.

It is this "chill" that intensified under the Harper administration. For example, new rules for reporting political activities led many groups to conduct less advocacy or to temporarily give it up entirely. As one executive director observed, "It is just not a nice situation right now, especially with CRA audits and how not-for-profits are seen in Ottawa" (R4). Another interview respondent saw this chill as a deliberate campaign against them and cited the elimination of funding. The respondent also stated that it was useless to go to the media "with your story [given] it is more likely to provoke retaliative destruction of your funding than civil attempts to resolve your complaint" (R6). It was little surprise that groups celebrated the warming of government relations when the Trudeau government announced an end to the "political harassment" of charities (Goar 2016).

All six respondents noted a dramatic increase in working collaboratively through coalitions when approaching the government. Coalition leadership is typically shared among two to four disability organizations, depending on the issue at hand. This allows them to capitalize on scarce resources while maximizing their impact. However, as one respondent stated, success is contingent on having a clearly defined and specific goal with the right people involved to increase the legitimacy of the demands put forward. The same interviewee also mentioned that it is equally important to ensure coalitions remain nimble and not become bureaucratically heavy and interested in maintaining their existence. Rather, coalitions need to know when to go away (R3). As another official noted, "The challenge for these types of collaborations or coalitions is getting below 60,000 feet. When you start considering all the different mandates of the different groups, that's where the challenge is" (R4). How, then, can common issues be identified?

Indeed, many difficulties remain for disability organizations in moving forward, which the third set of questions probed. First, financial and human resources remain a significant problem that can be mitigated in part through increased collaboration or work through coalitions (though they bring their own challenges). Second, timelines are excruciatingly long. For example, all respondents raised the challenge of keeping organization member expectations reasonable. The battle, often years in the making, is not won in getting a legislative change; rather, that is simply round one. Round two involves the development and implementation of regulations (which can take as long), from which policies and programs can then flow. All told, the process can take a decade or more, placing major stress on financial resources. To overcome these difficulties, compete in a permanent-campaign environment, and sustain themselves while under heightened scrutiny of political activities, disability organizations have transformed themselves in two ways.

First, they have increasingly become coaches working to activate individual organization members to lobby on their own, which involves the demanding task of educating and training members on the issues and processes. Such advocacy should target the different levels of government, which all respondents agreed should be emphasized. Second, disability organizations have also become facilitators (policy entrepreneurs) who work to connect their members and sister organizations with decision makers.

Looking broadly across the interviews, we found that respondents are keenly aware of the changed environment within which they now operate. This era of permanent campaigning, to which disability organizations have been slow to respond, has necessitated the use of new tools (e.g., digital media) and a reinvention of the role of disability organizations in the policy process. Now that these changes are largely entrenched, future campaign efforts should be more focused and strategic, though results may be less predictable, as interview respondents noted.

Permanent Campaigning in Canada

At the heart of this volume are three questions. The first seeks to illuminate similarities and differences in the actions of various actors during times of governance and campaign periods. For vulnerable populations and their representatives scrutinized in this chapter, there is no difference, except for the fact that they try to conduct more political activities, a demand stemming from the permanent-campaign environment. The extent to which this can be done successfully is greatly undercut by the ideological disposition of our elected governments; the differences in political-activity monitoring and enforcement between the Harper Conservatives and the Trudeau Liberals are a clear example. To address this limitation, disability organizations are increasingly developing counter strategies such as activating members into action. In this sense and in relation to the volume's second question, the move to permanent campaigning – particularly as it is coupled with technological changes – has led to a more informed and engaged citizenry, yet one that is increasingly cynical about the government's strategies towards disability organizations and disability issues. While better educated on issues, citizens' leadership on disability issues is undercut given the multi-member-based approach to advocacy that is now the norm. For ideologically driven governments, this makes it easy to divide and conquer groups when pressed with a multitude of claims. After all, whose information should they deem credible? The lack of agreement among claims seekers also provides the federal government with an opportunity to move forward with its own agenda. A premium is thus placed on disability organizations' ability to act in coalitions with clearly defined goals.

Kingdon's (1984) multiple streams framework of the policy process highlights these dynamics. Problems matter and are plentiful and complex. Here we see disability organizations working to address long-identified issues. New challenges are hard to identify due to cuts in funding to disability organizations or cuts to research, such as statistics gathering by the federal government. For example, the cancellation of the Participation and Activity Limitation Survey in 2006 and its replacement with the Canadian Survey on Disability in 2012, which is methodologically challenged, is undercutting any new claims that groups can advance. Even the cancellation and recent reinstatement of the long-form census presents challenges (*CBC News* 2016).

Policies are also problematic and unclear. The move to boutique programs under the Harper administration in place of an integrated planning approach or larger framework initiatives limited coordinated action. On the one hand, the government may be truly searching for solutions, yet on the other hand, it may be trying to divide and conquer by target-funding individual causes to appear to be addressing the issues while maximizing electoral considerations. It remains to be seen what the Trudeau government plans to do with such programs.

Politics also loom large. The Harper government's lack of desire for consultation and penchant for a small social policy role created a chilly climate in Ottawa for disability organizations. This was reinforced by changes in advocacy rules to require increased reporting of political activities and CRA audits, the elimination of funding to disability organizations, and the cancellation of the Court Challenges Program, among other things. This led organizations to cut staff and drastically reduce the amount of advocacy they conducted, thus limiting the effectiveness of their permanent campaigning. Interview respondents also emphasized the importance of party stripe to the extent that it affects how disability organizations craft their demands; ideology matters. The Trudeau Liberals have reversed many of the Conservative initiatives, thus warming relations.

The changing role of disability organizations in the policy process is another factor. No longer are they at the policy development table; instead, they are acting as policy entrepreneurs. It is in this role that they attempt to bring together the different streams (politics, problems, policies) in order to take advantage of a window of opportunity. As interview respondents revealed, they were forced to largely abandon bureaucratic advocacy because bureaucratic officials needed a political signal to proceed. As such, disability advocates targeted elected officials and their staff, but their efforts were limited by changes in advocacy rules and increased threats of CRA audits in the background. In response, disability organizations have curtailed much of their advocacy work or turned inwards to work with each other through coalitions on fewer issues. Also notable is the closeness with which organizations reviewed government policies and platforms to see how they could fit their demands into government priority areas. Similarly, they regularly monitored media coverage of politics to potentially identify events, or windows of opportunity, to publicly react, as with the fake interpreter incident. Lastly, disability organizations increasingly prioritized activating their members into action through training or by helping them connect with officials.

Looking broadly at the situation, we have used Kingdon's (1984) framework to reveal the opportunities and challenges of lobbying under conditions of permanent campaigning within government. The organizations we studied have become more active, have adopted a more diversified repertoire of tactics, including the use of digital tools, and have been generally constrained by the restrictions on political activity imposed by the CRA. In largely abandoning agenda-setting activities in response to a changing situational environment, they now assume the role of policy entrepreneurs, continually redefining their solutions and problems to meet the politics of the day. Thus, disability organizations have been co-opted along the incremental path and have tailored their permanent campaign accordingly.

Lastly, questions arise on the applicability of Kingdon's (1984) model to the Canadian context, given the different institutional structure (among other things) when compared to the United States, on which the model was based. The case study here reveals that any difference was minimal prior to 2006, given the embeddedness of disability groups in decision making. However, with some of the Harper Conservative changes (e.g., funding cuts to groups and the Court Challenges Program, as well as increased auditing and limits on political activities), access points in Canada have greatly decreased. Yet we notice that with the new Trudeau government, access points are in the process of being reopened: the reinstatement of the Court Challenges Program, the end of targeted auditing of interest groups, and a junior cabinet portfolio for persons with disabilities. These changes suggest that access points are fluid and that the relationship is thawing. More time is required before a final determination can be made, including the extent to which disability groups themselves use the permanent campaign as a tool.

NOTES

1 Canada (Attorney General) v. Jodhan v., 2012 FCA 161, A-478-1.
2 Sauvé v. Canada (Chief Electoral Officer), [2002] 3 S.C.R. 519, 2002 SCC 68.

REFERENCES

Associated Press. 2013. "Nelson Mandela Ceremony Sign Language Interpreter a 'Fake.'" *CBC News*, December 11. http://www.cbc.ca/news/world/nelson-mandela-ceremony-sign-language-interpreter-a-fake-1.2459469.

Battle, Ken, and Sherri Torjman. 1995. "Saving the Review." Caledon Institute of Social Policy. http://www.caledoninst.org/Publications/PDF/393ENG.pdf.

Berry, Jeffrey M., and Clyde Wilcox. 2009. *The Interest Group Society*, 5th ed. Toronto: Pearson Longman.

Blumberg, Mark. 2015. "Political Activity Audits and the CRA Program Update 2015." *Canadian Charity Law* (blog), April 24. http://www.canadiancharitylaw.ca/blog/cra_program_update_2015_and_political_activity_audits.

Brodie, Ian. 2016. "The Court Challenges Program Rises Once Again." *Policy Options* 37 (4). http://policyoptions.irpp.org/magazines/april-2016/the-court-challenges-program-rises-once-again/.

Canada Revenue Agency. 2003. "Political Activities." Policy Statement CPS-022. Accessed February 23, 2015. http://www.cra-arc.gc.ca/chrts-gvng/chrts/plcy/cps/cps-022-eng.html.

–. 2014. "T3010 Registered Charity Information Return." Accessed February 23, 2015. http://www.cra-arc.gc.ca/E/pbg/tf/t3010/.

–. 2015. "Charities Program Update – 2015." Accessed February 23, 2015. http://www.cra-arc.gc.ca/chrts-gvng/chrts/bt/chrtsprgrm_pdt-2015-eng.html.

Canadian Centre on Disability Studies. 2002. *Disability Community Capacity: A Framework for Preliminary Assessment*. Analysis Paper to HRDC, Social Policy Unit. http://disabilitystudies.ca/wp-content/uploads/2010/08/community-capacity-report-to-hrdc-may-31st-2002.pdf.

Carter, Terrance S., and Karen J. Cooper. 2012. "Playing by the Rules: Political Activities Fair Game for Charities." *Charity Law Bulletin* 286, June 28. http://www.carters.ca/pub/bulletin/charity/2012/chylb286.htm.

CBC News. 2016 (May 02). The long-form census is back, it's online — and this time, it's mandatory. http://www.cbc.ca/news/politics/mandatory-census-mail-out-1.3557511.

Chouinard, Vera, and Valorie A. Crooks. 2008. "Negotiating Neoliberal Environments in British Columbia and Ontario, Canada: Restructuring of State-Voluntary Sector Relations and Disability Organizations' Struggles to Survive." *Environment and Planning C: Government & Policy* 26 (1): 173–90. http://dx.doi.org/10.1068/c0502r.

Cobb, Chris. 2015. "After 35 Years, Federal Government Takes Jobs from Developmentally Disabled Workers." *Ottawa Citizen*, March 19. http://ottawacitizen.com/news/local

-news/after-35-years-federal-government-takes-jobs-from-developmentally-disabled
-workers-with-video.

Department of Finance. 2007. "Budget 2007." Accessed March 3, 2015. http://www.budget.gc.ca/2007/index-eng.html.

–. 2012. "Budget 2012." Accessed March 3, 2015. http://www.budget.finances.gouv.qc.ca/budget/2012-2013/index_en.asp.

Employment and Social Development Canada. 2013. "Organizational Structure." Accessed February 10, 2015. http://www.esdc.gc.ca/eng/about/branches/index.shtml.

Esselment, Anna. 2012. "Market Orientation in a Minority Government: The Challenges of Product Delivery." In *Political Marketing in Canada*, edited by A. Marland, T. Giasson, and J. Lees-Marshment, 123–39. Vancouver: UBC Press.

Flanagan, Tom. 2010. "Political Communication and the 'Permanent Campaign.'" In *How Canadians Communicate IV: Media and Politics*, edited by D. Taras and C. Waddell, 129–48. Edmonton: Athabasca University Press.

Foster, Émilie, and Patrick Lemieux. 2012. "Selling a Cause: Political Marketing and Interest Groups." In *Political Marketing in Canada*, edited by A. Marland, T. Giasson, and J. Lees-Marshment, 156–71. Vancouver: UBC Press.

Goar, Carol. 2016. "'Charity Chill' Melts under Friendly Government." *Toronto Star*, January 20. https://www.thestar.com/opinion/commentary/2016/01/20/charity-chill-melts-under-friendly-government-goar.html.

Graefe, Peter, and Mario Levesque. 2010. "Accountability and Funding as Impediments to Social Policy Innovation: Lessons from the Labour Market Agreements for Persons with Disabilities." *Canadian Public Policy* 36 (1): 45–62. http://dx.doi.org/10.3138/cpp.36.1.45.

Grosenick, Georgina C. 2014. "Opportunities Missed: Non-Profit Public Communication and Advocacy in Canada." In *Political Communication in Canada: Meet the Press and Tweet the Rest*, edited by A. Marland, T. Giasson, and T. A. Small, 179–93. Vancouver: UBC Press.

Hendriks, Carolyn M. 2006. "When the Forum Meets Interest Politics: Strategic Uses of Public Deliberation." *Politics & Society* 34 (4): 571–602. http://dx.doi.org/10.1177/0032329206293641.

Human Resources Development Canada. 1998. In Unison: A Canadian Approach to Disability Issues. http://www.publications.gc.ca/site/eng/9.647159/publication.html.

Human Resources and Skills Development Canada. 2011. "Disability in Canada: A 2006 Profile." http://www.esdc.gc.ca/eng/disability/arc/disability_2006.shtml.

Imagine Canada. 2012 (May 28). Charities' Engagement in public policy. Issue Alert. http://us1.campaign-archive1.com/?u=005f6731841412b698044ce64&id=9d00ac1cb5.

Kingdon, John W. 1984. *Agendas, Alternatives and Public Policies*. Boston: Little, Brown and Company.

Klandermans, Bert, and Suzanne Staggenborg. 2002. *Methods of Social Movement Research*. Minneapolis: University of Minnesota Press.

Klingbeil, Annalise. 2016. "Federal Budget Commits to Creating a Canadians with Disabilities Act." *Calgary Herald*, March 24. http://calgaryherald.com/news/local-news/federal-budget-commits-to-creating-a-canadians-with-disabilities-act.

Kloegman, Larissa. 2007. "A Democratic Defence of the Court Challenges Program." *Constitutional Forum Constitutionnel* 16 (3): 107–15.

Levesque, Mario. 2012. "Assessing the Ability of Disability Organizations: An Interprovincial Comparative Perspective." *Canadian Journal of Nonprofit and Social Economy Research* 3 (2): 82–103.

Levesque, Mario, and Peter Graefe. 2013. "'Not Good Enough': Canada's Stalled Disability Policy." In *How Ottawa Spends, 2013–14*, edited by B. Doern and C. Stoney, 172–83. Montreal/Kingston: McGill-Queen's University Press.

Meadowcroft, J. 2004. "Deliberative Democracy." In *Environmental Governance Reconsidered: Challenges, Choices, and Opportunities*, edited by R.F. Durant, D.J. Fiorino, and R. O'Leary, 183–217. Cambridge, MA: MIT Press.

Neufeldt, Aldred H. 2003. "Disability in Canada: An Historical Perspective." In *In Pursuit of Equal Participation: Canada and Disability at Home and Abroad*, edited by Henry Enns and Aldred H. Neufeldt, 22-80. Toronto: Captus Press.

Prince, Michael J. 2004. "Canadian Disability Policy: Still a Hit-and-Miss Affair." *Canadian Journal of Sociology* 29 (1): 59–82. http://dx.doi.org/10.2307/3341945.

–. 2010. "Engaging in Disability Policy Development and Advocacy with the Canadian State." Paper presented at the Canadian Disability Policy Alliance Meeting of CURA Partners. Regina, April 28th.

Public Safety Canada. 2000. "Bullying in Canada: National Strategy on Community Safety and Crime Prevention." Accessed January 7, 2016. http://canadiancrc.com/Bullying_Canada-Public_Safety_Canada.aspx.

Smith, D. 1981. *Obstacles: Report of the Special Committee on the Disabled and the Handicapped*. Ottawa: Minister of Supply and Services Canada.

Statistics Canada. 2012. *Disability in Canada: Initial Findings from the Canadian Survey on Disability*. Publication 89–654-X. http://www.statcan.gc.ca/pub/89-654-x/89-654-x2013002-eng.htm.

–. 2014. *Canadian Survey on Disability, 2012: Concepts and Methods Guide*. http://www.statcan.gc.ca/pub/89-654-x/89-654-x2014001-eng.htm.

Turcotte, Martin. 2014. *Persons with Disabilities and Employment: Insights on Canadian Society*. Statistics Canada Publication 75–006-X. http://www.statcan.gc.ca/pub/75-006-x/2014001/article/14115-eng.htm.

Young, Lisa, and Joanna Everitt. 2004. *Advocacy Groups*. Vancouver: UBC Press.

16

Permanent Campaigning: Changing the Nature of Canadian Democracy

Anna Lennox Esselment, Alex Marland, and Thierry Giasson

The Canadian political class is obsessed with campaigning, whether or not there is an election on. Every advantage is put to use. Sophisticated electoral planning and preparation begin years in advance of an election call. Party organizations are modernized. Data-driven analytics inform campaign strategy, policy design, and messaging. Techniques such as market intelligence, voter segmentation, branding, and microtargeting are ubiquitous. Methods of communication are more sophisticated, tactical, and intense. Online social media platforms are blended with traditional communications, such as TV and radio advertising, to simultaneously broadcast and narrowcast messages to targeted voters. The party strategists who direct electoral warfare have a growing expertise in all of these areas and are often subsumed into the highest offices of government. They recognize that combining aspects of political marketing, data, and political communication – financed through public resources wherever it is possible to do so – can create a winning campaign and vault a party into power. In short, political parties have largely abandoned parochial approaches to winning hearts and minds in favour of more hardnosed, expensive, and continuous methods of securing support. This goes well beyond the practices honed by Tom Flanagan and his collaborators as described in the book's foreword. In today's Canada, constant communication occurs no matter the party's label, leadership, or ideological orientation. The campaigning never lets up.

This volume investigates these phenomena outside the official campaign period, wrapped within the umbrella term of "permanent campaigning." Its chapters demonstrate that fundamental aspects of electioneering during the writ period evolve but do not cease in the absence of an official election campaign. Party organizations maintain a state of perpetual readiness. Building the infrastructure required to stay in touch with key voter groups does not end with the election of a government; rather, each campaign provides a burst of data that inform the next sortie. Parties are under intense pressure to continually feed their databases with voter information to optimize message targeting, reach out to new voter groups, stockpile research on the opposition, commission opinion research, send their leaders on carefully planned tours, and, especially, fundraise. In recent years, we have witnessed just how purposefully the party in power employs campaign techniques to maintain the support of their voter base. Driven from the centre of government, this involves undermining opponents, promoting the initiatives of the governing party using taxpayer dollars, rapidly responding to criticism as would occur in a campaign war room, surveying public opinion, and mounting mini-contests in the inter-election period. Every tool is used to secure electoral advantage; every political activity is viewed through the lens of winners and losers. Canadian political parties are looking and behaving in ways usually associated with their American counterparts. The question for Canadians is whether this development is a boon or bane to their system of democracy.

Permanent Campaigning and the Lead-Up to Campaign 2015

The chapters in this book are a repository of the variety of forms of permanent campaigning that have been practised in Canada in recent years. Authors render opinions on each practice's broader relevance, principally during the Conservative era of governance. Here we supplement their efforts by remarking on the pre-campaign electioneering that ramped up as the scheduled October 19, 2015, election approached, and touch on the early days of the new Liberal government.

For the first time in Canadian history, a national election was held on a fixed date. Elements that collided to intensify permanent campaigning include knowing when the election will be held, the winding down of the per-vote subsidy, and a "brazen" publicity machine to promote government initiatives (Burgess 2015b). In Chapter 9, Philippe Lagassé closely examines the impact of fixed dates, arguing that the reform of prerogative power was intended to shift decision making out of the hands of the executive branch to the legislative branch. The most important day in the parliamentary calendar had the effect of intensifying permanent campaigning by the government, opposition parties, and special interests for months before the election. This is not causal; but, as he observes, it has normalized constant campaigning by all parties. In theory, instead of media speculation about when an election will be held, the media have more meaty policy initiatives to report on because of greater certainty in the parliamentary calendar. Conversely, the chicanery that is usually found in the legislature is elevated as hyper-partisan competitiveness takes over. In practice, the slew of pre-campaign electioneering in 2015 illustrates that the dynamics of politicking are not equal during the ebbs and flows of the electoral cycle. The relative absence of rules and the considerable access to resources during governance are fertile ground for permanent campaigning.

Historically, governments follow a timeworn tactic of making controversial and unpopular decisions early in their mandate, which is followed by good news in an election-year budget. This played out in 2015, with the Conservatives doing financial gymnastics to table a balanced budget (Curry and McKenna 2015). But this time, there was the added element of a maelstrom of campaign-like politicking. Pollster Nik Nanos summed up what was going on during this period: "The unofficial campaign is on. This is one of the manifestations of a fixed election date. There is no summer break and no stoppage in campaigning" (quoted in McKenna 2015). Before we reflect on the book's overarching research questions, we itemize some of the pre-campaigning activities that were deployed in June and July in the lead-up to the election call. We cluster the pre-campaign activities that caught our eye during the early summer within the five components of permanent campaigning that we presented in Chapter 1 (see Table 1.1). It is important to recall that these are not mutually exclusive categories; quite the contrary, they are interloping. Any given activity exhibits multiple characteristics associated with diverse aspects of permanent campaigning. As well, our casual scan of media stories by no means produced an exhaustive list. One need only consult Chapter 4 by Andrea Lawlor to recognize that political parties (through press releases and other tools) and the media (by reporting on events) operate a lead-follow relationship to determine what makes the news.

Our framework submits that *communication control* is among the strategic objectives of permanent campaigning in Canada. Controlling communication is expressed through activities such as candidate screening, political advertising, tight media protocols, and direct marketing. We observe that there was nothing exceptional with respect to message control in the lead-up to the 2015 campaign. Noteworthy is that the dissolution of Parliament marked a *relinquishment* of control, particularly for the governing party. The official campaign had the effect of increasing the accessibility of all major party leaders, the prime minister especially. As has been well documented in this book and elsewhere, Stephen Harper routinely avoided media questioning in a bid to control the agenda. But an election campaign brings a public expectation of daily media access on the leaders' tours. For this reason, NDP leader Thomas Mulcair was panned for not accepting any questions on the first day of the campaign. He had previously employed such a clampdown in the final days of his leadership campaign, and he would do so again at the conclusion of the federal election. The Conservatives were experts at this, continuing their practice of accepting only four questions from national media who had paid to be on the tour, and one from a local journalist. That level of control was new in 2011, when the Conservatives were widely labelled as running a bubble campaign, but by 2015, the five-question protocol was their norm. By comparison, the Liberals positioned themselves as a pro-democracy party by being accessible to the media and, as the campaign went on, by drawing large crowds to events compared with the guarded control surrounding all facets of the Conservative leader's tour.

What interests us here is that the official campaign resulted in Prime Minister Harper being more accessible than he ever was as head of government. He participated in five national leaders' debates and almost every day was subjected to questioning from journalists about hot topics outside of the party's control. In an inter-election scenario, Harper would have been unreachable; as Anna Lennox Esselment and Paul Wilson detail in Chapter 12, a minister or parliamentary secretary would have been dispatched as the government's spokesperson, and the message delivered to stakeholders and voters would have been carefully coordinated from the Prime Minister's Office (PMO). Strategists would argue that a government cannot advance policy if the prime minister is continually knocked off message by others who are controlling the public agenda. Moreover, focused communication helps to ensure that election platform commitments are upheld, that the priorities of (select) voters are advanced, and that information is communicated with clarity. Likewise, Lawlor's chapter on media-party parallelism links to the observation that the prime minister was certainly aware that in late August, the trial of Senator Mike Duffy would leap to the top of the media's agenda and that vultures would circle, looking for evidence of PMO wrongdoing. During that period, Harper attempted to limit his accessibility by campaigning in Northern Canada, but it proved impossible to escape the intensity of a national contest and the drama of the Duffy trial. Other breaking developments during the campaign, notably those related to the Syrian refugee crisis, would ordinarily have the Conservatives using the levers available to government to control the message. Instead, Harper was often caught in unscripted moments dealing with controversies in the heat of the campaign trail. During governance, debate about the command-and-control approach is confined to small circles, but during an election campaign, it is magnified by being portrayed by the press as a disturbing antidemocratic manoeuvre. There is some truth to this, for as Esselment and Wilson observe, the executive branch and government MPs become disinterested in two-way dialogue with citizens. Regardless, these examples are reminders that the tools of campaigning can be more potent during governance than within the rules and norms of the official election period.

A second component of permanent campaigning is *resource exploitation.* Political operatives with access to state resources find ways to manipulate them for electioneering purposes. This often leads to new practices, because the party is working within institutional constraints that limit their freedom to deploy the resources. Examples include government advertising, parliamentary newsletters, satellite offices, and a leader touring the country on the public dime.

Far and away, stories of resource exploitation were the most prevalent in the run-up to the official campaign. The Conservative government leveraged public resources in a number of ways. Not only did they have privileged access to public opinion research, but they authorized an increase in public opinion polling spending in 2015, with the Privy Council Office adding new polls beyond its allotted budget (Beeby 2015a). This seems to be foremost a political ploy, given that government-funded opinion research studies are meant to inform policy that is introduced by the government, and the Conservatives could not be certain of being returned to office to act on the data. Amassing this type of survey information, as André Turcotte and Simon Vodrey show in Chapter 7, is of increasing value to political parties both in and out of power – and is causing more money to be spent. For the Conservatives, their commissioning of government polls paled in comparison to their seeking of public favour by dispensing public goods. Much publicity was generated about the issuance of $3 billion in Universal Child Care Benefit payments, with cheques mailed as of July 20, less than two weeks before the Conservatives called the election. Eligible parents received $160 per month per child under six, an increase of $60, and an additional $60 for every child older than six but under eighteen, which was paid in a lump sum retroactive to the start of the year. Conservative ministers and MPs busied themselves holding media events to publicize the payouts. The government's lead spokesperson on the policy, federal employment minister Pierre Poilievre, wore a blue golf shirt adorned with the Conservative Party logo at a government news conference marking the launch of the cheques. For his part, Mulcair, at the helm of a modernized and prepared party machine, as detailed by David McGrane in Chapter 8, launched a tour of Ontario that felt like a campaign: two daily media events, granting local media interviews, and attending partisan rallies in the evenings (Canadian Press 2015). He urged wealthy parents to donate their benefit payments to the New Democrats, a message that was repeated in the party's email blasts to supporters. All of this washed away over time and appears to have largely faded from public memory by election day.

During this period, much of the Conservative government's $10 billion allocated for provincial, territorial, and local infrastructure projects had not yet been spent. As speculation of an election call mounted, Conservatives held a flurry of events across the country to announce spending initiatives. There was so much spending that a number of MPs and senators held their own announcements without a minister present. All told, in the six weeks between the House rising and the prime minister visiting Rideau Hall, Conservatives made 670 announcements and $14 billion in spending pledges. Of these, 109 announcements were made on July 31 alone (Aiello and Ryckewaert 2015). Of the funds that were awarded, over half were earmarked for Conservative-held ridings (Press 2015), and of the projects that were announced, 83 percent were located in Conservative districts (Curry and Hannay 2015). It had all the feel of an election campaign, except that the media events were coordinated and funded by government, and they shifted the focus away from the CEO to a regional sales team, whose jobs would soon be on the line.

The exploitation of public resources for electoral gain did not stop when the official campaign began. Government advertising continued to air and appeared online for several days during the election period. This was the latest in a dubious history of taxpayer money financing government ads that involve political persuasion. The advertising is not for public safety reasons or foremost about information on government programs and services. Rather, it is meant to advance the innate value of a particular initiative and showcase what the government is "doing" for Canadians. When the election was called, Public Works and Government Services Canada immediately directed its media-buying agency to pull all government advertising. However, contracts are not instantly broken, and it can take up to five days for all publicity to cease. There was an added delay caused by a civic holiday in early August in some provinces. As a result, official campaigning was under way, yet Health Canada's antimarijuana advertising was airing during prime time, to name one example (Mas 2015). As Denver McNeney and David Coletto note in Chapter 10, this advertising can have the desired effect of winning over targeted supporters and is thus an unreasonable incumbent advantage. Some parliamentarians' publicity materials also carried on into the official campaign. A number of MPs seeking re-election sent out parliamentary newsletters that touted their accomplishments and their party's, which arrived in electors' mailboxes well after the official campaign was under way. The partisan nature of the newsletters is consistent with McGrane's warning that parliamentary activities and party headquarter initiatives are increasingly entwined. An egregious form of resource exploitation that occurs within the rules is when a sitting MP holds office and campaigns to be elected at a different level of government. Earlier in the year, Liberal MP Gerry Byrne declared his intention to seek office in the Newfoundland provincial election to be held in November. He won the provincial party nomination and stayed on as MP for approximately six months while campaigning for a provincial seat. In a roundabout way, this harkens to the manner in which party pollsters are planted in the upper echelons of government, as Turcotte and Vodrey describe. Thus, we have local politicos carrying on like those at the top: exploiting resources to the fullest potential within the boundaries of the law.

Whereas resource exploitation is foremost about pushing campaigning boundaries within rules, *redefining norms* involves changing the rules to accommodate additional campaigning. This favours the governing party, particularly if they have a majority government. The stricter rules that the Conservative government brought down to limit political activities by organizations with charitable status, whose implications Mario Levesque discusses in Chapter 15, is an example. Changes introduced through the *Fair Elections Act* sought to redefine the norms of the official election campaign period (for a summary, see Shepherd 2015). Harper's decision to initiate a seventy-eight-day contest was another case of redefining norms. The prime minister caught many off guard when he visited the governor general on August 2; a visit after Labour Day would have led to the usual thirty-six-day operation. Harper was correct that campaigning was already under way, so it might as well be governed by the rules and norms of elections. Nevertheless, he was the one who decided when to visit Rideau Hall, and he calculated that campaigning under the *Canada Elections Act* was to his party's advantage. These advantages were chiefly money-related, because the rules favoured the Conservatives as the better-financed party and they disadvantaged the special interests who were unable to spend their war chests. In July, Engage Canada launched a negative television and radio advertising campaign to persuade Canadians that it was time for a change of government. The so-called super PAC (an acronym for political action committee) comprised of a group of Liberal and NDP strategists, whose financiers included labour unions (Radwanski 2015). Within weeks, a group called HarperPAC emerged and initiated negative advertising against Liberal leader Justin Trudeau. It was devised by former Harper government political staff, but was quickly disbanded after public consternation and a rebuke by a Conservative Party spokesperson. This goes along with Lawlor's thinking about a catch-22 of campaign politics, echoed by McGrane: that constant electioneering does more to engage electors, but its substance and tone turn them off.

During this period, senior mandarins were thinking about ways to re-institute norms concerning the public service bargain that Jonathan Craft discusses in Chapter 2. The clerk of the Privy Council assembled deputy ministers in May and directed them to read up about New Political Governance. A summary prepared by the Privy Council Office for the meeting encapsulated that government today "is characterized by integration of governance and campaigning, partisan-political staff as a third force in public administration, politicization of appointments to the senior public service, and expectation that public servants should be promiscuously partisan" (Beeby 2015b). The clerk was right to initiate such a conversation. However, we should not confuse the public service's interpretation of "normal" with its membership's unwavering commitment to upholding the public service bargain. Moreover, Amanda Clarke and Mary Francoli observe in Chapter 13 that the Government of Canada's use of social media is hardly wrapped under the thumb of political elites, raising questions about whether perceptions of political manipulation are overwrought. The PMO's video magazine described by Mireille Lalancette and Sofia Tourigny-Koné in Chapter 14 is an example of the challenge of arriving at a definitive conclusion   about when permanent campaigning is unacceptable. To some, the *24 Seven* videos were blatant misuse of public funds for party propaganda; to others, they were an innovative way to use digital media to show a side of the prime minister that would otherwise never have come to light.

This raises questions about what "normal" is, and ought to be, in the public service and in government communication. Somehow it was acceptable post-election that new Prime Minister Trudeau and ministers were mobbed by adoring civil servants in the foyer of the Global Affairs headquarters in Ottawa. Hundreds of them – mostly women – clapped, hooted, and sought selfies. A reporter who asked a minister a difficult question was booed, while a minister's response to another question was met with applause. The government employees reached out to touch Trudeau, who waded through the crowd as he had at campaign events; the throng was so intense that he stopped to give a spontaneous address to his admirers. A Canadian Press reporter observed that "Conservatives have long complained of Liberal sympathies in the federal civil service but the Harper government's penchant for picking fights – on everything from scientific advice to collective bargaining – appears to have pushed the normally reserved bureaucracy past the point of caring about partisan optics" (Cheadle 2015). In that same lobby, soon after forming government, the Liberals unceremoniously removed the portrait of Canada's head of state that had been instituted by the Conservatives. Artwork first installed during the Pierre Trudeau era was put back. It is all a reminder that the concept of normal in the public service and the values of Canada's so-called natural governing party must not be confused with what is impartial or proper. The one thing that is now normal irrespective of partisanship is a penchant to get wrapped up in constant campaigning. It is an open question whether the Conservatives pushing an agenda on a recalcitrant public service is necessarily worse than star-crazed civil servants, of their own volition, publicly exhibiting a partisan bias.

Another component of permanent campaigning is *database management*. Steve Patten's contribution in Chapter 3 effectively details the considerable emphasis that political strategists place on the collection and refinement of information about supporters, potential supporters, and non-supporters. The use of database marketing technology is a cost-efficient way to communicate specific messages with targeted groups, who can be contacted by email, by telephone, by mail, by social media, and on their doorsteps. Within government, this involves employing political staff with specialized skill sets funded by the public purse; within the extra-parliamentary wing, the emphasis on technology requires raising funds to finance outsourcing and capital costs. As McGrane notes, in electoral districts, this pushes aside local volunteers in decision making and marginalizes them as a door-knocking sales force, albeit one that comes to life in between elections. This changes the nature of political engagement.

Thierry Giasson and Tamara Small draw particular attention to how opposition parties have used online platforms in the inter-election period to advance their strategic objectives. In Chapter 6, they refer to a hybrid process of old and new communications tactics, whereby digital media supplement traditional modes of communication, without straying far from the standard practice of sharing information and personalizing leaders. Parties constantly tweet out their missives, post announcements and achievements on Facebook, and maintain their brand through focused YouTube channels and Instagram accounts. They build voter profiles by mining data from Canadians who like party posts, retweet their messages, or leave comments on YouTube or other media platforms. Even amid a flurry of dynamic social media options, some aspects of a political organization's most important electronic communication still occurs through email. As Alex Marland and Maria Mathews set out in Chapter 5, email communication has the potential to fulfill civic knowledge and political activation functions. However, more often than not, it is used to satiate the party's hunger for resources. This is most obvious at the end of every fundraising quarter, when listserv members are bombarded with urgent requests to donate, only to hear very little once the deadline passes. They note that the commodification of leadership, which is particularly prevalent with Trudeau, is worth monitoring. Expanding on their data, we find that throughout early 2015, the three major parties regularly sent emails to their listserv members, constantly raising the spectre of an early election call and urging donations to help the party prepare for the October election. Oddly, the Liberal listserv was nearly dormant in July, explained only by the fervency by which the parties prioritize fundraising at the end of quarters (i.e., the end of June) and the possibility that party staff were on vacation.[1] This contradicts notions of non-stop campaigning, suggesting that just as there are peaks and valleys during the parliamentary calendar, there are certain times of year that campaigners take a break too. Not so when government resources are available. During that month, subscribers to the Conservative PMO's *24 Seven* listserv received an email trumpeting that the child-care benefit payments were about to begin, in lieu of the regular message highlighting that week's *24 Seven* video.

Political parties do not have a monopoly on microtargeting. With opinion polls suggesting that any one of the three major parties could form government, interest groups refined their pressure tactics as the inter-election period drew to a close. The activity by these groups, however, high-lights how the permanent campaign can advantage some interests over others, as Levesque explores. In this case, interests with healthy finances – such as the Canadian Medical Association and the Federation of Canadian Municipalities – used NationBuilder database tracking software[2] to manage and monitor lists of supporters. "The whole idea is using the database soft-ware to build a nation of supporters, capture their interest around their hometowns, and then start feeding them content," explained the municipal-ity organization's CEO (quoted in Burgess 2015a, 21). The medical associa-tion went a step further, commissioning Nanos Research to collect opinion survey data in marginal seats and using social media to identify potential supporters in those ridings so that it could communicate with them in-expensively during the campaign. These resources are not equally available to other groups, such as non-profit organizations, who cannot compete on the same footing in the era of permanent campaigning. But the protection of personal data is a serious privacy concern no matter who is compiling a political database. It is even more significant for political parties, because as Patten points out, they fall outside of protections offered to Canadians in the *Personal Information Protection and Electronic Documents Act* and the *Privacy Act*. In academia, obtaining informed consent is an important eth-ical value when collecting data from human subjects. But ethical standards are considerably lower in politics. Whether during NDP days of action, dur-ing a by-election, or throughout a general election campaign, local party canvassers input data into apps on their smartphones that sync with the party databases that are then used to assist with persuasion and mobiliza-tion efforts. Most Canadians likely have no comprehension whatsoever that any of the information they offer to political organizations ends up in a data-base that is stored, accessed, and manipulated by untold numbers of people for countless reasons over an indefinite period of time.

An argument could be made that, as a result of these party databases, voters are receiving much better service, perhaps even to the advantage of civic literacy. Political parties are amassing enough information to know which voters will be interested in their health-care policy (and will promptly be provided with information about the party's plans) and which voters would prefer to discuss how the budget will be balanced. What's more,

Canadians are less likely to be bothered by phone calls or door knocks from parties that they like the least, since parties are becoming more aware of which voters are beyond their party's reach. This saves the party valuable time and financial resources, but it diminishes the pluralistic engagement that should occur between political parties and citizens. The earlier point is the more important one: for the most part, citizens do not know what information about them is gathered and stored by political parties, nor how it is used. This poses an important ethical problem that requires some resolution.

Finally, *coalition building* brings together clusters of the electorate who share common values and mobilize to support the agenda of a political party. Communications activities are structured around appeasing these stakeholders and constituents and leveraging database information to persuade political action. In June 2015, the Liberal Party slipped to third place in public opinion polls and was grappling with public anger that they had supported Bill C-51, the Conservatives' controversial antiterrorism law. The unofficial campaign was on, but the party's lack of policy commitments made it difficult to build a coalition of supporters. The party braintrust determined that Trudeau should make a major policy speech each week through to October (Rana 2015). Strategists suggested that this was part of their plan all along. Regardless, knowing when the election would be held put the party on war footing for months. "The reality is, because we all knew when the election was coming, the campaign began so long ago – really, last spring or even last winter," said Liberal candidate Mark Holland (quoted in Kirkup 2015). Coalition building is much less tangible than other aspects of permanent campaigning. It requires strategic thinking and laying groundwork. It is less susceptible to jolts of activity that make the news.

The early period of the Trudeau Liberal government offers an abundance of evidence that the practice of permanent campaigning is continuing. The new prime minister's media acumen has leveraged government resources to generate positive publicity on both the international and domestic fronts, notably a proclivity for media events and social media communication. This was noticeable as Canada's new handsome leader was discovered on the world stage. He was mobbed for selfies by many attendees at the G20 conference in Turkey. He spoke to a packed UN crowd about climate change in New York. At the World Economic Forum in Davos, Switzerland, Trudeau earned positive press in numerous global newspapers. He also brought an entourage on an official visit to Washington, DC, and held court in a New York City boxing ring, all at taxpayer expense. The PMO pounces on these successful forays and uses digital media to speedily post and circulate pictorials, photographs, and videos about Trudeau and his government. Perpetual communication is still the order of the day, and the pursuit of digital government will continue apace, as Clarke and Francoli explore.

Constant communication and interactivity are not confined to splashy international events. The promise of the Liberal government to be more open and accessible demands a communications operation to demonstrate that it is fulfilling this promise. Inviting Canadians to the grounds of Rideau Hall for the official swearing-in of the new cabinet was a start. The new prime minister and his cabinet waved to the crowds gathered on the lawn as they walked up to Rideau Hall, epitomizing what openness means for a Liberal administration, while making it a splashy pomp-and-circumstance presidential affair. As well, Trudeau's ministerial mandate letters (instructions to new ministers on what they are to achieve over the term in office) were posted on the PMO website. The letters are soaked in campaign rhetoric; they are therefore valuable not only as a process of transparency (through the act of making them public), but also in their content. The letters repeat key messages from the campaign. They also instruct ministers to engage with the parliamentary press gallery, noting that questions from journalists "contribute in an important way to the democratic process" (Prime Minister's Office 2015b). To this point, ministers have been far more accessible to the press than their Conservative predecessors, and Trudeau has made a point of using the National Press Theatre for various government announcements. It is the art of striking a balance between traditional political communication as presented by the press gallery and political communication disseminated through the various digital platforms that provide for unfiltered messages and images directly to Canadians. Whatever the approach, we believe that the strategic shape and intensity of a prime minister's and other ministers' publicity activities are enveloped in permanent campaigning.

Regulating the Permanent Campaign

If there is one common theme that runs throughout this book, it is the conclusion arrived at independently by its various contributors: that more research about permanent campaigning in Canada is needed. We are only beginning to understand its practice, its implications, and what if anything must be done about it. In the introductory chapter of this book, we asked:

1   To what extent are the tactics, tools, or channels used by political actors
    in Canada during governance the same or different than what occurs
    during the official election campaign period?
2   To what extent does permanent campaigning result in a more informed,
    engaged, or cynical citizenry in Canada?
3   What are the corresponding implications of permanent campaigning for
    political parties, the media, parliamentary government, and Canadian
    democracy?

To our first question, many chapters indicate that tactics, tools, and
channels are increasingly the same regardless of the campaigning context.
Campaign strategists in the PMO and the Office of the Leader of the Official Opposition develop and implement strategic communications and
issues management to guide Parliament as they would in a campaign. Each
party has people charged with carrying the permanent campaign. Parties
are modernizing and are taking advantage of emergent online platforms to
communicate with supporters, to constantly fundraise, to manage the image
and brand of their leaders and organizations, and to collect and manage
voter information within databases. None of this is going to disappear. The
practices discussed in this book will become more, not less, sophisticated
and accurate and more, not less, valuable to political parties and governments. The main difference concerns the ferocity with which different leaders and parties choose to prioritize certain techniques.

How, then, is permanent campaigning affecting the citizenry in Canada?
Citizens are likely more informed and more engaged, but more critical. The
fallout of the 2015 federal election could be interpreted as a rejection of
permanent campaigning practices, or at least the way that the Harper
Conservatives practised them. Were Canadians tired of being spoon-fed
controlled party lines? Were they disturbed by Harper's treatment of Parliament as an electoral battlefield? Of the Conservative government's barrage
of partisan-leaning ads and the Conservative Party's negative advertising?
Of the silencing of some ministers and most public servants? Whatever the
reason, Canadians never had access to so many channels of political information and expression, and parties have never invested as much in strategies and tools that would allow them to communicate more efficiently
with Canadians. Our concern is that this efficient communication is narrow-
casted, specialized, and targeted, even when it appears otherwise. It is not

aimed at all Canadians and it does not speak of the common good. It foremost addresses the needs and wants of the party and of some segments of the citizenry that parties need to win the next election. Some Canadians are therefore very well informed, and personally informed, by party communication that is directed at them during the permanent campaign. Others, less desirable citizens, are left behind. Patten observes that this fractures the public sphere and pits individual interests against the collective. Yet more Canadians voted in 2015 than in the previous two federal elections. Whether they voted for a change of regime, against permanent campaigning or as a result of it, the fact is that more citizens got involved and engaged.

Finally, how is the permanent campaign affecting Canadian political institutions? Some chapters in this collection indicate that an area related to the exploitation of government resources is how the rules of the game change. Parliamentary procedures are challenged and then normalized, and new legislation is written that either accommodates or perpetuates a state of constant campaigning. The regular tabling of omnibus bills is a case in point. While still considered antithetical to good governance and effective scrutiny, omnibus bills became common during the Harper era. These types of bills are efficient in the sense that they bundle amendments to dozens of pieces of legislation into a monster bill running into the hundreds of pages. This limits the ability of parliamentarians to carefully consider each amendment; consequently, the government "wins" by effecting changes to numerous laws in one fell swoop. Other parliamentary procedures, such as time allocation and closure of debate, are also commonplace no matter which party is in power. Limiting debate helps to fit parliamentary processes into the timetable of government announcements that are used to highlight achievements and delivery of the governing party's commitments, primarily coordinated within the PMO. On the heels of public anger about the Harper Conservatives' style of governing, most observers thought the Trudeau Liberals would shy away from such practices. Within the first seven months of governing, however, the Liberals used their majority three times to cut legislative debate short. The new normal in Parliament continues, despite assurances to the contrary. It is clear that, no matter the party label, resources will be exploited to the advantage of the governing party. This is a troubling trajectory for Canada's parliamentary institutions.

A further implication of ongoing campaigning is that it impacts the public service and the public policy process. The traditional bargain, as Craft sets out, provides a clear demarcation between non-partisan public servants and their elected, political masters. Tensions inevitably arise when the imperatives of the permanent campaign, pursued by ministers and their political staff, place the impartiality of the public service at risk. Policy making is more compressed to satisfy partisan-political interests, ministers have a greater propensity to name and blame public servants when files are mishandled, and there is a growing expectation that top mandarins should be enthusiastic supporters of the government's agenda. He even suggests that permanent campaigning and its tensions constitute their own form of subsidiary public service bargain.

It is notable that Craft focuses on the internal relationship between the government and the bureaucracy. We must not overlook that the permanent campaign has implications for outside groups who want to have an effect on policy. Levesque's chapter on disability organizations highlights how they are trying to accommodate, or fit into, a permanent-campaign framework. The people whom he interviewed were clear that involvement in policy making had shifted dramatically from a period when broad consultation and collaborative involvement between the public service and interested groups was standard, to a new norm where any potential change to existing policy must have the political buy-in of a minister's political staff. Such an approach to governing leaves many organizations, especially those representing vulnerable Canadians, at the margins of policy making.

As constant electioneering settles into a way of life for Canadian politics, it is natural for us to consider the question of whether regulating aspects of the permanent campaign is appropriate. This has implications for citizens, political parties, and governance. As noted earlier, the real issue for citizens is one of personal privacy. Patten's chapter highlights how parties are using data and technology to create files with hundreds of pieces of information on each individual voter. While both companies and the Government of Canada are required to abide by privacy protection laws, political parties are essentially free to collect and use personal information as they see fit (Bennett and Bayley 2012). There are also few rules regarding how MPs use data that pertain to their constituents. While Canadians must be vigilant about how they choose to share details of their lives, the growing sophistication of data gathering and storing tools requires us to rethink whether the protection of citizens' information is important enough that political parties should fall under the same privacy legislation that regulates government institutions.

The effects of the permanent campaign could also be limited by regulating political parties in other ways. Party advertising is a case in point, and three approaches could be considered here. The first is to encourage parties to adhere to the same kind of standards for their advertising as businesses. Canada does have the *Canadian Code of Advertising Standards* to which corporations willingly sign on to ensure truthful, fair, and accurate competition with regard to advertising. Much like privacy legislation, the *Code* does not currently apply to political parties because the free expression of political ideas is a founding pillar of liberal democracies. But Canadians have numerous complaints about the state of party advertising, particularly their negative slant (Advertising Standards Canada 2014, 7). Negative political ads may include more facts than positive ads, but there is a tendency to take issues or words out of context to make a point (Akin 2013). This contravenes the business standards of being truthful, fair, and accurate and can have a deleterious impact on citizens' feelings of efficacy and trust in political institutions (Lau et al. 2007). The permanent campaign will witness more advertising from Canadian parties, both during and outside the confines of the official writ period. Requesting that they voluntarily agree to follow the *Canadian Code of Advertising Standards* is one way to manage the kind of party appeals to which Canadians will be subjected on TV, on the radio, in print, and online.

A second approach would introduce further limits on party finance. Parties are restricted in their spending only during the writ period. Considering the seventy-eight-day campaign in 2015, the spending limit was close to $52 million, more than double what it would have been with the usual thirty-six-day election. The advent of the permanent campaign has also been witness to heavy assaults by parties against each other outside the writ period. Legislating caps on the amount they could spend each year would scale this back. Furthermore, the controversy over so-called "pay to play" fundraising (Thompson 2016) is evidence of a permanent fundraising ethos. Banning the appearance of the first minister and ministers at fundraising events and in fundraising emails would go even further towards levelling the playing field and improving the ethics of money in politics.

A third approach would target government advertising. For many years, the governing party could promote its agenda and the value of its programs to Canadians through taxpayer-funded partisan advertising. The Harper Conservatives spent hundreds of millions of dollars on quasi-partisan ads funded through the public purse. The Ontario government banned this type of advertising in 2004 and gave the provincial Auditor General the responsibility of reviewing government commercials before their release, though they later watered down many of the provisions. In 2016, the federal Liberals initiated action on this issue. The government implemented an interim policy that requires Advertising Standards Canada to review all federal ads in an attempt to ensure that they are non-partisan, objective, factual, and reflective of a "legitimate public service announcement" (Cheadle 2016). Other aspects of the new regulation include a complete ban on government ads in the three months prior to a fixed election date, as well as a prohibition on advertising government policies that have not yet received royal assent. Generally speaking, these are welcome developments. However, the temptation to exploit government resources to promote government policies or MPs quickly resulted in a dispute between the Liberal government and the opposition parties, with accusations that the Liberals broke their own advertising policy just weeks after announcing the new safeguards. Trudeau was prominently featured in a government video that promoted Canadian tourism, which is contrary to the prohibition of appearances by MPs and ministers in government advertisements. The Liberals defended the ad, arguing that the video was part of a social media campaign and thus not subject to the new rules (McGregor 2016). It is clear that the compulsion to continuously campaign is such that even a party with a professed commitment to regulating certain types of communication cannot help but engage in those same banned activities and contorting the rules to suit its own agenda.

How can the permanent campaign be regulated within government? Craft points out the danger of bureaucratic politicization, while Esselment and Wilson detail the growing ranks of communications staff in the PMO and their campaign-oriented perspectives. They and other authors, such as Lalancette and Tourigny-Koné, argue that the PMO is preoccupied with strategic communications and issues management. Similarly, government resources can be employed to amplify the permanent campaign as part of an overall branding effort. This is the point made by J.P. Lewis and Kenneth Cosgrove in Chapter 11. They describe how the party in power neatly ties its partisan stripe to the government. The hue of government websites, for example, is changed to match party colours, a practice that we note has since been curbed by the new Treasury Board safeguards that affect partisan advertising – although we will have to see how the conflation of Liberal Party colours and Government of Canada colours (both red and white) will play out. Political staffers charged with enforcing and implementing these approaches to government communication are effectively campaigning from the seat of government. The partisan enthusiasm of political staff can transgress the boundaries that separate them from the non-political service provided by public servants.

To this end, the Gomery Commission (Public Works and Government Services Canada 2006) recommended that better training is required of political staff about the division between what is political and what is under the proper purview of the public service. Among the options for reform is ensuring that political staff do not direct public servants, interfere in the jobs that they do, or withhold information from their own MPs to extend them political protection from potential scandals. This would contribute to better governance and less politicking overall. The code of conduct for political staff that the Trudeau Liberals introduced in the guide for ministers is a positive start (Prime Minister's Office 2015a).

What about parliamentary reforms? As detailed earlier, the preoccupation with permanent campaigning has dealt parliamentary procedures a heavy blow. Several options are available to salvage the internal workings of the House of Commons. Omnibus bills, for example, could be prohibited through a change to the standing orders of the House. A commitment from the government House leader to permit the exhaustion of all substantive debate before holding votes would significantly reduce the imposition of time allocation and closure. Empowering the role of the Speaker to sanction members and compel more direct answers from cabinet would reduce hyperpartisanship during question period and make way for greater accountability. But resisting the temptation to manipulate parliamentary procedure is a real challenge in an atmosphere of permanent campaigning. It requires the good faith of elected representatives and a renewed commitment to our institutions of democratic government.

Conclusion: Permanent Campaigning and the State of Canadian Democracy

The permanence of campaigning in Canada is a troubling development for scholars, as this volume attests. Concerns range from how the private information of citizens is collected and used by political parties, to the closing-off of the executive branch to the public to wield tight control over its message. The ramp-up to an official election campaign illustrates the intensity with which parties approach these contests. The synthesis of all of the information presented here is that an official election neither really begins, nor ends, political party electioneering.

Perhaps the most worrisome mechanisms are the exploitation of government resources and the procedural processes in Parliament that curtail the scrutiny and accountability functions of the legislative branch. In large part there is an expectation that political parties will inform, persuade, and mobilize voters, and perhaps they can be forgiven for employing the most sophisticated tools available to them for this purpose. When only one party has access to the levers of power, however, the playing field is no longer level. The resources of the public, including their democratic institutions, become part of the arsenal of weapons to use against opponents. The potential damage to Canada's system of government must be taken seriously.

While the chapters in this collection focus primarily on the Conservative government of Stephen Harper, the solidifying of a permanent-campaign environment should be viewed more as a continuum. The centralization of power in the PMO and other central agencies began more than forty years ago (Savoie 1999). Distrust in government and a decline of deference by citizens towards those in authority have their roots at about the same time. The focus on party leaders, as opposed to local representatives, became much sharper as the television became a regular household item and political leaders could be beamed into voters' living rooms. And now, in a technologically advanced world where every word, every promise, every gesture, and every stumble can be captured and broadcast across the globe, parties and leaders have become far more adept at carefully controlling their political communication. To do so effectively means that discipline is the order of the day. There must be one core message, talking points to support the message, and little that blocks the way of delivering that message to Canadians. This applies as much to an actual campaign setting as it does to a governing party's performance in front of the press gallery, at government announcements, or in the House of Commons. The Harper administration perfected many aspects of the permanent campaign because it felt that it had to. Brian Mulroney and Jean Chrétien had the luxury of governing before avenues for political communication burst into dozens of directions and threatened the ability of the prime minister and cabinet to tell their own story to Canadians. But the Harper Conservatives brought a preoccupation, if not an obsession, for communication and message control since it was manoeuvring in the unforgiving realm of digital media. The instantaneous and interactive nature of social media technologies transformed how governments and parties developed their communications strategies.

The Liberal government of Justin Trudeau claims that it will revitalize Canadian democracy. In spite of its initial forays into greater openness and accessibility, it would be surprising to see the new federal Liberal government engage in a radically different communications approach from the Conservatives, and, there are more similarities between the two administrations than meets the eye. The Liberals must also manage the perilous, antagonistic, and ever-evolving communications environment. Current social media platforms such as Twitter and Instagram are gaining Canadian users daily, and even newer technologies appear almost every day that bring novel challenges for communications and campaigning strategies. Prime Minister Trudeau, we must not forget, is himself a brand that must be managed. His office is large and staffed with partisans from his campaign who are savvy with digital communication. They are tasked with ensuring the implementation of platform promises. The Trudeau PMO wants the delivery of their commitments to be communicated in a way that permits maximum media impact. The Liberal team is every bit as interested in speaking directly, and in an unfiltered manner, to their supporters as Prime Minister Harper and his team were to theirs. They will carry on with strongly coordinated and controlled communications because the next election is always right around the corner.

When we combine the precepts of New Political Governance with what we also know about the centralization of power in Canada and, now, the advent of permanent campaigning, the ingredients for a diminished democratic system are clearly evident. In his recent book *What Is Government Good At?*, Donald Savoie (2015, 63–64) remarks that "being good at managing permanent election campaigns deters Parliament and political parties from engaging Canadians in a sustained debate about the national interest and holding government to account in delivering programs. Members of Parliament and local candidates ... are no match for the political and marketing experts around party leaders and their close advisors." He has a point. If election campaigns increasingly revolve around the party leader, then it follows that the Canadian system of government will continue to experience increasing concentration of authority in the leader's inner circle generally and the leader specifically. Conversely, at least permanent campaigning engages citizens in new ways, and it does provide new opportunities for getting Canadians involved in governance. As the chapters throughout this volume indicate, we are only beginning to understand the consequences of the non-stop campaigning mentality that is pervading Canadian politics.

NOTES

1   Email data collected under the identical parameters described in Chapter 5 revealed a noticeable frequency variance. In 2013 and 2014, the Liberal email machine went into a lull during July and August. This reoccurred in July 2015, when there was a pronounced difference between the communication consistency of Conservative messages (May $n = 11$, June $n = 16$, July $n = 21$, August $n = 21$), Liberal messages (May $n = 24$, June $n = 34$, July $n = 4$, August $n = 43$), and NDP messages (May $n = 40$, June $n = 59$, July $n = 41$, August $n = 69$).

2   See http://nationbuilder.com/.

REFERENCES

Advertising Standards Canada. 2014. *Consumer Perspectives on Advertising.* Toronto: Advertising Standards Canada. http://www.adstandards.com/en/ASCLibrary/2014 ASCConsumerResearch.pdf.

Aiello, Rachel, and Laura Ryckewaert. 2015. "Tories Announced $14-Billion in Spending Six Weeks before Election Call, 670 Announcements." *Hill Times*, August 10, 1, 21.

Akin, David. 2013. "Conservatives Take Trudeau out of Context in Ad. Surprised?" *David Akin's On the Hill* (blog), April 15. http://blogs.canoe.com/davidakin/politics/ conservatives-take-trudeau-out-of-context-in-ad-surprised/.

Beeby, Dean. 2015a. "Harper Government Cranks Up Polling in Run-Up to Election." CBC News, July 14. http://www.cbc.ca/news/politics/harper-government-cranks-up -polling-in-run-up-to-election-1.3109766.

–. 2015b. "Top Bureaucrats Met to Resist Partisanship Imposed on Public Service." *CBC News*, November 2. http://www.cbc.ca/news/politics/top-bureaucrats-met-to-resist -partisanship-imposed-on-public-service-1.3294972.

Bennett, Colin J., and Robin M. Bayley. 2012. *Canadian Federal Political Parties and Personal Privacy Protection: A Comparative Analysis.* Report to the Office of the Privacy Commissioner of Canada. Victoria, BC: Linden Consulting Inc. https:// www.priv.gc.ca/information/research-recherche/2012/pp_201203_e.asp.

Burgess, Mark. 2015a. "Fixed Election Date Gives Interest Groups Head Start." *Hill Times*, June 1, 1, 21.

–. 2015b. "The Permanent Campaign Meets the 78-Day Campaign, and Falls Apart." In *Canadian Election Analysis: Communication, Strategy and Democracy*, edited by A. Marland and T. Giasson, 18–19. Vancouver: UBC Press. http://www.ubcpress.ca/ canadianelectionanalysis2015/CanadianElectionAnalysis2015.pdf.

Canadian Press. 2015. "Mulcair Hits Campaign Trail Early in Ontario." *Globe and Mail*, July 19. http://www.theglobeandmail.com/news/politics/mulcair-hits-campaign-trail -early-in-ontario/article25584103/.

Cheadle. 2015. "Foreign Affairs Employees Give Trudeau Out of This World Reception." *Maclean's*, November 6. http://www.macleans.ca/politics/ottawa/foreign-affairs -employees-give-trudeau-out-of-this-world-reception/.

–. 2016. "Liberals Move to Curb Partisan Government Advertising." *Huffington Post*, May 12. http://www.huffingtonpost.ca/2016/05/12/federal-liberals-make-interim -move-to-curb-partisan-government-advertising_n_9929940.html.

Curry, Bill, and Chris Hannay. 2015. "Government Favours Infrastructure Projects to Conservative Ridings." *Globe and Mail*, July 14. http://www.theglobeandmail.com/news/politics/government-favours-infrastructure-projects-to-conservative-ridings/article25492064/.

Curry, Bill, and Barrie McKenna. 2015. "Conservatives Deliver Balanced Budget ahead of Election." *Globe and Mail*, April 21. http://www.theglobeandmail.com/news/politics/budget-main/article24046411/.

Gomery Commission. 2006. "Restoring Accountability: Recommendations." Ottawa: Commission of Inquiry into the Sponsorship Program and Advertising Activities.

Kirkup, Kristy. 2015. "Liberals, Conservatives Both Made Most of Marathon Election Campaign." *Globe and Mail*, October 14. http://www.theglobeandmail.com/news/politics/liberals-conservatives-both-made-most-of-marathon-election-campaign/article26812772/.

Lau, Richard R, Lee Sigelman, and Ivy Brown Rovner. 2007. "The Effects of Negative Political Campaigns: A Meta-Analytic Reassessment." *The Journal of Politics* 69 (4): 1176-1209.

Mas, Susana. 2015. "Why Government Ads Were Still Running after Federal Election Call." *CBC News*, August 6. http://www.cbc.ca/news/politics/canada-election-2015-government-ads-aug5-1.3180167.

McGregor, Glen. 2016. "Liberals Spent $24,000 on Tourism Video That Tories Say Broke Ban on Partisan Ads." *CTV News*, May 24. http://www.ctvnews.ca/politics/glen-mcgregor-under-embargo/liberals-spent-24-000-on-tourism-video-that-tories-say-broke-ban-on-partisan-ads-1.2914998.

McKenna, Barrie. 2015. "Conservatives Hand Out Child Benefit Cheques as Campaign Ramps Up." *Globe and Mail*, July 20. http://www.theglobeandmail.com/news/national/conservatives-hand-out-child-benefit-cheques-as-campaign-ramps-up/article25588705/.

Press, Jordan. 2015. "Data Show Conservatives Using Marquee Infrastructure Fund as Campaign Fodder, Liberal MP Says." *National Post*, July 3. http://news.nationalpost.com/news/canada/slow-pace-of-federal-governments-marquee-infrastructure-fund-prompts-complaints-of-playing-politics-with-cash.

Prime Minister's Office. 2015a. "Open and Accountable Government." News backgrounder, November 27. http://pm.gc.ca/eng/news/2015/11/27/open-and-accountable-government.

–. 2015b. "Prime Minister Announces Canada's Growth and Investment Strategies." PMO listserv email, November 15.

Public Works and Government Services Canada. 2005. "Who Is Responsible? Summary." Ottawa: Commission of Inquiry into the Sponsorship Program and Advertising Activities. http://epe.lac-bac.gc.ca/003/008/099/003008-disclaimer.html?orig=/100/206/301/pco-bcp/commissions/sponsorship-ef/06-03-06/www.gomery.ca/en/phase1report/summary/es_full_v01.pdf.

Radwanski, Adam. 2015. "Unions, Centre-Left Interests to Begin Ad Campaign Attacking Harper's Tories." *Globe and Mail*, June 11. http://www.theglobeandmail.com/news/

politics/unions-centre-left-interests-to-begin-ad-campaign-attacking-harpers
-tories/article24924913/.

Rana, Abbas. 2015. "Trudeau to Make New Policy Announcements Almost Every Week." *Hill Times*, June 22, 1, 16.

Savoie, Donald J. 1999. *Governing from the Centre: The Concentration of Power in Canadian Politics*. Toronto: University of Toronto Press.

–. 2015. *What Is Government Good At? A Canadian Answer*. Montreal/Kingston: McGill-Queen's University Press.

Shepherd, Robert P. 2015. "Partisans and Elections: Electoral Reform Is for Parliament to Address." In *Canadian Election Analysis: Communication, Strategy and Democracy*, edited by A. Marland and T. Giasson, 12–13. Vancouver: UBC Press. http://www.ubcpress.ca/canadianelectionanalysis2015/CanadianElectionAnalysis2015.pdf.

Thompson, Elizabeth. 2015. "Ethics Commissioner Wants Tighter Rules on 'Pay-To-Play' Fundraisers." CBC News, October 27. http://www.cbc.ca/news/politics/political-fundraising-liberals-ethics-money-1.3824260.

Glossary

The following key communications-related concepts are used in *Permanent Campaigning in Canada*. This list provides important contextual relevance. It is partially derived from *Political Marketing in Canada* (UBC Press, 2012, 257–63), *Political Communication in Canada* (UBC Press, 2014, 247–54) and *Brand Command* (UBC Press, 2016, 405–14).

access to information (or freedom of information): The legislated provision that citizens have the right to request and obtain records from their government within a reasonable period, subject to reasonable limitations. Among the limitations are files received from other governments in confidence, files that might harm diplomatic or military activities, files that might injure a person, or files that might harm the jurisdiction's economic interests. Advice and recommendations prepared for senior government officials, including ministers, are normally exempt. Coordinators interpret the legislation to determine what must be released verbatim, what must be redacted, and what must be withheld.

advertising: Any controlled, mediated (print, television, radio, and Internet), and paid form of communication whose objective is to influence the opinion, choice, or behaviour of its destined audience. See also *attack ad* and *government advertising*.

agenda setting: Agenda setting occurs when extensive media coverage of an issue increases people's perceptions of its importance. The more coverage an issue receives, the more likely people are to perceive that it is important. The amount of attention devoted to particular issues in the news can influence political priorities and policy responses.

attack ad: Negative advertising that emphasizes the personal characteristics of an opponent rather than just political or policy aspects. One notorious example in Canada was the Jean Chrétien "face" ads featured during the 1993 federal election campaign.

attentive public: The small proportion of citizens who actively follow and gather information on politics, including issues and events not treated as leading news stories.

blog: Short for weblog, a low-cost, publicly available, single- or multiauthored web publication that has limited external editorial oversight. It provides updated mixed-media information, comments, and opinions archived in reverse chronological order, and it regularly comprises interactive elements such as hyperlinks. Blog writers (bloggers) post content on a wide variety of subjects, including politics. The aggregation of all blogs is known as the blogosphere. See also *social media.*

branding: The overall perception of a product or organization and often employs familiar logos or slogans to evoke meanings, ideas, and associations in the consumer. In politics, branding involves creating a trustful, long-term relationship with electors. A political brand is deeper than a political image because brands comprise tangible and non-tangible components, including personal experiences, emotional attachments, and partisan loyalties. See also *image.*

centralization: This concept posits that information, power, and communications strategy are clustered among core decision makers. In the federal government, centralization normally refers to central agencies, such as the Prime Minister's Office, Privy Council Office, Treasury Board, and Department of Finance. Within political parties, it normally refers to a leader's concentration of power and inner circle. Centralization constrains the independence of line departments, junior ministers, parliamentarians, and election candidates.

data analytics: The examination of data through machine learning to identify patterns, trends, and correlations within that data. For political parties, the identified patterns can then be used for predictive modelling to ascertain how an individual voter is likely to behave, particularly with regard to which party that person will support.

database marketing: Quantitative data on electors stored in a database and used to create targeted marketing messages. In Canada, political parties begin with information obtained from the list of electors, to which they add information collected when people contact the party, take out a membership, make a donation, put up a lawn sign, or respond to get-out-the-vote contact efforts, along with other data sources. Information can also be obtained from Statistics Canada, telemarketing companies, and list providers. Increasingly, database marketing is supplemented by scouring the web and social media for information on electors. See also *direct marketing; microtargeting; relationship marketing; voter file.*

digital government: The application of digital technologies to the functions of the public sector.

direct marketing: The communication of precise messages in a cost-efficient manner – via direct mail, telemarketing, direct dialogues, personalized emails, or texts to portable communications devices – directly to targeted individuals, thereby bypassing filters such as the mass media.

election platform/manifesto: A document identifying a political party's commitments and policy proposals that, should the party form government, will guide the government's agenda.

election turnout: The proportion of electors who voted in an election. Voter turnout in Canada has been decreasing over time.

fixed election date: A date set in legislation that governs when an election will be held to fill seats in a representative assembly. At the federal level in Canada, the fixed date is once every four years on the third Monday in October. Even with legislation that sets out a four-year election cycle, the calling of an election remains at the discretion of the prime minister and the law does not affect an early election, particularly if there is a minority government.

focusing event: An event (usually sudden, emotional, or calamitous) that trains public attention on a particular problem of public policy. The episode results in citizens calling on their elected representatives to find solutions to address the problem. A focusing event can affect government agenda setting by vaulting an unexpected incident to the front of a policy mandate.

frames: Interpretive cues used to present and give meaning to social and political issues by emphasizing or excluding specific elements. The political elite and the media develop frames to define political debates. Frames provide targeted audiences with definitions of social and political problems or issues along with the agendas of political actors involved in the debates and their proposed solutions or potential outcomes. See also *framing; image.*

framing: A strategic communicative process and an effect of the mediatization of politics. As a strategic process, it is the act of shaping or presenting issues, such as political ones, by using frames to reflect particular agendas and influence public opinion. As an effect, it is the indirect consequence of exposure to media coverage of politics over public opinion. The frames used by media to depict political issues lead citizens to cast different forms of responsibility on policy makers or interpret political and social issues in varying ways. The public's understanding of political issues is therefore influenced by the dominant frames used to define them. See also *frames; image.*

game frame: The media's treatment of politics and issues as a game that reduces complex matters to an assessment of winners and losers. This extends to media analysis of the strategy behind political decisions, particularly those involving political marketing. See also *horse-race journalism; strategy frame.*

gatekeeping: A process in which news editors select and favour certain types of stories over others, thereby controlling the flow and content of information, political or otherwise, and ultimately determining the news. Gatekeeping is highly influenced by the subjective attitudes or biases of journalists and editors and results in a hierarchy of news stories presented to the public. See also *agenda setting.*

get out the vote (GOTV): Mobilization strategies designed to ensure that supporters turn out to cast ballots on election day. GOTV increasingly uses segmentation and voter profiling to identify whom to target, and direct marketing (emails, mobile texts, or phone calls) is often employed to reach key segments by drawing on information stored in party databases.

government advertising: Political communication by a government to its citizens about public programs and services through various media, including print, television, radio, and online. Government advertising can be categorized as partisan if, according to a law in Ontario banning the practice, it is self-congratulatory, timed for political gain, or inappropriately uses the colour associated with the governing party.

horse-race journalism: The tendency of news media to report predominantly on opinion polls, campaign events, or leaders at the expense of electoral issues. This results in media coverage of even routine political events becoming mini-contests in which the focus is on winning and losing. As an election campaign climaxes, there is less coverage of contestants who are behind in opinion polls, and thus cannot influence the outcome of the race, and a fascination with who is leading in the polls. See also *gatekeeping*; *politainment*.

image: The mental impression or perception of an object, being, or concept, such as a politician, political party, or public policy. Images are subjective because of the ways in which their target audiences receive, absorb, process, and evoke political communication. The public images of political actors are actually imaginary constructs shaped by information and visuals controlled and filtered by political parties, public relations personnel, the media, pundits, and others. See also *branding*; *framing*.

image bites: Visual snippets, often in the form of digital visual files (photographs, videos) whose brevity accommodates the media's demand for succinct visuals easily accessible at no cost. See also *sound bites*.

infotainment: The treatment of information in an entertaining manner to attract and sustain audience interest. See also *politainment*.

inter-election period: The time between official election campaign periods. In Canada, the inter-election period, unlike campaign periods, is not regulated by extraordinary limitations on fundraising activities, spending, or political communication. See also *permanent campaign*.

interest group: A voluntary or non-profit organization that forms due to a shared connection or cause by its members. Interest groups seek to influence legislation by meeting with and persuading government policy makers about their common interest.

Internet marketing: The use of digital technologies to achieve marketing objectives. Electronic communications platforms and tactics include websites, wikis, emailing, texting, social networking, online file sharing, social bookmarking, and microblogging.

issues management: The way in which political parties or the government (particularly the Prime Minister's Office) identify potentially harmful stories and rapidly develop a response to combat them.

lobbying: The act of communicating with public officeholders about issues or legislation on behalf of a client, corporation, or organization. While viewed as a legitimate activity, in Canada, lobbyists who work for compensation must register with the government as a lobbyist and track their interactions with politicians and public servants.

market intelligence: Empirical data on the political marketplace and public views, also known as market research. Collecting market intelligence involves quantitative and qualitative methods such as polls, opinion surveys, focus groups, role playing, consultation, and analysis of existing public census data and election records. A political party relies on market intelligence to prioritize issues, develop and refine communications strategies, and present itself as the most competent party to address those issues.

market orientation: A willingness to use market intelligence and other data to assist in the identification and understanding of audience concerns and priorities and to incorporate them into the design of the product or service. A market-oriented organization therefore engages in far more consultation and dialogue with the public than does an organization that is product- or sales-oriented, and is more responsive to audiences' needs and wants. See also *product orientation; sales orientation.*

mass media/news media: Print and broadcast news outlets that reach a mass audience, such as newspapers, magazines, radio, and television. They are also referred to as the mainstream/traditional/conventional media because of the growing presence of alternative information channels, including blogs, online media, community news outlets, transit publications, and social media.

media logic: The theory that institutional actors change their behaviour in response to how journalists gather and report news.

media management: The strategies and techniques employed by public relations personnel in their interactions with the media, particularly tactics designed to control the message and frame.

media-party parallelism: The degree to which media outlets track party messaging (either positively or negatively).

media relations: Activities undertaken to manage and optimize interactions with the news media, such as news releases, pseudo-events, and fielding questions from journalists.

message event proposal (MEP): A policy instrument created by communications personnel in Stephen Harper's PMO that requires departments to provide media information to the PCO and PMO on their plans for public events, such as ministerial announcements. MEPs identify details of the planned event, the spokesperson(s), attendees, desired media headlines, intended audiences, key messages, photos, and attire. This strategy allows personnel at the apex of government to ensure that all spokespersons' messages are consistent in style, tone, and substance with those of the prime minister. See also *centralization*.

microtargeting: A strategic use of resources, uncovered through market intelligence, designed to focus communication on small segments of the electorate whose profiles indicate a propensity to support the sponsor. Sometimes called hypersegmentation, this process relies on complex voter-profiling activities or databases. One such example in Canada was the Conservatives' use of micropolicies such as boutique tax credits targeted at construction workers and truck drivers.

narrowcasting: The act of selecting media, based on the nature of the communication, most likely to reach targeted market segments – for example, communicating with target groups by advertising on sports or lifestyle specialty channels instead of via the broader mass media.

New Political Governance: A model of public sector management in which the governing party's pursuit of partisan gain leads to practices which betray the principles of impartial public administration in Westminster systems. See also *permanent campaign*.

New Public Management: A theory in public administration that governments have been adopting private sector practices since the 1980s in an effort to modernize their relationships with citizens while achieving cost efficiencies.

oppo: Short for opposition research, involves the collection of information on political opponents to discredit a target or defend oneself. Internet media have increased the ability to gather details and opportunities to disseminate findings.

partisanship: A person's psychological ties to a political party. Every party has a core of strong partisans who might or might not publicly self-identify as such.

party brand: All information that an individual has on a political party, including its name, logo, colour scheme, current and past leaders, candidates, policies, and overall record. A party brand generates emotional responses and loyalties and facilitates voter decision making. See also *branding; partisanship*.

permanent campaign: Electioneering throughout governance, which often involves leveraging public resources. This is more prevalent with fixed-date election legislation because all political parties maintain a state of election readiness that builds as the election approaches. Non-stop campaigning is most pronounced in the final year of a four-year cycle, during by-elections, and during the uncertainty of minority government when the possibility of a sudden election campaign is ever-present.

personal brand: All information that an individual has on a public figure, including his or her name, physical characteristics, attire, mannerisms, career path, political views, accomplishments and gaffes, and personal life. This includes impressions about, and feelings towards, a politician's image. See also *branding; personalization.*

personalization: The self-disclosure of private and personal details by politicians and the increased attention from the news media on the private lives of politicians, such as their families.

politainment: The media's treatment of politics as entertainment to stimulate audience interest. Market-oriented journalism is pressured by audiences' changing news habits and penchant for simplicity, which has evolving implications for news production.

political communication: The role of communication in politics, including the generation of messages by political actors (political organizations, non-profits, citizens, the media) and their transmission as well as reception. Communication occurs in a variety of forms (formal and informal), in a number of venues (public and private), and through a variety of media (mediated or unmediated content).

political marketing: The application of business marketing concepts to the practice and study of politics and government. With political marketing, a political organization uses business techniques to inform and shape its strategic behaviour, designed to satisfy citizens' needs and wants. Strategies and tools include branding, e-marketing, delivery, focus groups, get out the vote, internal marketing, listening exercises, opposition research, polling, public relations, segmentation, strategic product development, volunteer management, voter-driven communication, voter expectation management, and voter profiling.

political symbols: Visual icons that act as cognitive placeholders and simplify complex information, such as flags or colours.

press gallery: An organization composed of journalists accredited to cover the activities of the legislature, notably the Ottawa-based Canadian parliamentary press gallery.

priming: Communication tactic that seeks to influence the criteria that journalists and citizens employ when evaluating subject matter.

professionalism: Refers to the media's treatment of political actors' communication as a proxy for amateurism or political prowess.

propaganda: The subversive use of political communication to generate public support for an agenda or course of action. Propaganda is more manipulative than publicity because it methodically exploits socio-psychological levers, often through controlled images that provoke strong emotional responses.

pseudo-events: Events coordinated for no other reason than to maximize publicity by providing the media with something to report. See also *media logic.*

public opinion research: The collection of intelligence from a sample of the population designed to measure the public's views on issues, policies, leaders, and parties. The most common forms are opinion surveys and focus groups, which can be purchased on a customized or omnibus basis. See also *market intelligence.*

public relations (PR): Involves the strategic use of communications tools and media relations techniques to optimize interactions between an organization and its stakeholders.

public service bargain: The traditional bargain between public servants and elected politicians in which public servants give up blatant partisanship and some political rights in exchange for permanent careers, merit-based hiring, and anonymity in government.

publicity: The use of media relations and/or other communications to generate public awareness of a subject or topic.

relationship marketing: The use of marketing to build customer relationships and long-term associations sustained through commitment, loyalty, mutual benefit, and trust. See also *direct marketing.*

segmentation: Division of electors into new groups to allow more efficient targeting of political resources and creation of new segments, such as ethnic minorities or seniors, as society evolves. Segments can be targeted by policy, communication, or get-out-the-vote activities, as well as to encourage greater volunteer activity. See also *microtargeting.*

social media: Internet-based applications in which users create and share content. Includes applications such as social networking (Facebook, Google+, Instagram), blogs, microblogs (Tumblr, Twitter), online videos (YouTube, Vine), wikis (Wikipedia), and social bookmarking (Digg). They are also known as Web 2.0.

sound bites: The reduction of public remarks to short audio clips, usually from seven to fifteen seconds. This conditions public speakers to repeat their core messages and deliver quips in interesting ways. See also *image bites; media logic.*

spin: The framing of information to reflect a bias favourable to the sender, ideally without receivers noticing.

strategic communications: The proactive coordination of a communications strategy to help an organization stay on message and highlight what it is delivering to its targeted audience (clients, customers, citizens, voters). In government, this usually occurs within the Prime Minister's Office and takes into account all aspects of communication, including government announcements, advertising, speech writing, market research, ethnic outreach, and stakeholder relations.

strategy frame: The tendency of political journalism to report news through a strategy lens and to treat punditry about strategy as newsworthy in itself. This includes reporting on PR flacks' attempts to manipulate the media, speculating about the strategic implications of a political actor's options or chosen course of action, and so on. See also *game frame; politainment.*

voter file: The aggregation of data about a voter, including his/her partisan affiliation, marital status, level of education, occupation, policy concerns, and propensity to donate to a party, among many other points of data. These files are compiled in a party's database and contribute to voter targeting procedures. See also *database marketing; microtargeting.*

whole of government (WOG): An umbrella approach to government that seeks to unify the disparate departments and agencies into a cohesive agenda.

writ period: The period between the dissolution of Parliament and the election of a new Parliament. The official writ period lasts a minimum of thirty-six days and all campaign spending limits or other electoral rules apply.

Contributors

AMANDA CLARKE (Carleton University) teaches and researches in the fields of public administration and public policy, specializing in digital-era politics, government, and civic engagement. Her academic and public writing spans the topics of policy innovation, civic technology, and public service renewal. You can find her work at www.aclarke.ca or on Twitter @ae_clarke.

DAVID COLETTO (Carleton University) has published about political parties, political finance in Canada, and public opinion. His research interests include polling, public opinion, digital advertising, political finance, and elections.

KENNETH COSGROVE (Suffolk University) teaches and researches North American politics. He is the author of *Branded Conservatives* (Peter Lang, 2007) and was coeditor of *Political Marketing in the United States* (Routledge, 2014).

JONATHAN CRAFT (University of Toronto) specializes in comparative public policy, public administration, and Canadian politics. He authored *Backrooms and Beyond: Partisan Advisers and the Politics of Policy Work in Canada* (UTP, 2016) and has published widely on policy advice, political staff, and the executive. He previously worked as a federal public servant and a Legislative Assistant at the Legislative Assembly of Ontario.

ANNA LENNOX ESSELMENT (University of Waterloo) has published about parties, elections, and partisanship in the *Canadian Journal of Political Science*, *Canadian Journal of Public Administration*, and *Publius: The Journal of Federalism*. Her research interests include political parties, campaigns, Canadian institutions, and the role of partisanship in intergovernmental relations.

Tom Flanagan (University of Calgary) has managed national and provincial campaigns for conservative parties. He is the author of several books on Canadian political parties and campaigning.

Mary Francoli (Carleton University) has published about open government, social media and elections, and the impact of digital media on governance. Her research interests include political communication, access to information, and open data. She is a member of the Open Government Partnership's Independent Reporting Mechanism, International Expert Panel.

Thierry Giasson (Université Laval) is the coeditor, with Alex Marland, of the series *Communication, Strategy, and Politics* at UBC Press. His research investigates online forms of political campaigning and citizenship, transformations in political journalism, the mediatization of social crises, as well as political marketing practices in Canada and Québec. His work has been published in, among others, the *Canadian Journal of Political Science, Politique et sociétés,* and the *Canadian Journal of Communication.*

Philippe Lagassé (Carleton University) researches executive-legislative relations and prerogative powers in the Westminster system. His recent articles have appeared in *West European Politics, Parliamentary Affairs, Commonwealth and Comparative Politics, Review of Constitutional Studies,* and *Canadian Public Administration.* He is currently researching the relationship between Crown prerogatives and prime ministerial power.

Mireille Lalancette (Université du Québec à Trois-Rivières) has published about the construction of the mediatized image of politicians, gender, and representation, and has studied the use and impact of social media by citizens, grassroots organizations, and Canadian political actors. Researcher for the groupe de recherche en communication politique (GRCP), she is the author, with Marie-Josée Drolet and Marie-Ève Caty, of *ABC de l'argumentation pour les professionnels de la santé ou toute autre personne qui souhaite convaincre* (PUQ).

Andrea Lawlor (King's University College at Western University) studies the role of media in the policy process, with a particular focus on immigration and refugee politics, as well as public policy more broadly with an emphasis on electoral finance and personal finance policy. Her work has appeared in the *Journal of Social Policy, Canadian Journal of Political Science, Canadian Public Administration*, and *Journal of Ethnic and Migration Studies*, among others.

MARIO LEVESQUE (Mount Allison University) researches disability politics and policy in Canada related to political participation, leadership, accessible transit, and labour market programming. He is currently working on a SSHRC funded study on disability leadership in Atlantic Canada.

J.P. LEWIS (University of New Brunswick) has published about cabinet and political elites in the *Canadian Journal of Political Science, Canadian Public Administration, Canadian Parliamentary Review,* and *Governance*. He was coeditor, with Joanna Everitt, of *The Blueprint: Conservative Parties and their Impact on Canadian Politics* (University of Toronto Press, 2017).

ALEX MARLAND (Memorial University of Newfoundland) publishes about Canadian politics, political marketing, and political communication. He leads teams of academics on collaborative research projects and towards resolving complex problems within university administration. He is the author of *Brand Command: Canadian Politics and Democracy in an Age of Message Control* (UBC Press, 2016).

MARIA MATHEWS (Memorial University of Newfoundland) is an applied health services researcher with expertise in building datasets from non-traditional data sources to evaluate public policy. She uses both quantitative and qualitative research methods in projects that routinely involve knowledge translation components.

DAVID McGRANE (St. Thomas More College and the University of Saskatchewan) researches political marketing, political theory, public opinion, and multiculturalism policy. His most recent book is *Remaining Loyal: Social Democracy in Quebec and Saskatchewan* (MQUP, 2014), and he is currently working on a book about the federal NDP in the 2000s.

DENVER McNENEY (McGill University) is a doctoral candidate at the Centre for the Study of Democratic Citizenship. His research connects media content analysis with political behaviour to better understand how citizens update their political attitudes in light of new information.

Steve Patten (University of Alberta) has published on the evolving character of Canadian conservatism, party politics, Alberta politics, and the challenges of deepening democracy in policymaking. He is also coeditor, with Lois Harder, of *Patriation and Its Consequences: Constitution-Making in Canada* (UBC Press, 2015).

Tamara A. Small (University of Guelph) researches digital politics: the use and impact of the Internet by Canadian political actors. She is coauthor of *Fighting for Votes: Parties, the Media and Voters in an Ontario Election* (UBC Press, 2015) and the co-editor of *Political Communication in Canada: Meet the Press, Tweet the Rest* (UBC Press, 2014) and *Mind the Gaps: Canadian Perspectives on Gender and Politics* (Fernwood Press, 2013).

Sofia Tourigny-Koné (Université du Québec à Trois-Rivières) is a doctoral student in communication and a member of the groupe de recherche en communication politique (GRCP). She has published in *Revue approches inductives* and in *French Politics*. Her research interests include interest group uses of social media.

André Turcotte (Carleton University) lectures in research methods, political communication and public opinion research. He has given numerous speeches to professional and academic audiences. His recent publications include studies of boutique populism in the age of digital politics, the Conservative Party's use of market intelligence, the measurement of public opinion in Canadian elections, and co-authorship of *Dynasties and Interludes: Past and Present in Canadian Electoral Politics* (Dundurn Press, 2010).

Simon Vodrey (Carleton University) is a PhD candidate in Communication. His research interests include the historical development of journalism; political marketing; polling and market research; and the shifting patterns and traffic flows of influence in the political, commercial, and civil society arenas. He is assistant editor of the *Canadian Journal of Communication*.

Paul Wilson (Carleton University) served as director of policy in the Prime Minister's Office from 2009–11. His research interests include core executive governance, ministerial political advisors, and parliamentary processes. He has published in the *Canadian Journal of Political Science* and *Canadian Public Administration*.

Index

172–73; Harper and, 173, 304–5;
lieutenant governors and, 173; loss of
confidence votes and, 173, 174; and
partisanship, 177–78; prime ministers
and, 173–75, 178, 179; reform of, 168;
and relinquishment of communication
control, 300; in UK, 180
Donolo, Peter, 226
Duffy, Mike, 301
Durkheim, Emile, 128

earned media: and branding, 207–8;
incumbent advantage with, 213
Economic Action Plan (EAP), 43, 213,
215, 225
Eichbaum, Chris, 242, 244
election campaigns: advertising and
agenda setting for, 185–86; command-
and-control approach in, 302; conflation of governing with campaigning,
4–5; and constant campaigning, 299;
electoral expense regulations, 21;
fixed-date elections and length of, 167;
fixed-date elections and spending on,
167, 177; and governing vs. electioneering, 8, 216; local, 50, 54, 57; and
obsessional campaigning, 298; party-
media relationship in, 67, 69; permanent campaign, and governing vs.,
216; permanent campaigning and
length of, 179; personalization of politics in, 260; phases in modernization
of, 145–46; post-mortems, 152, 161;
revolving around party leaders, 318;
similarity of tactics/tools/channels
regardless of context, 311; spending
limits, 19
election preparation: as constant in postmodern campaigning, 146; defined,
146; fixed-date elections and, 179;
fixed-date elections and length of, 178;
length of time for, 160–61; modernization and length of campaign, 146;
NDP and, 147, 152–54; opposition
parties and, 179; and opposition

research, 156; parties and, 145, 147;
and permanent campaign, 145; political market orientation and, 159–60;
political parties and, 160; professionalization vs. amateurism in, 147, 152–54;
traditional vs. perpetual, 146, 148–
49(t), 152. *See also* perpetual election
preparation
election readiness: by-elections and, 92;
disability organizations' need for
constant communication in, 288–89;
emails and, 88, 100; fundraising and,
91, 100, 106
election timing: media and, 179; prime
ministers and, 174, 177, 178; in US
vs. Canada, 207. *See also* fixed-date
elections/legislation
Elections Canada: and anonymous small
cash donations, 90; parties provided
with data identifying which electors
voted, 106; party fundraising reports
to, 91; quarterly party financing
reports, 155; voters list, 55
electoral cycles: fixed-date election legislation and, 180; length of, 11. *See also*
fixed-date elections/legislation
Elmer, Greg, *The Permanent Campaign*,
15
email communication: address collection,
91–92; authorship of, 98, 99(t), 100;
by-elections and, 92, 102–4; Canadian
government participation in, 90;
characteristics, 98–100; and civic
education/engagement, 93, 100; communication functions, 88; Conservative Party and, 13, 96(f); content of,
100–1, 106; customization of, 89, 92;
democratic upside to, 88; and election
readiness, 88, 100; features of, 89; frequency variance of, 319n1; Harper
government media relations and, 13;
and issue-based debate communications, 118; list prospecting/refinement,
87; listserv, and political marketing,
106; message-testing procedures in,